DEFINING DOCUMENTS
IN WORLD HISTORY

The Middle East
(141 BCE–2017)

DEFINING DOCUMENTS
IN WORLD HISTORY

The Middle East
(141 BCE–2017)

Editor

Michael Shally-Jensen, PhD

Volume 2

SALEM PRESS
A Division of EBSCO Information Services, Inc.
Ipswich, Massachusetts

GREY HOUSE PUBLISHING

Publisher's Cataloging-In-Publication Data
(Prepared by The Donohue Group, Inc.)

Names: Shally-Jensen, Michael, editor.
Title: The Middle East (141 BCE-2017) / editor, Michael Shally-Jensen, PhD.
Other Titles: Defining documents in world history.
Description: [First edition]. | Ipswich, Massachusetts : Salem Press, a division of EBSCO Information Services ; [Amenia, New York] : Grey House Publishing, [2018] | Includes bibliographical references and index.
Identifiers: ISBN 9781682177020 (set) | ISBN 9781642650075 (v.1) | ISBN 9781642650082 (v.2)
Subjects: LCSH: Middle East--History--Sources.
Classification: LCC DS62 .M54 2018 | DDC 956--dc23

FIRST PRINTING
PRINTED IN THE UNITED STATES OF AMERICA

Table of Contents

Volume 1

EARLY, MEDIEVAL, AND EARLY MODERN HISTORY

OTTOMAN ENDURANCE AND COLLAPSE

Volume 2

TWENTIETH-CENTURY TROUBLES

Recent Realities

Appendixes

TWENTIETH-CENTURY TROUBLES

By the end of World War II, the United States had begun to emerge as the major outside power in the Middle East, the European powers having either been forced out (the Axis Powers) or eased out by internal politics and new developments in the region. France sought to hang on to its colony in Algeria, but after a long, dirty war there (1954-62) it lost control and left the country, which became independent. As nationalism took root and swept through the region, Britain, too, exited under pressure from Egypt's Gamal Abdel Nasser (ruled 1956-70). The United States viewed the nationalist movement as aligned with the Soviet Union and communism, which was only partially true yet served as a motivating factor. Washington's intervention in Iran, where a U.S. and British-backed coup ousted Prime Minister Mohammad Mossadegh in 1953, added to mistrust of the United States in the Arab world. The action would come back to roost when, in 1979, Iran ousted the U.S.-backed shah Mohammed Reza Pahlavi (ruled 1941-79) and declared an Islamic republic there.

In the case of the United States, the three main interests in the region were Persian Gulf oil, support and protection of the new state of Israel (from 1948), and containment of the Soviet Union. These goals proved difficult to manage, especially with the rise of Arab nationalism, three Arab-Israeli wars (1948, 1967, and 1973), and an Arab oil embargo (1973). Oil had been a U.S. priority in the Middle East since President Franklin Roosevelt discussed oil when he met with the Saudi king Abdul Aziz ibn Saud (ruled 1932-53) before the close of World War II. The United States was also among the first nations to recognize Israel in 1948, even as the United Nations voted to partition Palestine into Jewish and Arab states. That problematic partition has continued to vex the region to this day.

By the mid-1960s, the United States had not yet formed close relationships with Arab nations beyond Saudi Arabia. The Six-Day War (1967) between Israel and several Arab states only toughened Washington's position. The war left Israel in control of Jerusalem, the West Bank (adjacent to Jerusalem), and other Palestinian territories, most of which it still occupies today.

The distrust between Washington and the Arabs hardened by the time President Richard Nixon took office. Some of that troubled relationship had to do with continued U.S.-Soviet competition. By the end of the 1970s, little good will existed between the United States and the Arab world. The Americans were seen as being on the side of the status quo, of conservativism, while the Soviet Union aimed for disruption and new alignments, and the Arab movement sought regional unity, political change, and modest social reform, albeit largely under the control of elites.

With U.S. support, peace agreements were signed between Egypt and Israel in 1979 and between Jordan and Egypt in 1994. In addition, the Oslo Accords (1993 and 1995) sought peace between the Israelis and the Palestinians. The latter agreements, bound to a two-state solution, seemed to hold great promise at the time but ultimately proved to be troubled in the context of ongoing hostilities between the two parties and events occurring in the surrounding region.

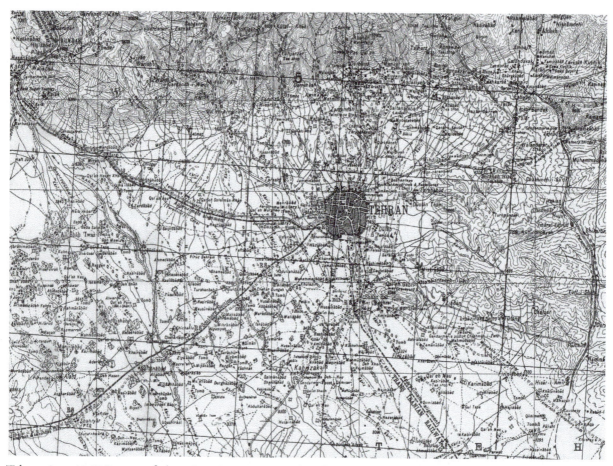

Tehran Area 1947 Portion of sheet I-39 D Iran. Original scale 1:250,000 Compiled and published originally under the direction of the Surveyor-General of India 1910 and Revised to 1940. Published by the U.S. Army Map Service November, 1947. Courtesy of The General Libraries, The University of Texas at Austin.

■ White Paper of 1939

Date: May 23, 1939
Author: Malcolm MacDonald
Geographic region: Middle East, Palestine
Genre: Treaty; memorandum; proclamation

Summary Overview

The significance of the document examined here is not so much who authored it but which government produced it and when and why. On the eve of World War II, the 1939 White Paper was issued. It was not accepted—and then World War II broke out.

To understand the historical context, one needs to go back to the end of World War I, when Great Britain was given (and desired) a role in the Middle East. Britain was given control over Iraq and what was then Palestine. Palestine was made up of the current state of Israel and the land governed by the current Palestinian authority. Britain, in requesting the mandate (i.e., controlling authority), wanted to maintain its own power in the world, limit the influence of France, and preserve its pipeline to India. However, the British, particularly in Palestine, had their hands full. Jewish forces believed that they had been promised a Jewish homeland in the area under the Balfour Declaration of 1917, and Arab forces believed that they had been promised control under the exchange of letters known as the Hussein-McMahon correspondence. Jewish forces decided to migrate to the area and take control, and the British between 1919 and 1939 tried to limit that process while also balancing domestic political concerns. By 1939, the British were desperate for an answer, and this White Paper was their attempt at it.

Defining Moment

The drafting of the White Paper represents a defining moment in Middle Eastern history as far as the British are concerned because they needed to establish a policy regarding Palestine that work for all parties. They had largely created the problem themselves by announcing, in the 1917 Balfour Declaration, the intent to establish a Jewish homeland; and by agreeing, through the Hussein-McMahon correspondence, to allow Arab control over Palestine. Between 1919 and 1939, Jews immigrated to the area and started buying land in order to assume control. In the 1920s, their goal was to buy enough land to control it. However, by the

1930s immigration was low yet problems mounted in Europe, as the threat of a major new war loomed. Soon, Jews sought to migrate anywhere outside of Europe, and Palestine was desirable because it overlapped with the ancient Jewish homeland. Arabs in the area, however, did not want more Jewish settlers, even though they were hardly consulted on the matter.

By 1939, the situation had become critical, as there were enough Jewish settlers in Palestine to be represent a sizable bloc of residents, but Britain was not yet prepared to commit to a two-state solution—one Arab/Palestinian and one Jewish. The British called a conference to try to negotiate a solution; but when the conference led to no significant change in Palestinian opinion (the Palestinians were not willing to accept the British ideas), the British simply announced their own intention to move ahead as they saw fit. The Palestinians did not accept the solution and so the situation remained at a standstill when World War II broke out. Complicating the issue was the fact that many European Jews had hoped to reach Palestine both before and during the outbreak of hostilities. Most nations would not accept Jewish migrants, and the British limited immigration in Palestine in order not to anger the Palestinians further. The Jews pointed out that they faced a grave danger in Europe, while the Palestinians pointed out that no one had asked them about giving up their land to help solve a problem they had not created.

Author Biography

The author of the White Paper of 1939 was Malcolm MacDonald, the British Colonial Secretary at the time. MacDonald was 37 years old then, fairly young for a high position. He was originally in the Labour Party, but joined the national government in the mid-1930s and was expelled. He became Colonial Secretary and oversaw an agreement with the Irish Free State, settling affairs there. He then oversaw the attempt to settle the issue of Palestine. In 1940, MacDonald left the office of Colonial Secretary, serving as Minister of Health for a while under Winston Churchill. In 1941 he served as

High Commissioner to Canada. After 1946, he continued his career in colonial affairs, serving until the late 1960s in various roles.

The British government was led by Neville Chamberlain at the time. Chamberlain had become prime minister in 1937, when Stanley Baldwin, who had won election as Prime Minister in 1935, resigned. (This was after George VI became king when Edward VII abdicated to marry Wallis Simpson.) Chamberlain had a number of crises to deal with, including the Munich Crisis, in which Hitler demanded the Sudetenland and Chamberlain bowed to Hitler's wishes. Chamberlain worked hard to avoid war, but after France fell in 1940, he abdicated and Winston Churchill came to power.

HISTORICAL DOCUMENT

In the statement on Palestine, issued on 9 November, 1938, His Majesty's Government announced their intention to invite representatives of the Arabs of Palestine, of certain neighboring countries and of the Jewish Agency to confer with them in London regarding future policy. It was their sincere hope that, as a result of full, free and frank discussions, some understanding might be reached. Conferences recently took place with Arab and Jewish delegations, lasting for a period of several weeks, and served the purpose of a complete exchange of views between British Ministers and the Arab and Jewish representatives. In the light of the discussions as well as of the situation in Palestine and of the Reports of the Royal Commission and the Partition Commission, certain proposals were formulated by His Majesty's Government and were laid before the Arab and Jewish Delegations as the basis of an agreed settlement. Neither the Arab nor the Jewish delegation felt able to accept these proposals, and the conferences therefore did not result in an agreement. Accordingly His Majesty's Government are free to formulate their own policy, and after careful consideration they have decided to adhere generally to the proposals which were finally submitted to and discussed with the Arab and Jewish delegations.

The Mandate for Palestine, the terms of which were confirmed by the Council of the League of Nations in 1922, has governed the policy of successive British Governments for nearly 20 years. It embodies the Balfour Declaration and imposes on the Mandatory four main obligations. These obligations are set out in Article 2, 6 and 13 of the Mandate. There is no dispute regarding the interpretation of one of these obligations, that touching the protection of and access to the Holy Places and religious building or sites. The other three main obligations are generally as follows:

To place the country under such political, administrative and economic conditions as will secure the establishment in Palestine of a national home for the Jewish People. To facilitate Jewish immigration under suitable conditions, and to encourage, in cooperation with the Jewish Agency, close settlement by Jews on the Land.

To safeguard the civil and religious rights of all inhabitants of Palestine irrespective of race and religion, and, whilst facilitating Jewish immigration and settlement, to ensure that the rights and position of other sections of the population are not prejudiced.

To place the country under such political, administrative and economic conditions as will secure the development of self governing institutions.

The Royal Commission and previous commissions of Enquiry have drawn attention to the ambiguity of certain expressions in the Mandate, such as the expression `a national home for the Jewish people', and they have found in this ambiguity and the resulting uncertainty as to the objectives of policy a fundamental cause of unrest and hostility between Arabs and Jews. His Majesty's Government are convinced that in the interests of the peace and well being of the whole people of Palestine a clear definition of policy and objectives is essential. The proposal of partition recommended by the Royal Commission would have afforded such clarity, but the establishment of self supporting independent Arab and Jewish States within Palestine has been found to be impracticable. It has therefore been necessary for His Majesty's Government to devise an alternative policy which will, consistent with their obligations to Arabs and Jews, meet the needs of the situation in Palestine. Their views and proposals are set forth below under three heads, Section I, "The Constitution", Section II. Immigration and Section III. Land.

Section I. "The Constitution"

It has been urged that the expression "a national home for the Jewish people" offered a prospect that Palestine might in due course become a Jewish State or Commonwealth. His Majesty's Government do not wish to contest the view, which was expressed by the Royal Commission, that the Zionist leaders at the time of the issue of the Balfour Declaration recognized that an ultimate Jewish State was not precluded by the terms of the Declaration. But, with the Royal Commission, His Majesty's Government believe that the framers of the Mandate in which the Balfour Declaration was embodied could not have intended that Palestine should be converted into a Jewish State against the will of the Arab population of the country. That Palestine was not to be converted into a Jewish State might be held to be implied in the passage from the Command Paper of 1922 which reads as follows

> "Unauthorized statements have been made to the effect that the purpose in view is to create a wholly Jewish Palestine. Phrases have been used such as that 'Palestine is to become as Jewish as England is English.' His Majesty's Government regard any such expectation as impracticable and have no such aim in view. Nor have they at any time contemplated . . . the disappearance or the subordination of the Arabic population, language or culture in Palestine. They would draw attention to the fact that the terms of the (Balfour) Declaration referred to do not contemplate that Palestine as a whole should be converted into a Jewish National Home, but that such a Home should be founded IN PALESTINE."

But this statement has not removed doubts, and His Majesty's Government therefore now declare unequivocally that it is not part of their policy that Palestine should become a Jewish State. They would indeed regard it as contrary to their obligations to the Arabs under the Mandate, as well as to the assurances which have been given to the Arab people in the past, that the Arab population of Palestine should be made the subjects of a Jewish State against their will.

The nature of the Jewish National Home in Palestine was further described in the Command Paper of 1922 as follows:

> "During the last two or three generations the Jews have recreated in Palestine a community now numbering 80,000, of whom about one fourth are farmers or workers upon the land. This community has its own political organs; an elected assembly for the direction of its domestic concerns; elected councils in the towns; and an organization for the control of its schools. It has its elected Chief Rabbinate and Rabbinical Council for the direction of its religious affairs. Its business is conducted in Hebrew as a vernacular language, and a Hebrew press serves its needs. It has its distinctive intellectual life and displays considerable economic activity. This community, then, with its town and country population, its political, religious and social organizations, its own language, its own customs, its own life, has in fact 'national' characteristics. When it is asked what is meant by the development of the Jewish National Home in Palestine, it may be answered that it is not the imposition of a Jewish nationality upon the inhabitants of Palestine as a whole, but the further development of the existing Jewish community, with the assistance of Jews in other parts of the world, in order that it may become a center in which the Jewish people as a whole may take, on grounds of religion and race, an interest and pride. But in order that this community should have the best prospect of free development and provide a full opportunity for the Jewish people to display its capacities, it is essential that it should

know that it is in Palestine as of right and not on sufferance. That is the reason why it is necessary that the existence of a Jewish National Home in Palestine should be internationally guaranteed, and that it should be formally recognized to rest upon ancient historic connection."

His Majesty's Government adhere to this interpretation of the (Balfour) Declaration of 1917 and regard it as an authoritative and comprehensive description of the character of the Jewish National Home in Palestine. It envisaged the further development of the existing Jewish community with the assistance of Jews in other parts of the world. Evidence that His Majesty's Government have been carrying out their obligation in this respect is to be found in the facts that, since the statement of 1922 was published, more than 300,000 Jews have immigrated to Palestine, and that the population of the National Home has risen to some 450,000, or approaching a third of the entire population of the country. Nor has the Jewish community failed to take full advantage of the opportunities given to it. The growth of the Jewish National Home and its achievements in many fields are a remarkable constructive effort which must command the admiration of the world and must be, in particular, a source of pride to the Jewish people.

In the recent discussions the Arab delegations have repeated the contention that Palestine was included within the area in which Sir Henry McMahon, on behalf of the British Government, in October, 1915, undertook to recognize and support Arab independence. The validity of this claim, based on the terms of the correspondence which passed between Sir Henry McMahon and the Sharif of Mecca, was thoroughly and carefully investigated by the British and Arab representatives during the recent conferences in London. Their report, which has been published, states that both the Arab and the British representatives endeavored to understand the point of view of the other party but that they were unable to reach agreement upon an interpretation of the correspondence. There is no need to summarize here the arguments presented by each side. His Majesty's

Government regret the misunderstandings which have arisen as regards some of the phrases used. For their part they can only adhere, for the reasons given by their representatives in the Report, to the view that the whole of Palestine west of Jordan was excluded from Sir Henry McMahon's pledge, and they therefore cannot agree that the McMahon correspondence forms a just basis for the claim that Palestine should be converted into an Arab State.

His Majesty's Government are charged as the Mandatory authority "to secure the development of self governing institutions" in Palestine. Apart from this specific obligation, they would regard it as contrary to the whole spirit of the Mandate system that the population of Palestine should remain forever under Mandatory tutelage. It is proper that the people of the country should as early as possible enjoy the rights of self-government which are exercised by the people of neighbouring countries. His Majesty's Government are unable at present to foresee the exact constitutional forms which government in Palestine will eventually take, but their objective is self government, and they desire to see established ultimately an independent Palestine State. It should be a State in which the two peoples in Palestine, Arabs and Jews, share authority in government in such a way that the essential interests of each are shared.

The establishment of an independent State and the complete relinquishment of Mandatory control in Palestine would require such relations between the Arabs and the Jews as would make good government possible. Moreover, the growth of self governing institutions in Palestine, as in other countries, must be an evolutionary process. A transitional period will be required before independence is achieved, throughout which ultimate responsibility for the Government of the country will be retained by His Majesty's Government as the Mandatory authority, while the people of the country are taking an increasing share in the Government, and understanding and cooperation amongst them are growing. It will be the constant endeavor of His Majesty's Government to promote good relations between the Arabs and the Jews.

In the light of these considerations His Majesty's Government make the following declaration of their intentions regarding the future government of Palestine:

The objective of His Majesty's Government is the establishment within 10 years of an independent Palestine State in such treaty relations with the United Kingdom as will provide satisfactorily for the commercial and strategic requirements of both countries in the future. The proposal for the establishment of the independent State would involve consultation with the Council of the League of Nations with a view to the termination of the Mandate.

The independent State should be one in which Arabs and Jews share government in such a way as to ensure that the essential interests of each community are safeguarded.

The establishment of the independent State will be preceded by a transitional period throughout which His Majesty's Government will retain responsibility for the country. During the transitional period the people of Palestine will be given an increasing part in the government of their country. Both sections of the population will have an opportunity to participate in the machinery of government, and the process will be carried on whether or not they both avail themselves of it.

As soon as peace and order have been sufficiently restored in Palestine steps will be taken to carry out this policy of giving the people of Palestine an increasing part in the government of their country, the objective being to place Palestinians in charge of all the Departments of Government, with the assistance of British advisers and subject to the control of the High Commissioner. Arab and Jewish representatives will be invited to serve as heads of Departments approximately in proportion to their respective populations. The number of Palestinians in charge of Departments will be increased as circumstances permit until all heads of Departments are Palestinians, exercising the administrative and advisory functions which are presently performed by British officials. When that stage is reached consideration will be given to the question of converting the Executive Council into a Council of Ministers with a consequential change in the status and functions of the Palestinian heads of Departments.

His Majesty's Government make no proposals at this stage regarding the establishment of an elective legislature. Nevertheless they would regard this as an appropriate constitutional development, and, should public opinion in Palestine hereafter show itself in favour of such a development, they will be prepared, provided that local conditions permit, to establish the necessary machinery.

At the end of five years from the restoration of peace and order, an appropriate body representative of the people of Palestine and of His Majesty's Government will be set up to review the working of the constitutional arrangements during the transitional period and to consider and make recommendations regarding the constitution of the independent Palestine State.

His Majesty's Government will require to be satisfied that in the treaty contemplated by sub-paragraph (6) adequate provision has been made for:

The security of, and freedom of access to the Holy Places, and protection of the interests and property of the various religious bodies.

The protection of the different communities in Palestine in accordance with the obligations of His Majesty's Government to both Arabs and Jews and for the special position in Palestine of the Jewish National Home.

Such requirements to meet the strategic situation as may be regarded as necessary by His Majesty's Government in the light of the circumstances then existing. His Majesty's Government will also require to be satisfied that the interests of certain foreign countries in Palestine, for the preservation of which they are at present responsible, are adequately safeguarded.

His Majesty's Government will do everything in their power to create conditions which will enable the independent Palestine State to come into being within 10 years. If, at the end of 10 years, it appears to His Majesty's Government that, contrary to their hope, circumstances require the postponement of the establishment of the independent State, they will consult with representatives of the people of Palestine, the Council of the League of Nations and the neighboring Arab States before deciding on such a postponement. If His Majesty's Government come to the conclusion that postponement is unavoidable, they will invite the co-operation of these parties in framing plans for the future with a view to achieving the desired objective at the earliest possible date.

During the transitional period steps will be taken to increase the powers and responsibilities of municipal corporations and local councils.

Section II. Immigration

Under Article 6 of the Mandate, the Administration of Palestine, "while ensuring that the rights and position of other sections of the population are not prejudiced," is required to "facilitate Jewish immigration under suitable conditions." Beyond this, the extent to which Jewish immigration into Palestine is to be permitted is nowhere defined in the Mandate. But in the Command Paper of 1922 it was laid down that for the fulfilment of the policy of establishing a Jewish National Home:

"It is necessary that the Jewish community in Palestine should be able to increase its numbers by immigration. This immigration cannot be so great in volume as to exceed whatever may be the economic capacity of the country at the time to absorb new arrivals. It is essential to ensure that the immigrants should not be a burden upon the people of Palestine as a whole, and that they should not deprive any section of the present population of their employment."

In practice, from that date onwards until recent times, the economic absorptive capacity of the country has been treated as the sole limiting factor, and in the letter which Mr. Ramsay MacDonald, as Prime Minister, sent to Dr. Weizmann in February 1931 it was laid down as a matter of policy that economic absorptive capacity was the sole criterion. This interpretation has been supported by resolutions of the Permanent Mandates Commissioner. But His Majesty's Government do not read either the Statement of Policy of 1922 or the letter of 1931 as implying that the Mandate requires them, for all time and in all circumstances, to facilitate the immigration of Jews into Palestine subject only to consideration of the country's economic absorptive capacity. Nor do they find anything in the Mandate or in subsequent Statements of Policy to support the view that the establishment of a Jewish National Home in Palestine cannot be effected unless immigration is allowed to continue indefinitely. If immigration has an adverse effect on the economic position in the country, it should clearly be restricted; and equally, if it has a seriously damaging effect on the political position in the country, that is a factor that should not be ignored. Although it is not difficult to contend that the large number of Jewish immigrants who have been admitted so far have been absorbed economically, the fear of the Arabs that this influx will continue indefinitely until the Jewish population is in a position to dominate them has produced consequences which are extremely grave for Jews and Arabs alike and for the peace and prosperity of Palestine. The lamentable disturbances of the past three years are only the latest and most sustained manifestation of this intense Arab apprehension. The methods employed by Arab terrorists against fellow Arabs and Jews alike must receive unqualified condemnation. But it cannot be denied that fear of indefinite Jewish immigration is widespread amongst the Arab population and that this fear has made possible disturbances which have given a serious setback to economic progress, depleted the Palestine exchequer, rendered life and property insecure, and produced a bitterness between the Arab and Jewish populations which is deplorable between citizens of the same country. If in these circumstances immigration is continued up to the economic absorptive capacity of the country, regardless of all other considerations, a fatal enmity between the two peoples will be perpetuated, and the situation in Palestine may become a permanent source of friction amongst all peoples in the Near and Middle East. His Majesty's Government cannot take the view that either their obligations under the Mandate, or considerations of common sense and justice, require that they should ignore these circumstances in framing immigration policy.

In the view of the Royal Commission the association of the policy of the Balfour Declaration with the Mandate system implied the belief that Arab hostility to the former would sooner or later be overcome. It has been the hope of British Governments ever since the Balfour Declaration was issued that in time the Arab population, recognizing the advantages to be derived from Jewish settlement and development in Palestine, would become reconciled to the further growth of the Jewish National Home. This hope has not been fulfilled. The alternatives before His Majesty's Government are either (i) to seek to expand the Jewish National Home indefinitely by immigration, against the strongly expressed will of the Arab people of the country; or (ii) to permit further expansion of the Jewish National Home by immigration only if the Arabs are prepared to acquiesce in it. The former policy means rule by force. Apart from other considerations, such a policy seems to His Majesty's Government to be contrary to the whole spirit of Article 22 of the Covenant of the League of Nations, as well as to their specific obligations to the Arabs in the Palestine Mandate. Moreover, the relations between the Arabs and the Jews in Palestine must be based sooner or later on mutual tolerance and goodwill; the peace, security and progress of the Jewish National Home itself requires this. Therefore His Majesty's Government, after earnest consideration, and taking into account the extent to which the growth of the Jewish National Home has been facilitated over the last twenty years, have decided that the time has come to adopt in principle the second of the alternatives referred to above.

It has been urged that all further Jewish immigration into Palestine should be stopped forthwith. His Majesty's Government cannot accept such a proposal. It would damage the whole of the financial and economic system of Palestine and thus effect adversely the interests of Arabs and Jews alike. Moreover, in the view of His Majesty's Government, abruptly to stop further immigration would be unjust to the Jewish National Home. But, above all, His Majesty's Government are conscious of the present unhappy plight of large numbers of Jews who seek refuge from certain European countries, and they believe that Palestine can and should make a further contribution to the solution of this pressing world problem. In all these circumstances, they believe that they will be acting consistently with their Mandatory obligations to both Arabs and Jews, and in the manner best calculated to serve the interests of the whole people of Palestine, by adopting the following proposals regarding immigration:

Jewish immigration during the next five years will be at a rate which, if economic absorptive capacity permits, will bring the Jewish population up to approximately one third of the total population of the country. Taking into account the expected natural increase of the Arab and Jewish populations, and the number of illegal Jewish immigrants now in the country, this would allow of the admission, as from the beginning of April this year, of some 75,000 immigrants over the next five years. These immigrants would, subject to the criterion of economic absorptive capacity, be admitted as follows:

For each of the next five years a quota of 10,000 Jewish immigrants will be allowed on the understanding that a shortage one year may be added to the quotas for subsequent years, within the five year period, if economic absorptive capacity permits.

In addition, as a contribution towards the solution of the Jewish refugee problem, 25,000 refugees will be admitted as soon as the High Commissioner is satisfied that adequate provision for their maintenance is ensured, special consideration being given to refugee children and dependents.

The existing machinery for ascertaining economic absorptive capacity will be retained, and the High Commissioner will have the ultimate responsibility for deciding the limits of economic capacity. Before each periodic decision is taken, Jewish and Arab representatives will be consulted.

After the period of five years, no further Jewish immigration will be permitted unless the Arabs of Palestine are prepared to acquiesce in it.

His Majesty's Government are determined to check illegal immigration, and further preventive measures are being adopted. The numbers of any Jewish illegal immigrants who, despite these measures, may succeed in coming into the country and cannot be deported will be deducted from the yearly quotas.

His Majesty's Government are satisfied that, when the immigration over five years which is now contemplated has taken place, they will not be justified in facilitating, nor will they be under any obligation to facilitate, the further development of the Jewish National Home by immigration regardless of the wishes of the Arab population.

Section III. Land

The Administration of Palestine is required, under Article 6 of the Mandate, "while ensuring that the rights and position of other sections of the population are not prejudiced," to encourage "close settlement by Jews on the land," and no restriction has been imposed hitherto on the transfer of land from Arabs to Jews. The Reports of several expert Commissions have indicated that, owing to the natural growth of the Arab population and the steady sale in recent years of Arab land to Jews, there is now in certain areas no room for further transfers of Arab land, whilst in some other areas such transfers of land must be restricted if Arab cultivators are to maintain their existing standard of life and a considerable landless Arab population is not soon to be created. In these circumstances, the High Commissioner will be given general powers to prohibit and regulate transfers of land. These powers will date from the publication of this statement of policy and the High Commissioner will retain them throughout the transitional period.

The policy of the Government will be directed towards the development of the land and the improvement, where possible, of methods of cultivation. In the light of such development it will be open to the High Commissioner, should he be satisfied that the "rights and position" of the Arab population will be duly preserved, to review and modify any orders passed relating to the prohibition or restriction of the transfer of land.

In framing these proposals His Majesty's Government have sincerely endeavored to act in strict accordance with their obligations under the Mandate to both the Arabs and the Jews. The vagueness of the phrases employed in some instances to describe these obligations has led to controversy and has made the task of interpretation difficult. His Majesty's Government cannot hope to satisfy the partisans of one party or the other in such controversy as the Mandate has aroused. Their purpose is to be just as between the two people in Palestine whose destinies in that country have been affected by the great events of recent years, and who, since they live side by side, must learn to practice mutual tolerance, goodwill and co operation. In looking to the future, His Majesty's Government are not blind to the fact that some events of the past make the task of creating these relations difficult; but they are encouraged by the knowledge that as many times and in many places in Palestine during recent years the Arab and Jewish inhabitants have lived in friendship together. Each community has much to contribute to the welfare of their common land, and each must earnestly desire peace in which to assist in increasing the well being of the whole people of the country. The responsibility which falls on them, no less than upon His Majesty's Government, to co operate together to ensure peace is all the more solemn because their country is revered by many millions of Moslems, Jews and Christians throughout the world who pray for peace in Palestine and for the happiness of her people.

GLOSSARY

Holy Places: the sacred areas of Jerusalem that were important to the three major faiths (Judaism, Christianity, and Islam) in the region

Jewish Agency: an organization representing the Jews of the world and seeking to help those wanting to relocate to Palestine

Jewish State: a state in Palestine run by Jews and promoting Jewish culture

Mandate: a grant of power under the League of Nations; an area so controlled or administered

National Home: in this context, a Jewish homeland in Palestine, but one that is not necessarily a sovereign state

Document Analysis

The document first notes why it was created. It lays out the conference and how it failed. To put a positive spin on it, the document argues that the failure of that meeting leaves the British government free to announce policy. The White Paper then looks at the history of the mandate and the original goals. It also honestly notes the difficulties with the mandate (these difficulties might have also been noted in order to give the British an out for not being any more successful there). The paper comments that the term "a national home for the Jewish people" was unclear and that a two-state solution was not possible. To justify this, in the first part of the paper, the author goes back to previous documents and argues that neither the Arabs, under the Hussein-McMahon correspondence, nor the Jews, under the Balfour Declaration, should get the entire area. The paper also argues that in line with the original League of Nations mandate, the whole area remains together. It states that only such a solution will allow the British the way out of the mandate, which, by this point, they were coming to desire.

After this, the White Paper moves into its goals, noting that the British wish to establish an independent state with both Arabs and Jews in it. This would be a government with "shared governance" involving both groups. The white paper notes the plan for creating such a government after a transitional period. The British would first lead and would then hand off the departments to the Palestinians, which here means both Arabs and Jews of the area. Unlike the executive, no plan is presented for a legislature, but the paper does indicate that the latter might be a good idea. A five-year transition period is proposed and the paper notes that Britain would need to be satisfied with the plans for protections of religious minorities and the holy sites of various religions before power was finally transferred. That period could take as long as ten years, it is noted.

On the subject of immigration, the White Paper notes that a continuation of the overall level of immigration is not desirable. After discussing why the Arabs are unhappy with the immigration currently, and noting the negative effects of the current level, the paper outlines three options. The first is to continue to allow immigration, which is not ideal given the wishes of the populace and also is contrary to the League of Nations. The second is to ban all immigration of Jews, which the paper denounces as contrary to the economic health of the region. Therefore, the paper proposes allowing 75,000 migrants in, with 10,000 per year and 25,000 refugees (at least under the first five years of the proposed transfer of power).

As for the land, the paper proposes that there should be no more transfers of land from the Arabs to the Jews. The two sides, in fact, are to be responsible for settling the issue of land rather than the British. The British basically have decided to end transfers and let the two sides sort out the past, as they will have to live together in the future. This is in accordance with the growing British interest in figuring a way out of the mandate, rather than continuing to be responsible for fixing all the problems regarding it.

Essential Themes

This document shows what the British might have done (or might have attempted to do) had World War II not broken out. Recall that there were various efforts afoot to prevent or limit a second world war from unfolding. Thus, the writers of this document were announcing what they wanted to do. It should be noted though that the British were trying to do this on their own, and their chances of success might have been limited because of it. After all, the reason why the British had to issue their own White Paper, rather than working with the local population, was that the Arabs had refused the agreement that the British suggested at the time. Thus, what the British were announcing had already been refuted.

There is also the matter of World War II, the threat of which was then looming over Europe. That threat shifted the focus of the British and most of the rest of the world. On the other hand, it caused the Jewish people in Europe to want to migrate more than ever. Although they were barred from entering a number of other countries, Jews did begin pouring into Palestine. This only increased the difficulty of the situation, and reduced the chance for finding an easy solution.

It is clear from the White Paper that the British wanted out of the area and also thought that there should be a Jewish homeland that could be governed jointly by Arabs and Jews. While that solution may have been unworkable, it was never really tried because of the British desire to be done with the matter and the onset of world war.

The paper, in fact, was written with an eye toward maintaining British influence in the region. That included relationships with Egypt, Iraq, and Saudi Arabia—even if these were not independent states at the time. If they had broken away, it could create an Axis powerhouse in the area given increased incursions from Germany and Italy. Moreover, much of the oil that the British planned to use in war came out of this area.

For the Arabs and the Jews, the White Paper did not serve their long-term interests. The Arabs were not ready to accept a Jewish homeland in the area, especially one thrust upon them; and the Jews considered that the homeland concept was not enough, that a state was what they needed. This conundrum would persist through the founding of Israel in 1948 and beyond.

—*Scott A. Merriman, PhD*

Bibliography and Additional Reading

Cohen, Michael Joseph. *Britain's Moment in Palestine: Retrospect and Perspectives, 1917-48.* London: Routledge/Taylor & Francis Group, 2014.

Matthews, Weldon C. *Confronting an Empire, Constructing a Nation: Arab Nationalists and Popular Politics in Mandate Palestine.* London: I.B. Tauris, 2006.

Neill, Lochery. "Review Article: Lion in the Sand: British Policy in the Middle East, 1945–67." *Middle Eastern Studies*, no. 5, 2008, p. 807.

Segev, Tom. *One Palestine, Complete: Jews and Arabs under the Mandate.* New York: Metropolitan Books, 2000.

Zweig, R. W. "British Policy to Palestine, May 1939 to 1943: The Fate of the White Paper." 1978. PhD Dissertation.

■ Charter of the Arab League

Date: March 22, 1945
Author: Mustafa al-Nahhas Pasha
Geographic region: Syria, Transjordan, Iraq, Saudi Arabia, Lebanon, Egypt, and Yemen
Genre: Charter

Summary Overview

The Charter of the Arab League lists the founding principles for a pan-Arab organization stretching across North Africa and the Middle East. The original members of the league gathered in response to the dissolution of the Ottoman Empire and concerns about divisions of territory after World War II, in particular regarding the creation of a Jewish state in Palestine. The purpose of the league has been to strengthen ties between countries within the region and to coordinate among members on matters of common interest. This charter provides for members to cooperate on shared economic, political, and social issues; it also endows the League with the ability to mediate military conflicts between or with member states. However, the charter's emphasis on recognizing national sovereignty above all else has drawn criticism since it limits the ability of the member states to act collectively. Since the original countries ratified the pact in 1945, the League has grown to twenty-two members and has attempted to reorganize into a more potent international organization after a wave of popular uprisings across the Arab world in 2011.

Defining Moment

The origins of the Arab League can be traced at least to the end of World War I and the "balkanization," i.e. division into smaller parts, of the Ottoman Empire. The Treaty of Lausanne, which was signed in 1923, defined the borders of the modern Turkish state and ceded many former territories in the Levant and North Africa into the control of the Allies as zones of influence. Arab leaders were immediately dissatisfied since the dissolution of Ottoman power resulted not in Arab independence, but an exchange of colonial control. Additionally, the Sykes-Picot Agreement of 1916, in which the United Kingdom, France, and Russia determined which Middle Eastern regions would fall under their spheres of influence, appeared to be a motivating force in how the European leaders divided the former Ottoman Empire among themselves with little attention to

regional differences. The Balfour Declaration, in which Britain expressed support for the creation of a new Jewish state in 1917, would also have huge ramifications for nascent Arab nationalism.

Several Arab leaders had been considering the merits of a pan-Arab state, or at very least promulgated the ideology of pan-Arab unity. Major proponents of pan-Arabism included Zaki al-Arsuzi and Michel Aflaq, two Syrians thinkers who helped establish the Ba'ath Party, as well as Abdullah I of Jordan, a ruler with expansionist hopes who was first Emir under a British Mandate and later king of the independent nation. Surprisingly, Britain became a supporter of a pan-Arab organization to foment unity at the start of World War II. The Allies needed to secure support against the Axis drive into North Africa, and they could not combat both anti-British sentiment in the Middle Eastern territories or risk losing local support to the Axis powers. The League of Nations, although it had failed in its mission to prevent another world war, provided a paradigm for a consortium of governments that could gather to work on shared issues. In 1941 British Foreign Minister Anthony Eden announced his country's support for recognizing the independence of the Lebanese and Syrians, and he expressed hope that these new Arab countries would build economic and political ties with each other.

It was only during the spring of 1943 that an Arab leader, Nuri al-Said of Iraq, came forward with a plan for Arab unity. Al-Said proposed that Iraq and Syria initially form an "Arab League" that would be open to other Arab states to join; he also suggested that this "Arab League" would have a permanent council that could pass decisions on many issues, including currency control, foreign affairs, education, and protection of minority rights. The leaders of Egypt and Transjordan had different ideas about what Arab unity would look like, and serious questions about the form of this new organization stymied progress. Nahhas Pasha, the premier of Egypt, decided that his government ought to mediate the question of regional Arab cooperation; he announced a joint conference that would be held in Alexandria on September 25, 1944. The Alexandria Protocol resulted from this conference, and became the prototype of the later Charter of the League of Arab States. In this earlier protocol, five nations (Egypt, Iraq, Syria, Jordan, and Lebanon) set the groundwork for strengthening relations between themselves. However, this protocol also stressed protection for independent sovereignty, a right that had been relatively recently acquired for all participating member states. This concern would become one of the fundamental organizing guidelines for the later Charter and one of the greatest obstacles in encouraging political unity and more concerted action between member states.

Author Biography

Seven countries signed the initial charter to form the League of Arab States, but the composition of the pact was due in large part to the work of Nahhas Pasha, Egyptian premier at the time. Mustafa al-Nahhas Pasha (1879-1965) began his career first as a lawyer and then as a judge until he was dismissed and exiled in 1919 for joining the Wafd, an Egyptian nationalist party. He rejoined Egyptian government in 1923, and climbed the ranks of government quickly; he first served as prime minister for a short tenure in 1928. Nahhas Pasha frequently clashed with both the Egyptian king and the British over his nationalist sympathies and desire to curtail the sovereign's power. When he was appointed prime minister for a third time in 1936, Nahhas Pasha helped negotiate the Anglo-Egyptian Treaty in London, which ended British occupation of Egypt and established an alliance. He would not hold onto his third premiership for long, since the new king Farouk I disagreed with his domestic and foreign policies. The outbreak of World War II and British pressure compelled the king to appoint the controversial Nahhas Pasha again to be prime minister in 1942. During this premiership, he instituted important social policies on labor and played a central role in gathering Arab leaders to the conference that resulted in the Alexandria Protocol in 1944. He studied the activities of other nascent pan-regional conferences, such as the Organization of American Republics, in order to help draft the document that would serve as the blueprint for the later Charter of the Arab League. However, two days after the Alexandria Protocol was signed in order to guide a new pan-Arab association, the Egyptian king removed Nahhas Pasha from his position; the Syrian and the Jordanian prime ministers who had joined the conference were also dismissed from their posts in their respective countries. Nahhas Pasha served one last term as prime minister in 1950, during which time he abrogated the Anglo-Egyptian Treaty in favor of the Egyptian king, but growing dissatisfaction with the Wafd Party led to his final dismissal in 1952. Nahhas Pasha and his wife were arrested and charged with corruption and imprisoned for a year, after which he lived out the rest of his life as a private citizen.

HISTORICAL DOCUMENT

His Excellency the President of the Syrian Republic,
His Royal Highness the Emir of Transjordan,
His Majesty the King of Iraq,
His Majesty the King of Saudi-Arabia,
His Excellency the President of the Lebanese Republic,
His Majesty the King of Egypt;
His Majesty the King of Yemen,

With a view to strengthen[ing] the close relations and numerous ties which bind the Arab States,

And out of concern for the cementing and reinforcing of these bonds on the basis of respect for the independence and sovereignty of theme Stated,

And in order to direct their efforts toward[s] the goal of the welfare of all the Arab States, their common weal, the guarantee of their future and the realization of their aspirations,

And in response to Arab public opinion in all the Arab countries,

Have agreed to conclude a pact to this effect and have delegated as their plenipotentiaries those whose names are given below:

Who, after the exchange of the credentials granting them full authority, which were found valid and in proper form, have agreed upon the following:

Article 1.

The League of Arab States shall be composed of the: independent Arab States that have signed this Pact.

Every independent Arab State shall have the right to adhere to the League. Should it desire to adhere, it shall present an application to this effect which shall be filed with the permanent General Secretariat and submitted to the Council at its first meeting following the presentation of the application.

Article 2.

The purpose of the League is to draw closer the relations between member States and co-ordinate their political activities with the aim of realizing a close collaboration between them, to safeguard their independence and sovereignty, and to consider in a general way the affairs and interests of the Arab countries.

It also has among its purposes a close co-operation of the member States with due regard to the structure of each of these States and the conditions prevailing therein, in the following matters:

- (a) Economic and financial matters, including trade, customs, currency, agriculture and industry;
- (b) (communications, including railways, roads, aviation, navigation, and posts and telegraphs;
- (c) Cultural matters;
- (d) Matters connected with nationality, passports, visas, execution of judgments and extradition;
- (e) Social welfare matters;
- (f) Health matters.

Article 3.

The League shall have a Council composed of the representatives of the member States. Each State shall have one vote, regardless of the number of its representatives.

The Council shall be entrusted with the function of realizing the purpose of the League and of supervising the execution of the agreements concluded between the member States on matters referred to in the preceding article or on other matters.

It shall also have the function of determining the means whereby the League will collaborate with the international organizations which may be created in the future to guarantee peace and security and organize economic and social relations.

Article 4.

A special Committee shall be formed for each of the categories enumerated in article 2, on which the member States shall be represented. These Committees shall be entrusted with establishing the basis and scope of co-operation in the form of draft agreements which shall be submitted to the Council for its consideration preparatory to their being submitted to the States referred to.

Delegates representing the other Arab countries may participate in these Committees as members. The Council shall determine the circumstances in which the participation of these representatives shall be allowed as well as the basis of the representation.

Article 5.

The recourse to force for the settlement of disputes between two or more member States shall not be allowed. Should there arise among them a dispute that does not involve the independence of a State, its sovereignty or its territorial integrity, and should the two contending parties apply to the Council for the settlement of this dispute, the decision of the Council shall then be effective and obligatory.

In this case, the States among whom the dispute has arisen shall not participate in the deliberations and decisions of the Council.

The Council shall mediate in a dispute which may lead to war between two member States or between a member State and another State in order to conciliate them

The decisions relating to arbitration and mediation shall be taken by a majority vote.

Article 6.

In case of aggression or threat of aggression by a State against a member State, the State attacked or threatened with attack may request an immediate meeting of the Council.

The Council shall determine the necessary measures to repel this aggression. Its decision shall be taken unanimously. If the aggression is committed by a member State the vote of that State will not be counted in determining unanimity.

If the aggression is committed in such a way as to render the Government of the State attacked unable to communicate with the Council, the representative of that State in the Council may request the Council to convene for the purpose set forth in the preceding paragraph. If the representative is unable to communicate with the Council, it shall be the right of any member State to request a meeting of the Council.

Article 7.

The decisions of the Council taken by a unanimous vote shall be binding on all the member States of the League; those that are reached by a majority vote shall bind only those that accept them.

In both cases the decisions of the Council shall be executed in each State in accordance with the fundamental structure of that State.

Article 8.

Every Member State of the League shall respect the form of government obtaining in the other States of the League, and shall recognize the form of government obtaining as one of the rights of those States, and shall pledge itself not to take any action tending to change that form.

Article 9.

The States of the Arab League that are desirous of establishing among themselves closer collaboration and stronger bonds than those provided for in the present Pact, may conclude among themselves whatever agreements they wish for this purpose.

The treaties and agreements already concluded or that may be concluded in the future between a member State and any other State shall not be binding on the other members.

Article 10.

The permanent seat of the League of Arab States shall be Cairo. The Council of the League may meet at any other place it designates.

Article 11.

The Council of the League shall meet in ordinary session twice a year, during the months of March and October. It shall meet in extraordinary session at the request of two member States whenever the need arises.

Article 12.

The League shall have a permanent General Secretariat, composed of a Secretary-General, Assistant Secretaries and an adequate number of officials.

The Secretary-General shall be appointed by the Council upon the vote of two-thirds of the States of the League. The Assistant Secretaries and the principal officials shall be appointed by the Secretary-General with the approval of the Council.

The Council shall establish an internal organization for the General Secretariat as well as the conditions of service of the officials.

The Secretary-General shall have the rank of Ambassador; and the Assistant Secretaries the rank of Ministers Plenipotentiary.

The first Secretary-General of the League is designated in an annex to the present Pact.

Article 13.

The Secretary-General shall prepare the draft of the budget of the League and submit it for approval to the Council before the beginning of each fiscal year.

The Council shall determine the share of each of the States of the League in the expenses. It shall be allowed to revise the share if necessary.

Article 14.

The members of the Council of the League, the members of its Committees and such of its officials as shall be designated in the internal organization, shall enjoy, in the exercise of their duties, diplomatic privileges and immunities.

The premises occupied by the institutions of the League shall be inviolable.

Article 15.

The council shall meet the first time at the invitation of the Head of the Egyptian Government. Later meetings shall be convoked by the Secretary-General.

In each ordinary session the representatives of the States of the League shall assume the chairmanship of the Council in rotation.

Article 16.

Except for the cases provided for in the present Pact, a majority shall suffice for decisions by the Council effective in the following matters:

(a) Matters concerning the officials.
(b) The approval of the budget of the League.
(c) The internal organization of the Council, the Committees and the General Secretariat.
(d) The termination of the sessions.

Article 17.

The member States of the League shall file with the General Secretariat copies of all treaties and agreements which they have concluded or will conclude with any other State, whether a member of the League or otherwise.

Article 18.

If one of the member States intends to withdraw from the League, the Council shall be informed of its intention one year before the withdrawal takes effect.

The Council of the League may consider any State that is not fulfilling the obligations resulting from this Pact as excluded from the League, by a decision taken by a unanimous vote of all the States except the State referred to.

Article 19.

The present Pact may be amended with the approval of two-thirds of the members of the League in particular for the purpose of strengthening the ties between them, of creating an Arab Court of Justice, and of regulating the relations of the League with the international organizations that may be created in the future to guarantee security and peace

No decision shall be taken as regards an amendment except in the session following that in which it is proposed.

Any State that does not approve an amendment may withdraw from the League when the amendment becomes effective, without being bound by the provisions of the preceding article.

Article 20.

The present Pact and its annexes shall be ratified in accordance with the fundamental form of government in each of the contracting States.

The instruments of ratification shall be filed with the General Secretariat and the present Pact shall become binding on the States that ratify in fifteen days after the Secretary-General receives instruments of ratification from four States.

The present Pact has been drawn up in the Arabic language in Cairo and dated 8 Rabi al Thani 1364 (March 22, 1945), in a single text which shall be deposited with the General Secretariat.

A certified copy shall be sent to each of the States of the League.

ANNEX ON PALESTINE

At the end of the last Great War, Palestine, together with the other Arab States, was separated from the Ottoman Empire. She became independent, not belonging to any other State.

The Treaty of Lausanne proclaimed that her fate should be decided by the parties concerned in Palestine.

Even though Palestine was not able to control her own destiny, it was on the basis of the recognition of her independence that the Covenant of the League of Nations determined a system of government for her.

Her existence and her independence among the nations can, therefore, no more be questioned de jure than the independence of any of the other Arab States.

Even though the outward signs of this independence have remained veiled as a result of force majeure, it is not fitting that this should be an obstacle to the participation of Palestine in the work of the League.

Therefore, the States signatory to the Pact of the Arab League consider that in view of Palestine's special circumstances, the Council of the League should designate an Arab delegate from Palestine to participate in its work until this country enjoys actual independence.

ANNEX ON CO-OPERATION WITH ARAB COUNTRIES NOT MEMBERS OF THE COUNCIL OF THE LEAGUE

Whereas the member States of the League will have to deal either in the Council or in the Committees with questions affecting the interests of the entire Arab world.

And whereas the Council cannot fail to take into account the aspirations of the Arab countries not members of the Council and to work toward their realization, the States signatory to the Pact of the Arab League strongly urge that the Council of the League should cooperate with them as far as possible in having them participate in the Committees referred to in the Pact, and in other matters should not spare any effort to learn their needs and understand their aspirations and should moreover work for their common weal and the guarantee of their future by whatever political means available.

ANNEX ON THE APPOINTMENT OF SECRETARY-GENERAL OF THE LEAGUE

The States signatory to the present Pact have agreed to appoint Abd Al Rahman Azzam Bey Secretary-General of the League of Arab States.

His appointment shall be for a term of two years. The Council of the League shall later determine the future organization of the General Secretariat.

Document Analysis

Many of the critiques of the Arab League focus on its inability to foment positive unity and change among the relations of its member states. However, the wording of the Charter itself clarifies that the League was never meant to have its own supranational ideology: the terms characterize the League as a reactive device for solving disputes rather than a proactive entity in international affairs.

Even in the preamble of the charter, it is clear that there is no overarching political ideology guiding the organization. The first two lines of the preamble show how the pact intends to create a device for improving regional relations. The signatory countries have agreed upon the following articles "With a view to strengthen[ing] the close relations and numerous ties which bind the Arab States," which reveals that the charter intends to confirm the existing relationships, rather than create new ties that may transcend existing connections or divisions. The next line of the preamble is even clearer regarding this purpose: "And out of concern for the cementing and reinforcing of these bonds on the basis of respect for the independence and sovereignty of theme Stated": the Charter does not restrict which types of sovereignty the League respects, but leaves the language general. This permitted the League to include authoritarian regimes among its members for many years. Article 8 reinforces that the League will not attempt to change the form of a member state's government, and yet does not consider the ramifications should a member state's government be repressive. Furthermore, Article 7 undermines the ability of the League to take any proactive stance, since it stipulates that decisions of the Council will only apply to the members who vote on a decision. Article 9 similarly negates any possibility for the League to have a proactive function, since this article stipulates that member states "may conclude among themselves whatever agreements they wish" for the purposes of collaboration. Again, this does not guard against potentially unjust alliances, and has permitted factionalism within the League to stymie its efforts to proactively resolve military confrontations.

The Charter comes closest to stipulating a guiding ideology for the Arab League in its Annex on Palestine. By agreeing to this addendum, members of the Arab League profess to the right of sovereign self-determination in the face of unjust occupation. However, the previous articles of the Charter do not bind the Arab states to cooperate on this principle. Thus, Egypt was free to make independent peace agreements with Israel, and the League had difficulty in forcefully responding to Iraq's invasion of Kuwait. In this way, the Arab League has reflected its most immediate predecessor, the League of Nations, in its ability to respond to difficult political and military matters; in smaller economic and social matters, the Charter has reflected its close contemporary, the United Nations, in creating substantive change.

Essential Themes

The Charter's emphasis on recognizing the sovereignty of its member states above all has contributed to charges of disunity, disorganization, and ineffectiveness against the League. The decline of British and French spheres of influence, the rise of the strategic importance of oil reserves, and Cold War rivalries undermined the message of Arab unity. The issue of Palestine has remained one of the few ideologically unifying components of the Charter's principles. After the Six-Day War with Israel in 1967, the Arab League passed the Khartoum Resolution: this stipulated that the League would have no peace with Israel, would not recognize Israel, and would not negotiate with it; the League has also maintained an official boycott of Israeli goods since 1948, although recent enforcement has not been as strict. Egypt's leadership in the League in particular has been tested by the nation's evolving relationship with Israel. In 1977 Egyptian President Anwar Sadat opened up unilateral peace negotiations with Israel; in turn, the League voted to suspend Egypt's membership and moved its headquarters from Cairo to Tunis. Egypt was only readmitted into the League in 1989 and the headquarters moved back to Cairo in 1990. Internal divisions similarly beset the Arab League during Iraq's invasion of Kuwait in 1990, the United States' involvement during the first Gulf War (1990-1991), and the American invasion of Iraq in 2003. Some members approved of Western involvement, including powerful members like Egypt, Saudi Arabia, and Syria; others opposed foreign encroachment, and some members took neither side.

The failure of the Arab League to coordinate on military issues rendered important bodies like the Joint Defense Council effectively purposeless. However, popular uprisings across the Arab world in 2011 gave the League an opportunity to reform its policies; the appointment of Egyptian Nabil al-Araby as secretary-general in the same year was also seen as a turning point in the organization. Not only did the League support U.N. action against Muammar Gaddafi, the former authoritarian leader of Libya, but the League also supported a no-fly zone over Libya that helped in Gaddafi's overthrow. After Gaddafi's end, the League approached the deteriorating civil war in Syria. After Bashar al-Assad, President of Syria, continued to oppress peaceful protesters of his regime and violated the Arab League's peace agreement, the League stripped Syria of its membership. Still, the old divisions remain: allies of Assad have blocked the Syrian opposition government from fully participating in the organization, and others have looked askance at the League's willingness to work with the United Nations as "internationalizing" a regional problem. Although the original principles of the League's charter were in response to a time when spheres of influence and external aggression were serious threats to the independence of the new Arab states, the stress on independent sovereignty continues to hamper the ability of the member states to rise above their regional differences and act together as a supranational entity.

—*Ashleigh Fata, MA*

Bibliography and Additional Reading

Addi, Lahouari. *Radical Arab Nationalism and Political Islam.* Translated by Anthony Roberts, Washington, D.C.: Georgetown University Press, 2017.

Doran, Michael. *Pan-Arabism Before Nasser: Egyptian Power Politics and the Palestinian Question.* New York: Oxford University Press, 1999.

MacDonald, Robert W. *The League of Arab States: A Study in Dynamics of Regional Organization.* Princeton: Princeton University Press, 1965.

Wien, Peter. *Arab Nationalism: The Politics of History and Culture in the Modern Middle East.* New York: Routledge, 2017.

■ Truman Statement on Immigration into Palestine

Date: October 4, 1946
Author: Harry S. Truman
Geographic region: Palestine
Genre: Government document

Summary Overview

In 1946, as the debate over whether Jews should be allowed to establish a homeland in Palestine raged, President Harry S. Truman advocated strongly in favor of the Jews' position. However, when a London conference on the issue abruptly ended without a clear series of recommendations for resolution, Truman issued a statement on the eve of Yom Kippur (the Day of Atonement in Judaism) expressing his disappointment about that conference's outcome. Truman reiterated his position that 100,000 displaced Jews should be allowed to immigrate to Palestine. He urged world leaders to endorse a peaceable solution to the Palestine issue and to create liberal immigration policies that would welcome Jews and other displaced groups to take up residence in their respective nations.

Defining Moment

When Adolf Hitler published his book *Mein Kampf* (1925, 1927), he outlined a personal philosophy that the Jews and other racial minorities were to be eradicated. Upon assuming power as chancellor (or Fuhrer) of Germany in 1933, Hitler quickly moved to make this idea a reality. By 1945, about six million of Europe's nine-and-a-half million Jews (a 1933 estimate) had died as a result of the Holocaust, with hundreds of thousands more displaced before and during World War II. Most of the survivors moved to the Western Hemisphere, but a sizable population still sought refuge in Europe.

One option for them had been under consideration for decades. In 1917, Russian-born Zionist Chaim Weizmann convinced the British government to honor the Jews, who had supported Britain against the Turks during World War I, by calling for a Jewish state in Palestine. However, by the 1930s, Jews escaping Hitler's genocide began entering Palestine, inciting a political backlash from the Arabs living there. Because Arabs already enjoyed a strong relationship with Britain (which, after World War I, controlled the region), Great Britain withdrew its support of the Jewish state. Zionist coali-tions, feeling betrayed by the British change of course, turned to the United States for support.

President Franklin D. Roosevelt was supportive of the idea, particularly as the Holocaust showed the world the horrors to which the Jews were subjected. Near the end of World War II, Roosevelt's successor, Harry Truman, also showed great sympathy for the Zionist cause. He was, however, cognizant of the political risks of dividing Palestine into two distinct, autonomous states. In 1946, Truman worked with the Anglo- American Committee of Inquiry to address the issue in two areas: first, the Palestine issue, and second, the travel arrangements for 100,000 Jews who would be taken there.

In the United States, Congress was increasingly in favor of the idea of a Jewish state in Palestine. However, the manner by which the state would be established— whether a singular, all-inclusive state or a divided nation (one for Jews, the other for Arabs)—could not be settled. Truman, himself an advocate of a single state, believed that the partitioned model invited conflict and war. In an election year, Truman made the difficult decision of turning down the partition plan in Congress. Nevertheless, he continued to call for a Jewish state, which would be essential to harboring the 100,000 Jewish refugees whose fate had yet to be decided. In September 1946, a conference was held in London to bring a resolution to the Palestinian issue. However, the conference only lasted three weeks, as a large number of its participants looked to attend the meeting of the United Nations General Assembly on October 23. The conference was adjourned abruptly, with its organizers planning to reconvene after the middle of December, though they did not ultimately meet again until February. Truman, in response, issued a statement in which he presented his thoughts on the adjournment and the issue as a whole.

Author Biography

Harry S. Truman was born on May 8, 1884, in Lamar, Missouri. He spent most of his childhood living in Independence, Missouri, outside of Kansas City. He enlisted in the National Guard and served from 1905 to 1911, rising to the rank of captain by World War I. In 1922, he won election as judge in Jackson County, Missouri. In 1934, Truman was elected to the U.S. Senate and won reelection in 1940. In 1944, he was nominated Franklin D. Roosevelt's running mate in the presidential election. In 1945, after Roosevelt's sudden death, Truman assumed the role of president, overseeing the end of World War II and introducing the Fair Deal domestic economic reform package. He won reelection in 1948, faced with the Cold War, and during this term helped form the North Atlantic Treaty Organization (NATO). After his second term, Truman retired to Independence. He died on December 26, 1972.

HISTORICAL DOCUMENT

I have learned with deep regret that the meetings of the Palestine Conference in London have been adjourned and are not to be resumed until December 16, 1946. In the light of this situation it is appropriate to examine the record of the administration's efforts in this field, efforts which have been supported in and not of Congress by members of both political parties, and to state my views on the situation as it now exists.

It will be recalled that, when Mr. Earl Harrison reported on September 29, 1945, concerning the condition of displaced persons in Europe, I immediately urged that steps be taken to relieve the situation of these persons to the extent at least of admitting 100,000 Jews into Palestine. In response to this suggestion the British Government invited the Government of the United States to cooperate in setting up a joint Anglo-American Committee of Inquiry, an invitation which this Government was happy to accept in the hope that its participation would help to alleviate the situation of the displaced Jews in Europe and would assist in finding a solution for the difficult and complex problem of Palestine itself. The urgency with which this Government regarded the matter is reflected in the fact that a 120-day limit was set for the completion of the Committee's task.

The unanimous report of the Anglo-American Committee of Inquiry was made on April 20, 1946, and I was gratified to note that among the recommendations contained in the Report was an endorsement of my previous suggestion that 100,000 Jews be admitted into Palestine. The administration immediately concerned itself with devising ways and means for transporting the 100,000 and caring for them upon their arrival. With this in mind, experts were sent to London in June 1946 to work out provisionally the actual travel arrangements. The British Government cooperated with this group but made it clear that in its view the Report must be considered as a whole and that the issue of the 100,000 could not be considered separately.

On June 11, I announced the establishment of a Cabinet Committee on Palestine and Related Problems, composed of the Secretaries of State, War, and Treasury, to assist me in considering the recommendations of the Anglo-American Committee of Inquiry. The alternates of this Cabinet Committee, headed by Ambassador Henry F. Grady, departed for London on July 10, 1946, to discuss with British Government representatives how the Report might best be implemented. The alternates submitted on July 24, 1946 a report, commonly referred to as the "Morrison plan," advocating a scheme of provincial autonomy which might lead ultimately to a bi-national state or to partition. However, opposition to this plan developed among members of the major political parties in the United States—both in the Congress and throughout the country. In accordance with the principle which I have consistently tried to follow, of having a maximum degree of unity within the country and between the parties on major elements of American foreign policy, I could not give my support to this plan.

I have, nevertheless, maintained my deep interest in the matter and have repeatedly made known and have urged that steps be taken at the earliest possible moment to admit 100,000 Jewish refugees to Palestine.

In the meantime, this Government was informed of the efforts of the British Government to bring to London representatives of the Arabs and Jews, with a view to finding a solution to this distressing problem. I expressed the hope that as a result of these conversations a fair solution of the Palestine problem could be found. While all the parties invited had not found themselves able to attend, I had hoped that there was still a possibility that representatives of the Jewish Agency might take part. If so, the prospect for an agreed and constructive settlement would have been enhanced.

The British Government presented to the Conference the so-called "Morrison plan" for provincial autonomy and stated that the Conference was open to other proposals. Meanwhile, the Jewish Agency proposed a solution of the Palestine problem by means of the creation of a viable Jewish state in control of its own immigration and economic policies in an adequate area of Palestine instead of in the whole of Palestine. It proposed furthermore the immediate issuance of certificates for 100,000 Jewish immigrants. This proposal received wide-spread attention in the United States, both in the press and in public forums. From the discussion which has ensued it is my belief that a solution along these lines would command the support of public opinion in the United States. I cannot believe that the gap between the proposals which have been put forward is too great to be bridged by men of reason and good-will. To such a solution our Government could give its support.

In the light of the situation which has now developed I wish to state my views as succinctly as possible:

1. In view of the fact that winter will come on before the Conference can be resumed I believe and urge that substantial immigration into Palestine cannot await a solution to the Palestine problem and that it should begin at once. Preparations for this movement have already been made by this Government and it is ready to lend its immediate assistance.

2. I state again, as I have on previous occasions, that the immigration laws of other countries, including the United States, should be liberalized with a view to the admission of displaced persons. I am prepared to make such a recommendation to the Congress and to continue as energetically as possible collaboration with other countries on the whole problem of displaced persons.

3. Furthermore, should a workable solution for Palestine be devised, I would be willing to recommend to the Congress a plan for economic assistance for the development of that country.

In the light of the terrible ordeal which the Jewish people of Europe endured during the recent war and the crisis now existing, I cannot believe that a program of immediate action along the lines suggested above could not be worked out with the cooperation of all people concerned. The administration will continue to do everything it can to this end.

Document Analysis

Even prior to his first term as president, Harry Truman had a reputation as a Zionist advocate. Truman and the rest of the international community had an opportunity to reach this goal at the end of World War II, as millions of refugees (a large number of whom were Jewish) sought safe havens after years of Nazi persecution. However, Truman was surprised and disappointed to learn that the international community could not come to an agreement on whether to allow 100,000 Jewish refugees to immigrate to Palestine. On the eve of Yom Kippur, Truman issued this statement, underscoring his commitment to peaceably enabling Jewish refugees to settle in the predominantly Arab region.

Truman begins his statement by expressing regret that the September Palestine Conference in London adjourned with no resolution and would not reconvene until the winter. Truman suggests that such an impasse undid the groundwork that he and other leaders laid over the course of decades. The preceding year, he says, Earl Harrison (the U.S. representative of the Intergovernmental Committee on Refugees and dean of the University Pennsylvania Law School) issued a moving report depicting the plight of the Jews immediately after the Holocaust. Given the treatment the Jews had received by the Nazis and their continuing misery, Truman and the British government looked to relieve at least some of this suffering by giving 100,000 Jews entry into Palestine. As part of a bilateral commission, the U.S. and British governments worked to generate attention about the Jews; Truman says that that commission's report suggested that these 100,000 refugees and their potential entry into Palestine could not be made a separate issue from the larger issue of postwar refugees.

Truman acknowledges, however, that the notion of moving a large number of Jews into the predominantly Arab area of Palestine was politically charged. The initial plan, dubbed the Morrison plan, entailed the division of Palestine into either two federated parts or two autonomous states. Truman says that, although he supports the Morrison plan in theory, neither the Republican nor the Democratic Party in Congress would agree to such a plan. He, therefore, begrudgingly abstains from supporting it. Nevertheless, he says, he will continue to advocate for the Palestine option. Other versions of the Morrison plan still existed, each of which calling for a Jewish state in Palestine and for the immigration of Jewish refugees to that state. Such proposals received a great deal of attention from the media and political leaders, he adds, ensuring that the issue itself remained highly relevant.

He argues that the U.S. and other governments should liberalize their immigration policies to give safe haven to Jews and other wartime refugees. Second, according to him, the Palestine proposal should be immediately revisited and settled. Given the experiences of the Jews before and during the war, Truman says, it was only right that they be given prompt attention.

Essential Themes

President Harry Truman's statement served as a reiteration of his position on the plight of Europe's Jews. Truman expressed disappointment that the London conference adjourned without resolution. Keenly aware of the reports that came out of German-occupied territories before and during the war, Truman reiterated his call for to allow 100,000 Jewish refugees to enter and live in Palestine as well as the liberalization of international immigration policy to address the broader refugee crisis.

Truman used the opportunity to summarize the work that he, the U.S. government, and their counterparts in Great Britain had performed to date in order to resolve this issue. He stated that there appeared to be forward momentum on the matter, particularly as the world was becoming increasingly aware of and sympathetic toward the plight of the Jews. However, he acknowledged, there were political forces at work that impeded the process. At home, during an election year, there was congressional partisanship with which to contend; Truman knew that were his effort to succeed, he needed not only congressional support, but the support of the voters as well. Internationally, the landscape was also challenging: the Arabs had successfully lobbied against the effort before, and the pressure was on the president to encourage a peaceful, diplomatic solution that would ensure that both Arabs and the increasing Jewish population would live in peace. Regardless how the Palestine concept would take shape—whether as a single state or as a bi-national state—it was imperative to address the refugees' welfare promptly.

The decisions made at that time continue to have resonance in the twenty-first century. The Palestinians were ultimately promised a state of their own, alongside that established for the Jewish people, Israel. However, wars soon ensued between the Palestinians and the Israelis, and the contentious debate over the "one-state solution" and the "two-state solution" remains.

—*Michael P. Auerbach, MA*

Bibliography and Additional Reading

Benson, Michael T. *Harry S. Truman and the Founding of Israel*. Westport: Greenwood, 1997. Print.

"Jewish Population of Europe in 1945." *Holocaust Encyclopedia*. United States Holocaust Memorial Museum, 20 Jun. 2014. Web. 2 Jan. 2015.

Judis, John B. "Seeds of Doubt: Harry Truman's Concerns about Israel and Palestine Were Prescient—and Forgotten." *New Republic*. The New Republic, 15 Jan. 2014. Web. 2 Jan. 2015.

"London Conference on Palestine Suddenly Adjourns until after U.N. General Assembly." *JTA*. Jewish Telegraphic Agency, 2015. Web. 2 Jan. 2015.

McCullough, David. *Truman*. New York: Simon, 2003. Print.

"The Recognition of the State of Israel." *Harry S. Truman Library and Museum*. Harry S. Truman Library and Museum, 2014. Web. 2 Jan. 2015.

■ Truman Doctrine Speech

Date: March 12, 1947
Author: Harry S. Truman
Geographic region: Global
Genre: Speech

Summary Overview

Less than two years after the end of World War II, President Harry S. Truman gave a speech in which he articulated a new American foreign policy that would become known as the Truman Doctrine, intended to address the postwar geopolitical climate. Since the end of World War II, the Soviet Union had expanded its reach throughout Eastern Europe and was threatening to spur Communist revolutions in the Middle East. The focus of Truman's speech was the situation in Greece and Turkey, two nations that were threatened in different ways by the spread of Communism. Though the threats were different, the response, Truman argued, needed to be the same—financial aid to help contain the tide of Communist expansion. The United States was only just becoming accustomed to its new role as a world superpower; in the postwar order, Truman asserted, the United States was the only nation able to provide such aid, and the country had an ongoing responsibility to safeguard the world from the spread of Communism.

Defining Moment

In the two years following the defeat of Nazi Germany, U.S. relations with its wartime ally the Soviet Union had changed dramatically. At the Yalta Conference in February 1945, the leaders of the United States, Great Britain, and the Soviet Union had agreed that the nations Germany had conquered during the war should be able to freely choose their governments through democratic elections. Very quickly after the conclusion of the war, however, it became clear that the Soviet Union was doing everything it could to ensure that all of the nations along its borders came under Communist rule. This direct disregard for the Yalta Agreement meant that the United States now had a new foe in a "cold war," which pitted democracy against totalitarianism.

American foreign policy experts struggled to determine the best course of action; George F. Kennan, who had perhaps the most familiarity with the Soviet government, having served as a U.S. diplomat in Moscow for seven years, articulated what he saw as the reasons for Soviet aggressiveness in his "long telegram" in February 1946. To Kennan, Soviet expansionism was shaped by Russia's history of imperialistic conquest as well as by Marxist ideology, which saw Communism in an ongoing war against capitalism. He believed the only policy that could stop the Soviets' expansionist influence was one of containment, which required a commitment by the United States to the long-term limitation of the Soviets to their own sphere of influence. This had dramatic implications for American policy, as Kennan had no doubt that the Soviets would continue their drive to expand for the foreseeable future.

The need to articulate a new policy came to a head in February 1947, when the British government, which had suffered far greater economic hardship than the United States during World War II, informed American officials that it would no longer be able to provide economic and military aid to Greece and Turkey, both of which were facing important threats related to Communist expansionism. In Greece, leftist rebels, supported by Yugoslavia and the Soviet Union, had waged an insurgency against the Greek royal government. In Turkey, the Soviet Union was aggressively seeking to share control over the Dardanelles and the Bosporus straits, which connect the Mediterranean to the Black Sea, where the Soviets had large naval bases. Truman administration officials believed that if Greece and Turkey were overtaken by Communists, the appeasement of Soviet demands would only embolden the Soviets to go further, and country after country would fall to Communism— an idea that became popularly known as the "domino theory." The only way to stop the dominos from falling—or to contain the Soviet threat to Greece, Turkey, and the rest of the free world—was for the United States to take an active role in international affairs by meeting Soviet aggression with countervailing political, economic, and military force whenever necessary. With this policy in mind, Truman spoke to a joint session of Congress on March 12, 1947.

Author Biography

Following the death of President Franklin D. Roosevelt in April 1945, in the last days of World War II, Harry S. Truman became president of the United States. The peace that followed the war was short-lived, however, as, almost immediately; Truman was faced with a new kind of war, a "cold war," pitting the United States against its wartime ally the Soviet Union. Relations began to break down even before World War II had ended, due to the ideological differences between the two nations, with the United States supporting capitalism and democracy, while the Soviet Union championed socialism and an authoritarian form of government. Though these differences had existed since the Russian Revolution in 1917, they took on geopolitical overtones after World War II and became a much more pressing concern for Truman. Much of Truman's presidency was defined by the nascent Cold War, and in 1947, Truman sought to define what the U.S. government's response to the Soviet threat would be.

HISTORICAL DOCUMENT

The gravity of the situation which confronts the world today necessitates my appearance before a joint session of the Congress. The foreign policy and the national security of this country are involved.

One aspect of the present situation, which I wish to present to you at this time for your consideration and decision, concerns Greece and Turkey.

The United States has received from the Greek Government an urgent appeal for financial and economic assistance. Preliminary reports from the American Economic Mission now in Greece and reports from the American Ambassador in Greece corroborate the statement of the Greek Government that assistance is imperative if Greece is to survive as a free nation.

I do not believe that the American people and the Congress wish to turn a deaf ear to the appeal of the Greek Government.

Greece is not a rich country. Lack of sufficient natural resources has always forced the Greek people to work hard to make both ends meet. Since 1940, this industrious and peace loving country has suffered invasion, four years of cruel enemy occupation, and bitter internal strife.

When forces of liberation entered Greece they found that the retreating Germans had destroyed virtually all the railways, roads, port facilities, communications, and merchant marine. More than a thousand villages had been burned. Eighty-five per cent of the children were tubercular. Livestock, poultry, and draft animals had almost disappeared. Inflation had wiped out practically all savings.

As a result of these tragic conditions, a militant minority, exploiting human want and misery, was able to create political chaos which, until now, has made economic recovery impossible.

Greece is today without funds to finance the importation of those goods which are essential to bare subsistence. Under these circumstances the people of Greece cannot make progress in solving their problems of reconstruction. Greece is in desperate need of financial and economic assistance to enable it to resume purchases of food, clothing, fuel and seeds. These are indispensable for the subsistence of its people and are obtainable only from abroad. Greece must have help to import the goods necessary to restore internal order and security, so essential for economic and political recovery.

The Greek Government has also asked for the assistance of experienced American administrators, economists and technicians to insure that the financial and other aid given to Greece shall be used effectively in creating a stable and self-sustaining economy and in improving its public administration.

The very existence of the Greek state is today threatened by the terrorist activities of several thousand armed men, led by Communists, who defy the government's authority at a number of points, particularly along the northern boundaries. A Commission appointed by the United Nations Security Council is at present investigating disturbed conditions in northern Greece and alleged border violations along the frontier between Greece on the one hand and Albania, Bulgaria, and Yugoslavia on the other.

Meanwhile, the Greek Government is unable to cope with the situation. The Greek army is small and poorly equipped. It needs supplies and equipment if it is to restore the authority of the government throughout Greek territory. Greece must have assistance if it is to become a self-supporting and self-respecting democracy.

The United States must supply that assistance. We have already extended to Greece certain types of relief and economic aid but these are inadequate. There is no other country to which democratic Greece can turn.

No other nation is willing and able to provide the necessary support for a democratic Greek government. The British Government, which has been helping Greece, can give no further financial or economic aid after March 31. Great Britain finds itself under the necessity of reducing or liquidating its commitments in several parts of the world, including Greece.

We have considered how the United Nations might assist in this crisis. But the situation is an urgent one requiring immediate action and the United Nations and its related organizations are not in a position to extend help of the kind that is required.

It is important to note that the Greek Government has asked for our aid in utilizing effectively the financial and other assistance we may give to Greece, and in improving its public administration. It is of the utmost importance that we supervise the use of any funds made available to Greece; in such a manner that each dollar spent will count toward making Greece self-supporting, and will help to build an economy in which a healthy democracy can flourish.

No government is perfect. One of the chief virtues of a democracy, however, is that its defects are always visible and under democratic processes can be pointed out and corrected. The Government of Greece is not perfect. Nevertheless it represents eighty-five per cent of the members of the Greek Parliament who were chosen in an election last year. Foreign observers, including 692 Americans, considered this election to be a fair expression of the views of the Greek people.

The Greek Government has been operating in an atmosphere of chaos and extremism. It has made mistakes. The extension of aid by this country does not mean that the United States condones everything that the Greek Government has done or will do. We have condemned in the past, and we condemn now, extremist measures of the right or the left. We have in the past advised tolerance, and we advise tolerance now.

Greece's neighbor, Turkey, also deserves our attention.

The future of Turkey as an independent and economically sound state is clearly no less important to the freedom-loving peoples of the world than the future of Greece. The circumstances in which Turkey finds itself today are considerably different from those of Greece. Turkey has been spared the disasters that have beset Greece. And during the war, the United States and Great Britain furnished Turkey with material aid.

Nevertheless, Turkey now needs our support.

Since the war Turkey has sought financial assistance from Great Britain and the United States for the purpose of effecting that modernization necessary for the maintenance of its national integrity.

That integrity is essential to the preservation of order in the Middle East.

The British government has informed us that, owing to its own difficulties can no longer extend financial or economic aid to Turkey.

As in the case of Greece, if Turkey is to have the assistance it needs, the United States must supply it. We are the only country able to provide that help.

I am fully aware of the broad implications involved if the United States extends assistance to Greece and Turkey, and I shall discuss these implications with you at this time.

One of the primary objectives of the foreign policy of the United States is the creation of conditions in which we and other nations will be able to work out a way of life free from coercion. This was a fundamental issue in the war with Germany and Japan. Our victory was won over countries which sought to impose their will, and their way of life, upon other nations.

To ensure the peaceful development of nations, free from coercion, the United States has taken a leading part in establishing the United Nations. The United Nations is designed to make possible lasting freedom and independence for all its members. We shall not realize our objectives, however, unless we are willing to help free peoples to maintain their free institutions and their national integrity against aggressive movements that seek to impose upon them totalitarian regimes. This is no more than a frank recognition that totalitarian regimes imposed on free peoples, by direct or indirect aggression, undermine the foundations of international peace and hence the security of the United States.

The peoples of a number of countries of the world have recently had totalitarian regimes forced upon them against their will. The Government of the United States has made frequent protests against coercion and intimidation, in violation of the Yalta agreement, in Poland, Rumania, and Bulgaria. I must also state that in a number of other countries there have been similar developments.

At the present moment in world history nearly every nation must choose between alternative ways of life. The choice is too often not a free one.

One way of life is based upon the will of the majority, and is distinguished by free institutions, representative government, free elections, guarantees of individual liberty, freedom of speech and religion, and freedom from political oppression.

The second way of life is based upon the will of a minority forcibly imposed upon the majority. It relies upon terror and oppression, a controlled press and radio; fixed elections, and the suppression of personal freedoms.

I believe that it must be the policy of the United States to support free peoples who are resisting attempted subjugation by armed minorities or by outside pressures.

I believe that we must assist free peoples to work out their own destinies in their own way.

I believe that our help should be primarily through economic and financial aid which is essential to economic stability and orderly political processes.

The world is not static, and the status quo is not sacred. But we cannot allow changes in the status quo in violation of the Charter of the United Nations by such methods as coercion, or by such subterfuges as political infiltration. In helping free and independent nations to maintain their freedom, the United States will be giving effect to the principles of the Charter of the United Nations.

It is necessary only to glance at a map to realize that the survival and integrity of the Greek nation are of grave importance in a much wider situation. If Greece should fall under the control of an armed minority, the effect upon its neighbor, Turkey, would be immediate and serious. Confusion and disorder might well spread throughout the entire Middle East.

Moreover, the disappearance of Greece as an independent state would have a profound effect upon those countries in Europe whose peoples are struggling against great difficulties to maintain their freedoms and their independence while they repair the damages of war.

It would be an unspeakable tragedy if these countries, which have struggled so long against overwhelming odds, should lose that victory for which they sacrificed so much. Collapse of free institutions and loss of independence would be disastrous not only for them but for the world. Discouragement and possibly failure would quickly be the lot of neighboring peoples striving to maintain their freedom and independence.

Should we fail to aid Greece and Turkey in this fateful hour, the effect will be far reaching to the West as well as to the East.

We must take immediate and resolute action.

I therefore ask the Congress to provide authority for assistance to Greece and Turkey in the amount of $400,000,000 for the period ending June 30, 1948. In requesting these funds, I have taken into consideration the maximum amount of relief assistance which would be furnished to Greece out of the $350,000,000 which I recently requested that the Congress authorize for the prevention of starvation and suffering in countries devastated by the war.

In addition to funds, I ask the Congress to authorize the detail of American civilian and military personnel to Greece and Turkey, at the request of those countries, to assist in the tasks of reconstruction, and for the purpose of supervising the use of such financial and material assistance as may be furnished. I recommend that authority also be provided for the instruction and training of selected Greek and Turkish personnel.

Finally, I ask that the Congress provide authority which will permit the speediest and most effective use, in terms of needed commodities, supplies, and equipment, of such funds as may be authorized.

If further funds, or further authority, should be needed for purposes indicated in this message, I shall not hesitate to bring the situation before the Congress. On this subject the Executive and Legislative branches of the Government must work together.

This is a serious course upon which we embark.

I would not recommend it except that the alternative is much more serious. The United States contributed $341,000,000,000 toward winning World War II. This is an investment in world freedom and world peace.

The assistance that I am recommending for Greece and Turkey amounts to little more than 1 tenth of 1 per cent of this investment. It is only common sense that we should safeguard this investment and make sure that it was not in vain.

The seeds of totalitarian regimes are nurtured by misery and want. They spread and grow in the evil soil of poverty and strife. They reach their full growth when the hope of a people for a better life has died. We must keep that hope alive.

The free peoples of the world look to us for support in maintaining their freedoms.

If we falter in our leadership, we may endanger the peace of the world—and we shall surely endanger the welfare of our own nation.

Great responsibilities have been placed upon us by the swift movement of events.

I am confident that the Congress will face these responsibilities squarely.

Document Analysis

The Truman Doctrine represents a dramatic turning point in the history of American foreign policy. President Harry S. Truman spoke to a joint session of Congress and announced a new direction in U.S. foreign policy, marking what many consider to be the beginning of the Cold War. In his speech, he speaks directly about the situation faced by Greece and Turkey as they sought to avoid Communist domination. In a larger sense, however, Truman used the speech to articulate a new vision of the United States' role in the world. According to Truman, the United States could no longer shrink back to an isolated existence as it had at the conclusion of previous wars. A new geopolitical landscape, a new position as a world superpower, and the spread of Communism created the need for a new strategy to deal with the situation.

Truman begins by explaining the two crises in Greece and Turkey. The Communist-led insurgency in Greece, funded by the Communist government of Yugoslavia, threatened to overthrow the pro-Western monarchy. Great Britain had been providing financial assistance to the Greek government but, due to their own economic crisis, were unable to continue. Truman asserts that, without American aid, Greece could very well fall to the Communists. In Turkey, the Soviet Union was pressuring the small, weak nation to share control over the Dardanelles and the Bosporus. Without assistance from the United States, the Soviet Union could dominate the eastern Mediterranean Sea and the Middle East. Truman speaks briefly about how he had considered asking the United Nations (U.N.) to assist Greece and Turkey, as the settlement of international disputes was the very reason for its existence, but he came to the conclusion that the situation needed immediate assistance of a greater extent than the U.N. could provide.

The larger issue, however, was the choice the nations of the world faced between a way of life "based upon the will of the majority" that had free elections and institutions as well as guaranteed protection of individual freedoms, and a way of life "based upon the will of a minority forcibly imposed upon the majority," where the state is coercive and totalitarian, suppressing individual and social freedoms. The role of the United States in this new world was to contain Soviet expansion by helping nations such as Greece to "become a self-supporting and self-respecting democracy." Truman sums up his intentions by stating that "it must be the policy of the United States to support free peoples who are resisting attempted subjugation by armed minorities or by outside pressures." According to Truman, the United States must meet any challenge put forward by the Soviet Union and its desire to expand Communist control, arguing that "there is no other country to which democratic Greece can turn. No other nation is willing and able to provide the necessary support."

Essential Themes

The Truman Doctrine outlined the ideas that shaped America's foreign policy during the early years of the Cold War, particularly the idea that the Soviet Union needed to be contained and that the United States was the only nation in the world capable of doing so. The United States relied primarily on political and economic means, though the fact that the American military was kept on a permanent war-footing demonstrated that armed conflict was always a possibility. Though Congress approved the aid package that Truman requested for Greece and Turkey, not everyone was convinced by Truman's long-term strategy. Former vice president Henry A. Wallace, who had been the secretary of commerce until he gave a speech in 1946 critical of the Truman administration's foreign policy toward the Soviet Union, thought that cooperation with the Soviets would be far more effective. Others thought the Truman Doctrine too soft and argued that the Soviets would only respect military power in equal measure to its own.

In retrospect, the results of the aid package to Greece and Turkey were ambiguous. Both countries were able to stand firm in the face of the Communist threats they faced, but the aid did not guarantee a more democratic government in either country, as both saw the rise of authoritarian right-wing governments. However, the die was cast, and the Truman Doctrine inspired the Marshall Plan that, beginning in 1948, provided large amounts of financial aid to friendly governments in Europe, with the idea being that when the people of a nation are not economically threatened, they would be far less likely to succumb to Communist propaganda or support an overthrow of their government. The military component of the Truman Doctrine began to take shape with the administration's approval of NSC-68 in 1950, a document that set in motion plans to strengthen the U.S. military as a counterweight to the massive Soviet military.

Though later presidents recast the conflict in ways that suited their own style, the basic ideas contained in the Truman Doctrine formed the basis of the United States' Cold War strategy from the beginning to the end, and the second half of the twentieth century was to be dominated by the global showdown between the two superpowers.

—*Steven L. Danver, PhD*

Bibliography and Additional Reading

Bostdorff, Denise M. *Proclaiming the Truman Doctrine: The Cold War Call to Arms*. College Station: Texas A&M UP, 2008. Print.

Jones, Howard. "A New Kind of War": *America's Global Strategy and the Truman Doctrine in Greece*. New York: Oxford UP, 1989. Print.

Mastny, Vojtech. *The Cold War and Soviet Insecurity: The Stalin Years*. New York: Oxford UP, 1996. Print.

Offner, Arnold A. *Another Such Victory: President Truman and the Cold War, 1945–1953*. Stanford: Stanford UP, 2002. Print.

Pechatnov, Vladimir O. "The Soviet Union and the World, 1944–1953." *The Cambridge History of the Cold War: Origins*. Vol. 1. Ed. Melvyn P. Leffler and Odd Arne Westad. New York: Cambridge UP, 2010. 90–111. Print.

■ Declaration of the Establishment of the State of Israel

Date: May 14, 1948
Authors: David Ben-Gurion, Zvi Berenson, Yehuda Leib Maimon, Pinchas Rosen, Moshe Sharett, Aharon Zisling
Geographic region: Israel
Genre: Speech; declaration

Summary Overview

The declaration that the Jewish community living in the British protectorate of Palestine was forming an independent nation transformed international politics, not only in the Middle East, but across the world. Although it would take a few months to formally adopt a constitution, and even longer to gain control of its territories, the modern state of Israel began its existence on Mary 14, 1948, the last day the British ruled the area under a mandate given after World War I. During the seven decades since the declaration by the Jewish People's Council, the state of Israel has undergone major changes in its population, territory, and economy. Beginning with a war to secure the independence that had been declared, Israel's military has almost always been involved in ongoing operations, including four major wars against neighboring Arab states. The creation of the state of Israel, without the Palestinian Arabs taking the opportunity to create their own state in 1948, created uncertainty and an imbalance of power that has contributed to the ongoing hostility between Israel and its neighbors.

Defining Moment

With the Allied victory in World War II, the time came for the United Kingdom and France to make good on promises given to people in the Middle East during that war and during World War I. The British had governed the protectorate of Palestine since the end of World War I, directly, west of the Jordan River, and through a compliant monarchy east of the Jordan. In 1946, the territory east of the Jordan River became fully independent as the state of Jordan. West of the river, two groups had competing claims on the land and for statehood. Although Jewish groups and individuals had migrated throughout the world since antiquity, in the second century C.E., most Jews remaining in the Romans province of Palestine were expelled by the authorities. Since that time, the Jewish population in the region

had been relatively small. However, the Zionist movement (which began in the late nineteenth century) had encouraged Jews to return to the area in which the Biblical states of Israel and Judea had been located, with the goal of creating a Jewish state. This goal had been reinforced by the Balfour Declaration (1917) in which the British government had endorsed the creation of a "national home for the Jewish people."

In 1946, a joint British-American commission recommended the creation of two states, one Jewish and one Arab, within the territory west of the Jordan River. However, President Truman made a statement supporting Jewish interests and ignoring the Arabs. The British stated that they would no longer administer the Palestinian Mandate, effective by August, 1948. In 1947, the United Nations passed Resolution 181 which suggested the creation of two states in Palestine. The Arab states were opposed to this resolution and to later attempts to establish a Palestinian Arab state at the same time as the new Jewish state, because the proposed divisions seemed to favor the Jewish population. With civil unrest increasing, and a U.N. proposal in place, the United Kingdom announced that it was ending its protectorate at the end of the day on May 14, 1948. Thus, the Jewish leadership arranged for this declaration to be made that day, creating a temporary government for the territory identified as the new Jewish state of Israel in the United Nations' plan for partition. No comparable Arab government was in place, as the Palestinian Arabs and neighboring Arab states believed that the entire territory should be one state, which would have an Arab majority. (In 1945, the population was approximately 60 percent Muslim and 31 percent Jewish.) With the declaration that the state of Israel was established, conflict between Israel and its neighbors began with more than 13,000 Arab troops moving into Palestine to stop the creation of Israel as a viable state. When an armistice was finally negotiated, in 1949, between Israel and its four neighbors, Israel

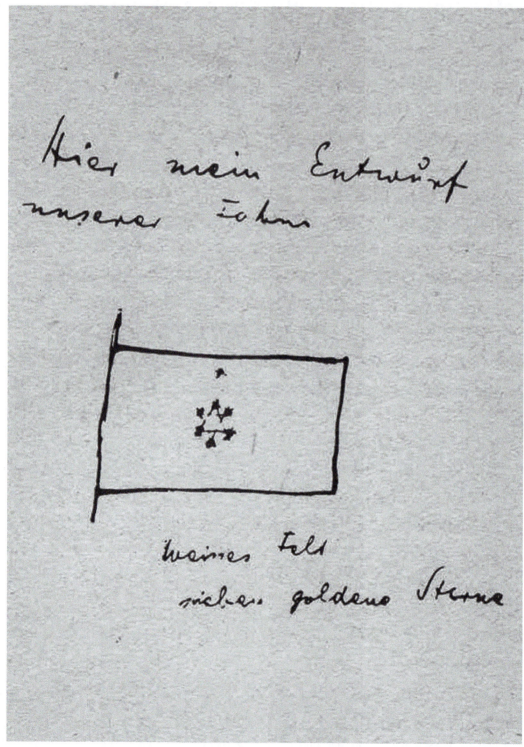

The Seven Stars flag, drawn by Herzl Translation: Here (is) my design for our flag, white field, seven gold stars.

had increased in size by one third with the remainder of what had been proposed to be the Palestinian state then under the control of Jordan (West Bank) and Egypt (Gaza).

Author Biographies

David Ben-Gurion (1886-1973) was born (as David Gruen) in the Russian Empire/Poland. Raised in a Zionist family, by age 18 he was teaching a socialist form of Zionism in Warsaw. In 1906, he moved to Palestine and continued his activism. Exiled by the Ottoman Empire, he returned to Palestine after World War I. By 1935, he was the chairman of the principle Zionist organization in Palestine. After World War II, Ben-Gurion strengthened his work to create a Jewish state. He became Israel's first prime minister and defense minister. He served as prime minister from May 1948 to January 1954, and November 1955 to June 1963.

Zvi Berenson (1901-2001) was born in Palestine/Israel. A lawyer by training, he was an advisor to the General Labor Federation in Palestine, under the British. He wrote the first draft of the Declaration of the Establishment of the State of Israel. He served as Minister of Labor and later as a Supreme Court justice from 1954-1977.

Yehuda Leib Maimon (1875-1962) was born in the Russian Empire. A rabbi, he became a leader within the religious Zionist movement. He moved to Palestine in 1913, and was expelled by the Ottoman Empire, returning after World War I. He participated in every Zionist Congress from 1909 to 1948. After Israel was formed, he became the first Minister of Religions, serving until 1951.

Pinchas Rosen (1887-1978) was born in Germany and was a lawyer. Prior to World War I, he helped found a Zionist organization in Germany, and after the war became chairman of the Zionist Federation in Germany. Moving to Palestine, he was active in politics under the British, creating the New Aliyah Party. Upon independence, he became the first Minister of Justice, serving from 1948-51, 1952-56, and 1956-61.

Moshe Sharett (1894-1965) was born in the Russian Empire/Ukraine. He moved to Palestine in 1906 and later studied law in Constantinople. He worked in the Zionist movement, becoming a leader in 1933. Upon the creation of Israel, he was the first Foreign Minister and the second Prime Minister when Ben-Gurion retired.

Aharon Zisling (1901-1964) was born in the Russian Empire/Belarus. He moved to Palestine, in 1904, becoming a leader in the Haganah, the Zionist paramilitary organization, which was the foundation for the Israel Defense Force. He initially served as Agricultural Minister, but broke with Ben-Gurion because of Ben-Gurion's treatment of Arab civilians in the 1948 Arab-Israeli War.

HISTORICAL DOCUMENT

ERETZ-ISRAEL (Hebrew—the Land of Israel, Palestine) was the birthplace of the Jewish people. Here their spiritual, religious and political identity was shaped. Here they first attained to statehood, created cultural values of national and universal significance and gave to the world the eternal Book of Books.

After being forcibly exiled from their land, the people kept faith with it throughout their Dispersion and never ceased to pray and hope for their return to it and for the restoration in it of their political freedom.

Impelled by this historic and traditional attachment, Jews strove in every successive generation to re-establish themselves in their ancient homeland. In recent decades they returned in their masses. Pioneers, ma'pilim (Hebrew—immigrants coming to Eretz-Israel in defiance of restrictive legislation0 and defenders, they made deserts bloom, revived the Hebrew language, built villages and towns, and created a thriving community controlling its own economy and culture, loving peace but knowing how to defend itself, bringing the blessings of progress to all the country's inhabitants, and aspiring towards independent nationhood.

In the year 5657 (1897), at the summons of the spiritual father of the Jewish State, Theodore Herzl, the First Zionist Congress convened and proclaimed the right of the Jewish people to national rebirth in its own country.

This right was recognized in the Balfour Declaration of the 2nd November, 1917, and re-affirmed in the Mandate of the League of Nations which, in particular, gave international sanction to the historic connection between the Jewish people and Eretz-Israel and to the right of the Jewish people to rebuild its National Home.

The catastrophe which recently befell the Jewish people—the massacre of millions of Jews in Europe—was another clear demonstration of the urgency of solving the problem of its homelessness by re-establishing in Eretz-Israel the Jewish State, which would open the gates of the homeland wide to every Jew and confer upon the Jewish people the status of a fully privileged member of the comity of nations.

Survivors of the Nazi holocaust in Europe, as well as Jews from other parts of the world, continued to migrate to Eretz-Israel, undaunted by difficulties, restrictions and dangers, and never ceased to assert their right to a life of dignity, freedom and honest toil in their national homeland.

In the Second World War, the Jewish community of this country contributed its full share to the struggle of the freedom- and peace-loving nations against the forces of Nazi wickedness and, by the blood of its soldiers and its war effort, gained the right to be reckoned among the peoples who founded the United Nations.

On the 29th November, 1947, the United Nations General Assembly passed a resolution calling for the establishment of a Jewish State in Eretz-Israel; the General Assembly required the inhabitants of Eretz-Israel to take such steps as were necessary on their part for the implementation of that resolution. This recognition by the United Nations of the right of the Jewish people to establish their State is irrevocable.

This right is the natural right of the Jewish people to be masters of their own fate, like all other nations, in their own sovereign State.

Accordingly we, members of the People's Council, representatives of the Jewish community of Eretz Israel and of the Zionist Movement, are here

assembled on the day of the termination of the British Mandate over Eretz Israel and, by virtue of our natural and historic right and on the strength of the resolution of the United Nations General Assembly, hereby declare the establishment of a Jewish state in Eretz Israel, to be known as the State of Israel.

We declare that, with effect from the moment of the termination of the Mandate being tonight, the eve of Sabbath, the 6th Iyar, 5708 (15th May, 1948), until the establishment of the elected, regular authorities of the State in accordance with the Constitution which shall be adopted by the Elected Constituent Assembly not later than the 1st October 1948, the People's Council shall act as a Provisional Council of State, and its executive organ, the People's Administration, shall be the Provisional Government of the Jewish State, to be called "Israel".

The State of Israel will be open for Jewish immigration and for the Ingathering of the Exiles; it will foster the development of the country for the benefit of all its inhabitants; it will be based on freedom, justice and peace as envisaged by the prophets of Israel; it will ensure complete equality of social and political rights to all its inhabitants irrespective of religion, race or sex; it will guarantee freedom of religion, conscience, language, education and culture; it will safeguard the Holy Places of all religions; and it will be faithful to the principles of the Charter of the United Nations.

The State of Israel is prepared to cooperate with the agencies and representatives of the United Nations in implementing the resolution of the General Assembly of the 29th November, 1947, and will take steps to bring about the economic union of the whole of Eretz-Israel.

We appeal to the United Nations to assist the Jewish people in the building-up of its State and to receive the State of Israel into the comity of nations.

We appeal—in the very midst of the onslaught launched against us now for months—to the Arab inhabitants of the State of Israel to preserve peace and participate in the upbuilding of the State on the basis of full and equal citizenship and due representation in all its provisional and permanent institutions.

We extend our hand to all neighbouring states and their peoples in an offer of peace and good neighbourliness, and appeal to them to establish bonds of cooperation and mutual help with the sovereign Jewish people settled in its own land. The State of Israel is prepared to do its share in a common effort for the advancement of the entire Middle East.

We appeal to the Jewish people throughout the Diaspora to rally round the Jews of Eretz-Israel in the tasks of immigration and upbuilding and to stand by them in the great struggle for the realization of the age-old dream—the redemption of Israel.

Placing our trust in the Almighty, we affix our signatures to this proclamation at this session of the provisional Council of State, on the soil of the Homeland, in the city of Tel-Aviv, on this Sabbath eve, the 5th day of Iyar, 5708 (14th May, 1948).

GLOSSARY

Herzl, Theodor: Austrian Jew who rejected assimilation and advocated for the creation of a Jewish state; he is considered the father of the modern Jewish state, although he died in 1904

Iyar, 5708: eighth month of the Jewish calendar from Rosh Hashanah, second counting from Nissan (month in which Passover falls), with the year based on ancient calculations of either creation or the expulsion of Adam from the Garden of Eden

Zionist: a supporter of the late nineteenth- and early twentieth-century political movement advocating the creation of a Jewish state; the term is derived from a Biblical name for the hill on which the Jewish temple was located

Document Analysis

This declaration was made to formally announce the creation of the state of Israel as well as to give justification for its creation. The authors sought to outline the long history of the Jewish people, as well as the origins of the Jewish state. Moving to more recent events, they gave their understanding of why a Jewish state was needed and why it should be located in what had been the British protectorate of Palestine. The Zionist forces within Judaism had been growing stronger each decade since the modern movement was established. Finally, they outlined what would be the transitional government, as well as giving assurances to all people that Israel would be a modern democracy, with rights extended to all its citizens, regardless of "religion, race or sex."

The declaration began with a statement of what had occurred in the ancient past, recounting Biblical stories of the development of the Jewish people, religion, and state. The fact that most of these things had occurred in this location (British Protectorate of Palestine) gave them, in their minds, a strong foundation for establishing the modern state of Israel in Palestine. In their declaration, the authors made indirect reference to parts of the Jewish liturgy in which those praying sought to celebrate holy days in Jerusalem, when they stated that Jews "in every successive generation" hoped to return to their homeland. In 1917, when the British Foreign Secretary, Arthur Balfour, communicated his government's support for the eventual establishment of a "national home for the Jewish people" in Palestine, it was an affirmation of these Jewish hopes. Thus, the committee established, to their satisfaction, that the protectorate of Palestine was the proper location of the new state.

The need for such a state was seen from two directions. For some, the temptation to assimilate into mainstream Western society was the primary reason a Jewish state was needed. The revival of the Hebrew language was but one illustration of the transformation that could happen in a Jewish state. However, for the majority, it was the Holocaust perpetuated by Nazis in World War II that illustrated the need for a Jewish state. While Jews had been somewhat assimilated in Western Europe, this had never been the case in Eastern Europe, nor did it seem, in Germany. Because there was no safe haven for Jews, many who hoped to flee persecution could not. By creating a state in which all Jews would automatically be eligible for citizenship, it was hoped that a repeat of the horrors of the concentration and extermination camps could be avoided.

The time for its creation was now, in 1948, in the eyes of the declaration's authors. World War II had ended and there was great support for the Jews who had suffered so much at the instigation of the Nazi leaders. It had been thirty years since the British had taken control of Palestine, and they were tiring of the financial and military costs of ruling the protectorate. The United Kingdom's announcement that it would no longer govern this portion of the Middle East had precipitated a crisis for many, due to the uncertainty that lay ahead. Negotiations at the newly formed United Nations resulted in Resolution 181, which called for a Jewish and an Arab (Muslim) state to be established in the territory that had been ruled by Britain. (The authors of the declaration conveniently forgot to mention the latter part of the United Nations' resolution.) While a resolution did not force the creation of these states, it did give a sense of what the world community thought would be best, even if the world community was only fifty-seven nations at that time. (The vote was thirty-three in favor, thirteen opposed—including all five Arab states; ten abstained, and one was not present.) Even though the British did not have a plan for the future of their protectorate of Palestine, once they left, they were among those voting against the resolution. Without any real alternative put forward by the British, or the United Nations, the Jewish leaders' decision to move forward in May 1948, seemed to them to be the best move.

With the creation of Israel, the authors of the declaration understood that there were certain responsibilities that would be placed upon the new government. As such, they pledged the new state to the ideals of the United Nations and the recommendations contained in Resolution 181. The committee pledged that the new state would act in the mold of modern liberal democracies, by respecting religious freedom and granting all equality before the law. Although they were consciously creating a Jewish state, and spent much time debating exactly how this should be reflected in the declaration and the government of the new state, the authors understood what it meant to be persecuted for one's religion. Thus, they pledged "freedom of religion, conscience, language, education, and culture." Even while ignoring the sections of Resolution 181 which recommended the creation of an Arab state, they did pledge that they would uphold the economic recommendations of Resolution 181, which had suggested that the two new states be unified in their economic development, creating an "economic union" such as was just starting

in Western Europe. The committee offered "peace and good neighbourliness" to the surrounding Arab states, even though a low scale conflict had been simmering ever since the British had announced their departure from Palestine. (Within hours of the announcement of this declaration, this turned into a much larger military conflict.) With the public proclamation of this declaration creating the state of Israel, it was up to the Jewish people whether or not the state had a future.

Essential Themes

Having gathered in the Tel Aviv Museum of Art to announce this declaration to the world (this meeting was kept secret until almost the last minute due to security concerns), the Jewish People's Committee, which became the Provisional State Council, officially created the modern state of Israel. Gaining official recognition from the United States the day it was created, and the Union of Soviet Socialist Republics shortly thereafter, the leaders hoped that the future would be bright and that the conflict with the Arab states might be short-lived. However, as the decades have passed, it became clear that this was not the case. The fact that this was designated as a Jewish state has been one of the core issues of this conflict, just as it was one of the central points of the declaration. The suffering of the Jews down through the centuries was seen by Zionists as partially the result of not having a state to which they could immigrate, if needed. Reflecting Biblical history, as well as twentieth-century statements and events, the declaration sought to create Israel as a Jewish state, even while granting religious freedom to all people.

Although the United Nations was an untested organization, the Jewish leaders were hopeful that Resolution 181 would provide the foundation for international support for the state of Israel. By additionally pledging that all people would have basic human rights, the council hoped that this would increase support for the new state, as well as change the minds of some Arab leaders. The pledge of economic cooperation was another step in this direction. Although they recognized that the impending conflict was most probably going to occur, the council projected an optimistic vision for the future, even as they saw the "onslaught launched against us." However, for these individuals, their hope for the "redemption of Israel" was worth any struggle that might lie ahead.

—Donald A Watt, PhD

Bibliography and Additional Reading

Ben-Arieh, Alex. "Independence Day 1948" *Historama.* Tel Aviv: Historama, 2018. Web. 27 February 2018.

Morris, Benny. *1948: A History of the First Arab-Israeli War.* New Haven: Yale University Press, 2008. Print.

Office of the Historian. "The Arab-Israeli War of 1948" *Milestones in U.S. Foreign Relations.* Washington: Department of State, 2018. Web. 27 February 2018.

SchlichimMetrowest. "Declaration of Independence of the State of Israel (English subtitles)" *YouTube.* San Bruno CA: YouTube, 2010. Web. 27 February 2018.

Shapira, Anita. (Anthony Berris, trans.) *Ben-Gurion: Father of Modern Israel.* (Jewish Lives) New Haven: Yale University Press, 2014. Print.

Shinder, Colin. *A History of Modern Israel.* 2nd ed. Cambridge: Cambridge University Press, 2013. Print.

Proclamation of the Algerian National Liberation Front

Date: November 1, 1954
Author: National Liberation Front
Geographic region: Algeria
Genre: Proclamation; political tract; speech

Summary Overview

The Algerian War of Independence was a war of de-colonization between the Algerian National Liberation Front (FLN) and the French government from 1954 to 1962. The FLN fought to free Algeria from the control of the French, who had occupied Algeria since the 1840s. The war ended when the French withdrew from Algeria and handed over rule of the country to an Algerian-run government.

The war is famous for the use of guerrilla tactics by the FLN and of brutal retaliations against Algerians by the French. The FLN realized the importance of having public opinion on their side, and they attempted throughout the war to gain the support of Algerians and of the international community. The French, on the other hand, quickly lost the moral high ground with their indiscriminate violence and publicized killings of civilians. After nearly eight years of war, the French government negotiated a truce with Algeria that led to the cessation of hostilities and the establishment of an independent Algerian government.

The FLN was founded by Algerians who had been active in revolutionary groups prior to the outbreak of war. The group announced its existence and the beginning of the War of Independence on November 1, 1954 by releasing a Proclamation that lays out their objectives, demands for independence, and plans for war if the French do not withdraw.

Defining Moment

The French had established a colonial government in Algeria in 1840. French colonists controlled political and social policies, and they held much of the fertile and developed land in the country after having seized it from native Algerians in the first wave of colonialism. By 1900, France had a colonial empire that reached as far as the Pacific Ocean, but the Algerian colony was their longest-held possession and a defining part of France's identity as an imperialist power.

Islamic and nationalist movements were founded in Algeria in the early twentieth century to oppose France, but they made little progress under the colonist-dominated system. One early voice in favor of Algerian independence was Messali Hadj (1898-1974), who founded one of the first nationalist parties. As anti-French activism had been banned in Algeria, he travelled Europe promoting the Algerian cause, spending time in jail and under house arrest. Despite these early efforts, it was not until World War II that the first major anti-French resistance movements gained traction. When France had been invaded by Nazi Germany and the pro-Nazi Vichy government ruled France and the colonies, an Allied force invaded Algeria to free it from German rule. The Allies repealed many of the repressive Vichy laws that had been unpopular with native Algerians, but they also demanded that Algeria supply soldiers to fight against the Germans. Muslim leaders were unwilling to encourage their people to fight on behalf of the French without having a say in their own government.

The French government ignored Algerian calls for self-government. Dissatisfaction with the status quo, intensified by famine and unemployment, continued to grow in Algeria until 1945; riots and police violence broke out even at celebrations to mark the end of the European war. In retaliation, the French government attacked suspected revolutionaries as well as civilian areas.

Despite the violence and Algerian calls for self-government, French public opinion was very much in favor of preserving Algeria as a French colony. Messali Hadj, who had been under house arrest for much of the war, founded another independence movement (called the Movement for the Triumph of Democratic Liberties, or MTDL), this time with a military branch. The movement was wildly successful in the 1947 elections despite electoral interference by French colonists.

In response to their political defeat, the French government developed an assembly consisting of two groups: one to represent the Muslim majority and the other to represent the colonists, a small minority of the general population. In addition, the 1948 assembly elections were once again rigged in favor of the colonists.

The obvious interference with the political system spurred widespread political activism. Anti-French demonstrations broke out across the country. Older party leaders who had fought to be treated equally by the French began to be pushed aside in favor of younger revolutionaries who advocated pushing the French out of Algerian society altogether. At the same time, French colonists who saw these movements as a threat to their political and social power began to fear the loss of privilege that a more egalitarian society would bring. Algerian society became even more polarized than it already had been, and violence frequently broke out at protests.

After one such protest in 1952, Messali Hadj was arrested and deported to France. His MTDL was soon dissolved, with many of its members going underground and founding new committees with a stronger focus on the military arm. By 1954, several anticolonial revolutionary groups were ready to take aim at the French government by organized military means. The most successful of these groups was to be a small group known as the National Liberation Front.

Author Biography

The *Fronte de Libération Nationale* (abbreviated as the FLN; anglicized as the National Liberation Front) was founded by members of the MTLD who were committed to an armed revolution against French colonial rule of Algeria. They planned to continue their predecessors' opposition to French rule by political means, but they added an organized strategy of military resistance. The FLN sprang into the fight against France on November 1, 1954 with the issuance a proclamation urging all Algerians to join their cause against the French. With the FLN's call to arms, the Algerian War of Independence officially began.

The eight-year war was a bloody and complicated revolution that led to hundreds of thousands of deaths, millions of refugees, and the eventual collapse of France's overseas empire. Both sides used guerilla tactics, targeted civilians, and tortured their opponents. Throughout the war, members of the FLN directed military actions against the French while attempting to get the support of the international community, including the United Nations. At the same time, the French quickly alienated the world by using brutal tactics against the Algerian people, militants, and civilians alike.

The FLN slowly shifted the war from rural areas into the cities. Beginning in 1956, the main theater of action was the capital city of Algiers. The rebels bombed several popular French cafes in 1956 and increased acts violence in the city, including shootings and bombings. They also agitated for a nationwide general strike. The French responded by instituting total martial law over the city: they used soldiers to break the strike, imposed a curfew, and tortured detainees. Their brutal methods caused a near-universal shift in Algerian opinion to the side of the rebels and increased global support for the FLN. In their attempt to regain control of the colony, the French made their rule intolerable to its inhabitants.

The war intensified until 1958. In that year, voters in France expressed their dissatisfaction with the politicians who had been unable to quell the violence and ensure the safety of the French colonists in Algeria. Charles de Gaulle, who had himself been a guerrilla leader during World War II and was the most respected man in French politics, reentered government. He toured Algeria in an attempt to appeal to both colonists and native Algerians, promising safety to the former and reform to the latter. He called for suffrage for all Algerians (including women) and set up a committee to draft a new constitution that would treat the colony more equally. When pressed, however, he revealed that Algerians would always be second-class citizens in a French-run society. His lack of commitment to total equality alienated Algerians and his attempt to compromise alienated French colonists.

Seizing the moment, the FLN established their own government-in-exile in Tunisia. Their public relations campaign was beginning to take hold in France and abroad: intellectuals and private citizens wrote and provided financial aid to the revolution, and the United Nations began to take an interest. By 1961, negotiations for a peace had begun.

In a February referendum, Algerians voted by a large majority for independence. Violence continued until a ceasefire was decreed in March 1962. The negotiations that followed led to a truce in June and then the decree on July 3, 1962 of Algerian independence from France. After 132 years of colonization and a traumatic eight-year war, Algeria was free to determine its own government.

The FLN immediately seized political control of Algeria, established itself as the ruling party, and outlawed opposition. Despite some internal conflicts, the party reigned for over 25 years under the control of various long-term leaders; no multi-party elections were held. It was not until 1990 that the FLN, pressured by strikes and protests, allowed other parties to participate in elections. They were defeated in the first open local elections, but political and religious divisions soon led to the Algerian Civil War, another brutally bloody war marked by drawn-out conflict and atrocities. At the end of the war, which lasted from 1991 to 2002, the FLN reestablished itself as a major political party, and FLN politicians currently hold about a third of the elected seats in Algeria's national government.

HISTORICAL DOCUMENT

To the Algerian people
To the Militants of the National Cause

To you who are called upon to judge us, the Algerian people in a general way, the militants more particularly, our purpose in distributing this proclamation is to enlighten you concerning the profound reasons which have impelled us to act by revealing to you our program, the meaning of our action, and the cogency of our views the, goal of which remains National Independence within the North African framework. Our wish as well is to help you avoid the confusion maintained by imperialism and its corrupt political and administrative agents.

Before all else, we consider that after decades of struggle the National Movement has reached its final stage of realization. In fact, as the goal of the revolutionary movement is to create all the favorable conditions needed for the launching of operations for liberation, we believe that internally the people are united behind the sign of independence and action; and externally the climate of détente is favorable for the settling of minor problems (among them ours) with the support of our Arab and Muslim brothers above all. The events in Morocco and Tunisia are significant in this regard, and profoundly mark the process of the liberation struggle in North Africa. It is worth noting that for quite some time we have been, in this regard, precursors in the unity of action, unfortunately never realized among the three countries.

Today, many are resolutely engaged on this path and we, relegated to the rear, suffer the fate of those who events have passed by. It is thus that our national movement, overwhelmed by years of immobilisme and routine, poorly oriented, deprived of the indispensable support of public opinion, and overtaken by events, has progressively disintegrated, to the great satisfaction of colonialism, which thinks it has carried off its greatest victory in its struggle against the Algerian vanguard. The hour is serious.

Facing this situation, which risks becoming irreparable, a group of young leaders and conscious activists, rallying around it the majority of the healthy and decisive elements, has judged that the moment has arrived to move the National Movement out of the impasse into which it was backed by personal struggles and fights over influence, in order to launch it, at the side of the Moroccan and Tunisian brothers, into the true revolutionary struggle.

To this end, we insist on specifying that we are independent of the two clans that are fighting over power. Placing national interest above all petty and erroneous considerations of personality and prestige, in conformity with revolutionary principles, our action is directly solely against colonialism, our only blind and obstinate enemy, which has always refused to grant the least freedom by peaceful means.

These are, we think, sufficient, reasons for a movement of renewal to present itself under the name of National Liberation Front, releasing itself in this way from all possible compromises, and offering the possibility to all Algerian patriots of all social classes, of all the purely Algerian parties and movements, to integrate themselves into the struggle for liberation, without any other consideration.

In summary, we spell out below the major elements of our political program:

Goal: National Independence by:

The restoration of the sovereign, democratic and social Algerian state, within the framework of Islamic principles.

The respect of all fundamental liberties without distinction of race or religion.

Internal Objectives:

Political reform by the returning of the National Revolutionary Movement to its true path and by the wiping-out of the vestiges of corruption and reformism, the causes of our current regression.

The gathering together and organization of all the healthy energies of the Algerian people for the liquidation of the colonial system.

External Objectives:

The internalization of the Algerian problem.

The realization of North African unity within its natural Arabo-Islamic framework.

Within the framework of the U.N. Charter, the affirmation of our active sympathy with regard to all nations who support our operations for liberation.

Means of Struggle:

In conformity with revolutionary principles, and taking into account the internal and external situations, the continuation of the struggle by all possible means until the realization of our goal.

In order to reach these objectives, the National Liberation front will have two essential tasks to carry out simultaneously: an internal action, on the fronts of politics and action, and an external action, with the goal of the making of the Algerian problem a reality for the entire world, with the support of all our natural allies.

This is a heavy task which necessitates the mobilization of all national energy and resources. It is true that the struggle will be long, but the result is certain.

In the last place, in order to avoid all false interpretations and subterfuges, in order to prove our real desire for peace, to limit the number of human lives lost and the amount of blood spilled, we propose to French authorities an honorable platform of discussion, if these latter are animated by good faith and recognize once and for all in the people they subjugate the right to dispose of themselves:

The opening of negotiations with the authorized spokesmen of the Algerian people on the basis of the recognition of sovereignty through Algerian liberation, one and indivisible.

The creation of a climate of confidence through the liberation of all political prisoners, the lifting of all measures of exception, and the ceasing of all pursuit of the fighting forces.

The recognition of Algerian nationality by an official declaration abrogating the edicts, decrees and laws making Algeria a "French land," which is a denial of the History, the geography, the language, the religion, and the mores of the Algerian people.

In return:

French cultural and economic interests, honestly acquired, will be respected, as will persons and families.

All Frenchmen wishing to remain in Algeria will have the choice between their nationality of origin, in which case they will be considered foreigners vis à vis the laws in place, or they will opt for Algerian nationality, in which case they will be considered such in rights and obligations.

The bonds between France and Algeria will be defined and will be the object of an agreement between the two powers on the basis of equality and mutual respect.

Algerians! We invite you to think over our above Charter. Your obligation is to join with it in order to save our country and restore to it its freedom. The National Liberation Front is your front. Its victory is yours.

As for us, resolved to pursue the struggle, sure of your anti-imperialist sentiments, we give the best of ourselves to the Fatherland.

The Secretariat

GLOSSARY

abrogating: repealing, removing, denying

cogency: coherence, clearness

détente: lessening of hostilities

mores: customs, habits

sovereign: self-governing, self-determining

vestiges: traces

vis a vis: with respect to, in regard to

Document Analysis

The FLN's issuance of this Proclamation is today considered the first action of the Algerian War of Independence. The authors are prepared for a long-term, all-out, radical revolution that would completely overturn the existing society. They are aware that they will be fighting against the full power of the French establishment and French society, which has exploited Algerians and considered them second-class citizens for over a hundred years. They also realize the importance of international opinion and of winning not only battles but the respect and loyalty of the Algerian people. To that end, they use this proclamation to lay out their objectives, acknowledge the magnitude of their undertaking, and win public opinion to their side.

The first part of the speech also addresses the issue of public opinion. Creation of "favorable conditions" for the liberation movement depends on the support of the people being liberated, and the authors state that the unity of the Arab and Muslim societies is of primary importance. "Placing national interest above all," the FLN states that their aim is to support all those who support the revolution. They appeal to shared values and virtues—"independence and action," "freedom by peaceful means," patriotism, and liberation—in addressing an audience unified by opposition to imperialism.

The next part of the speech lays out the goal of the revolution: the establishment of Algerian self-government, free of external influences. The inclusion of both internal and external objectives is an important part of the FLN's strategy. For the duration of the war, they fought the French at home while also trying to get support for their cause abroad. As the war went on, their appeals to the United Nations were especially important in gaining international sympathy.

In the final section of the proclamation, the FLN offers an ultimatum and warns their opponents that they are willing to fight to the death for freedom. They speak directly to the French to request "recognition of Algerian nationality" and the elimination of French claims. The FLN states openly that the labeling of Algeria as French is a harmful construct invented to support French interests at the expense of Algerian. They offer an olive branch—if the French cooperate, Algeria will support a peaceful transition for the French colonists still in Algeria. Though they do not explicitly state what will happen if their demands are not met, they state their desire to limit—but not eliminate— "the number of human lives lost and the amount of blood spilled." If the French continue their colonization, the FLN will "give the best of ourselves" to the struggle.

Essential Themes and Impact

The Proclamation was published on November 1, 1954. On that day, the FLN attacked several police and military locations around Algeria, killing seven people total. The day became known as *Toussaint Rouge* ("Red All Saints' Day", after the Catholic holiday on which it took place). French authorities increased the number of troops stationed in Algeria, but the French government did not acknowledge the demands of the revolutionaries. In a speech addressing the attacks, the French president continued to state that Algeria was a French land and would remain French forever.

It took a few years for the revolutionary movement to gain traction abroad, but the FLN worked on all fronts to gain support in Algeria. Their military arm launched attacks against French bases and their intellectuals wrote and spoke in favor of liberation. At first, the French viewed the revolution as a problem to suppress by military action, but the FLN worked on both military and social fronts to gain support. As the war went on, the French realized that they would not be able to win by violence alone. After eight years of terror and bloodshed in Algeria and (to a lesser extent) France, the revolution led to the liberation of Algeria and the creation of the modern Algerian state.

—*Hannah Rich, MA*

Bibliography and Additional Reading

McDougall, James. 2017. *A History of Algeria*. Cambridge University Press.

Shepard, Todd. 2008. *The Invention of Decolonization: The Algerian War and the Remaking of France*. Cornell University Press.

Stone, Martin. 1997. *The Agony of Algeria*. Columbia University Press.

CIA Summary of the Overthrow of Premier Mossadeq of Iran

Date: March 1954
Author: Donald N. Wilber
Geographic region: Iran
Genre: Government document

Summary Overview

In the late summer of 1953, British and American intelligence services worked together to orchestrate a coup to overthrow the democratically elected prime minister of Iran, Mohammad Mossadeq (also spelled Mosaddegh or Mosaddiq). The British relied heavily on Iranian oil, which they had controlled since 1909, and Mossadeq led a popular movement to nationalize the oil fields. The British responded to nationalization with a boycott, removing trained personnel from Iranian refineries and refusing to purchase or transport Iranian oil. This led to an economic crisis, and fears in the West that the Soviet Union would exploit this instability to gain influence in Iran through the Tudeh Party, Iran's Communist party. The shah, or monarch, of Iran was reluctant to support the coup plot, which hinged on a royal decree that would remove Mossadeq and install a pro-Western prime minister, Fazlollah Zahedi. After significant pressure from the CIA, the shah agreed to support the coup, which replaced Mossadeq with Zahedi and reopened Iranian oil to Western investment. The following year, one of the main CIA organizers of the coup, Donald N. Wilber, wrote a classified history of the event that was not made public until the year 2000.

Defining Moment

Great Britain's interest in Iranian oil began in earnest on May 28, 1901, when the shah granted the petroleum rights over vast areas of territory to a British citizen, William Knox D'Arcy. When oil was not immediately discovered, D'Arcy was forced to accept other investors. Significant quantities of oil were discovered in 1908, and in 1909, the Anglo-Persian Oil Company (APOC) which would later become British Petroleum, was formed. By 1913, a massive refinery in Abadan was pumping oil destined for the British Empire. Under the agreement with D'Arcy, the Iranian government's share of the oil profits was just 16 percent, and the company declined to open its books for inspection.

Just before World War I, the British navy upgraded their ships from coal to oil, and the British government gained a controlling interest in the APOC. The British economy and military were dependent on a steady flow of inexpensive Iranian oil. During the war, the British stationed troops in Iran to protect their pipelines and proposed in 1919 that Iran become a British protectorate. Though this was not accepted by Iran, the British continued to control the vast majority of Iranian territory, but not without opposition. In the 1920s and 1930s, the Iranian government fought to renegotiate the D'Arcy agreement and regain greater control of the nation's resources. In 1933, a new sixty-year agreement was reached, which increased payments to the Iranian government and reduced the amount of land under direct APOC control.

Britain's relationship with Iran became even more complicated during World War II. The Soviet Union was a key British ally and was holding the Axis armies at bay on the Eastern Front; this two-front war was key to Britain's survival. The Soviet Union depended on Iranian oil to resupply its army, and though Iran was neutral, the shah was suspected of Nazi sympathies. British and Soviet forces therefore invaded Iran in 1941. The ruler, Reza Shah, was deposed and replaced by his son, Mohammad Reza Pahlavi, who remained in power until 1979.

After the war, the Iranian parliament wanted greater control over the country's oil reserves. Mossadeq was the leader of the nationalization movement and was elected prime minister of Iran in 1951. On May 2, Mossadeq declared the oil fields to be the property of Iran alone. The response from Britain was to remove all trained personnel from the refineries and organize and international boycott of Iranian oil. Production and sales dropped precipitously, leading to an economic crisis and internal unrest. By 1952, British and American intelligence officers had begun to develop a plan to oust Mossadeq. Dwight D. Eisenhower, the newly elected president of the United States, was afraid that the Soviet Union would be able to take advantage of the instability in Iran and decided to support the coup.

Author Biography

Donald Newton Wilber was born in Wisconsin on November 14, 1907. He attended New Trier High School and then went to Princeton University, where he graduated with a BA in 1929, as well as an MFA and PhD in architecture in 1949. Wilber's area of scholarly expertise was the Middle East, and he traveled and wrote extensively in Iran, Afghanistan, and Sri Lanka. Wilber's book *Iran, Past and Present* was published in 1948, establishing him as an expert on Iranian history. These scholarly endeavors gave Wilbur cover for his activities with the CIA, which he joined in 1948. He was a primary planner of the overthrow of Mossadeq in favor of a government friendlier to Western interests. Wilber served in the CIA until 1970, while working with various prestigious universities. He died on February 2, 1997, in Princeton, New Jersey, survived by his wife and two daughters.

HISTORICAL DOCUMENT

SECRET

Summary

By the end of 1952, it had become clear that the Mossadeq government in Iran was incapable of reaching an oil settlement with interested Western countries; was reaching a dangerous and advanced stage of illegal, deficit financing; was disregarding the Iranian constitution in prolonging Premier Mohammed Mossadeq's tenure of office; was motivated mainly by Mossadeq's desire for personal power; was governed by irresponsible policies based on emotion; had weakened the Shah and the Iranian Army to a dangerous degree; and had cooperated closely with the Tudeh (Communist) Party of Iran. In View of these factors, it was estimated that Iran was in real danger of falling behind the Iron Curtain; if that happened it would mean a victory for the Soviets in the Cold War and a major setback for the West in the Middle East. No remedial action other than the covert action plan set forth below could be found to improve the existing state of affairs.

It was the aim of the TPAJAX project to cause the fall of the Mossadeq government; to reestablish the prestige and power of the Shah; and to replace the Mossadeq government with one which would govern Iran according to constructive policies. Specifically, the aim was to bring power to a government which would reach equitable oil settlement, enabling Iran to become economically sound and financially solvent, and which would vigorously prosecute the dangerously strong Communist Party.

Once it had been determined definitely that it was not in American interests for the Mossadeq government to remain in power and CIA had been so informed by the Secretary of State in March 1953, CIA began drafting a plan whereby the aims state above could be realized through covert action. An estimate entitled "Factors Involved in the Overthrow of Mossadeq" was completed on 16 April 1953. It was here determined that an overthrow of Mossadeq was possible through covert operations. In April it was determined that CIA should conduct the envisioned operation jointly with the British Secret Intelligence Service (SIS). By the end of April, it was decided that CIA and SIS officers would draw up a plan on Cyprus which would be submitted to CIA and SIS Headquarters, and to the Department of State and the Foreign Office for final approval. On 3 June 1953, U.S. ambassador Loy Wesley Henderson arrived in the United States where he was fully consulted with regard to the objective and aims, as stated above, as well as CIA's intentions to design covert means of achieving the objective and aims.

The plan was completed by 10 June 1953 at which time Mr. Kermit Roosevelt, Chief of the Near East and Africa Division, CIA (who carried with him the views of the Department of State, CIA, and Ambassador Henderson); Mr. Roger Goiran, CIA Chief of Station, Iran; and two CIA planning officers met in Beirut to consider the plan. With minor changes the operational proposal was submitted to the SIS in London on 14 June 1953.

On 19 June 1953, the final operational plan, agreed upon by Mr. Roosevelt for the CIA and by British Intelligence in London, was submitted in Washington to the Department of State; to Mr. Allen W. Dulles, Director of CIA; and to Ambassador Henderson for approval. Simultaneously, it was submitted to the British Foreign Office by SIS for approval. The Department of State wanted to be assured of two things before it would grant approval of the plan:

1. That the United States Government could provide adequate grant aid to a successor Iranian Government so that such a government could be sustained until an oil settlement was reached.

2. That the British Government would signify in writing, to the satisfaction of the Department of State, its intentions to reach an early oil settlement with a successor Iranian Government in a spirit of good will and equity.

The Department of State satisfied itself on both of these scores.

In mid-July 1953, the Department of State and the British Foreign Office granted authorization for the implementation of the TPAJAX project, and the Director of CIA obtained the approval of the President of the United States. The SIS, with the concurrence of the CIA Director and Ambassador Henderson, proposed that Mr. Roosevelt assume field command in Tehran of the final phases of the operation. It was determined by the Department of State that it would be advisable for Ambassador Henderson to postpone his return to Iran, from Washington consultation, until the operation had been concluded. Arrangements were made jointly with SIS whereby operational liaison would be conducted on Cyprus where a CIA officer would be temporarily stationed, and support liaison would be conducted in Washington. Rapid three-way communications were arranged through CIA facilities between Tehran, Cyprus, and Washington. The time set for the operation was mid-August.

In Iran, CIA and SIS propaganda assets were to conduct an increasingly intensified propaganda effort through the press, handbills, and the Tehran clergy in a campaign designed to weaken the Mossadeq government in any way possible. In the United States, high-ranking U.S. officials were to make official statements which would shatter any hopes held by Premier Mossadeq that American economic aid would be forthcoming, and disabuse the Iranian public of the Mossadeq myth that the United States supported his regime.

General Fazlollah Zahedi, a former member of Mossadeq's cabinet, was chosen as the most suitable successor to the Premier since he stood out as the only person of stature who had consistently been openly in opposition to Mossadeq and who claimed any significant following. Zahedi was to be approached by CIA and be told of our operation and its aim of installing him as the new prime minister. He was to name a military secretariat with which CIA would conclude a detailed staff plan of action.

From the outset, the cooperation of the Shah was considered to be an essential part of the plan. His cooperation was necessary to assure the action required of the Tehran military garrisons, and to legalize the succession of a new prime minister. Since the Shah had shown himself to be a man of indecision, it was determined that pressure on him to cooperate would take the following forms:

1. The Shah's dynamic and forceful twin sister, Princess Ashraf Pahlavi, was to come from Europe to urge the Shah to dismiss Mossadeq. She would say she had been in contact with U.S. and U.K. officials who had requested her to do so.

2. Arrangements were made for a visit to Iran by General H. Norman Schwarzkopf, former head of the U.S. Gendarme Mission, who the Shah liked and respected. Schwarzkopf was to explain the proposed project and get from the Shah signed firmans (royal decrees) dismissing Mossadeq,

appointing Zahedi, and calling on the Army to remain loyal to the crown.

3. The principal indigenous British agent, who bona fides had been established with the Shah, was to reinforce the Shah that this was a joint U.S.-U.K. action.

4. Failing results from the above, Mr. Roosevelt, representing the President of the United States, would urge the Shah to sign the above-mentioned firmans. When received, the firmans would be released by CIA to Zahedi on the day called for in the plan. On D-Day, the Shah was to be at some location outside of Tehran so that Zahedi, armed with the royal firmans and with military support, could take over the government without danger of the Shah's reversing his stand, and to avoid any attempt on the Shah's life.

Through agents in the Tehran military, CIA was to ensure, to the degree possible, Tehran Army cooperation in support of the Shah-appointed new prime minister.

The following public statements made in the United States had tremendous impact on Iran and Mossadeq, and contributed greatly to Mossadeq's downfall:

1. The publication, on 9 June 1953, of President Eisenhower's 29 June 1953 letter to Premier Mossadeq made it clear that increased aid would not be forthcoming to Iran.

2. The Secretary of State's press conferences of 28 July 1953 stated that " . . The growing activities of the illegal Communist Party in Iran and the toleration for them by the Iranian Government has caused our government concern. These developments make it more difficult to grant aid to Iran."

3. The President's Seattle speech at the Governors' convention, in which he stated that the United States would not sit by and see Asian countries fall behind the Iron Curtain, had definite effect.

In cooperation with the Department of State, CIA had several articles planted in major American newspapers and magazines which, when reproduced in Iran, had the desired psychological effect in Iran and contributed to the war of nerves against Mossadeq.

After considerable pressure from Princess Ashraf and General Schwarzkopf, and after several meetings with Mr. Roosevelt, the Shah finally signed the required firmans on 15 August 1953. Action was set for 16 August. However, owing to a security leak in the Iranian military, the chief of the Shah's bodyguard, assigned to seize Mossadeq with the help of two truckloads of pro-Shah soldiers, was overwhelmed by superior armed forces still loyal to Mossadeq. The balance of the military plan was thus frustrated for that day. Upon hearing that the plan has misfired, the Shah flew to Baghdad. This was an act of prudence and had been at least partially foreseen in the plan. Zahedi remained in hiding in CIA custody. With his key officers, he eluded Mossadeq's security forces which were seeking to apprehend the major opposition elements.

Early in the afternoon of 17 August 1953 Ambassador Henderson returned to Tehran. General Zahedi, through a CIA-arranged secret press conferences and through CIA covert printing facilities, announced to Iran that he was legally prime minister and that Mossadeq had staged an illegal coup against him. CIA agents disseminated a large quantity of photographs of the firmans, appointing Zahedi prime minister and dismissing Mosssadeq. This had tremendous impact on the people of Tehran who had already been shocked and angered when they realized that the Shah had been forced to leave Iran because of Mossadeq's actions. U.S. Ambassador Burton Y. Berry, in Baghdad, contacted the Shah and stated that he had confidence that the Shah would return soon to Iran despite the apparent adverse situation at the time. Contact was also established with the Shah in Rome after he had flown there from Baghdad. Mr. Roosevelt and the station consistently reported that Mossadeq's apparent victory was misleading; that there were very concrete signs that the Army was still loyal to the Shah; and that a favorable reversal of the situation was possible. The station further urged both the British Foreign Office and the Department of State to make a maximum effort to persuade the Shah to make public statements encouraging the Army and populace to reject Mossadeq and to accept Zahedi as prime minister.

On 19 August 1953, a pro-Shah demonstration, originating in the bazaar area, took on overwhelming proportions. The demonstration appeared to start partially spontaneously, revealing the fundamental prestige of the Shah and the public alarm at the undisguised republican move being started by the Communists as well as by certain National Frontists. Station political action assets also contributed to the beginnings of the Pro- Shah demonstrations. The Army very soon joined the pro-Shah movement and by noon of that day it was clear that Tehran, as well as certain provincial areas, were controlled by pro-Shah street groups and Army units. The situation was such that the above-mentioned military plan could then be implemented. At the station's signal, Zahedi came out of hiding to lead the movement. He first broadcast over Radio Tehran and announced that the government was his. The General Staff offices were then seized, Mossadeq's home was gutted, and pro-Mossadeq politicians and officers arrested. By the end of 19 August, the country was in the hands of the new Premier, Zahedi, and members of the Mossadeq government were either in hiding or were incarcerated.

The Shah returned shortly to Iran where he was given a rousing popular reception. The Shah was deeply moved by the fact that his people and Army had revolted in the face of adversity against a vindictive Mossadeq and a Communist Party riding the crest of a temporary victory and clearly planning to declare Iran a republic. The Shah felt for the first time that he had the mandate of his people, and he returned determined to regain firm control of the Army.

In order to give Zahedi badly needed immediate financial assistance so that the month-end payrolls could be met before the United States could provide large scale grant aid, CIA covertly made available $5,000,000 within two days of Zahedi's assumption of power.

[The C.I.A.'s secret history of the 1953 coup in Iran was a nearly 200-page document, comprising the author's own account of the operation and a set of planning documents he attached. The New York Times on the Web is publishing the introduction and many of the planning documents. But the Times decided not to publish the main body of text after consulting prominent historians who believed there might be serious risk that some of those named as foreign agents would face retribution in Iran.

Because the introductory summary and the main body of the document are inconsistent on a few dates and facts, readers may note discrepancies between accounts. In its reporting, the Times as relied upon details in the C.I.A. document not published here. In addition, certain names and identifying descriptions have been removed from the documents available on the Web.]

Document Analysis

This selection is the introduction and summary of Wilber's CIA history of the coup. It begins with a brief recap of the reasons that the CIA and British intelligence had decided to remove Mossadeq from power. The first sentence outlines perhaps the principal British concern: "By the end of 1952, it had become clear that the Mossadeq government in Iran was incapable of reaching an oil settlement with interested Western countries." They believed furthermore that Mossadeq was acting recklessly, contrary to the constitution of Iran, and was in danger of leading the nation "behind the Iron Curtain," or into Soviet-style Communism—perhaps the principal American concern. If Iran turned to Communism, it would advance Soviet interests in the Middle East at the expense of the West, and so the decision was made to replace the Mossadeq government with one that would "govern Iran according to constructive policies." By April 1953, a coup was agreed upon as the best course of action, and plans were drawn up for a joint operation between the CIA and British Secret Intelligence Services. By mid-July 1953, the plan was approved by both governments; in the United States, the operation was named TPAJAX, or Operation Ajax.

The lead-up to the coup involved a propaganda war, with U.S. officials making clear in public statements that economic aid would not be offered to Mossadeq's Iran. At the same time, opposition to Mossadeq was fomented inside the country, particularly through the media. A top army general, Fazlollah Zahedi, was picked to replace Mossadeq as prime minister. However, the plot also hinged on the cooperation of the shah, Mohammad Reza Pahlavi, who was extremely reluctant to involve himself in a plot by foreign powers and is described by Wilber as "a man of indecision." The report lays out the ways that pressure was brought to bear on the shah, from bringing his sister and U.S. Army general H. Norman Schwarzkopf Sr. to negotiate with him, to readying the orders for him to sign and promising to spirit him away while the coup was taking place. On August 15, under considerable pressure, the shah signed the decrees needed to oust Mossadeq.

The plot seemed doomed from the beginning. A security leak meant that the element of surprise was lost, and Mossadeq initially escaped capture. The shah fled to Iraq, and the CIA worked to gather support for the newly appointed Zahedi by disseminating copies of the decrees replacing Mossadeq. On August 19, with the help of some CIA agents, a pro-shah demonstration in the streets of Tehran gathered momentum. By the end of the day, the capital was in the hands of supporters of Zahedi and the shah, and Mossadeq and his supporters were arrested.

The report ends by noting that the CIA secretly transferred five million dollars to Zahedi's government within two days in order to keep the government running until promised U.S. grant aid was forthcoming.

Essential Themes

The Iranian coup of 1953 was the first of several CIA operations that sought to encourage rivals of obstreperous or Communist-leaning leaders during the Cold War; for example, the following year, in 1954, the CIA engineered a coup in Guatemala to overthrow the democratically elected government of Jacobo Árbenz, and in 1961, the CIA backed the ill-fated Bay of Pigs Invasion intended to oust Fidel Castro, the Communist leader of Cuba. When the extent of U.S. intervention in these countries was suspected, or confirmed, it led to long-term resentment and distrust of U.S. policy in these regions. The overthrow of Mossadeq was no exception. The shah continued to rule until 1979 in close association with the United States and Britain. When he was overthrown by militants led by Ayatollah Khomeini in 1979, the depth of animosity toward the United States in Iran was made clear. The American Embassy was attacked and the staff taken hostage, accused of spying and manipulating the Iranian people. Tensions with Iran remain high in part because of the historical distrust sewn during the 1953 coup.

—*Bethany Groff Dorau, MA*

Bibliography and Additional Reading

Abrahamian, Ervand. *The Coup: 1953, the CIA, and the Roots of Modern US-Iranian Relations*. New York: New, 2013. Print.

Bowie, Robert R. & Richard H. Immerman. *Waging Peace: How Eisenhower Shaped an Enduring Cold War Strategy*. New York: Oxford UP, 1998. Print.

Gasiorowski, Mark J. *Mohammad Mosaddeq and the 1953 Coup in Iran*. Syracuse, NY: Syracuse UP, 2004. Print.

■ Baghdad Pact

Date: February 25, 1955
Authors: Various
Geographic region: Kingdom of Iraq; Republic of Turkey; United Kingdom; Dominion of Pakistan; Kingdom of Iran
Genre: Treaty

Summary Overview

In the 1950s, United States foreign policy was concerned primarily with halting the spread of Communism throughout the world. Asia, Europe, and the Middle East all bordered the Soviet Union, and had great strategic importance for the United States, Great Britain, and their allies. The Middle East, in particular, with its vast oil reserves and its proximity to the Soviet Union, seemed ripe for a Communist incursion, and the maintenance of pro-Western governments was of great concern to the United States and Great Britain.

In 1953, U.S. secretary of state John Foster Dulles traveled to several Middle Eastern capitals, gathering support for a pro-Western defense alliance similar to the North Atlantic Treaty Organization (NATO). This ultimately led to the formation of the Baghdad Pact, or Middle East Treaty Organization (METO), between Turkey, Pakistan, Iraq, Iran, and the United Kingdom. The United States did not ultimately sign the treaty, as it was reluctant to antagonize Egypt and wary of being perceived as anti-Israel, but remained involved in the organization. Though it was a milestone in the containment policies of the United States, the agreement proved to be short-lived and generally unsuccessful. After Iraq withdrew from the pact in 1959, the alliance changed its name to the Central Treaty Organization (CENTO), but when Iran withdrew in 1979 it dissolved completely.

Defining Moment

The United States and the Soviet Union had clashed over control of the oil-rich land of the Middle East since the end of World War II. Initially allies, Russian, British, and American forces occupied Iran to keep its resources out of German hands. After the war, however, relations between the Soviet Union and its former allies were in precipitous decline, and the Soviet Union refused to withdraw its troops from the region. Under increasing international pressure, they withdrew in March 1946, but their interest in the Middle East was clear. Later that month, Turkey and Iraq signed a Treaty of Friendship and Good Neighbourhood, the first in a sequence of separate mutual assistance treaties signed over the following decade between Turkey, Pakistan, Iraq, Iran, the United Kingdom, and the United States.

The United States eventually signed separate agreements with all of the nations who would join the Baghdad Pact. In 1954 Pakistan and Turkey signed a security agreement, followed by Iraq and Turkey in February 1955. Yet both the United States and the United Kingdom wanted a broader regional mutual defense pact, along the lines of NATO or the Southeast Asia Treaty Organization (SEATO). Such alliances were vital to the Western powers' strategy of containment of Communism, which relied on pro-Western governments in nations surrounding the Soviet Union in order to block the spread of Soviet influence. Containment was the main policy of the United States during the Cold War, and would significantly shape international relations. The United States and Great Britain were hopeful that Jordan and Syria would also join a potential agreement, which would complete the regional barrier to Communist expansion in what became known as the Northern Tier area of the Middle East.

Direct negotiation with Middle Eastern nations was tricky for the United States, however, as it enjoyed a special relationship with Israel, which was suspicious of Western treaties with nations antagonistic toward it. In addition, the pact faced strong opposition from Arabs in the anti-colonialist movement, especially Egyptian president Gamal Abdel Nasser and his followers. Nasser saw the Baghdad Pact as a threat to his leadership in the Middle East and resented Western influence in the region. He denounced it in the press. Jordan and Syria, facing significant public pressure, did not join. The United Kingdom joined Iraq and Turkey's earlier alliance in February 1955 along with Pakistan and Iran, forming the official Baghdad Pact, but the United States did not sign the agreement.

Bagdad City bus map, 1961.

Although not formally a member, the United States was intimately involved in the creation of the Baghdad Pact. It achieved a major strategic goal for the United States policy of containment, linking Turkey, the southernmost member of NATO, with the westernmost member of SEATO, Pakistan, to form a bloc along the southwestern border of the Soviet Union.

Document Information

The Baghdad Pact, as a multinational treaty, had no single author, but was crafted through the work of the governments involved. It began in February 1955 as a cooperation agreement between Turkey and Iraq, designed to provide a framework for mutually opposing any aggression from foreign powers. The two allies then invited other nations to join; the United Kingdom did so in April 1955, followed by Pakistan in September and Iran in October. The place of signing—Iraq's capital, Baghdad—lent the pact its name.

Although the United States did not sign the Baghdad Pact, it was instrumental in forming the alliance. Most notably, U.S. secretary of state John Foster Dulles, appointed by President Dwight D. Eisenhower in 1953, played a key role in shaping the agreement in accord with U.S. goals in the region. British foreign secretary Anthony Eden was another important figure representing the Western powers in the development of the Baghdad Pact.

HISTORICAL DOCUMENT

Whereas the friendly and brotherly relations existing between Iraq and Turkey are in constant progress, and in order to complement the contents of the Treaty of Friendship and Good Neighbourhood concluded between His Majesty the King of Iraq and his Excellency the President of the Turkish Republic signed in Ankara on March 29, 1946, which recognised the fact that peace and security between the two countries is an integral part of the peace and security of all the nations of the world and in particular the nations of the Middle East, and that it is the basis for their foreign policies;

Whereas article 11 of the Treaty of Joint Defence and Economic Co-operation between the Arab League States provides that no provision of that treaty shall in any way affect, or is designed to affect, any of the rights and obligations accruing to the Contracting Parties from the United Nations Charter;

And having realised the great responsibilities borne by them in their capacity as members of the United Nations concerned with the maintenance of peace and security in the Middle East region which necessitate taking the required measures in accordance with article 51 of the United Nations Charter;

They have been fully convinced of the necessity of concluding a pact fulfilling these aims, and for that purpose have appointed as their plenipotentiaries . . . who having communicated their full powers, found to be in good and due form, have agreed as follows:-

ARTICLE 1

Consistent with article 51 of the United Nations Charter the High Contracting Parties will co-operate for their security and defence. Such measures as they agree to take to give effect to this co-operation may form the subject of special agreements with each other.

ARTICLE 2

In order to ensure the realization and effect application of the co-operation provided for in article 1 above, the competent authorities of the High Contracting Parties will determine the measures to be taken as soon as the present pact enters into force. These measures will become operative as soon as they have been approved by the Governments of the High Contracting Parties.

ARTICLE 3

The High Contracting Parties undertake to refrain from any interference whatsoever in each other's internal affairs. They will settle any dispute between themselves in a peaceful way in accordance with the United Nations Charter.

ARTICLE 4

The High Contracting Parties declare that the dispositions of the present pact are not in contradiction with any of the international obligations contracted by either of them with any third State or States. They do not derogate from and cannot be interpreted as derogating from, the said international obligations. The High Contracting Parties undertake not to enter into any international obligation incompatible with the present pact.

ARTICLE 5

This pact shall be open for accession to any member of the Arab League or any other State actively concerned with the security and peace in this region and which is fully recognized by both of the High Contracting Parties. Accession shall come into force from the date of which the instrument of accession of the State concerned is deposited with the Ministry for Foreign Affairs of Iraq.

Any acceding State party to the present pact may conclude special agreements, in accordance with article 1, with one or more States parties to the present pact. The competent authority of any acceding State may determine measures in accordance with article 2. These measures will become operative as soon as they have been approved by the Governments of the parties concerned.

ARTICLE 6

A Permanent Council at ministerial level will be set up to function within the framework of the purposes of this pact when at least four Powers become parties to the pact.

The Council will draw up its own rules of procedure.

ARTICLE 7

This pact remains in force for a period of five years renewable for other five-year periods. Any Contracting Party may withdraw from the pact by notifying the other parties in writing of its desire to do so six months before the expiration of any of the above-mentioned periods, in which case the pact remains valid for the other parties.

ARTICLE 8

This pact shall be ratified by the contracting parties and ratifications shall be exchanged at Ankara as soon as possible. Thereafter it shall come into force from the date of the exchange of ratifications.

In witness whereof, the said plenipotentiaries have signed the present pact in Arabic, Turkish and English, all three texts being equally authentic except in the case of doubt when the English text shall prevail.

Done in duplicate at Bagdad this second day of Rajab 1374 Hijri corresponding to the twenty-fourth day of February 1955.

Document Analysis

The Baghdad Pact begins by referencing the Treaty of Friendship and Good Neighbourhood signed by Iraq and Turkey in 1946. It recognizes that the earlier treaty acknowledged that world peace was not possible without peace in the Middle East, and that "the friendly and brotherly relations existing between Iraq and Turkey are in constant progress." It also mentions the signing nations' submission to the authority of both the Arab League and the United Nations, and their adherence to international law, reinforcing the Baghdad Pact as one of many interrelated treaties and alliances created after World War II.

Critically, the pact references the primary goal of "the maintenance of peace and security in the Middle East region." The pact's eight articles outline the ways in which this goal is intended to be achieved. Signers will "cooperate for their security and defense," and "refrain from any interference whatsoever in each other's internal affairs." It states that special agreements between individual members are allowed as long as they work toward cooperation. Likewise, the pact ensures that it does not interfere with any member's agreements or alliances with other nations outside the pact. The governments of each participant are left responsible for enacting the treaty at the practical level—significantly, no mention is made of an overarching hierarchy of command or shared armed forces. This meant the pact did not provide an outright structure for mutual defense.

The pact is left open to anyone who has an active interest in the security of the Middle East, particularly members of the Arab League. It further states that once four nations have ratified the pact, a permanent council will be set up to administer its application, though it leaves the procedure of the council open. For a long-term structure, the pact states that it can be renewed every five years after it comes into force. It also confirms the right of any member to withdraw, and that it will remain valid even after a member leaves the treaty.

The treaty was ratified by all parties by October 1955.

Essential Themes

The United States was pursuing a policy of containment in 1955, encouraging the formation of alliances to thwart the Soviet Union's ability to expand and spread. The Middle East seemed particularly vulnerable, but was also a sensitive area for U.S. foreign policy. The Baghdad Pact was designed, encouraged, and promoted by the United States, working closely with Great Britain, but in the end the United States was not a signatory. This absence points to the complex political climate in the region, with Arab nationalism, pro-Western dictatorships, Israeli territorial instability, and encroaching Communism all in the mix.

After the pact went into effect, the United States continued to support the alliance, even joining as an associate member and serving on its military committee in an attempt to bolster its influence. However, the Baghdad Pact never proved effective in containing Communism or promoting peace in the Middle East. The seizure of the Suez Canal in 1956 by Egyptian forces under Nasser led to the decline of British influence in the region, and the Soviet Union successfully aligned itself with several Middle Eastern countries. Iraq withdrew from the pact in 1959 after its government was overthrown, and the other nations abandoned the Baghdad Pact title in favor of the Central Treaty Organization, or CENTO.

The headquarters of CENTO were moved to Ankara, Turkey, and the organization generally served as a vehicle for economic cooperation rather than a military alliance. Although Pakistan attempted to gain the support of other members during its 1965 war with India, no mutual defense was provided. CENTO officially disbanded in 1979 after the Iran withdrew following its revolution and Pakistan also left.

—*Bethany Groff Dorau, MA*

Bibliography and Additional Reading

Ashton, Nigel John. "The Hijacking of a Pact: The Formation of the Baghdad Pact and Anglo-American Tensions in the Middle East, 1955–1958." *Review of International Studies* 19.2 (1993): 123–37. Print.

Lansford, Tom. *The Lords of Foggy Bottom: American Secretaries of State and the World They Shaped.* Baldwin Place: Encyclopedia Soc., 2001. Print.

Sanjian, Ara. "The Formulation of the Baghdad Pact." *Middle Eastern Studies* 33.2 (1997): 226–66. Print.

Yeşilbursa, B. Kemal. *The Baghdad Pact: Anglo-American Defence Policies in the Middle East, 1950–1959.* New York: Cass, 2005. Print.

■ Gamal Abdel Nasser on the Nationalization of the Suez Canal

Date: July 26, 1956
Author: Gamal Abdel Nasser
Geographic region: Egypt
Genre: Speech

Summary Overview

From its opening in 1869, the Suez Canal was a vital link for European trade with Asia and many parts of the Middle East. Anything that might upset the flow of ships, and the goods they transported, would precipitate a major crisis. Thus, when Nasser created great uncertainty by announcing the nationalization of the Suez Canal Company, many members of the global community reacted strongly. While the speech Nasser gave on July 26, 1956, dealt with the economic matter of the purchase of all shares of the Universal Company of the Suez Maritime Canal by the government of Egypt, and the continuation of operations, it also represented a political slap in the face to the British and French, who had been running the canal. The turmoil that developed among members of the international community resulted in the political and military conflict known as the Suez Crisis. Within months, British, French, and Israeli forces invaded Egypt to try to force Egypt to relinquish control of the canal to its previous owners (mainly British and French), and hopefully to overthrow Nasser. By obtaining the backing of the United States and the Soviet Union, Egypt not only successfully weathered these events, kept control of the canal, and strengthened its position in the Middle East, but also pushed the country into a leadership role within the non-aligned movement.

Defining Moment

The Suez Canal Company was originally developed in 1858 as a joint venture between French entrepreneurs and the Ottoman Empire's regional governor in Egypt. However, under political pressure, the Ottoman Empire gave Egypt partial independence in 1867, and then financial problems forced the Egyptian viceroy (khedive) to sell Egypt's 44 percent of the company's stock to the British government in 1875. From that point forward the British, which controlled trade going around the horn of Africa, sought to control trade going through the canal as well. Invited in to help the Egyptian gov-

ernment put down a revolt, British troops took control not only of that situation but of the canal as well. Thus, from 1882 the Suez Canal was both owned by European interests and managed on a day-to-day basis by them. Several times in the decades prior to 1956 the British had been asked to leave, and Egyptian leaders had sought a larger role in canal operations. The British had been slowly removing their troops and had agreed to the transfer of leadership in canal operations in the future. The final withdrawal of British troops (negotiated with Nasser in 1954) occurred on July 18, 1956.

Nasser had come into power after a 1952 coup against King Farouk, who had lost popular support owing to his lavish lifestyle. Nasser sought to develop Egypt economically, through the construction of a dam on the Nile River at Aswan. As a former military leader, he also wanted to strengthen the military for possible use against Israel. Trying to be neutral in the Cold War, Nasser traded with, and accepted assistance from, both Western and Communist nations. While the United States and the United Kingdom had initially pledged funds to build the dam, when Nasser bought weapons from a Communist source, both nations pulled out of the project. Nasser had previously pressed for greater Egyptian control of the Suez Canal, and the end of U.S. support for the dam gave him one excuse to take over the operations of the canal. The money earned from its operations would, according to Nasser's plan, be used to build the Aswan Dam. With the last foreign troops (British) having been withdrawn from Egypt eight days prior to this speech, Nasser felt secure in making the move. His dramatic step not only resulted in Egypt gaining control of canal operations (technically, it had always owned the land on which the canal was built) but helped Egypt and Nasser become leaders within the Arab and non-aligned communities.

Author Biography

Gamal Abdel Nasser (January 15, 1918—September 28, 1970) was born into what might be considered a

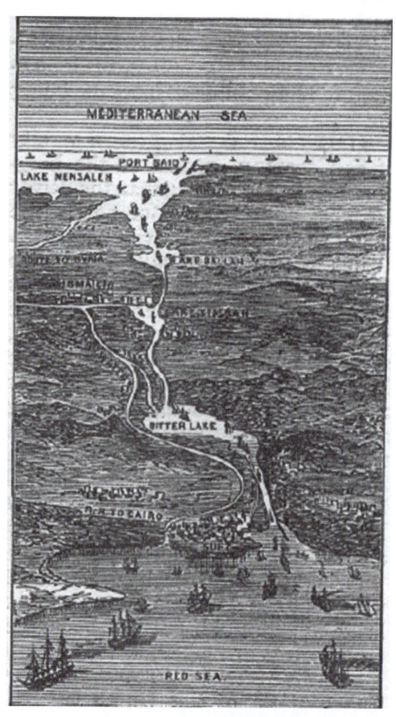

Suez Canal drawing 1881

middle-class family, with his father working as a postal supervisor in a variety of offices. While in school, Nasser became active in anti-British, anti-colonial demonstrations that ended up with him being wounded and acquiring a criminal record. Although he remained a strong nationalist, when demonstrations died out after a new British-Egyptian treaty was signed, Nasser completed school and began to study law. Dropping out, he sought entrance into the military but was denied owing to his criminal record. Gaining support from a high government official, he was admitted to the military college and was commissioned in 1938. At his first posting (Mankabad) he met other young officers with a similar nationalist orientation and they began discussing how to rid the nation of the British and to advance a modern political/economic agenda. During the 1948 Arab-Israeli War, Nasser became a national hero as commander of a small Egyptian force surrounded by Israeli troops, which held its position until negotiations for that territory were concluded between the

leaders of the respective governments. Later, He was among those sent to negotiate the final agreement ending hostilities.

After the war, Nasser expanded the group that had formed in Mankabad, with it becoming the Association of Free Officers. Slowly developing his network of allies, Colonel Nasser finally led a coup in 1952, although politically he remained in the background and pushed General Naguib to be the head of the government. Nasser was more radical in the economic reforms he desired, and by 1954 he had pushed Naguib out of power, although he did not himself become president until June 1956. The nationalization of the canal made Nasser very popular among Egyptians. During his reign he pushed through many economic changes and major construction projects. He was a leader in the Arab world and a major player on the world stage. However, his strong leadership also meant that many human right violations occurred during his rule. He ruled until his death in 1970.

HISTORICAL DOCUMENT

In the Name of the Nation

The President of the Republic,

Considering the two firmans issued on November 30, 1854 and January 5, 1856 (respectively) concerning the preferential rights relating to the administration of the Suez Canal Transit Service and the establishment of an Egyptian joint-stock company to operate it; and Law No. 129 of 1947 concerning public utility concessions; and Law No. 317 of 1952 concerning individual labor contracts; and Law No. 26 of 1954 concerning joint-stock companies, limited partnerships by shares and limited liability companies; with the advice of the State Council; has issued the following law:

Article I

The Universal Company of the Suez Maritime Canal (Egyptian joint-stock company) is hereby nationalized. All its assets, rights and obligations are transferred to the Nation and all the organizations

and committees that now operate its management are hereby dissolved.

Stockholders and holders of founders' shares shall be compensated for the ordinary or founders shares they own in accordance with the value of the shares shown in the closing quotations of the Paris Stock Exchange on the day preceding the effective date of the present law.

The payment of said indemnity shall be effected after the Nation has taken delivery of all the assets and properties of the nationalized company.

Article II

An independent organization endowed with juristic personality and annexed to the Ministry of Commerce, shall take over the management of the Suez Canal Transit Service. The composition of the organization and the remuneration of its members shall be fixed in an order of the President of the Republic. In so far as managing the Transit Service is concerned the organization shall have all the necessary powers required for the purpose without being restricted by Government regulations and procedures.

Without prejudice to the auditing of its final accounts by the State Audit Department, the organization shall have an independent budget prepared in accordance with the rules in force for commercial concerns. Its financial year shall begin on July 1 and end on June 30 each year. The budget and final accounts shall be approved by an order of the President of the Republic. The first financial year shall begin on the effective date of the present law and end with June 30, 1957.

The organization may delegate one or several of its members to implement its decisions or to discharge any duty assigned to these members.

It may also set up from among its own members or from among other people, a technical committee to assist it in its own research work and studies.

The chairman of the organization shall represent it before the courts, government agencies, and other places, and in its dealings with third parties.

Article III

The assets and rights of the nationalized company in the Republic of Egypt and abroad are hereby frozen. Without specific permission obtained in advance from the organization provided for in Article II above, banks, organizations and private persons are hereby prohibited from disposing of those assets or making any payment requested them or due by them.

Article IV

The organization shall retain all the present officials, employees and laborers of the nationalized company at their posts; they shall have to continue with the discharge of their duties; no one will be allowed to leave his work or vacate his post in any manner and for any reason whatsoever except with the permission of the organization provided for in Article II above.

Article V

All violations of the provisions of Article III above shall be punished by imprisonment and a fine equal to three times the value of the amount involved in the offense. All violations of the provisions of Article IV shall be punished by imprisonment in addition to the forfeiture by the offender of all rights to compensation, pension or indemnity.

Article VI

The present order shall be published in the Official Gazette and shall have the force of law. It shall come into force on the date of its publication. The Minister of Commerce shall issue the necessary administrative orders for its implementation.

It shall bear the Seal of the State and be implemented as one of the State laws.

Given this 18th day of Zull Heggah, 1375 A.H. [July 26, 1956]
Gamal Abdel Nasser

GLOSSARY

firman: a ruler's administrative order or edict; the term originated during the Ottoman Empire

juristic personality: a legal entity capable of making all forms of legal agreements and undertaking corporate operations

Document Analysis

On July 26 Nasser spoke to a large crowd for more than two and a half hours, with the central point of his speech being the nationalization of the Suez Canal. Nasser had been studying politics, especially the politics of revolution, for more than twenty years when he made the decision to take control of canal operations. He understood the repercussions of taking control from the Europeans, and sought to mitigate these by paying the previous owners a fair price for their asset.

In addition, he made it clear that the canal would continue to function and that Egypt was totally committed to this move. Contemporaneous records indicated that Nasser only fully developed this plan a few days prior to its announcement; he was seeking to give his action a basic legal foundation and a means to domestically enforce the decision.

Egyptian leaders since the time of the pharaohs had desired, and some attempted, to build a canal connecting the Red Sea and the Nile River or Mediterranean Sea. A few attempts had been successful in temporarily connecting the Nile and the Red Sea, but none were lasting. Thus, when Europeans entrepreneurs proposed the creation of a canal in the 1850s, they were following in the footsteps of previous generations. As part of his speech, Nasser pointed out that most of the canal had been dug by Egyptians, and used this as part of the underlying reason why Egypt should have control of the canal operations. (He conveniently ignored the fact that Egypt had originally owned part of the company operating the canal.) In the introduction to this official document, Nasser outlined the executive orders that had created the "joint-stock company" operating the canal. Thus, he made certain there could be no legal action based on a lack of clarity as to what was being nationalized.

Articles I and III stated that all assets of the operating company were being nationalized, not just those within Egypt. Nasser understood that it would be harder to nationalize things outside of Egypt, but their clear inclusion in Article III gave a legal foundation for any legal actions necessary in other countries. In Article I, the Universal Company of the Suez Maritime Canal was told that what might be termed a hostile takeover had occurred, with the assets of this company being merged into Egypt's Ministry of Commerce. As in normal mergers/takeovers, the stockholders of the company would be paid for their stock, based on the last price of the previous day's trading on, in this case, the Paris Stock Exchange. Nasser was trying to smooth the takeover of the canal, by doing away with what would have been a major obstacle, if no payment had been made. Nasser anticipated that some shareholders, and European politicians, would object to his action. He believed that this compensation would weaken these objections substantially. Paying for the stock was a key step—the carrot—in the eventual acceptance of his action by the global community. Conversely, the stick that he wielded was contained in Article V, which allowed for

"imprisonment and a fine" for those who failed to follow the orders dictated by Article III.

Articles II, IV, and V outlined how the continuing operation of the canal would be implemented. The second article specified the relationship between the new "Suez Canal Transit Service" and the government of Egypt. It also made provision for replacing the private corporation's board of directors with "an independent organization endowed with juristic personality" that would oversee the operations of the canal. The fourth and fifth articles insured that those handling the day to day operations of the canal would remain in their positions, until the new management decided to replace them. Article IV mandated that these individuals remain in place, while Article V outlined the types of punishments that could be imposed upon individuals who failed to follow the regulations outlined in Article IV. The scope of possible punishment ranged from "forfeiture" of monetary items to actual incarceration. While virtually all Egyptians working for the canal would have no reason to quit their jobs because of the nationalization, Nasser hoped that this would keep the foreign workers in place until an orderly transition could be established to replace those who might desire to leave.

The last article, Article VI, was included to follow a common legal formulation in which a new law, or executive order, had to be announced publically through an established process. While Nasser's speech in Alexandria told people what was happening, and it did happen on the day of the speech, the written publication of the edict "in the Official Gazette" made it clearly a law under the established procedures of the Egyptian government. Nasser wanted to ensure that this dramatic act, which would transform the international shipping industry and global commerce, was not thwarted by a legal technicality. (By following the technicalities in the process for the implementation of a new law, Nasser hoped it would quiet some international and domestic objections.) Whether or not under Egyptian law Nasser had the power to nationalize the canal operations and abrogate an international agreement, he did have the backing of the military and Egyptian people when he nationalized the canal. Domestically, this was all that was needed for the nationalization to be successful.

Essential Themes

When Nasser stepped forward in Alexandria to speak to the audience gathered to hear him, his primary message was simple: The operation of the Suez Canal was being taken over by the Egyptian government. However, he added two auxiliary messages that he hoped would insure a tranquil transition, in canal operations and in Egypt's relationships with other nations. Nasser's statement that the company running canal operations "is hereby nationalized" gave the essential point of this speech. Even though the agreement that had established the company running the canal had another twelve years on its lease, and the owners of the company had expected another twelve years of income from this concession, Nasser put an end to this arrangement. While he went on to clarify how the canal company was being brought into the government (via the Ministry of Commerce), this was secondary to the fact that canal operations were being nationalized.

Nasser understood that there would be resistance to this dramatic action. In order to try to keep friendly relations with the United Kingdom and France and various influential individuals, Nasser clearly stated that the current owners of company stock would be paid for their shares, based on the value from the preceding day's transactions. By making this secondary point a part of the speech, he hoped to undercut any negative reaction from stock owners or the European governments. Obviously, the invasion by British and French forces three months later showed that this was a false hope in terms of the governments. However, for the individuals who owned the stock, his decision to pay market value for their shares reduced many complications that might have arisen had he seized the assets of the company without payment.

The other secondary message was that canal operations would continue without interruption, by his proclamation that anyone working for the canal had to remain working for the canal administration, unless the Egyptian government gave permission for a worker to leave. This was a multi-purpose point, assuring workers that they still had jobs, assuring the shipping industry that competent individuals would still be running the canal, and ensuring that the operations could not be sabotaged by certain key individuals leaving their posts. Although foreign workers had less to fear, by holding their pensions hostage Nasser made sure that they would remain during the transition.

As Nasser announced this bold step, undertaken to make Egypt more self-sufficient, he was establishing himself, and his nation, as a role model for others seeking to move from colonial status to true independence. Although the move did not go as smoothly as he had hoped—for example, the Sinai was temporarily lost to invading forces—Nasser was ultimately successful in nationalizing the canal's operations and, except in times of warfare, it has operated efficiently under Egyptian control. While there were at first some serious obstacles to overcome, in the long run the nationalization of the canal has worked out well for Egypt.

—*Donald A Watt, PhD*

Bibliography and Additional Reading

Aburish, Said K. *Nasser: The Last Arab*. New York: Thomas Dunne Books, 2004. Print.

Adel, Ezzat. "The Day Nasser Nationalised the Canal." *BBC News*. London: The British Broadcasting Corporation, 2006. Web. 2 March 2018.

Doran, Michael. *Ike's Gamble: American's Rise to Dominance in the Middle East*. New York: Free Press, 2016. Print.

Kyle, Keith. *Suez*. New York: St. Martin's Press, 1991. Print.

Milner, Laurie. "History: The Suez Crisis." *BBC*. London: The British Broadcasting Corporation, 2014. Web. 28 February 2018.

Slany, William Z. "Foreign Relations of the United States, 1955-1957, Suez Crisis, July 26-December 31, 1956, Volume XVI." *Office of the Historian: Department of State*. Washington: United States Department of State, 2018. Web. 2 March 2018.

■ The Eisenhower Doctrine

Date: January 5, 1957
Author: Dwight D. Eisenhower
Geographic region: Middle East
Genre: Speech

Summary Overview

President Eisenhower announced what would become known as the Eisenhower Doctrine in January 1957 in a speech to a joint session of Congress. He called for a new relationship with nations in the increasingly unstable Middle East, in order to protect them from the threat of Communist incursion. Eisenhower made funds and military support available to any nation that felt that its independence was threatened, and he singled out the Soviet Union as being particularly eager for control of the area. Congress approved the spending and the authority necessary to carry this out in March 1957. The Eisenhower Doctrine placed the Middle East squarely in the middle of the Cold War conflict between the United States and the Soviet Union. Where the French and English had previously been the controlling Western powers in the Middle East, the United States was now pledged to defend the volatile region from Soviet incursion.

Defining Moment

The Middle East was increasingly unstable in the months leading up to Eisenhower's speech. In particular, Egyptian leader Gamal Abdel Nasser had sparked an anti-Western, anti-Israeli, pan-Arab movement that threatened to undermine U.S. and European interests in the area; his provocations came to an explosive head in the Suez Canal Crisis of October 1956.

The crisis began on July 19, 1956, when the United States announced that it would not offer Egypt financial aid in the construction of the Aswan Dam over the Nile River. Nearly seventy million dollars had been pledged by the United States and Great Britain in December 1955 to Nasser's government, but the offer was revoked because of both Nasser's increasing ties to the Soviet Union and vitriolic anti-Western agenda. It was hoped that financial aid would temper Nasser's nationalist goals and weaken his ties to the Soviets, but Nasser continued to purchase Soviet weapons through Czechoslovakia, and his attacks on Western colonialism and imperialism continued unabated. Nasser was enraged

by the withdrawal of support, and the Soviet Union quickly offered aid of its own. The British were also taken by surprise at the U.S. announcement and saw it as a dangerous maneuver, destined to strengthen Nasser and further damage British relations with the Egypt.

Nasser responded to the withdrawal of U.S. support for the Aswan Dam by announcing, on July 26, 1956, that the Suez Canal Company, the operators of a vital trade route for Middle Eastern petroleum that was managed by the French and British governments and was held by the British, would be nationalized—that is, declared the property of the Egyptian government. All the company's assets were seized, and Egypt closed the canal to all Israeli shipping. The British and French were outraged, and the United States, hoping to avoid an armed conflict that could ignite hostilities with the Soviet Union and perhaps even lead to a nuclear war, attempted to broker a compromise deal that would divide ownership equally between Egypt, France, and Britain, along with other interested nations. None of the parties involved were interested in this compromise, and Britain, France, and Israel began secretly planning an invasion of Egypt to retake the Suez Canal.

On October 29, 1956, Israel attacked Egypt across the Sinai Peninsula and advanced rapidly toward the Suez Canal. Two days later, British and French forces joined the Israeli army. The United States was in the difficult position of condemning recent Soviet intervention in Hungary, which was also in turmoil, but not wishing to condemn its allies in Egypt or support an escalation that would lead to increased Soviet involvement in the conflict. The Eisenhower administration urged the belligerents to accept United Nations intervention, with a ceasefire on November 6, and even voted for a measure in the U.N. condemning the invasion. The Americans urged the Soviet Union not to involve itself in the conflict and pressured U.S. allies to withdraw from Egypt. The British and French left in December. The Israeli army remained in Egypt until March 1957, after the declaration of the Eisenhower Doctrine. Relations between the United States and its allies Britain and France were cooled by this episode, with both sides feeling that they had been deceived by the other. The Eisenhower Doctrine was articulated just two months after the end of hostilities as a U.S. effort to fill the power vacuum left by receding British and French influence in the region.

Author Biography

Dwight David Eisenhower was born in Denison, Texas, on October 14, 1890. He was the third of seven sons, and when he was two years old, his parents moved to Abilene, Kansas. Eisenhower graduated from Abilene High School in 1909 and was accepted to West Point in 1911. He was an officer in the U.S. Army during World War I but was not sent overseas. He continued his military career after the war and became a brigadier general on October 3, 1941. Eisenhower went on to command

the Allied landing in North Africa in November 1942. In 1943, President Franklin D. Roosevelt made Eisenhower supreme Allied commander in Europe, and he was in charge of the Allied forces that invaded occupied France on June 6, 1944, D-Day. After a postwar position as the military commander of occupied Germany, Eisenhower was named chief of staff of the Army, until becoming president of Columbia University in 1948. He was named supreme commander of the North Atlantic Treaty Organization (NATO) in 1950, but he retained the presidency of Columbia until 1953, when he became president of the United States. After serving a second term as president, Eisenhower retired to Pennsylvania, where his German American family originated. He died of congestive heart failure on March 28, 1969, and is buried on the grounds of the Eisenhower Presidential Library in Abilene, Kansas.

HISTORICAL DOCUMENT

First may I express to you my deep appreciation of your courtesy in giving me, at some inconvenience to yourselves, this early opportunity of addressing you on a matter I deem to be of grave importance to our country.

In my forthcoming State of the Union Message, I shall review the international situation generally. There are worldwide hopes which we can reasonably entertain, and there are worldwide responsibilities which we must carry to make certain that freedom—including our own—may be secure.

There is, however, a special situation in the Middle East which I feel I should, even now, lay before you.

Before doing so it is well to remind ourselves that our basic national objective in international affairs remains peace—a world peace based on justice. Such a peace must include all areas, all peoples of the world if it is to be enduring. There is no nation, great or small, with which we would refuse to negotiate, in mutual good faith, with patience and in the determination to secure a better understanding between us. Out of such understandings must, and eventually will, grow confidence and trust, indispensable ingredients to a program of peace and to

plans for lifting from us all the burdens of expensive armaments. To promote these objectives, our government works tirelessly, day by day, month by month, year by year. But until a degree of success crowns our efforts that will assure to all nations peaceful existence, we must, in the interests of peace itself, remain vigilant, alert and strong.

I.

The Middle East has abruptly reached a new and critical stage in its long and important history. In past decades many of the countries in that area were not fully self-governing. Other nations exercised considerable authority in the area and the security of the region was largely built around their power. But since the First World War there has been a steady evolution toward self-government and independence. This development the United States has welcomed and has encouraged. Our country supports without reservation the full sovereignty and independence of each and every nation of the Middle East.

The evolution to independence has in the main been a peaceful process. But the area has been often troubled. Persistent crosscurrents of distrust and fear with raids back and forth across national boundaries have brought about a high degree of instability in much of the Mid East. Just recently there have been hostilities involving Western European nations that once exercised much influence in the area. Also the relatively large attack by Israel in October has intensified the basic differences between that nation and its Arab neighbors. All this instability has been heightened and, at times, manipulated by International Communism.

II.

Russia's rulers have long sought to dominate the Middle East. That was true of the Czars and it is true of the Bolsheviks. The reasons are not hard to find. They do not affect Russia's security, for no one plans to use the Middle East as a base for aggression against Russia. Never for a moment has the United States entertained such a thought.

The Soviet Union has nothing whatsoever to fear from the United States in the Middle East, or anywhere else in the world, so long as its rulers do not themselves first resort to aggression.

That statement I make solemnly and emphatically.

Neither does Russia's desire to dominate the Middle East spring from its own economic interest in the area. Russia does not appreciably use or depend upon the Suez Canal. In 1955 Soviet traffic through the Canal represented only about three fourths of 1% of the total. The Soviets have no need for, and could provide no market for, the petroleum resources which constitute the principal natural wealth of the area. Indeed, the Soviet Union is a substantial exporter of petroleum products.

The reason for Russia's interest in the Middle East is solely that of power politics. Considering her announced purpose of Communizing the world, it is easy to understand her hope of dominating the Middle East.

This region has always been the crossroads of the continents of the Eastern Hemisphere. The Suez Canal enables the nations of Asia and Europe to carry on the commerce that is essential if these countries are to maintain well-rounded and prosperous economies. The Middle East provides a gateway between Eurasia and Africa.

It contains about two thirds of the presently known oil deposits of the world and it normally supplies the petroleum needs of many nations of Europe, Asia and Africa. The nations of Europe are peculiarly dependent upon this supply, and this dependency relates to transportation as well as to production! This has been vividly demonstrated since the closing of the Suez Canal and some of the pipelines. Alternate ways of transportation and, indeed, alternate sources of power can, if necessary, be developed. But these cannot be considered as early prospects.

These things stress the immense importance of the Middle East. If the nations of that area should lose their independence, if they were dominated by alien forces hostile to freedom, that would be both a tragedy for the area and for many other free nations whose economic life would be subject to near strangulation. Western Europe would be endangered just as though there had been no Marshall Plan, no North Atlantic Treaty Organization. The free nations of Asia and Africa, too, would be placed in serious jeopardy. And the countries of the Middle East would lose the markets upon which their economies depend. All this would have the most adverse, if not disastrous, effect upon our own nation's economic life and political prospects.

Then there are other factors which transcend the material. The Middle East is the birthplace of three great religions-Moslem, Christian and Hebrew. Mecca and Jerusalem are more than places on the map. They symbolize religions which teach that the spirit has supremacy over matter and that the individual has a dignity and rights of which no despotic government can rightfully deprive him. It would be intolerable if the holy places of the Middle East should be subjected to a rule that glorifies atheistic materialism.

International Communism, of course, seeks to mask its purposes of domination by expressions of good will and by superficially attractive offers of political, economic and military aid. But any free nation, which is the subject of Soviet enticement, ought, in elementary wisdom, to look behind the mask.

Remember Estonia, Latvia and Lithuania! In 1939 the Soviet Union entered into mutual assistance pacts with these then dependent countries; and the Soviet Foreign Minister, addressing the Extraordinary Fifth Session of the Supreme Soviet in October 1939, solemnly and publicly declared that "we stand for the scrupulous and punctilious observance of the pacts on the basis of complete reciprocity, and we declare that all the nonsensical talk about the Sovietization of the Baltic countries is only to the interest of our common enemies and of all anti-Soviet provocateurs." Yet in 1940, Estonia, Latvia and Lithuania were forcibly incorporated into the Soviet Union.

Soviet control of the satellite nations of Eastern Europe has been forcibly maintained in spite of solemn promises of a contrary intent, made during World War II.

Stalin's death brought hope that this pattern would change. And we read the pledge of the Warsaw Treaty of 1955 that the Soviet Union would follow in satellite countries "the principles of mutual respect for their independence and sovereignty and noninterference in domestic affairs." But we have just seen the subjugation of Hungary by naked armed force. In the aftermath of this Hungarian tragedy, world respect for and belief in Soviet promises have sunk to a new low. International Communism needs and seeks a recognizable success.

Thus, we have these simple and indisputable facts:

1. The Middle East, which has always been coveted by Russia, would today be prized more than ever by International Communism.

2. The Soviet rulers continue to show that they do not scruple to use any means to gain their ends.

3. The free nations of the Mid East need, and for the most part want, added strength to assure their continued independence.

III.

Our thoughts naturally turn to the United Nations as a protector of small nations. Its charter gives it primary responsibility for the maintenance of international peace and security. Our country has given the United Nations its full support in relation to the hostilities in Hungary and in Egypt. The United Nations was able to bring about a cease-fire and withdrawal of hostile forces from Egypt because it was dealing with governments and peoples who had a decent respect for the opinions of mankind as reflected in the United Nations General Assembly. But in the case of Hungary, the situation was different. The Soviet Union vetoed action by the Security Council to require the withdrawal of Soviet armed forces from Hungary. And it has shown callous indifference to the recommendations, even the censure, of the General Assembly. The United Nations can always be helpful, but it cannot be a wholly dependable protector of freedom when the ambitions of the Soviet Union are involved.

IV.

Under all the circumstances I have laid before you, a greater responsibility now devolves upon the United States. We have shown, so that none can doubt, our dedication to the principle that force shall not be used internationally for any aggressive purpose and that the integrity and independence of the nations of the Middle East should be inviolate. Seldom in history has a nation's dedication to principle been tested as severely as ours during recent weeks.

There is general recognition in the Middle East, as elsewhere, that the United States does not seek either political or economic domination over any other people. Our desire is a world environment of freedom, not servitude. On the other hand many, if not all, of the nations of the Middle East are aware of the danger that stems from International Communism and welcome closer cooperation with the United States to realize for themselves the United Nations goals of independence, economic well-being and spiritual growth.

If the Middle East is to continue its geographic role of uniting rather than separating East and West; if its vast economic resources are to serve the well-being of the peoples there, as well as that of others; and if its cultures and religions and their shrines are to be preserved for the uplifting of the spirits of the peoples, then the United States must make more evident its willingness to support the independence of the freedom-loving nations of the area.

V.

Under these circumstances I deem it necessary to seek the cooperation of the Congress. Only with that cooperation can we give the reassurance needed to deter aggression, to give courage and confidence to those who are dedicated to freedom and thus prevent a chain of events which would gravely endanger all of the free world.

There have been several Executive declarations made by the United States in relation to the Middle East. There is the Tripartite Declaration of May 25, 1950, followed by the Presidential assurance of October 31, 1950, to the King of Saudi Arabia. There is the Presidential declaration of April 9, 1956, that the United States will within constitutional means oppose any aggression in the area. There is our Declaration of November 29, 1956, that a threat to the territorial integrity or political independence of Iran, Iraq, Pakistan, or Turkey would be viewed by the United States with the utmost gravity.

Nevertheless, weaknesses in the present situation and the increased danger from International Communism, convince me that basic United States policy should now find expression in joint action by the Congress and the Executive. Furthermore, our joint resolve should be so couched as to make it apparent that if need be our words will be backed by action.

VI.

It is nothing new for the President and the Congress to join to recognize that the national integrity of other free nations is directly related to our own security.

We have joined to create and support the security system of the United Nations. We have reinforced the collective security system of the United Nations by a series of collective defense arrangements. Today we have security treaties with 42 other nations which recognize that our peace and security are intertwined. We have joined to take decisive action in relation to Greece and Turkey and in relation to Taiwan.

Thus, the United States through the joint action of the President and the Congress, or, in the case of treaties, the Senate, has manifested in many endangered areas its purpose to support free and independent governments—and peace—against external menace, notably the menace of International Communism. Thereby we have helped to maintain peace and security during a period of great danger. It is now essential that the United States should manifest through joint action of the President and the Congress our determination to assist those nations of the Mid East area, which desire that assistance.

The action which I propose would have the following features.

It would, first of all, authorize the United States to cooperate with and assist any nation or group of nations in the general area of the Middle East in the development of economic strength dedicated to the maintenance of national independence.

It would, in the second place, authorize the Executive to undertake in the same region programs of military assistance and cooperation with any nation or group of nations which desires such aid.

It would, in the third place, authorize such assistance and cooperation to include the employment of the armed forces of the United States to secure and protect the territorial integrity and political independence of such nations, requesting such aid, against overt armed aggression from any nation controlled by International Communism.

These measures would have to be consonant with the treaty obligations of the United States, including the Charter of the United Nations and with any action or recommendations of the United Nations. They would also, if armed attack occurs, be subject to the overriding authority of the United Nations Security Council in accordance with the Charter.

The present proposal would, in the fourth place, authorize the President to employ, for economic and defensive military purposes, sums available under the Mutual Security Act of 1954, as amended, without regard to existing limitations.

The legislation now requested should not include the authorization or appropriation of funds because I believe that, under the conditions I suggest, presently appropriated funds will be adequate for the balance of the present fiscal year ending June 30. I shall, however, seek in subsequent legislation the authorization of $200,000,000 to be available during each of the fiscal years 1958 and 1959 for discretionary use in the area, in addition to the other mutual security programs for the area hereafter provided for by the Congress.

VII.

This program will not solve all the problems of the Middle East. Neither does it represent the totality of our policies for the area. There are the problems of Palestine and relations between Israel and the Arab States, and the future of the Arab refugees. There is the problem of the future status of the Suez Canal. These difficulties are aggravated by International Communism, but they would exist quite apart from that threat. It is not the purpose of the legislation I propose to deal directly with these problems. The United Nations is actively concerning itself with all these matters, and we are supporting the United Nations. The United States has made clear, notably by Secretary Dulles' address of August 26, 1955, that we are willing to do much to assist the United Nations in solving the basic problems of Palestine.

The proposed legislation is primarily designed to deal with the possibility of Communist aggression, direct and indirect. There is imperative need that any lack of power in the area should be made good, not by external or alien force, but by the increased vigor and security of the independent nations of the area.

Experience shows that indirect aggression rarely if ever succeeds where there is reasonable security against direct aggression; where the government disposes of loyal security forces, and where economic conditions are such as not to make Communism seem an attractive alternative. The program I suggest deals with all three aspects of this matter and thus with the problem of indirect aggression.

It is my hope and belief that if our purpose be proclaimed, as proposed by the requested legislation, that very fact will serve to halt any contemplated aggression. We shall have heartened the patriots who are dedicated to the independence of their nations. They will not feel that they stand alone, under the menace of great power. And I should add that patriotism is, throughout this area, a powerful sentiment. It is true that fear sometimes perverts true patriotism into fanaticism and to the acceptance of dangerous enticements from without. But if that fear can be allayed, then the climate will be more favorable to the attainment of worthy national ambitions.

And as I have indicated, it will also be necessary for us to contribute economically to strengthen those countries, or groups of countries, which have governments manifestly dedicated to the preservation of independence and resistance to subversion. Such measures will provide the greatest insurance against Communist inroads. Words alone are not enough.

VII.

Let me refer again to the requested authority to employ the armed forces of the United States to assist to defend the territorial integrity and the political independence of any nation in the area against Communist armed aggression. Such authority would not be exercised except at the desire of the nation attacked. Beyond this it is my profound hope that this authority would never have to be exercised at all.

Nothing is more necessary to assure this than that our policy with respect to the defense of the area be promptly and clearly determined and declared. Thus the United Nations and all friendly governments, and indeed governments which are not friendly, will know where we stand.

If, contrary to my hope and expectation, a situation arose which called for the military application of the policy which I ask the Congress to join me in proclaiming, I would of course maintain hour-by-hour contact with the Congress if it were in session. And if the Congress were not in session, and if the situation had grave implications, I would, of course, at once call the Congress into special session.

In the situation now existing, the greatest risk, as is often the case, is that ambitious despots may miscalculate. If power-hungry Communists should either falsely or correctly estimate that the Middle East is inadequately defended, they might be tempted to use open measures of armed attack. If so, that would start a chain of circumstances which would almost surely involve the United States in military action. I am convinced that the best insurance against this dangerous contingency is to make clear now our readiness to cooperate fully and freely with our friends of the Middle East in ways consonant with the purposes and principles of the United Nations. I intend promptly to send a special mission to the Middle East to explain the cooperation we are prepared to give.

IX.

The policy which I outline involves certain burdens and indeed risks for the United States. Those who covet the area will not like what is proposed. Already, they are grossly distorting our purpose. However, before this Americans have seen our nation's vital interests and human freedom in jeopardy, and their fortitude and resolution have been equal to the crisis, regardless of hostile distortion of our words, motives and actions.

Indeed, the sacrifices of the American people in the cause of freedom have, even since the close-of World War II, been measured in many billions of dollars and in thousands of the precious lives of our youth. These sacrifices, by which great areas of the world have been preserved to freedom, must not be thrown away.

In those momentous periods of the past, the President and the Congress have united, without partisanship, to serve the vital interests of the United States and of the free world.

The occasion has come for us to manifest again our national unity in support of freedom and to show our deep respect for the rights and independence of every nation—however great, however small. We seek not violence, but peace. To this purpose we must now devote our energies, our determination, ourselves.

Document Analysis

Eisenhower's speech to the joint session of Congress begins with a promise to review the most pressing international concern of the hour, the "special situation" in the Middle East. Eisenhower reiterates that the fundamental objective in all international relations is the pursuit of peace. He argues that the Middle East is at a particularly vulnerable stage in its development. It is emerging from centuries of colonial rule, which he downplays as "other nations exercis[ing] considerable authority in the area." While colonial powers had once been responsible for the defense and security of their Middle Eastern territory, the move toward independence and self-determination in these countries meant increasing conflict and border disputes. The Suez Canal Crisis, which he refers to as "hostilities involving Western European nations" has exacerbated these tensions, particularly with Israel. The Soviet Union, at the head of "international Communism," had also exploited these tensions and therefore has responsibility for some of the outbreak of violence.

The bulk of this speech addresses the Soviet Union's reasons for wanting to control the Middle East and the reasons it must be prevented from doing so. Eisenhower notes that unlike Western Europe, which depends heavily on Middle Eastern petroleum, Russia has its own oil reserves. Thus, they do not need to use the trade route that the Suez Canal provides. Their desire to control the Middle East is ideological and not born of economic necessity. He says the Soviet Union is motivated by its "announced purpose of Communizing the world." Eisenhower warns the nations of the Middle East not to fall for Soviet promises of aid with no strings attached. Independent nations had been absorbed by the Soviet Union by force after such promises had been made. He gives examples of the Baltic States during World War II and the Eastern European nations after the war, most notably Hungary, where the Soviet Union had intervened militarily to prop up the Communist puppet government there. The United Nations was unable to intervene, since the Soviet Union was able to use its veto on the U.N. Security Council. In addition, Eisenhower reminds Congress that the officially atheist Soviet Union does not respect religious freedom. He asks: How would it treat the holy sites of Christianity, Islam, and Judaism if it controlled the region?

It is no secret that the "national integrity of other free nations is directly related to our own security," and therefore, Eisenhower proposes a plan that would work with the United Nations to build economic support for the Middle East and to provide it with "programs of military assistance." Eisenhower indicates that he will ask for two hundred million dollars for aid to the Middle East in the upcoming years, a commitment that he felt would encourage nations in the region to resist Soviet overtures or aggression.

Essential Themes

The Eisenhower Doctrine firmly established the United States' interest in the Middle East, supplanting the influence of former colonial powers in the region, most notably France and Great Britain. The ongoing conflict between the United States and the Soviet Union would increasingly be played out in the Middle East (among other parts of the developing world), and the area remained unstable and volatile.

The military intervention promised in the Eisenhower Doctrine was requested once, by Lebanon, in July 1958. Lebanese president Camille Chamoun aroused the ire of Nasser and anti-Western pan-Arabs by refusing to cut diplomatic ties with Western nations during the Suez Crisis. Fearing a revolution with outside (Soviet) support, Chamoun went to the U.N. Security Council for help, and when that body failed to provide support, he called on the United States for help. The United States sent ships and troops to protect transportation and trade centers in Beirut, notably the seaport and airport. The troops were withdrawn in October 1958.

—Bethany Groff Dorau, MA

Bibliography and Additional Reading

Ambrose, Stephen E. *Eisenhower, Vol. II: The President*. New York: Simon, 1984. Print.

Thomas, Evans. *Ike's Bluff: President Eisenhower's Secret Battle to Save the World*. New York: Little, Brown, 2012. Print.

Walker, Martin. *The Cold War: A History*. New York: Holt, 1993. Print.

■ U.N. Security Council Resolution 242 on the Arab-Israeli Conflict

Date: November 22, 1967
Authors: Hugh M. Foot; Arthur Goldberg; Eugene Rostow
Geographic region: Middle East; Egypt; Jordan; Syria
Genre: Legislation; report

Summary Overview

In June, 1967, with tension rising in the Middle East, and Egyptian, Jordanian, and Syrian military forces being mobilized and stationed along their borders with Israel, Israel mobilized its forces and attacked these three nations, winning a decisive military victory in six days. Israel occupied territory belonging to these three nations when a cease-fire was signed. A solution was needed to ease, or perhaps end, the tensions between the Arabs and the Israelis. The U.N. resolution reprinted here was designed to address that situation.

Resolution 242 addressed both a basic problem from before the war (the existence of Israel) and a major problem as a result of the war (Israel occupying non-Israeli territory). The compromise offered through this resolution was that Israel would return the lands it had conquered in exchange for the Arab states recognizing Israel and its right to exist. Although this compromise would not have solved all the tensions that had arisen in the region since World War II, the full implementation of the resolution would have peacefully resolved major disputes that these nations were facing.

Defining Moment

One reason the United Nations was founded, as stated in its charter, was to settle "international disputes by peaceful means." Resolution 242 was one attempt to implement this aspect of the charter; in this instance by settling the dispute between Israel and its neighbors, Egypt, Jordan, and Syria. When the British had announced that they were giving up their protectorate of Palestine during 1948, the existing Arab countries in that region had desired the creation of one new state in that area, Palestine. If this had been done it would have been a majority Arab/Muslim state, with a significant Jewish minority. However, Jewish settlers in that area, and Jews around the world, advocated for the creation of a Jewish state in those sections of the protectorate in which Jews were the majority. A two-state division of

the area was recommended by the United Nations, and Jewish leaders declared the creation of Israel in 1948. After repelling Arab troops, Israel was established with most of the area that was to have been a Palestinian state incorporated into Egypt and Jordan.

During the spring of 1967, increased violence was directed toward Israel, in the form of both guerilla raids by Palestinians and larger efforts such as Syria's artillery bombardment of northern Israel. Egypt closed Israel's access to the Red Sea. By early June, when the Israeli leadership believed (as did most other global leaders) that the Arab states were about to attack Israel (reinforcements were on the way to Jordan from Iraq), Israel made a pre-emptive attack against them destroying their air forces and many of their tanks and other mechanized forces. Once the Israelis had advanced far enough to secure defensible physical borders, they accepted a cease-fire, ending the fighting but not ending the hostility between the two sides. As the organization that had brokered the cease-fire on June 11, the United Nations, and its leaders sought to find a way to create a more stable situation for Israel and its neighbors. After five months of discussion, debate, and negotiations, the fifteen members of the Security Council unanimously adopted Resolution 242 at the 1382nd meeting of the Security Council.

The resolution was directed toward the nations of the Middle East, where it received a cool reception. Although it contained points that each side could accept, those that were acceptable to the Israelis seemed to be unacceptable to the Arabs, and vice versa. As such, although it did contain a potential path toward long-term peace and stability, the resolution produced no great progress. However, the basic premise of the resolution, land for peace, was the foundation for later agreements that Israel made with individual Arab states. As such, it was a seed that eventually did bear fruit, even if not in the form that had been articulated by the Security Council.

Author Biographies

Hugh M. Foot (1907-1990) was a British diplomat who grew up in a liberal, politically active family. (His father and three brothers were all, at various times, members of Parliament.) He was an administrator in British Palestine and during World War II served as a military administrator in the Mediterranean. Except for a short time when he resigned over the British policy in Rhodesia, he served as a representative for the United Kingdom from 1961 to 1970. In 1964, he was made a life peer.

Arthur Goldberg (1908-1990) was the American ambassador to the United Nations. He grew up in a family of modest means but eventually earned a law degree. Prior to his work at the U.N., he had been a labor lawyer and Secretary of Labor, and had served as an Associate Justice of the Supreme Court. After his time at the U.N., Goldberg tried, and failed, to win elective office, subsequently returning to private practice.

Eugene Rostow (1913-2002) was from a socialist family but became a conservative Democrat and supported a number of unpopular causes. He became a law professor at Yale, and in 1945, as an advisor to the State Department, published an article against Japanese-American internment. He eventually became Dean of the Yale Law School, serving there until 1965. During the Johnson administration he was an under-secretary of state and a strong defender of U.S. actions in the Vietnam War. It was in this capacity, as under-secretary, that he became involved in the U.N. action regarding the Six Day War in the Middle East. Rostow later led the U.S. Arms Control and Disarmament Agency.

HISTORICAL DOCUMENT

The Security Council,

Expressing its continuing concern with the grave situation in the Middle East,

Emphasizing the inadmissibility of the acquisition of territory by war and the need to work for a just and lasting peace in which every State in the area can live in security,

Emphasizing further that all Member States in their acceptance of the Charter of the United Nations have undertaken a commitment to act in accordance with Article 2 of the Charter,

1. Affirms that the fulfillment of Charter principles requires the establishment of a just and lasting peace in the Middle East which should include the application of both the following principles:
   (i) Withdrawal of Israeli armed forces from territories occupied in the recent conflict;
   (ii) Termination of all claims or states of belligerency and respect for and acknowledgement of the sovereignty, territorial integrity and political independence of every State in the area and their right to live in peace within secure and recognized boundaries free from threats or acts of force;

2. Affirms further the necessity
   (a) For guaranteeing freedom of navigation through international waterways in the area;
   (b) For achieving a just settlement of the refugee problem;
   (c) For guaranteeing the territorial inviolability and political independence of every State in the area, through measures including the establishment of demilitarized zones;

3. Requests the Secretary General to designate a Special Representative to proceed to the Middle East to establish and maintain contacts with the States concerned in order to promote agreement and assist efforts to achieve a peaceful and accepted settlement in accordance with the provisions and principles in this resolution;

4. Requests the Secretary-General to report to the Security Council on the progress of the efforts of the Special Representative as soon as possible.

Document Analysis

The Security Council of the United Nations sought to end the tension in the Middle East caused by the withdrawal of the British from Palestine without the status of the territory, and borders of any new states, having been agreed to by all interested parties. In 1948, when the Jewish leaders announced the creation of the state of Israel within borders recommended by a 1947 U.N. resolution, there was not a comparable Arab/Palestinian organization ready to establish a government within the remaining territory, nor were the Arab Palestinians ready to accept the proposed arrangement. The resulting turmoil and new borders led to twenty years of ongoing tension between Israel and its neighbors. The members of the Security Council rightly understood that unless this underlying tension was resolved, the pressures that had brought about the Six Day War would result in future wars. Thus, the Council not only called for a "just and lasting peace in which every State in the area can live in security," but tried to provide a foundation on which this might occur. Without mandating a timeline or other specifics, the resolution proposed that a long-term peace would be attained through the resolution of basic four issues. These would be the withdrawal from occupied territory (Israel), mutual recognition of states and previous boundaries (all participants, but especially the Arab states), following agreements regarding international waterways (Egypt), and a solution to the refugee crisis resulting from the displacement of many Palestinians (mainly Jordan and Israel). While no specific temporal order was assigned to resolving these issues, it was understood that these were not totally independent concerns and certain solutions might have to be implemented simultaneously.

The creators of this resolution understood that the goal of peace was not simple, or it would have already been accomplished. However, with the Six Day War ceasefire a new opportunity presented itself. Both sides in the conflict had something the other wanted. The Arab states wanted their lands back, or at least for Israel not to have it, while Israel wanted diplomatic recognition and the ability to undertake normal economic endeavors. Those opposing Israel looked at the first major point in the introduction and the first clause, which stated that Israel should withdraw from "territories occupied in the recent conflict." The initial thought was that this was a first step, to be followed by other actions. These leaders demanded that Israel take the first step. Israel's response was to point to the next clause, which mandated that everyone in the Middle East should make an "acknowledgement of the sovereignty, territorial integrity and political independence of every State" within the region. Israel countered, then, that the first step should be the implementation of the second clause declaring that secure national borders must be established along with the acceptance of Israel's right to exist. Israel's position was that the Arab states' rejection of Israel had been the source of tension prior to the war. The Security Council, however, believed that with each side having something to trade, Israel should be able to obtain diplomatic recognition in exchange for giving up the occupied territory.

It was assumed that if the border issue were resolved, then opening the Straits of Tiran (connecting the Gulf of Aqaba and the Red Sea) would be assured, as was the case when Egypt and Israel signed a peace treaty in 1978. (Since Israel held the Sinai Peninsula after the Six Day War, this was temporarily not an issue.) The first three clauses laying out issues to be settled were all important to Israel—and to at least one of the Arab states. However, the fourth issue, "the refugee problem," was not a top concern for any national leader at the time. Israel seemed to think that the refugees could transform into residents in whatever nation they found themselves. The Arab nations believed that, while some refugees might meld into their populations, most would return to Palestine (the Gaza Strip or the West Bank) and become part of the new Palestinian state, whenever that was created. Thus, all of the leaders considered the refugees as someone else's problem, and therefore they took few steps to try to solve this issue.

Although a Special Representative was to be appointed to assist with any negotiations, and a report submitted to the Security Council, those measures were not expected to resolve any serious issues not otherwise addressed. Officials were sent and offers to mediate were made, but none of these efforts were eagerly received by the nations in the conflict. In addition, the exact meaning of this fairly simple resolution was debated. For example, a dispute over the exact meaning of the clause instructing Israel to withdraw seems to have been present from the start. Israel and Arthur Goldberg, one of the authors, interpreted this statement as meaning that Israel should withdraw from some of, but not necessarily all, the territory. On the other side, the Arab nations and Eugene Rostow, another author, believed that to fulfill the resolution Israel had to withdraw from all territory acquired during the 1967 war. While there are no modifiers on the term "withdrawal" in the resolution, those supporting a partial withdrawal pointed to the fact that the Security Council had voted against a Soviet Union proposal that had included the word "total" as a modifier to "withdrawal," instead adopting the British proposal without that modifier. The resolution was not complex, and clearly related to Article 2 Clause 3 of the U.N. Charter, which affirmed that settlement of disputes should be "by peaceful means," and Clause 4's affirmation of "territorial integrity." Nevertheless, exactly how the resolution was to be implemented to achieve this goal was not a matter of settled opinion.

Essential Themes

At the heart of Resolution 242 was the proposal to end the conflict by means of what has been called a "land for peace" deal. Israel held territory that had been part of, or was claimed by, the three major belligerents on the Arab side. Although none of the four active participants in the war responded to the resolution by giving it a wholehearted endorsement, Israel, Egypt, and Jordan were inclined to see it as a positive proposal and something that might work. Syria was adamant that it would not consider discussing other issues while Israel held Syrian territory. Although Resolution 242 initially received a tepid reception, it did play an important role in future talks and treaties.

The 1979 peace treaty signed by Egyptian and Israeli leaders reflected the core of Resolution 242. While additional issues and safeguards were included in the later agreement, Israel returned the Sinai Peninsula to Egypt and Egypt recognized Israel and its right to exist. The Gaza Strip, which had been governed by Egypt from 1948 to 1967, was left in Israel's control, to become a future Palestinian state. Although Jordan had annexed the West Bank after the 1948 Arab-Israeli conflict, in 1988 it officially renounced this annexation, turning over the territory to the Palestinian people, even though at that time it was under Israel's control. Thus, the Jordanian-Israeli treaty, signed in 1994, returned only a small amount of territory to Jordan in exchange for its recognition of Israel and normalization of economic and political relations between the two states. Syria and Israel have never signed a peace treaty, although they

did have an agreement leading to military "disengagement" along their border. The Syrian leadership has always demanded that Israel withdraw from all occupied territory before they would consider further discussions regarding a peace treaty. Still, even aspects of the "disengagement" plan echoed Resolution 242, in that Israel partially withdrew in return for a small move toward more peaceful relations between the two nations.

The final issue that Resolution 242 sought to advance was the "refugee problem." While Jordan had the largest group of displaced Palestinians within its borders, once Israel had taken control of the Gaza Strip and the West Bank it acquired not only this territory and the original inhabitants, but thousands of refugees as well. As illustrated by the situation more than fifty years later, the refugee issue was not then at the forefront of matters requiring a quick solution. Yet, on this issue, and on the related issue of a Palestinian state, Resolution 242 established the pattern for what was to be accomplished. The Palestinian slogan of the "right to return" was not in the resolution, nor was any specific reference to Palestinians. But under the 1993 Oslo Accords, Israel gave the Palestinian National Authority control over much of the occupied territory, and in exchange the PLO and the Palestinian National Authority recognized the right of Israel to exist. Thus, although no nation that participated in the Six Day War received Resolution 242 with enthusiasm, it has ended up playing a role in a variety of later events and agreements.

—*Donald A Watt, PhD*

Bibliography and Additional Reading

Black, Eric. "Resolution 242 and the Aftermath of 1967." *Frontline*. Boston: WGBH Educational Foundation, 1995. Web. 6 March 2018.

Gilbert, Martin. *Israel: A History*. New York: Harper Perennial, 1998 and 2008. Print.

Jewish Virtual Library. "U.N. Security Council: The Meaning of Resolution 242." *Jewish Virtual Library*. Chevy Chase MD: American-Israeli Cooperative Enterprise, 2018. Web. 7 March 2018.

Odeh, Adnan Abu (ed.) *U.N. Security Council Resolution 242: The Building Block of Peacemaking: A Washington Institute Monograph*. Washington: Washington Institute for Near East Policy. 1993. Print.

Robins, Philip. *A History of Jordan*. Cambridge: Cambridge University Press, 2004. Print.

Robenne, Meir. "Understanding U.N. Security Council Resolution 242." *Jerusalem Center for Public Affairs: Israeli Security, Regional Diplomacy, and International Law.* Jerusalem: Jerusalem Center for Public Affairs, 2018. Web. 7 March 2018.

Rostow, Eugene V. "The Drafting of Security Council Resolution 242: The Role of Non-Regional Actors." *Yale Law School Legal Scholarship Repository: Faculty Scholarship Series.* New Haven: Yale Law School, 1993. Web. 6 March 2018.

Palestinian National Charter

Date: July 1968
Author: Ahmed Shukeiri
Geographic region: Palestine
Genre: Charter

Summary Overview

Because Arab leaders refused to create a government in 1947-48, when the state and government of Israel were created, the Arab Palestinian people were left without a state and without established leaders. In 1964, with Egypt and Jordan ruling most of what had been the proposed Palestinian state, the Arab League held a meeting that recommended a Palestinian organization be established. It was to eventually create a Palestinian state, and in the interim to assist the Palestinian people in their conflict with Israel. The Palestinian National Council was thus created, which adopted the first version of the Palestinian National Charter. In 1968, after a decisive Arab military defeat by Israeli forces, this charter was expanded, generally with stronger statements against the existence of Israel.

The Palestinian National Charter was the first concrete step that Arab leaders had taken toward the creation of an Arab state in what had been the British protectorate west of the Jordan River. Prior to the charter's being written and adopted, Arab and Palestinian leaders had made statements about how an Arab majority state should exist in the region, yet no official group had come together to explicitly organize for that eventuality. While the charter was not a constitution, in terms of outlining the specifics of a system of government, it did recognize the Palestine Liberation Organization (PLO) as the official representative for all Palestinians. For the first time, there was an organization charged with the responsibilities of leadership of the Palestinians and with creating a situation in which a viable Palestinian state could come into existence.

Defining Moment

Under the League of Nations, the United Kingdom was given mandates to rule various areas in the Middle East, with the goal of helping them to prepare for independence. Civil unrest in the British protectorate of Palestine made the British eager to withdraw from that area after the end of World War II. The territory east of the Jordan River gained independence in 1946, with strong divisions west of the river inhibiting the creation of a state in that region. The United Kingdom announced that it was withdrawing from that region by the middle of 1948, turning the situation over to the United Nations. In November 1947, the United Nations passed a resolution recommending the division of the area west of the Jordan River into two states, one Jewish and one Arab (Muslim). On the day the British withdrew their last troops from the protectorate of Palestine, Jewish leaders announced the creation of the state of Israel, with its borders to be those recommended by the United Nations. The Arab leaders rejected the division and refused to create a government for the area which was to become the Arab state of Palestine. Neighboring nations attacked Israel, which successfully responded, repelling the invading armies and expanding the territory of Israel by about a third. The other areas that were to have been part of the Palestinian state were taken by Egypt and Jordan. This war created the first wave of Palestinian refugees.

Twenty years after the creation of Israel, there was still no Palestinian state. The Six Day War, in 1967, gave Israel control of the entire area that had been proposed as a Palestinian state, as well as parts of Egypt, Jordan, and Syria. This also created a second wave of Palestinian refugees. Without any Arab government in control of what had been considered Palestinian territory, many believed that a radical step was needed to confront Israel. The 1968 Palestinian National Charter included revisions that gave justification for military operations against any Israeli unit or locale, as well as abandoning the 1947 proposal for a two-state solution. The PLO intensified its efforts to wear down the Israeli government by a constant series of small attacks or conflicts, including targeting civilians. The Palestinian National Charter not only gave the PLO formal status, at least vis-à-vis Arab states and their allies, but the ability to fight or use peaceful means to reach the goal of defeating Israel. However, as stated in the charter, military actions were seen by the Palestinian leaders to be the only way in which Israel could be forced out of Palestine, and out of existence.

Author Biography

Ahmed Shukeiri (1908—1980) was born in the Ottoman Empire, where his father, an Ottoman legislator, represented part of what became the Palestine protectorate. Ahmed was well educated and went on to graduate from law school in Britain. As a respected lawyer, he advocated for independence, during the British rule. After World War II, he worked in various Arab causes, including as a delegate to the United Nations for Syria. As assistant Secretary General of the Arab League, in 1964, he was given the responsibility for organizing the Palestinians into a more united body. He convened the meeting which adopted the 1964 Charter, having written most of it himself. He was elected the Chairman of the PLO, and served until December 1967. Although he was not personally responsible for Israel's dramatic victory in the Six Day War, many Palestinian leaders blamed him for the loss. After his resignation he continued to support Palestinian and Arab causes, working as an author until his death.

HISTORICAL DOCUMENT

Article 1

Palestine is the homeland of the Arab Palestinian people; it is an indivisible part of the greater Arab homeland, and the Palestinian people are an integral part of the Arab nation.

Article 2

Palestine, with the boundaries it had during the British Mandate, is an indivisible territorial unit.

Article 3

The Palestinian Arab people possess the legal right to their homeland and to self-determination after the completion of the liberation of their country in accordance with their wishes and entirely of their own accord and will.

Article 4

The Palestinian identity is a genuine, essential, and inherent characteristic; it is transmitted from fathers to children. The Zionist occupation and the dispersal of the Palestinian Arab people, through the disasters which befell them, do not make them lose their Palestinian identity and their membership in the Palestinian community, nor do they negate them.

Article 5

The Palestinians are those Arab nationals who, until 1947, normally resided in Palestine regardless of whether they were evicted from it or stayed there. Anyone born, after that date, of a Palestinian father—whether in Palestine or outside it—is also a Palestinian.

Article 6

The Jews who had normally resided in Palestine until the beginning of the Zionist invasion are considered Palestinians.

Article 7

There is a Palestinian community and that it has material, spiritual, and historical connection with Palestine are indisputable facts. It is a national duty to bring up individual Palestinians in an Arab revolutionary manner. All means of information and education must be adopted in order to acquaint the Palestinian with his country in the most profound manner, both spiritual and material, that is possible. He must be prepared for the armed struggle and ready to sacrifice his wealth and his life in order to win back his homeland and bring about its liberation.

Article 8

The phase in their history, through which the Palestinian people are now living, is that of national (watani) struggle for the liberation of Palestine. Thus the conflicts among the Palestinian national forces are secondary, and should be ended for the sake of the basic conflict that exists between the forces of Zionism and of colonialism on the one hand, and the Palestinian Arab people on the other. On this basis the Palestinian masses, regardless of whether they are residing in the national homeland or in Diaspora (mahajir) constitute—both their organizations and the individuals—one national front working for the retrieval of Palestine and its liberation through armed struggle.

Article 9

Armed struggle is the only way to liberate Palestine. This is the overall strategy, not merely a tactical phase. The Palestinian Arab people assert their absolute determination and firm resolution to continue their armed struggle and to work for an armed popular revolution for the liberation of their country and their return to it. They also assert their right to normal life in Palestine and to exercise their right to self-determination and sovereignty over it.

Article 10

Commando (Feday'ee) action constitutes the nucleus of the Palestinian popular liberation war. This requires its escalation, comprehensiveness, and the mobilization of all the Palestinian popular and educational efforts and their organization and involvement in the armed Palestinian revolution. It also requires the achieving of unity for the national (watani) struggle among the different groupings of the Palestinian people, and between the Palestinian people and the Arab masses, so as to secure the continuation of the revolution, its escalation, and victory.

Article 11

Palestinians have three mottoes: national unity, national (al-qawmiyya) mobilization, and liberation.

Article 12

The Palestinian Arab people believe in Arab unity. In order to contribute their share toward the attainment of that objective, however, they must, at the present stage of their struggle, safeguard their Palestinian identity and develop their consciousness of that identity, oppose any plan that may dissolve or impair it.

Article 13

Arab unity and the liberation of Palestine are two complementary goals, the attainment of either of which facilitates the attainment of the other. Thus, Arab unity leads to the liberation of Palestine, the liberation of Palestine leads to Arab unity; and the work toward the realization of one objective proceeds side by side with work toward the realization of the other.

Article 14

The destiny of the Arab Nation, and indeed Arab existence itself, depend upon the destiny of the Palestinian cause. From this interdependence springs the Arab nation's pursuit of, and striving for, the liberation of Palestine. The people of Palestine play the role of the vanguard in the realization of this sacred (qawmi) goal.

Article 15

The liberation of Palestine, from an Arab viewpoint, is a national (qawmi) duty and it attempts to repel the Zionist and imperialist aggression against the Arab homeland, and aims at the elimination of Zionism in Palestine. Absolute responsibility for this falls upon the Arab nation—peoples and governments-with the Arab people of Palestine in the vanguard. Accordingly, the Arab nation must mobilize all its military, human, moral, and spiritual capabilities to participate actively with the Palestinian people in the liberation of Palestine. It must, particularly, in the phase of the armed Palestinian revolution, offer and furnish the Palestinian people with all possible help, and material and human support, and make available to them the means and opportunities that will enable them to continue to carry out their leading role in the armed revolution, until they liberate their homeland.

Article 16

The liberation of Palestine, from a spiritual viewpoint, will provide the Holy Land with an atmosphere of safety and tranquillity, which in turn will safeguard the country's religious sanctuaries and guarantee freedom of worship and of visit to all, without discrimination of race, color, language, or religion. Accordingly, the Palestinian people look to all spiritual forces in the world for support.

Article 17

The liberation of Palestine, from a human point of view, will restore to the Palestinian individual his dignity, pride, and freedom. Accordingly, the Palestinian Arab people look forward to the support of all those who believe in the dignity of man and his freedom in the world.

Article 18

The liberation of Palestine, from an international point of view, is a defensive action necessitated by the demands of self-defense. Accordingly, the Palestinian people, desirous as they are of the friendship of all people, look to freedom-loving and peace-loving states for support in order to restore their legitimate rights in Palestine, to re-establish peace and security in the country, and to enable its people to exercise national sovereignty and freedom.

Article 19

The partition of Palestine in 1947, and the establishment of the state of Israel are entirely illegal, regardless of the passage of time, because they were contrary to the will of the Palestinian people and its natural right in their homeland, and were inconsistent with the principles embodied in the Charter of the United Nations, particularly the right to self-determination.

Article 20

The Balfour Declaration, the Palestine Mandate, and everything that has been based on them, are deemed null and void. Claims of historical or religious ties of Jews with Palestine are incompatible with the facts of history and the conception of what constitutes statehood. Judaism, being a religion, is not an independent nationality. Nor do Jews constitute a single nation with an identity of their own; they are citizens of the states to which they belong.

Article 21

The Arab Palestinian people, expressing themselves by armed Palestinian revolution, reject all solutions which are substitutes for the total liberation of Palestine and reject all proposals aimed at the liquidation of the Palestinian cause, or at its internationalization.

Article 22

Zionism is a political movement organically associated with international imperialism and antagonistic to all action for liberation and to progressive movements in the world. It is racist and fanatic in its nature, aggressive, expansionist and colonial in its aims, and fascist in its methods. Israel is the instrument of the Zionist movement, and the geographical base for world imperialism placed strategically in the midst of the Arab homeland to combat the hopes of the Arab nation for liberation, unity, and progress. Israel is a constant source of threat vis-à-vis peace in the Middle East and the whole world. Since liberation of Palestine will destroy the Zionist and imperialist presence and will contribute to the establishment of peace in the Middle East. That is why the Palestinian people look to the progressive and peaceful forces and urge them all, irrespective of their affiliations and beliefs, to offer the Palestinian people all aid and support in their just struggle for the liberation of their homeland.

Article 23

The demand of security and peace, as well as the demand of right and justice, require all states to consider Zionism an illegitimate movement, to outlaw its existence, and to ban its operations, in order that friendly relations among peoples may be preserved, and the loyalty of citizens to their respective homelands safeguarded.

Article 24

The Palestinian people believe in the principles of justice, freedom, sovereignty, self-determination, human dignity, and the right of peoples to exercise them.

Article 25

For the realization of the goals of this Charter and its principles, the Palestine Liberation Organization will perform its role in the liberation of Palestine.

Article 26

The Palestine Liberation Organization, the representative of the Palestinian revolutionary forces, is responsible for the Palestinian Arab peoples movement in its struggle—to retrieve its homeland, liberate and return to it and exercise the right to self-determination in it—in all military, political, and financial fields and also for whatever may be required by the Palestinian cause on the inter-Arab and international levels.

Article 27

The Palestine Liberation Organization shall cooperate with all Arab states, each according to its potentialities; and will adopt a neutral policy among them in light of the requirements of the battle of liberation; and on this basis does not interfere in the internal affairs of any Arab state.

Article 28

The Palestinian Arab people assert the genuineness and independence of their national revolution and reject all forms of intervention, trusteeship, and subordination.

Article 29

The Palestinian people possess the fundamental and genuine legal right to liberate and retrieve their homeland. The Palestinian people determine their attitude toward all states and forces on the basis of the stands they adopt vis-à-vis the Palestinian revolution to fulfill the aims of the Palestinian people.

Article 30

Fighters and carriers of arms in the war of liberation are the nucleus of the popular army which will be the protective force for the gains of the Palestinian Arab people.

Article 31

This Organization shall have a flag, an oath of allegiance, and an anthem. All this shall be decided upon in accordance with a special law.

Article 32

A law, known as the Basic Statute of the Palestine Liberation Organization, shall be annexed to this Covenant. It will lay down the manner in which the Organization, and its organs and institutions, shall be constituted; the respective competence of each; and the requirements of its obligation under the Charter.

Article 33

This Charter shall not be amended save by [vote of] a majority of two-thirds of the total membership of the National Council of the Palestine Liberation Organization [taken] at a special session convened for that purpose.

GLOSSARY

commando action: small-scale raids, some of which might be called terrorist acts, intended to cause harm to Israelis or Israeli targets, without seeking to retain control of the area attacked

Zionism: the political movement during the late nineteenth and early twentieth centuries that advocated for the creation of a Jewish homeland in Palestine; once Israel was created, it was seen as the push for its full development

Document Analysis

The Arab League called together nearly four hundred representatives of the Palestinian people, in 1964, to begin the process of developing a Palestinian state. Knowing that this was a process, they included in their charter the provision that it could be amended. In 1968, the National Council of the PLO amended the original charter, adopting several more aggressive provisions in the struggle against Israel. The focus of this charter was the assertion that Israel had no right to exist, since all the territory west of the Jordan River was part of the yet to be formed Palestinian state. Israel was "illegal," from the Palestinian point of view. As such, "armed struggle" was the manner by which Palestine could be freed, since it was clear Israel was not going to voluntarily disband. All Arabs should be unified, according to the charter, especially in support of the Palestinian cause. Once Palestine was liberated, then Palestinians would work with other Arabs in creating a more unified Middle East. However, until that time the PLO would focus on opposing all who supported Israel and work toward gaining justice and freedom for the Palestinian people through any means which might lead to the collapse of Israel.

The Palestinian National Charter defined a Palestinian quite broadly, as any Arab who "normally" lived in Palestine, or was descended from a person who had lived in the territory as of 1947. (Jews who lived in Palestine prior to the beginnings of the Zionist movement, in the 1890s, were also defined as Palestinians.) These were the individuals to whom the land belonged, and who should be allowed to create a state that included all the territory of the British mandate west of the Jordan River. The gathering that adopted this document believed that these people had a "material, spiritual, and historical connection" with the land, and each with one another. Thus, the Diaspora created by the imposition of the state of Israel upon this territory, according

to the Palestinian National Council, needed to be tempered by educating the children as Palestinians not as citizens of wherever the family resided.

The charter was divided in terms of the view of the Palestinian leadership that it presented to the world. The main perception which was projected was one regarding the strong support which it gave to using violence to obtain the goal of a Palestinian state. This was clearly stated in Articles 7, 9, 10, 15, 21, 26, 29, and 30. The "revolutionary force," or the PLO's operational wing, was to bring a "war of liberation" to Israel. Stating that "commando action constitutes the nucleus of the Palestinian popular liberation war," the charter authorized virtually any type of armed action against Israel and its supporters. As noted, some of these articles were added in the 1968 version and others were strengthened. Through this process, the final vision became that of an all-or-nothing struggle. Either Israel was destroyed, or the Palestinian cause would fail.

At the same time that the charter supports strong military actions, it also tries to communicate the idea that the values of the Western democratic tradition are a part of the Palestinian worldview. Thus, the charter contains assurances that Palestinians believe in "justice, freedom, sovereignty, human dignity, and the right of peoples to exercise them." Variations of this statement were included in several articles of the charter. To many who read the charter, these ideals can seem overshadowed by the advocacy of violent action against Israel. The articles reflecting a firm resolve for the use of violent methods to achieve the goal of a Palestinian state tend to outweigh the promised "tranquility" that a Palestinian state would be expected bring.

Many articles (i.e. 3, 4, 8, 15, 19, 20, 22, and 23) illustrate a worldview holding that none of the arguments supporting the existence of Israel, or even Israel itself, are valid. Not just Palestinians, but the entire global community should understand, according to the charter, that Zionism is "an illegitimate movement." The division of the territory into two states, whether as the result of United Nations' actions, or by any other means, is deemed unacceptable, or illegal, according to the charter. All of this reflects the goal of the destruction of Israel and the institution of the state of Palestine in all the territory that the United Kingdom had given to the United Nations in 1948, when the state of Israel had been declared to exist. According to the charter, there is no room in the Middle East for the state of Israel.

In line with the thought of the 1960s, Arab unity plays a strong role within the charter. It serves a dual purpose. First, it is one justification for broader Arab support of the Palestinian cause and movement. If the broader Arab community accepts the assertion that "Arab existence itself" is possible only if Israel is destroyed and the new Arab state of Palestine replaces it, then a strong argument is created for all Arab states to contribute to the Palestinian cause. The Palestinians as the vanguard in the struggle against hostile forces are depicted as the first wave in the reunification of all Arabs, as well. Even though the military forces of the major Arab nations had recently been embarrassed in a war with Israel, the Palestinian charter advocates for putting the combined military and economic forces of the Arab community at the disposal of the leaders and allies of the Palestinian cause. The long-term pledge by the Palestinian leadership is that they will support a future pan-Arab order.

As might be expected in a charter of this kind, the focus of the Palestinian National Charter was the creation of a Palestinian state. However, in this case the Palestinians believed that the only way the state of Palestine could be created would be if Israel was totally destroyed. The "national struggle" outlined in this charter does not allow for a compromise on this score. Violent revolution was the path, the only path, to liberation, according to the Palestine National Council and its charter.

Essential Themes

When the Palestinian leaders watched all the territory they claimed come under Israeli control, they responded with a strong statement of opposition. They outlined who, in their eyes, had a legitimate claim to the territory that had been the "British Mandate," and then proclaimed not only the right for the Palestinian people to

use force against Israel, but indicated that it was their duty. "Armed struggle" would allow Palestine to come to life, or at least the Palestinian leaders hoped this would be the case. There was a strong global condemnation of the emphasis upon violence, as most nations had hoped that a negotiated settlement might have been possible. However, in the 1960s this was not considered by the Palestinians. With the statement that Israel was an illegal entity, Israeli leaders were not ready for negotiations either. Since reasonable people understood that Israel was not going to disappear, the Palestinian stance was not viable in the long-term.

When secret negotiations between the PLO and Israel became public negotiations in the early 1990s, the PLO had to renounce some or all of several articles in this charter. While PLO leaders have given written statements assuring this to be the case, it was unclear to some if the official text of the charter was ever changed according to the rule outlined in Article 33. However, the 1994 agreement between the PLO and Israel, leading to the creation of the Palestinian National Authority, was based in part upon the PLO renouncing the most militant articles of the charter. Although the Oslo Accords, as the 1994 agreement is known, have allowed Israel and the Palestinian Authority to cooperate, the issues of the borders outlined in the charter are far from resolved. There are also groups, such as Hamas, which have maintained a more militant stance, and have continued violent acts toward Israel. However, the PLO, in creating the Palestinian Authority and allowing it to cooperate with Israel, has moved the Palestinian cause forward by gaining control of some of the territory promised in the 1947 United Nations' resolution. Although the 1994 agreement proved that significant progress toward coexistence could be made, events since then have demonstrated that there is still a long way to go before any lasting solution is reached.

—*Donald A Watt, PhD*

Bibliography and Additional Reading

Baracskay, Daniel. *The Palestine Liberation Organization: Terrorism and Prospects for Peace in the Holy Land.* (Praeger Security International) Santa Barbara CA: Praeger, 2011. Print.

Jamal, Amal. *The Palestinian National Movement.* Bloomington IN: Indiana University Press, 2005. Print.

Palestine Ministry of Information. "The Palestinian Charter." *Palestine Affairs Council.* Houston: Palestine American Council, 2018. Web. 7 March 2018.

Shukeiry, Ahmed. "Palestine Liberation Organization: The Original Palestine National Charter (1964)." Jewish Virtual Library. Washington: American-Israeli Cooperative Enterprise, 2018. Web. 7 March 2018.

UCC Palestine Solidarity Campaign. "Ahmad Shukairi." *Palestine: Information with Provenance (PIWP database).* Cork IE: UCC Palestine Solidarity Campaign, 2018. Web. 7 March 2018.

■ Camp David Accords

Date: September 17, 1978
Authors: Anwar al-Sadat and Menachem Begin (signatories)
Geographic Region: Middle East
Genre: Treaty

Summary Overview1

In the fall of 1978, Egyptian president Anwar al-Sadat and Israeli prime minister Menachem Begin, with U.S. president Jimmy Carter acting as facilitator, signed a landmark peace accord that helped establish peace between Egypt and Israel. The Egypt-Israel peace framework formed one part of the agreement and was by far the most successful; the other part was a framework for resolution of the wider Arab-Israeli conflict, mainly the political and territorial issues between Israel and the Palestinian Arabs. This part of the agreement was far less successful, as it was rejected by the Palestinians, who were given no part in the negotiations, and by the United Nations, which objected to it on several grounds.

Defining Moment

When the United Nations voted in 1947 to partition Palestine into Jewish and Arab territories, the action helped foster decades of distrust, political instability, violence, and war. Shortly after Israel's declaration of independence in 1948, forces from multiple neighboring states (Egypt, Syria, Iraq, Lebanon, Saudi Arabia, and Jordan) invaded the new nation. Israel was able to repel the Arab attackers before a series of localized armistices temporarily halted the violence. Egypt retained control over the Gaza Strip, a piece of land along the southern coast of Israel, and Jordan held the West Bank along Israel's eastern border with that nation. This uneasy peace held until 1967.

In 1967, tensions rose again when Egypt moved troops into the Sinai Peninsula, which borders Israel, and compelled U.N. peacekeepers to leave. Israel responded by launching a pre-emptive strike against Egypt in June. Jordan, Syria, and Iraq then attacked Israel, and over the course of six days Israeli forces decisively defeated these powers, capturing the Gaza Strip and Sinai Peninsula from Egypt, the West Bank from Jordan, and the Golan Heights from Syria. In the wake of the Six-Day War, as it became known, the U.N. Security Council adopted Resolution 242, calling for Israel to return the territories it had occupied in exchange for the Arab nations' recognition of Israel's territorial integrity and political independence. This resolution became the foundation of future diplomatic efforts to resolve the Arab-Israeli conflict.

Those efforts were again interrupted by war, however, when Egypt and Syria again attacked Israel and were again repelled in the 1973 Yom Kippur War. Although defeated, Egyptian and Syrian forces performed better than expected in the conflict. Egyptian president Sadat opted to use his increased prestige following the conflict to try to move toward peace with Israel. Meanwhile, in 1977, Israel elected a new prime minister, Menachem Begin, who was also interested in a peace initiative. In November of 1977, Sadat became the first Arab leader to visit Israel. In the summer of 1978, Begin returned the gesture, visiting Cairo. In September of 1978, U.S. president Jimmy Carter, recognizing the opportunity that these gestures created, invited Begin and Sadat to Camp David, a presidential retreat in Maryland. Located a safe distance from the lights and publicity of Washington, D.C., Camp David would provide the three leaders with the seclusion needed for the frank exchange of ideas necessary to broker peace.

Author Biographies

Muhammad Anwar al-Sadat was born in Mit Abu al-Kawm, Egypt, on December 25, 1918. He played an active role in the fight against British dominance in Egypt, helping to depose the pro-British King Farouk in 1952. He became President Gamal Abdel Nasser's vice president in 1969, and when Nasser died the following year, Sadat became president. During his tenure, he loosened Egypt's ties to the Soviet Union and drew it closer to the United States. A strong proponent of the Middle East peace process, Sadat was assassinated in 1981 by Egyptian extremists who were opposed to his peace initiatives.

Menachem Wolfovitch Begin was born on August 16, 1913, in Brest-Litovsk in the Russian Empire (now in Belarus). Begin was a major figure in the Betar Zionist

From left to right: Menachem Begin, Jimmy Carter and Anwar Sadat in Camp David. Fitz-Patrick, Bill, photographer - Jimmy Carter Library: Carter White House Photographs Collection, 01/20/1977 - 01/22/1981

youth movement before World War II. During the war, he joined a Soviet-backed Polish army unit that was sent to Palestine, where he was released from service and joined the fight for an independent Israel. After in-dependence, he rose in Israeli politics, becoming chair-man of the conservative Likud party in 1973. In 1977, he became prime minister, a post he held until 1983. He died on March 9, 1992.

HISTORICAL DOCUMENT

The Framework for Peace in the Middle East

Muhammad Anwar al-Sadat, President of the Arab Republic of Egypt, and Menachem Begin, Prime Minister of Israel, met with Jimmy Carter, Presi-dent of the United States of America, at Camp Da-vid from September 5 to September 17, 1978, and have agreed on the following framework for peace in the Middle East. They invite other parties to the Arab-Israel conflict to adhere to it.

Preamble

The search for peace in the Middle East must be guided by the following:

The agreed basis for a peaceful settlement of the conflict between Israel and its neighbors is United Nations Security Council Resolution 242, in all its parts.

After four wars during 30 years, despite intensive human efforts, the Middle East, which is the cradle of civilization and the birthplace of three great re-ligions, does not enjoy the blessings of peace. The people of the Middle East yearn for peace so that the vast human and natural resources of the region can be turned to the pursuits of peace and so that this area can become a model for coexistence and cooperation among nations.

The historic initiative of President Sadat in vis-iting Jerusalem and the reception accorded to him by the parliament, government and people of Israel, and the reciprocal visit of Prime Minister Begin to Ismailia, the peace proposals made by both leaders, as well as the warm reception of these missions by the peoples of both countries, have created an un-precedented opportunity for peace which must not be lost if this generation and future generations are to be spared the tragedies of war.

The provisions of the Charter of the United Na-tions and the other accepted norms of international law and legitimacy now provide accepted stan-dards for the conduct of relations among all states. To achieve a relationship of peace, in the spirit of Article 2 of the United Nations Charter, future ne-gotiations between Israel and any neighbor prepared to negotiate peace and security with it are necessary for the purpose of carrying out all the provisions and principles of Resolutions 242 and 338.

Peace requires respect for the sovereignty, ter-ritorial integrity and political independence of ev-ery state in the area and their right to live in peace within secure and recognized boundaries free from threats or acts of force. Progress toward that goal can accelerate movement toward a new era of rec-onciliation in the Middle East marked by coopera-tion in promoting economic development, in main-taining stability and in assuring security.

Security is enhanced by a relationship of peace and by cooperation between nations which enjoy normal relations. In addition, under the terms of peace treaties, the parties can, on the basis of reci-procity, agree to special security arrangements such as demilitarized zones, limited armaments areas, early warning stations, the presence of international forces, liaison, agreed measures for monitoring and other arrangements that they agree are useful.

Framework

Taking these factors into account, the parties are determined to reach a just, comprehensive, and du-rable settlement of the Middle East conflict through the conclusion of peace treaties based on Security Council resolutions 242 and 338 in all their parts. Their purpose is to achieve peace and good neigh-borly relations. They recognize that for peace to endure, it must involve all those who have been most deeply affected by the conflict. They therefore agree that this framework, as appropriate, is intended by them to constitute a basis for peace not only between Egypt and Israel, but also between Israel and each of its other neighbors which is prepared to negotiate peace with Israel on this basis. With that objective in mind, they have agreed to proceed as follows:

West Bank and Gaza

Egypt, Israel, Jordan and the representatives of the Palestinian people should participate in negotiations on the resolution of the Palestinian problem in all its aspects. To achieve that objective, negotiations relating to the West Bank and Gaza should proceed in three stages:

Egypt and Israel agree that, in order to ensure a peaceful and orderly transfer of authority, and taking into account the security concerns of all the parties, there should be transitional arrangements for the West Bank and Gaza for a period not exceeding five years. In order to provide full autonomy to the inhabitants, under these arrangements the Israeli military government and its civilian administration will be withdrawn as soon as a self-governing authority has been freely elected by the inhabitants of these areas to replace the existing military government. To negotiate the details of a transitional arrangement, Jordan will be invited to join the negotiations on the basis of this framework. These new arrangements should give due consideration both to the principle of self-government by the inhabitants of these territories and to the legitimate security concerns of the parties involved. Egypt, Israel, and Jordan will agree on the modalities for establishing elected self-governing authority in the West Bank and Gaza. The delegations of Egypt and Jordan may include Palestinians from the West Bank and Gaza or other Palestinians as mutually agreed. The parties will negotiate an agreement which will define the powers and responsibilities of the self-governing authority to be exercised in the West Bank and Gaza. A withdrawal of Israeli armed forces will take place and there will be a redeployment of the remaining Israeli forces into specified security locations. The agreement will also include arrangements for assuring internal and external security and public order. A strong local police force will be established, which may include Jordanian citizens. In addition, Israeli and Jordanian forces will participate in joint patrols and in the manning of control posts to assure the security of the borders.

When the self-governing authority (administrative council) in the West Bank and Gaza is established and inaugurated, the transitional period of five years will begin. As soon as possible, but not later than the third year after the beginning of the transitional period, negotiations will take place to determine the final status of the West Bank and Gaza and its relationship with its neighbors and to conclude a peace treaty between Israel and Jordan by the end of the transitional period. These negotiations will be conducted among Egypt, Israel, Jordan and the elected representatives of the inhabitants of the West Bank and Gaza. Two separate but related committees will be convened, one committee, consisting of representatives of the four parties which will negotiate and agree on the final status of the West Bank and Gaza, and its relationship with its neighbors, and the second committee, consisting of representatives of Israel and representatives of Jordan to be joined by the elected representatives of the inhabitants of the West Bank and Gaza, to negotiate the peace treaty between Israel and Jordan, taking into account the agreement reached in the final status of the West Bank and Gaza. The negotiations shall be based on all the provisions and principles of U.N. Security Council Resolution 242. The negotiations will resolve, among other matters, the location of the boundaries and the nature of the security arrangements. The solution from the negotiations must also recognize the legitimate right of the Palestinian peoples and their just requirements. In this way, the Palestinians will participate in the determination of their own future through:

The negotiations among Egypt, Israel, Jordan and the representatives of the inhabitants of the West Bank and Gaza to agree on the final status of the

West Bank and Gaza and other outstanding issues by the end of the transitional period.

Submitting their agreements to a vote by the elected representatives of the inhabitants of the West Bank and Gaza.

Providing for the elected representatives of the inhabitants of the West Bank and Gaza to decide how they shall govern themselves consistent with the provisions of their agreement.

Participating as stated above in the work of the committee negotiating the peace treaty between Israel and Jordan.

All necessary measures will be taken and provisions made to assure the security of Israel and its neighbors during the transitional period and beyond. To assist in providing such security, a strong local police force will be constituted by the self-governing authority. It will be composed of inhabitants of the West Bank and Gaza. The police will maintain liaison on internal security matters with the designated Israeli, Jordanian, and Egyptian officers.

During the transitional period, representatives of Egypt, Israel, Jordan, and the self-governing authority will constitute a continuing committee to decide by agreement on the modalities of admission of persons displaced from the West Bank and Gaza in 1967, together with necessary measures to prevent disruption and disorder. Other matters of common concern may also be dealt with by this committee. Egypt and Israel will work with each other and with other interested parties to establish agreed procedures for a prompt, just and permanent implementation of the resolution of the refugee problem.

Egypt-Israel

Egypt-Israel undertake not to resort to the threat or the use of force to settle disputes. Any disputes shall be settled by peaceful means in accordance with the provisions of Article 33 of the U.N. Charter.

In order to achieve peace between them, the parties agree to negotiate in good faith with a goal of concluding within three months from the signing of the Framework a peace treaty between them while inviting the other parties to the conflict to proceed si-

multaneously to negotiate and conclude similar peace treaties with a view the achieving a comprehensive peace in the area. The Framework for the Conclusion of a Peace Treaty between Egypt and Israel will govern the peace negotiations between them. The parties will agree on the modalities and the timetable for the implementation of their obligations under the treaty.

Associated Principles

Egypt and Israel state that the principles and provisions described below should apply to peace treaties between Israel and each of its neighbors—Egypt, Jordan, Syria and Lebanon. Signatories shall establish among themselves relationships normal to states at peace with one another. To this end, they should undertake to abide by all the provisions of the U.N. Charter. Steps to be taken in this respect include:

full recognition;
abolishing economic boycotts;
guaranteeing that under their jurisdiction the citizens of the other parties shall enjoy the protection of the due process of law.

Signatories should explore possibilities for economic development in the context of final peace treaties, with the objective of contributing to the atmosphere of peace, cooperation and friendship which is their common goal.

Claims commissions may be established for the mutual settlement of all financial claims. The United States shall be invited to participate in the talks on matters related to the modalities of the implementation of the agreements and working out the timetable for the carrying out of the obligations of the parties.

The United Nations Security Council shall be requested to endorse the peace treaties and ensure that their provisions shall not be violated. The permanent members of the Security Council shall be requested to underwrite the peace treaties and ensure respect or the provisions. They shall be requested to conform their policies and actions with the undertaking contained in this Framework.

For the Government of Israel: Menachem Begin
For the Government of the Arab Republic of Egypt:
Muhammed Anwar al-Sadat
Witnessed by: Jimmy Carter, President of the United
States of America

Framework for the Conclusion of a Peace Treaty between Egypt and Israel

In order to achieve peace between them, Israel and Egypt agree to negotiate in good faith with a goal of concluding within three months of the signing of this framework a peace treaty between them: It is agreed that:

> The site of the negotiations will be under a United Nations flag at a location or locations to be mutually agreed.
> All of the principles of U.N. Resolution 242 will apply in this resolution of the dispute between Israel and Egypt.
> Unless otherwise mutually agreed, terms of the peace treaty will be implemented between two and three years after the peace treaty is signed.

The following matters are agreed between the parties:
> the full exercise of Egyptian sovereignty up to the internationally recognized border between Egypt and mandated Palestine;
> the withdrawal of Israeli armed forces from the Sinai;
> the use of airfields left by the Israelis near al-Arish, Rafah, Ras en-Naqb, and Sharm el-Sheikh for civilian purposes only, including possible commercial use only by all nations;
> the right of free passage by ships of Israel through the Gulf of Suez and the Suez Canal on the basis of the Constantinople Convention of 1888 applying to all nations; the Strait of Tiran and Gulf of Aqaba are international waterways to be open to all nations for unimpeded and nonsuspendable freedom of navigation and overflight;
> the construction of a highway between the Sinai and Jordan near Eilat with guaranteed free and peaceful passage by Egypt and Jordan; and the stationing of military forces listed below.

Stationing of Forces

No more than one division (mechanized or infantry) of Egyptian armed forces will be stationed within an area lying approximately 50 km. (30 miles) east of the Gulf of Suez and the Suez Canal. Only United Nations forces and civil police equipped with light weapons to perform normal police functions will be stationed within an area lying west of the international border and the Gulf of Aqaba, varying in width from 20 km. (12 miles) to 40 km. (24 miles).

In the area within 3 km. (1.8 miles) east of the international border there will be Israeli limited military forces not to exceed four infantry battalions and United Nations observers.

Border patrol units not to exceed three battalions will supplement the civil police in maintaining order in the area not included above.

The exact demarcation of the above areas will be as decided during the peace negotiations. Early warning stations may exist to insure compliance with the terms of the agreement.

United Nations forces will be stationed:

in part of the area in the Sinai lying within about 20 km. of the Mediterranean Sea and adjacent to the international border, and in the Sharm el-Sheikh area to insure freedom of passage through the Strait of Tiran; and these forces will not be removed unless such removal is approved by the Security Council of the United Nations with a unanimous vote of the five permanent members.

After a peace treaty is signed, and after the interim withdrawal is complete, normal relations will be established between Egypt and Israel, including full recognition, including diplomatic, economic and cultural relations; termination of economic boycotts and barriers to the free movement of goods and people; and mutual protection of citizens by the due process of law.

Interim Withdrawal

Between three months and nine months after the signing of the peace treaty, all Israeli forces will withdraw east of a line extending from a point east of El-Arish to Ras Muhammad, the exact location of this line to be determined by mutual agreement.

For the Government of the Arab Republic of Egypt: Muhammed Anwar al-Sadat
For the Government of Israel: Menachem Begin
Witnessed by: Jimmy Carter, President of the United States of America

Document Analysis

The first part of the Camp David Accords is an ambitious "Framework for Peace in the Middle East." It begins by recognizing U.N. Security Council Resolutions 242 as the basis for peace negotiations, and by further acknowledging that "peace requires respect for the sovereignty, territorial integrity and political independence of every state in the area." This framework, it is hoped, will not just lead to peace between the signatories, Israel and Egypt, but "between Israel and each of its other neighbors which is prepared to negotiate peace with Israel on this basis."

Following this preamble, the document attempts to address the heart of the Arab-Israeli conflict: the fate of the Palestinian territories of the West Bank and Gaza Strip, whose Arab inhabitants had essentially been stateless refugees ever since the establishment of Israel in 1948, and who had been living under Israeli occupation since 1967. Therefore, it is proposed that Egypt and Israel (as well as Jordan and representatives of the Palestinians themselves, although neither is a party to this agreement) work together to facilitate the granting of political autonomy to Gaza and the West Bank, over a transitional period of five years. As an independent Palestinian government is negotiated and elected, the Israeli occupation is to end, with Israeli forces withdrawn and mutual security arrangements put in place.

The second part of the agreement is a "Framework for the Conclusion of a Peace Treaty between Egypt and Israel." This treaty, with an ambitious timeline for conclusion of three months following the signing of this document, is to involve the full withdrawal of Israeli forces from the Sinai and the peninsula's return to Egyptian sovereignty. Israeli military airfields established in the Sinai are to be repurposed for civilian use, and the Suez Canal and other waterways around the Sinai are to be open to international travel. Detailed provisions are also laid out for the stationing of military forces a safe distance from sensitive borders. The United Nations is to maintain a peacekeeping presence near some key waterways to ensure they remain open. Once all of these provisions are implemented, Egypt and Israel are to establish normal diplomatic relations, "including full recognition, including diplomatic, economic and cultural relations; termination of economic boycotts and barriers to the free movement of goods and people; and mutual protection of citizens by the due process of law."

Essential Themes

The second part of the Camp David Accords—the part that applied exclusively to the two signatories—was carried out in full: the Egypt-Israel Peace Treaty was signed the following year, 1979, again by Sadat and Begin in the presence of Carter, in Washington, D.C. Egypt was the first Arab state to conclude a peace agreement with Israel, and the treaty remains in force. In recognition of this accomplishment, Begin and Sadat were jointly awarded the 1978 Nobel Peace Prize. Carter received the Nobel Peace Prize in 2002, and the Camp David Accords were listed among his accomplishments.

However, the first part of the agreement, aimed at resolving the status of the Palestinian Arabs, was roundly rejected by all the parties not present, including the Palestinians themselves and all the other Arab states. In fact, the United Nations itself rejected this portion of the agreement, as it was concluded without consulting the people it most directly affected, the Palestinians, thus violating the principle of self-determination, as well as a number of U.N. resolutions regarding the Palestinian issue. The other Arab states were outraged that Egypt had broken the united Arab front against Israel, and in 1979 Egypt's membership in the Arab League was suspended (it was readmitted in 1989). Sadat himself paid the ultimate price at the hands of Arab extremists when he was shot to death during a military parade in 1981 by members of his own presidential guard. However, Sadat also showed that peace with Israel was possible, and despite Jordan's umbrage at being named in the Camp David Accords, that country became the second Arab state to conclude peace with Israel, in 1994. The issue of Palestinian statehood, however, remains as unresolved and fraught with violence in the twenty-first century as it was in the twentieth.

—*Michael P. Auerbach, MA*

Bibliography and Additional Reading

Feron, James. "Menachem Begin, Guerilla Leader Who Became Peacemaker." *New York Times*. New York Times, 10 Mar. 1992. Web. 30 Mar. 2016.

Friedman, Uri. "The 'Peace Process': A Short History." *Foreign Policy*. Foreign Policy, 27 Feb. 2012. Web. 30 Mar. 2016.

Pace, Eric. "Anwar el-Sadat, the Daring Arab Pioneer of Peace with Israel." *New York Times*. New York Times, 7 Oct. 1981. Web. 30 Mar. 2016.

"Peace Talks at Camp David, September 1978." *PBS*. WGBH, n.d. Web. 30 Mar. 2016.

Pressman, Jeremy. "Explaining the Carter Administration's Israeli-Palestinian Solution." *Diplomatic History* 37.5 (2013): 1117–47. Print.

■ Ayatollah Khomeini on "The Great Satan"

Date: November 5, 1979
Author: Ruhollah Khomeini
Geographic region: Iran
Genre: Speech

Summary Overview

On November 4, 1979, a mob of Iranian militants, many of them university students, seized the United States Embassy in Tehran, Iran, taking over sixty people hostage. The following day, Ayatollah Ruhollah Khomeini, a cleric and leader of the Iranian Revolution, gave a speech praising the actions of the revolutionaries and denouncing the United States and its influence in Iran. He famously called the United States the Great Satan for its alleged role in manipulating Iran, including supporting the unpopular, authoritarian shah (king). The shah had been ousted in January 1979 amid widespread rioting, and the ayatollah installed a regime governed by Islamic law in his place. The ayatollah's anti-Western speech would set the tone for Iran's relations with the United States for decades to come.

Defining Moment

American involvement in Iran can be traced to Iran's ties to Great Britain and the discovery of significant quantities of oil in Iran in the early 1900s. In 1909 the Anglo-Persian Oil Company (APOC), which would later become British Petroleum (BP), was formed. The British economy and military were dependant on a steady flow of inexpensive Iranian oil, and during World War I the British stationed troops in Iran to protect their pipelines. Though Iran was technically an independent nation, the British controlled large amounts of its territory.

The United States became involved in Iran as an ally of Great Britain during World War II. Though Iran was neutral, the shah was suspected of Nazi sympathies. Combined British and other Allied forces invaded Iran and the shah, Reza Shah Pahlavi, was deposed and replaced by his son, Mohammad Reza Shah Pahlavi.

In 1951 the popular nationalist Mohammad Mossadeq was elected prime minister of Iran and announced that he would nationalize the nation's oil production. Fearing the loss of these strategic oil reserves, British and U.S. intelligence orchestrated a coup that replaced Mossadeq with a pro-Western leader and restored the power of the shah. The shah returned most of Iran's oil wealth to the United States and Britain and headed a secular government that attempted to modernize and westernize the nation. He received vast amounts of foreign aid in return for his loyalty, but was seen by many Iranians as a puppet of the United States who brutally suppressed his own people.

In 1963 the shah clashed with a group of conservative Islamic clerics led by Ayatollah Ruhollah Khomeini, who preached a return to a religious state that would throw off Western oppression. The uprising was suppressed, and Khomeini imprisoned and then exiled to Iraq, but discontent with the shah's autocratic regime continued to grow. Protests erupted throughout Iran during the 1970s, and government crackdowns could not prevent the growing instability. On January 6, 1979, the shah fled to Egypt, and on February 1, 1979, Khomeini returned to cheering crowds. Under his leadership an Islamic state was established, with the ayatollah declared its supreme leader for life. He reinstated Islamic law and purged the government and civil service of opposition to his new regime, killing thousands.

Anti-American fervor swept the country as Khomeini gave impassioned speeches about purging the nation of Western influence. On November 4, 1979, a group of militant protestors scaled the walls of the United States Embassy in Tehran and took more than sixty hostages, demanding the extradition of the shah, who was in the United States for cancer treatment. The next day Khomeini gave a memorable speech in support of their efforts against what he viewed as Iran's greatest enemy.

Author Biography

Ruhollah Khomeini was born on September 24, 1902 in Khomeyn, Iran. He was from a family of Shia Islamic mullahs and was educated in a series of Islamic schools. After World War I he studied at a seminary until he moved with his religious teacher to the city of Qom in 1922. He studied history, philosophy, and religion, and was a lecturer and noted scholar of Shia Islam in Qom. He wrote prodigiously on Islamic law and philosophy, and was an outspoken critic of the shah. He was made an ayatollah, or religious leader, in the 1950s, and a supreme religious leader or grand ayatollah, in 1963.

Khomeini was imprisoned for antigovernment protests in 1963 and then exiled, first to Iraq and then to France, where he continued to communicate with his followers in Iran and call for an Islamic republic. When the shah was overthrown in 1979, Khomeini returned to Iran as the leader of the revolution and installed a strict Islamic regime while suppressing opposition. He was the political and religious ruler of Iran until his death on June 3, 1989.

HISTORICAL DOCUMENT

In the name of God, the merciful, the compassionate

[America, the Great Satan]

I have in mind a story in which on the day the Prophet attained prophethood, that Great Satan shouted and gathered all the devils around himself to say that we are facing some difficulties. In this revolution, the Great Satan, which is the United States, is gathering the devils around himself with a shout. And he has gathered both the baby devils who are in Iran, and the devils outside of Iran, and has started a ruckus.

You all know that during the reign of these two evil men [reference to the two Shahs of the Pahalavi dynasty]—whose reign was also against the law— Iran was at one period captive to Britain, and at another, to the United States. I mean, mostly, the U.S.. The British brought Reza Khan and made him an officer over us, and Mohammad Reza, when the Allied Forces came to Iran—as they said—it was best that Mohammad Reza remains. Of course, they did not see what is best for the nation; they meant what is best for themselves. During this time extensive problems affected our nation—whether women or men—you all know. Many of you don't remember much of it, which I do remember, that they, during the time of Reza Khan, in the name of unity in form, in the name of lifting the veil, the things they did, what calamities they bestowed on this country. What bullying, what children were aborted as a result of their attacks on women to pull off their veils. That period passed in bitterness, and those same Allied Forces that had brought him—meaning the British—those same people took him from

here. And they announced it, too. On the Dehli Radio, which at that time was in their hands, they announced that we brought him and after he betrayed us, we took him. And later, he gathered up his jewelry and packed his bags and placed them in the ship to take with him, on the way—as told by one of his companions –they approached his ship with a special ship for carrying animals, and they took Reza Khan to that place where he belonged. And he said "the luggage?" and they said "they will come later." He was taken to that island and they took the luggage for themselves.

Then it was this second one's turn for plundering, which most of you remember. I mean, all of you remember the end. Also the beginning, many of you remember what they did, and what crimes they committed in this country, and with what deceptive names. Unfortunately, some people believed their extensive propaganda, and some who are partners in their crimes and are still active. These are those same devils who now, with the shouts of the U.S., have become active, who are busy with deviousness. And our nation must neutralize these conspiracies with vigilance and astuteness.

[Deception and gossip of the enemy]

It is important, these conspiracies . . . these deceptions, this gossip-mongering that is now common. Many rumors for weakening the spirits of the nation. Imagine several thieves kill some people in a place. Then we see that the news arrives that they've killed 100 people somewhere, they've beheaded 25 people. The second time, 400 people were killed, although none of this happened. They want to create rumors to weaken. "All the destroyed checkpoints, all that happened"; it's all to create some mischief and weaken your spirits, our spirits.

Including things that keep being said, and keep being promulgated from around that "a revolution has taken place, but nothing really happened, it's just a revolution and things went from a monarchy form to a mullah form. But nothing's changed." This is something that I also said yesterday. And again I submit to you: that what the nation wanted, all of that has taken place. What did the nation want? When the nation roared, what was it saying? Wasn't it saying "freedom and independence and Islamic Republic"? Which one hasn't happened? Right now there is freedom, such that you and I can sit here and talk. Could we do this five years ago? Independence is there. Right now, this ruckus that the U.S. has created and all this noise that this Great Satan screams and gathers the other devils around itself, this is because its hands have been tied. Its hands from taking our resources; they've been tied from its interest here. And it is afraid that its hands will be tied until the end; that's why it is conspiring.

[Occupying the American nest of spies (e.g. U.S. embassy)]

And that center that our youngsters went and took over—as they informed us—was the center of spying and conspiracy. America expects that it can take the Shah over there, to be busy with conspiracies, and also create a base here for conspiracies, and that our youngsters [will] just sit and watch. Again the rotten roots became active to get us to intervene and tell the youth that "you should come out of the place" where they went. The youth did something because they saw, because they upset these youngsters. A Shah that plundered this country for fifty years and looted it and gave it away, given others to take, and taken himself, and more important than this, has killed so much, has killed civilians—the 15th of *Khordad*—the way it became infamous—fifteen thousand people were murdered. On the day of the 15th of *Khordad* and from that time until now, maybe we have had one hundred thousand dead and several hundred thousand wounded, who we are everyday faced with these injured ones. Just now they told me that there are some injured here who, on the day of the *aid-e Qadir*, the injured are one segment of them. Many of them are the same ones injured during the revolution, at their hands. They said that on the day of *aid-e Qadir*, "they're having a meeting, you should come, too. " Of course I will also go there. They expect that a person who, for fifty years, has done that to this nation, and now the U.S., with a silly excuse, has taken him and is safeguarding him, and has provided his comfort, and in the name of being sick, or in reality being sick—it makes no difference—has taken him over there and is keeping him, and our youth that protested there, they dispersed them or jailed them. In these two or three days that on that Statue of Liberty—which is a bald-faced lie in the U.S., "liberty"—our young people went there and chained themselves there and placed a banner there that you must return the Shah. The police went and dispersed them and apprehended several of them. They expect to take our first-rate criminal and keep him there and support him, and also create a center of conspiracy here, and create a center for distributing things that are conspiracy, I don't know, do all the things they want to do, and our nation, and our youth, and our young people from the university, and our devout young people sit and watch so that the blood of this one hundred thousand people, approximately—more or less—is wasted, in order to show respect for Mr. Carter and others like him. There must be no conspiracies. But of course if there were no conspiracies, if these sabotages did not exist, if that corrupt act didn't exist, all the people are free to be present here. But when there is a conspiracy at play, when those kinds of corrupt acts take place, it upsets our youth. Young people expect that in this world where their country—for which they have made so much effort—is in their own hands. When they see a conspiracy where they want to return to the previous situation and again all their things are lost to the wind, they cannot sit still. There must not be an expectation that they sit still and watch. And they plundered, now carry out their conspiracies, and this conspiracy grows and whatnot. Our young people must destroy these conspiracies with all their focus and with strength.

[Underground and hidden conspiracies]

Today is not a day for us to sit and watch. Today, the situation is a little deeper, a little worse, than the time when Mohammad Reza was there. At that time, it was clear that this traitor was standing up against the nation. And the nation knew him and was standing up against him. Today, there are underground betrayals. Specifically, underground betrayals are being fomented in the very embassies that exist, the most important and the majority of which belong to the Great Satan, which is the U.S. And you cannot sit still and they carry out their conspiracy. One day we realize that a country was destroyed, and with irrelevant talk like 'democracy' and the like, deceives us that the country is a democracy, and anybody has the right to stay here; has the right to foment a conspiracy. This irrelevant talk has to be set aside. And our nation, just as it has happened up to now, must continue the same way from now on and cut off the hands of these people. And if these people don't get it, and don't return the Shah who has taken our treasures and placed large sums in banks—that we may be aware of some of them—has placed them in banks, and it all belongs to the nation, unless they return him, and if they don't return him, we will deal with them in a different way. We will deal with Britain in a different way, as well. They shouldn't imagine that we are just sitting still and listening and they can do whatever they damn please. No, it's not like this. The issue is, again, the revolution. A larger revolution than the first one will take place. They must sit in their place and return this traitor. And that other traitor; the traitor Bakhtiar, they must return him. Not that they take that traitor Bakhtiar there and he can sit down and foment a conspiracy and gather people around himself and—I submit to you—write a newspaper and create information, and the British government to arrest and incarcerate our young people for protesting against the Shah or against Bakhtiar. If they don't let go of them and deliver these criminals, or at least expel them from their countries, we have another duty and will act on that duty.

[Not showing weakness in front of conspiracies]

We must go forward with power. If we show weakness, if they sense that we have become weak, if these diminutions that our unfair writers make of our nation, if they feel that these writings have affected us, if they feel this, they will be emboldened and will attack. They will do worse things. Don't feel weakness in yourselves. The more these writers write that "Nothing's happened and this country is in the same place as before", and, like it's written in a piece that I saw the day before yesterday, that "in the previous regime, political activists were jailed, were imprisoned, and now too political activists are imprisoned, this has not changed with them, in the previous regime, there was suffocation and the like, now is the same way". Well, this is to weaken our spirits. Now we will take this under consideration.

[The difference between prisoners during the monarchy and the Islamic Republic]

In the previous regime, some people were imprisoned. Some people were captive. Now, too, some people are imprisoned. No doubt. But who are they? In the previous regime, who was imprisoned, and in the current regime, who are imprisoned? Which groups were executed in the previous regime? Let's look at who was executed in the previous regime and who is executed in the current regime? They don't look at that. They just say all this and think that our youth will be tricked by these words. In the previous regime, the ones they killed, [were] the best of our young people, committed, religious, because they said don't violate, they said don't ruin our country. They were Islamic scholars. This Mr. Montazeri was in jail for ages. That late Mr. Taleghani was in jail, and many like them. The ones who were executed, who were they? The late Sa'eidi was executed, and people like him. These same clerics that they took from around these people and sometimes, they were in jail. This, Mr. Lahouti who is now in the *Sepah*,

he was imprisoned for a long time. And what calamities has this man witnessed, and what insults
he has endured. In exile, scholars from this *howzeh,* the learned men of this *howzeh,* the scientists
of this *howzeh,* were in exile. Here, there, they took
them and exiled them. Those who were jailed back
then, were these kinds of people. And the ones who
were executed were these kinds of people. And the
ones exiled were these kinds of people. Now let's
look at this side of the story, that there is no difference between now and then. Has been executed:
Hoveyda, Nasiri. They are tearing their hearts out
for him. These who are writing that there has been
no change; these are the same people who in the
U.S., they speak of that why? Why? Why? And those
unjust advocates of human rights are calling out,
why is he executed? Those same people who when
he is writing "why are there executions in Iran?" do
not write about many places where there are geno-
cides by this corrupt U.S., and they don't say a word
about that. But here, that they executed Hovayda, or
executed Nasiri, or these corrupt individuals, they
are making a lot of noise. And the ones here who
are of their kind, they write that there is no difference; now there are executions, back then there
were executions, too. Who are the ones imprisoned?
Who were they back then? Do you find one imprisoned individual today who is a decent person and is
in prison? Do you find a person who is a religious
person, a nationalistic person, a person? Back then
when they were imprisoned, all the nationalists were
imprisoned. And all, I submit to you, like that. And
now, who is imprisoned? Those who have committed many crimes and all those crimes, these are in
prison. Now see the situation of the imprisonment of
these criminals, with the situation of presents back
then with those criminals, with these devout people.
The situation of then was such that you have to hear
from the people who were in prison how things were.
These things, as much as we have information, the
most important of which is Tehran, the people who
are there, and we have constantly instructed, will
never abuse anyone. Prison terms are not the kinds
that create dissatisfaction. It's prison, but these unfair [writers] write that the prisons are worse than

that time, at that place, in those prisons. In one of
those prisons, they sawed off the leg of one of our
scholars—as has been said. Now these prisons are
worse than those? These are all the same devils that
Carter has gathered around himself by a great shout,
because, in the same way that that Great Satan is
scared of the Quran and Islam, now they, too, are
afraid of this movement, which is an Islamic movement. And, following that Great Satan, are busy with
treachery to weaken the spirit of our people. Our nation, our valorous youth, must go forward with complete strength and not fear these conspiracies. These
are not humans that humans should be afraid of.

[Hands behind the veil in Kurdistan unrest]

And these disturbances that sometimes these same
devils cause, and the followers of these depraved
causes, resolving these, too, is not a problem. They
imagine that the situation of Kurdistan is a situation
that cannot be resolved. The situation in Kurdistan,
if they were not mixed with the Kurdish people, and
were not amongst the young and the women and
children, we don't want even one innocent person
to get killed, if they weren't there, then it would be
nothing to mow them down and annihilate them.
But unfortunately, it's like this, right now. You have
heard, for sure, that these unfair [people] use wom-
en and children as shields, and by using them as
shields, killed our young people. And those brave
young men, so as not to kill the innocent, did not resist. Well, if they were not mixed with them, it would
be no effort to destroy them. They are not much
of a force. They are a bunch of hoodlums. These
hoodlums, we were faced with them in the past,
too. These are a bunch of hooligans that are thieves.
Sometimes they kidnap, or kill people, too. They are
not a force now against the force of the government,
or against the force of the nation. We, whenever we
want, all the people may go up to Kurdistan and destroy them, but we want the situation to be fixed
in peace. These unfair [people] won't let us. Now a
group has gone to resolve the problem in peace, to
see "what do you want?" The things that they want,
we gave to them. Will give. But they want America.

They, if you ask them directly, what they want in their hearts, the Democrat Party [*Hezb-e democrat*] will say that we "want the interests of the masses." Meaning, they express a tendency for the Left, but all of them are right-wing, the dishonest right.

Be strong brothers, sisters, be strong with strength. Islam is behind you. The elevated and sublime God is behind you. Go forth with power and strength and build this country yourselves. The country must be build by your hands. May God bless you all.

Document Analysis

Khomeini begins his speech with a traditional Islamic invocation, known as the Basmala, which calls on the name of God. He relates a story from the Qur'an about the Prophet Mohammed, who challenged evil so much that Satan summoned his demons for assistance. He draws a parallel to Iran's challenge to the United States: the Iranian revolution has caused the United States, which he directly calls "the Great Satan," to attempt to gather support among "devils" both inside and outside of Iran. In this way he immediately positions the United States and Iran as mortal enemies grounded in religious conflict.

Khomeini then gives a brief overview of the history of Western involvement in Iran. He describes the last two shahs as "evil men" and pawns of the United States and Britain, who have only their own interests at heart. He describes the "calamities bestowed on this country" by the pro-Western shahs, focusing on the literal and symbolic "lifting of the veil," or traditional Islamic dress for women, as the destruction of moral and cultural values. Khomeini notes that there were some Iranians who cooperated with the shahs and now sympathize with the United States. He claims that these forces are still at work, and they must be found and destroyed.

Khomeini warns his audience not to listen to rumors and Western propaganda, particularly suggestions that the ayatollah's supporters are committing crimes or that the revolution has simply replaced the monarchy with religious authority. These are only the murmurs of a desperate United States, he claims, and proof that the Great Satan is worried. He asserts that the fact that he is able to make this speech, which surely would not have been allowed by the shah, is evidence that the revolution is succeeding in throwing off Western control and providing freedom.

The ayatollah then addresses the seizure of the U.S. Embassy—which he calls a "center of spying and conspiracy"—by revolutionaries as a noble act by young people who could not sit idly by and watch the shah escape punishment and continue to conspire with the United States against the Iranian people. Khomeini announces that he will not intervene to release the hostages or make the revolutionaries leave the embassy. The United States is defending a murderer, he argues, who for fifty years has executed his own countrymen. Western powers must return the shah and other figures from the pro-Western Iranian government for trial. Khomeini also warns that the enemies of the state are harder to identify but even more dangerous now that they are not in power and are trying to bring down the righteous government through spying and intrigue disseminated through embassies.

Khomeini also addresses the issue of the mass imprisonments and executions in Iran, drawing a distinction between those before and after the revolution. He argues that good people, especially religious leaders and scholars, were imprisoned and executed by the shah, but that the revolutionaries have only imprisoned and executed corrupt thieves and spies. He claims that Western onlookers and human rights activists criticizing his regime are hypocritical both for ignoring this difference and for failing to condemn atrocities committed by the United States.

He closes his speech with a description of the Kurdish rebellion, which he claims is incited by Western disruption. Khomeini says the rebellion is little threat and could be put down easily, except they use women and children as shields. The speech ends, as it began, with an Islamic invocation and the assurance that "Islam is behind you."

Essential Themes

The Iran hostage crisis and Khomeini's hostile rhetoric led to great tension between Iran and the United States and consequences on both sides, including American economic sanctions against Iran and the failure of U.S. President Jimmy Carter's re-election bid when he was unable to resolve the hostage situation. Of the sixty-six hostages taken, thirteen were quickly released and another was freed later. The remaining fifty-two hostages were held for 444 days and released soon after President Carter left office in 1981. Khomeini continued to lead an anti-Western theocracy and refer to the United States as Iran's greatest enemy, the Great Satan. He was also hostile to the world's other superpower, the Soviet Union, calling it the Lesser Satan, while Israel was termed the Little Satan. The ayatollah further encouraged militant Islamic revolution in neighboring countries, and Iran was at war with Iraq for eight years.

Khomeini dismantled many of the economic drivers that had supported Iran's prosperity under the shah. Trade with the West was virtually eliminated and oil production plummeted. During the war with Iraq, Khomeini liquidated much of the nation's gold reserves and inflation skyrocketed. Despite bread lines and war, Khomeini was the undisputed leader of Iran for the remainder of his life, and he embodied the principal of rule by those who carried out Islamic law. The term "Great Satan" would become a lasting symbol of Islamic resistance to Western power.

—*Bethany Groff Dorau, MA*

Bibliography and Additional Reading

Axworthy, Michael. *Revolutionary Iran: A History of the Islamic Republic*. New York: Oxford UP, 2016. Print.

Kinzer, Stephen. *All the Shah's Men: An American Coup and the Roots of Middle East Terror*. Hoboken: Wiley, 2003. Print.

Lesch, David W. *1979: The Year That Shaped the Modern Middle East*. Boulder: Westview, 2001. Print.

■ Egypt-Israel Peace Treaty

Date: March 26, 1979
Geographic Region: Middle East
Authors: Anwar al-Sadat and Menachem Begin (signatories)
Genre: Treaty

Summary Overview

On March 26, 1979, after three decades of declared war between their two nations, Egyptian president Anwar al-Sadat and Israeli prime minister Menachem Begin signed the Egypt-Israel Peace Treaty. The treaty was signed at the White House and was overseen by U.S. president Jimmy Carter, who had arranged for the meeting that led to the treaty and played a crucial role in negotiations. The framework for peace that led to the treaty, called the Camp David Accords, was a result of over a year of high-level diplomatic negotiations, culminating in a two-week summit at Camp David, in rural Maryland, beginning on September 5, 1978. Egypt and other Arab nations had been at war with Israel since the latter had declared its independence in 1948. After the Six-Day War of 1967, Israel occupied the Egyptian-controlled Gaza Strip and the Sinai Peninsula. The United Nations issued Resolution 242, which called for Israel's withdrawal from these and other occupied areas in exchange for peace with its Arab neighbors and an equitable settlement for displaced Palestinians. For a decade, no agreement was reached, and unrest in the Middle East continued. Sadat and Begin were awarded the 1978 Nobel Peace Prize for their work on the Camp David Accords and the treaty that followed.

Defining Moment

Conflict between Egypt and what became Israel can be traced back to the end of World War I. When the Ottoman Empire collapsed at the end of the war, Palestine, which it had controlled for four centuries, was placed under British control, and planning for a Jewish homeland in the region began. After World War II, the United Nations adopted a plan to partition the region into three separate areas, which was accepted by the Jewish community but not the Arab world. There would be an independent Israel, an independent Palestine, and the contested cities of Jerusalem and Bethlehem would be internationally administered by the United Nations. The region disintegrated into civil war after Israel declared its independence on May 14, 1948. The

fighting continued for ten months, and Israel was left in control of a larger area than had initially been included in the United Nations partition plan. There was no independent Palestinian state, and the remainder of the territory was divided up between Israel's neighbors. Hundreds of thousands of Palestinian Arabs left their lands in the newly created Israeli state and fled to neighboring countries, while hundreds of thousands of Jewish people from across the world settled in Israel. This massive demographic upheaval exacerbated longstanding resentment between Israel and its neighbors, and sporadic violence flared up in the decades that followed.

Arab resistance to Israel was led by Egyptian president Gamal Abdel Nasser until his death in 1970. During his tenure, Egypt lost the Sinai Peninsula and the Gaza Strip to Israel during the 1967 Six-Day War; Syria lost the Golan Heights and Jordan lost the West Bank. When hostilities ended on June 11, 1967, the Egyptian air force was destroyed, and Israel occupied more than three times as much territory as it had held before the war. The United Nations passed Security Council Resolution 242 in November, calling for Israel to leave occupied areas and settle the refugee crisis, and for Israel's neighbors to seek peace and recognize Israel's right to exist.

A stalemate quickly developed as Israel waited to withdraw its troops until it had received official recognition from its Arab neighbors, which was not forthcoming. When Sadat became president of Egypt after Nasser's death, he was eager to regain the territory lost in the Six-Day War, and also believed that even if unsuccessful, an attack could put him in a more favorable position to set terms of peace. On October 6, 1973, the Yom Kippur War began, as Egypt and Syria attacked Israel with support from Jordan and Iraq. Israel quickly mobilized and pushed back the allies, and on October 25, 1973, a cease-fire was declared. After the war, Sadat, who had been heavily supported by the Soviet Union, moved away from Soviet influence and made overtures toward Israel and the West. In 1974, a portion of the Sinai Peninsula was returned to Egypt, and in 1977, Sadat traveled to Jerusalem. He was the first Arab leader to ever visit Israel, and his visit outraged many hard-line pan-Arabists. After it seemed that peace talks were faltering, Carter, the president of the United States in 1977, invited Sadat and Begin to meet at Camp David, the presidential retreat in rural Maryland. There, they hashed out a road map that would lead to peace between the two nations, and both signed the Egypt-Israel Peace Treaty on March 26, 1979.

Author Biographies

The Egypt-Israel Peace Treaty was signed on March 26, 1979, in Washington, D.C. The treaty was witnessed by Jimmy Carter, president of the United States since 1977, and was signed by Egyptian president Anwar al-Sadat and Israeli prime minister Menachem Begin.

Sadat had played a major role in the fight against British rule in Egypt in the 1940s and 1950s, in some cases facing imprisonment. After aiding in Gamal Abdel Nasser's coup that overthrew the British in 1952, he succeeded in being named to the vice presidency under Nasser in 1964 and again in 1969. Upon Nasser's death, he was elected president in 1970 and quickly began making serious efforts to establish peace between Egypt and Israel. However, facing increased domestic disapproval following the treaty signed in 1979, he was assassinated in 1981.

Begin had been head of the Betar, a Revisionist-Zionist youth movement, and fought with an underground militant group to attain an independent Israeli state. In 1977, when his Likud party won a majority in the Knesset (the Israeli parliament), he was elected prime minister. He resigned from his post in 1983 and died in 1992.

HISTORICAL DOCUMENT

The Government of the Arab Republic of Egypt and the Government of the State of Israel;

PREAMBLE

Convinced of the urgent necessity of the establishment of a just, comprehensive and lasting peace in the Middle East in accordance with Security Council Resolutions 242 and 338;

Reaffirming their adherence to the "Framework for Peace in the Middle East Agreed at Camp David," dated September 17, 1978;

Noting that the aforementioned Framework as appropriate is intended to constitute a basis for peace not only between Egypt and Israel but also between Israel and each of its other Arab neighbors which is prepared to negotiate peace with it on this basis;

Desiring to bring to an end the state of war between them and to establish a peace in which every state in the area can live in security;

Convinced that the conclusion of a Treaty of Peace between Egypt and Israel is an important step in the search for comprehensive peace in the area and for the attainment of settlement of the Arab-Israeli conflict in all its aspects;

Inviting the other Arab parties to this dispute to join the peace process with Israel guided by and based on the principles of the aforementioned Framework;

Desiring as well to develop friendly relations and cooperation between themselves in accordance with the United Nations Charter and the principles of international law governing international relations in times of peace;

Agree to the following provisions in the free exercise of their sovereignty, in order to implement the "Framework for the Conclusion of a Peace Treaty Between Egypt and Israel";

ARTICLE I

The state of war between the Parties will be terminated and peace will be established between them upon the exchange of instruments of ratification of this Treaty. Israel will withdraw all its armed forces and civilians from the Sinai behind the international boundary between Egypt and mandated Palestine, as provided in the annexed protocol (Annex I), and Egypt will resume the exercise of its full sovereignty over the Sinai. Upon completion of the interim withdrawal provided for in Annex I, the parties will establish normal and friendly relations, in accordance with Article III (3).

ARTICLE II

The permanent boundary between Egypt and Israel in the recognized international boundary between Egypt and the former mandated territory of Palestine, as shown on the map at Annex II, without prejudice to the issue of the status of the Gaza Strip. The Parties recognize this boundary as inviolable. Each will respect the territorial integrity of the other, including their territorial waters and airspace.

ARTICLE III

The Parties will apply between them the provisions of the Charter of the United Nations and the principles of international law governing relations among states in times of peace. In particular: They recognize and will respect each other's sovereignty, territorial integrity and political independence; They recognize and will respect each other's right to live in peace within their secure and recognized boundaries; They will refrain from the threat or use of force, directly or indirectly, against each other and will settle all disputes between them by peaceful means. Each Party undertakes to ensure that acts or threats of belligerency, hostility, or violence do not originate from and are not committed from within its territory, or by any forces subject to its control or by any other forces stationed on its territory, against the population, citizens or property of the other Party. Each Party also undertakes to refrain from organizing, instigating, inciting, assisting or participating in acts or threats of belligerency, hostility, subversion or violence against the other Party, anywhere, and undertakes to ensure that perpetrators of such acts are brought to justice. The Parties agree that the normal relationship established between them will include full recognition, diplomatic, economic and cultural relations, termination of economic boycotts and discriminatory barriers to the free movement of people and goods, and will guarantee the mutual enjoyment by citizens of the due process of law. The

process by which they undertake to achieve such a relationship parallel to the implementation of other provisions of this Treaty is set out in the annexed protocol (Annex III).

ARTICLE IV

In order to provide maximum security for both Parties on the basis of reciprocity, agreed security arrangements will be established including limited force zones in Egyptian and Israeli territory, and United Nations forces and observers, described in detail as to nature and timing in Annex I, and other security arrangements the Parties may agree upon. The Parties agree to the stationing of United Nations personnel in areas described in Annex I. The Parties agree not to request withdrawal of the United Nations personnel and that these personnel will not be removed unless such removal is approved by the Security Council of the United Nations, with the affirmative vote of the five Permanent Members, unless the Parties otherwise agree. A Joint Commission will be established to facilitate the implementation of the Treaty, as provided for in Annex I. The security arrangements provided for in paragraphs 1 and 2 of this Article may at the request of either party be reviewed and amended by mutual agreement of the Parties.

ARTICLE V

Ships of Israel, and cargoes destined for or coming from Israel, shall enjoy the right of free passage through the Suez Canal and its approaches through the Gulf of Suez and the Mediterranean Sea on the basis of the Constantinople Convention of 1888, applying to all nations, Israeli nationals, vessels and cargoes, as well as persons, vessels and cargoes destined for or coming from Israel, shall be accorded non-discriminatory treatment in all matters connected with usage of the canal. The Parties consider the Strait of Tiran and the Gulf of Aqaba to be international waterways open to all nations for unimpeded and non-suspendable freedom of navigation and overflight. The parties will respect each other's right to navigation and overflight for access to either country through the Strait of Tiran and the Gulf of Aqaba.

ARTICLE VI

This Treaty does not affect and shall not be interpreted as affecting in any way the rights and obligations of the Parties under the Charter of the United Nations. The Parties undertake to fulfill in good faith their obligations under this Treaty, without regard to action or inaction of any other party and independently of any instrument external to this Treaty. They further undertake to take all the necessary measures for the application in their relations of the provisions of the multilateral conventions to which they are parties, including the submission of appropriate notification to the Secretary General of the United Nations and other depositaries of such conventions. The Parties undertake not to enter into any obligation in conflict with this Treaty. Subject to Article 103 of the United Nations Charter in the event of a conflict between the obligation of the Parties under the present Treaty and any of their other obligations, the obligations under this Treaty will be binding and implemented.

ARTICLE VII

Disputes arising out of the application or interpretation of this Treaty shall be resolved by negotiations. Any such disputes which cannot be settled by negotiations shall be resolved by conciliation or submitted to arbitration.

ARTICLE VIII

The Parties agree to establish a claims commission for the mutual settlement of all financial claims.

ARTICLE IX

This Treaty shall enter into force upon exchange of instruments of ratification. This Treaty supersedes the Agreement between Egypt and Israel of September, 1975. All protocols, annexes, and maps attached to this Treaty shall be regarded as an integral part hereof. The Treaty shall be communicated to the Secretary General of the United Nations for registration in accordance with the provisions of Article 102 of the Charter of the United Nations.

Annex I

Protocol Concerning Israeli Withdrawal and Security Agreements

ARTICLE I

CONCEPT OF WITHDRAWAL Israel will complete withdrawal of all its armed forces and civilians from the Sinai not later than three years from the date of exchange of instruments of ratification of this Treaty. To ensure the mutual security of the Parties, the implementation of phased withdrawal will be accompanied by the military measures and establishment of zones set out in this Annex and in Map 1, hereinafter referred to as "the Zones." The withdrawal from the Sinai will be accomplished in two phases: The interim withdrawal behind the line from east of El-Arish to Ras Mohammed as delineated on Map 2 within nine months from the date of exchange of instruments of ratification of this Treaty. The final withdrawal from the Sinai behind the international boundary not later than three years from the date of exchange of instruments of ratification of this Treaty. A Joint Commission will be formed immediately after the exchange of instruments of ratification of this Treaty in order to supervise and coordinate movements and schedules during the withdrawal, and to adjust plans and timetables as necessary within the limits established by paragraph 3, above. Details relating to the Joint Commission are set out in Article IV of the attached Appendix. The Joint Commission will be dissolved upon completion of final Israeli withdrawal from the Sinai.

ARTICLE II

DETERMINATION OF FINAL LINES AND ZONES In order to provide maximum security for both Parties after the final withdrawal, the lines and the Zones delineated on Map 1 are to be established and organized as follows:

Zone A

Zone A is bounded on the east by line A (red line) and on the west by the Suez Canal and the east coast of the Gulf of Suez, as shown on Map 1. An Egyptian armed force of one mechanized infantry division and its military installations, and field fortifications, will be in this Zone. The main elements of that Division will consist of: Three mechanized infantry brigades. One armed brigade. Seven field artillery battalions including up to 126 artillery pieces. Seven anti-aircraft artillery battalions including individual surface-to-air missiles and up to 126 anti-aircraft guns of 37 mm and above. Up to 230 tanks. Up to 480 armored personnel vehicles of all types. Up to a total of twenty-two thousand personnel.

Zone B

Zone B is bounded by line B (green line) on the east and by line A (red line) on the west, as shown on Map 1. Egyptian border units of four battalions equipped w1nd supplement the civil police in maintaining order in Zone B. The main elements in the four Border Battalions will consist of up to a total of four thousand personnel. Land based, short range, low power, coastal warning points of the border patrol units may be established on the coast of this Zone. There will be in Zone B field fortifications and military installations for the four border battalions.

Zone C

Zone C is bounded by line B (green line) on the west and the International Boundary and the Gulf of Aqaba on the east, as shown on Map 1. Only United Nations forces and Egyptian civil police will be stationed in Zone C. The Egyptian civil police armed with light weapons will perform normal police functions within this Zone. The United Nations Force will be deployed within Zone C and perform its functions as defined in Article VI of this annex. The United Nations Force will be stationed mainly in camps located within the following stationing areas shown on Map 1, and will establish its precise locations after consultations with Egypt: In that part of the area in the Sinai lying within about 20 Km. of the Mediterranean Sea and adjacent to the International Boundary. In the Sharm el Sheikh area.

Zone D

Zone D is bounded by line D (blue line) on the east and the international boundary on the west, as shown on Map 1. In this Zone there will be an Israeli limited force of four infantry battalions, their military installations, and field fortifications, and United Nations observers. The Israeli forces in Zone D will not include tanks, artillery and anti-aircraft missiles except individual surface-to-air missiles. The main elements of the four Israeli infantry battalions will consist of up to 180 armored personnel vehicles of all types and up to a total of four thousand personnel. Access across the international boundary shall only be permitted through entry check points designated by each Party and under its control. Such access shall be in accordance with laws and regulations of each country. Only those field fortifications, military installations, forces, and weapons specifically permitted by this Annex shall be in the Zones.

ARTICLE III

AERIAL MILITARY REGIME Flights of combat aircraft and reconnaissance flights of Egypt and Israel shall take place only over Zones A and D, respectively. Only unarmed, non-combat aircraft of Egypt and Israel will be stationed in Zones A and D, respectively. Only Egyptian unarmed transport aircraft will take off and land in Zone B and up to eight such aircraft may be maintained in Zone B. The Egyptian border unit may be equipped with unarmed helicopters to perform their functions in Zone B. The Egyptian civil police may be equipped with unarmed police helicopters to perform normal police functions in Zone C. Only civilian airfields maybe built in the Zones. Without prejudice to the provisions of this Treaty, only those military aerial activities specifically permitted by this Annex shall be allowed in the Zones and the airspace above their territorial waters.

ARTICLE IV

NAVAL REGIME Egypt and Israel may base and operate naval vessels along the coasts of Zones A and D, respectively. Egyptian coast guard boats, lightly armed, may be stationed and operate in the territorial waters of Zone B to assist the border units in performing their functions in this Zone. Egyptian civil police equipped with light boats, lightly armed, shall perform normal police functions within the territorial waters of Zone C. Nothing in this Annex shall be considered as derogating from the right of innocent passage of the naval vessels of either party. Only civilian maritime ports and installations may be built in the Zones. Without prejudice to the provisions of this Treaty, only those naval activities specifically permitted by this Annex shall be allowed in the Zones and in their territorial waters.

ARTICLE V

EARLY WARNING SYSTEMS Egypt and Israel may establish and operate early warning systems only in Zones A and D respectively.

ARTICLE VI

UNITED NATIONS OPERATIONS The Parties will request the United Nations to provide forces and observers to supervise the implementation of this Annex and employ their best efforts to prevent any violation of its terms. With respect to these United Nations forces and observers, as appropriate, the Parties agree to request the following arrangements: Operation of check points, reconnaissance patrols, and observation posts along the international boundary and line B, and within Zone C. Periodic verification of the implementation of the provisions of this Annex will be carried out not less than twice a month unless otherwise agreed by the Parties. Additional verifications within 48 hours after the receipt of a request from either Party. Ensuring the freedom of navigation through the Strait of Tiran in accordance with Article V of the Treaty of Peace. The arrangements described in this article for each zone will be implemented in ones A, B, and C by the United Nations Force and in Zone D by the United Nations Observers. United Nations verification teams shall be accompanied by liaison officers of the respective Party. The United Nations Force and observers will report their findings to both Parties. The United Nations Force and Observers operating in the Zones will enjoy freedom of movement and other facilities necessary for the performance of their tasks. The United Nations Force and Observers are not empowered to authorize the crossing of the international boundary. The Parties shall agree on the nations from which the United Nations Force and Observers will be drawn. They "will be drawn from nations other than those which are permanent members of the United Nations Security Council. The Parties agree that the United Nations should make those command arrangements that will best assure the effective implementation of its responsibilities.

ARTICLE VII

LIAISON SYSTEM Upon dissolution of the Joint Commission, a liaison system between the Parties will be established. This liaison system is intended to provide an effective method to assess progress in the implementation of obligations under the present Annex and to resolve any problem that may arise in the course of implementation, and refer other unresolved matters to the higher military authorities of the two countries respectively for consideration. It is also intended to prevent situations resulting from errors or misinterpretation on the part of either Party. An Egyptian liaison office will be established in the city of El-Arish and an Israeli liaison office will be established in the city of Beer-Sheba. Each office will be headed by an officer of the respective country, and assisted by a number of officers. A direct telephone link between the two offices will be set up and also direct telephone lines with the United Nations command will be maintained by both offices.

ARTICLE VIII

RESPECT FOR WAR MEMORIALS Each Party undertakes to preserve in good condition the War Memorials erected in the memory of soldiers of the other Party, namely, those erected by Egypt in Israel, and shall permit access to such monuments.

ARTICLE IX

INTERIM ARRANGEMENTS The withdrawal of Israeli armed forces and civilians behind the interim withdrawal line, and the conduct of the forces of the Parties and the United Nations prior to the final withdrawal, will be governed by the attached Appendix and Map 2 . . .

ANNEX II

Map of Israel-Egypt International Boundary

ANNEX III

Protocol Concerning Relations of the Parties

ARTICLE 1

DIPLOMATIC AND CONSULAR RELATIONS The Parties agree to establish diplomatic and consular relations and to exchange ambassadors upon completion of the interim withdrawal.

ARTICLE 2

ECONOMIC AND TRADE RELATIONS The Parties agree to remove all discriminatory barriers to normal economic relations and to terminate economic boycotts of each other upon completion of the interim withdrawal. As soon as possible, and not later than six months after the completion of the interim withdrawal, the Parties will enter negotiations with a view to concluding an agreement on trade and commerce for the purpose of promoting beneficial economic relations.

ARTICLE 3

CULTURAL RELATIONS The Parties agree to establish normal cultural relations following completion of the interim withdrawal. They agree on the desirability of cultural exchanges in all fields, and shall, as soon as possible and not later than six months after completion of the interim withdrawal, enter into negotiations with a view to concluding a cultural agreement for this purpose.

ARTICLE 4

FREEDOM OF MOVEMENT Upon completion of the interim withdrawal, each Party will permit the free movement of the nationals and vehicles of the other into and within its territory according to the general rules applicable to nationals and vehicles of other states. Neither Party will impose discriminatory restrictions on the free movement of persons and vehicles from its territory to the territory of the other. Mutual unimpeded access to places of religious and historical significance will be provided on a non-discriminatory basis.

ARTICLE 5

COOPERATION FOR DEVELOPMENT AND GOOD NEIGHBORLY RELATIONS The Parties recognize a mutuality of interest in good neighbourly relations and agree to consider means to promote such relations. The Parties will cooperate in promoting peace, stability and development in their region. Each agrees to consider proposals the other may wish to make to this end. The Parties shall seek to foster mutual understanding and tolerance and will, accordingly, abstain from hostile propaganda against each other.

ARTICLE 6

TRANSPORTATION AND TELECOMMUNICATIONS The Parties recognize as applicable to each other the rights, privileges and obligations provided for by the aviation agreements to which they are both party, particularly by the Convention on International Civil Aviation, 1944 ("The Chicago Convention") and the International Air Services Transit Agreement, 1944. Upon completion of the interim withdrawal any declaration of national emergency by a party under Article 89 of the Chicago Convention will not be applied to the other party on a discriminatory basis. Egypt agrees that the use of airfields left by Israel near El-Arish, Rafah, Ras El-Nagb and Sharm El-Sheikh shall be for civilian purposes only, including possible commercial use by all nations. As soon as possible and not later than six months after the completion of the interim withdrawal, the Parties shall enter into negotiations for the purpose of concluding a civil aviation agreement. The Parties will re-open and maintain roads and railways between their countries and will consider further road and rail links. The Parties further agree that a highway will be constructed and maintained between Egypt, Israel and Jordan near Eilat with guaranteed free and peaceful passage of persons, vehicles and goods between Egypt and Jordan, without prejudice to their sovereignty over that part of the highway which falls within their respective territory. Upon completion of the interim withdrawal, normal postal, telephone, telex, data facsimile, wireless and cable communications and television relay services by cable, radio and satellite shall be established between the two Parties in accordance with all relevant international conventions and regulations. Upon completion of the interim withdrawal, each Party shall grant normal access to its ports for vessels and cargoes of the other, as well as vessels and cargoes destined for or coming from the other. Such access will be granted on the same conditions generally applicable to vessels and cargoes of other nations. Article 5 of the Treaty of Peace will be implemented upon the exchange of instruments of ratification of the aforementioned treaty.

ARTICLE 7

ENJOYMENT OF HUMAN RIGHTS The Parties affirm their commitment to respect and observe human rights and fundamental freedoms for all, and they will promote these rights and freedoms in accordance with the United Nations Charter.

ARTICLE 8

TERRITORIAL SEAS Without prejudice to the provisions of Article 5 of the Treaty of Peace each Party recognizes the right of the vessels of the other Party to innocent passage through its territorial sea in accordance with the rules of international law . . .

For the Government of the Arab Republic of Egypt: Muhammed Anwar al-Sadat
For the Government of Israel: Menachem Begin
Witnessed by: Jimmy Carter, President of the United States of America

Document Analysis

The Egypt-Israel Peace Treaty begins with an affirmation of the need for peace between not only Israel and Egypt, but all of Israel's neighbors in the Middle Eastern region. The opening lines of the treaty also affirm the desire of both nations to come into compliance with U.N. Security Resolution 242, which called for the withdrawal of Israel from occupied lands and the recognition of Israel by Arab states. Egypt feels that it must lead other nations in this regard, as "a Treaty of Peace between Egypt and Israel is an important step in the search for comprehensive peace in the area and for the attainment of settlement of the Arab-Israeli conflict in all its aspects." Other Arab states are invited to join the peace process as outlined in the Camp David Accords, and both nations desire to comply with the U.N. Charter.

The two most contentious points in any conversation between Israel and its neighbors were always the return of occupied lands and the recognition of Israel's sovereignty. The body of the treaty deals primarily with the mechanics of the return of the Sinai Peninsula to Egypt and the simultaneous official recognition of the state of Israel. The withdrawal of Israeli troops and civilians is addressed in great detail, and the Egyptians agree to hold Sinai as a demilitarized area once they regain control of it. The treaty does not address the issue of the Palestinians, and leaves the issue of Gaza, the other occupied territory formerly under Egypt's control, to be revisited "without prejudice," exempting it from the required return of territory to Egypt. In fact, the Camp David Accords dealt with the transition of the West Bank and Gaza Strip to a self-governing Palestinian state, so there was no need to include such language in the treaty.

In addition to the agreement to withdraw from the Sinai Peninsula, with its very specific requirements for access and buffer zones on both sides, the treaty addresses two specific points crucial to a healthy trade relationship. Egypt agrees to free passage of Israeli vessels through the Suez Canal, the Strait of Tiran, and the Gulf of Aqaba. This access was crucial to the delivery of supplies, particularly oil, to Israel. In addition, Israel would now be allowed to purchase Egyptian oil on the open market, a trade relationship that was impossible during the declared war of the previous years. In further hope of preventing future conflicts related to such deep-seated issues, the treaty also specifies that any possible disputes over these stipulations should be handled through diplomacy rather than military action.

Essential Themes

Egypt was a very large and relatively developed and wealthy nation compared to some of its Arab neighbors, and the world had good reason to hope that the signing of the Egypt-Israeli Peace Treaty in 1979 would be the first step to a general thawing of tensions between Israel and its Middle Eastern neighbors. Egypt would be the only neighbor to recognize Israel for years, however. Sadat returned to find many of his former allies outraged at the treaty and refusing to accept the Camp David Accords and their peace process. In 1979, Egypt was suspended from membership in the Arab League, whose headquarters were moved to Tunisia, even as Sadat and Begin were jointly awarded the Nobel Peace Prize for their work on the Camp David Accords. Sadat was assassinated by members of the Egyptian Islamic Jihad on October 6, 1981, as he attended a parade commemorating Egypt's crossing of the Suez Canal during the Yom Kippur War of 1973. Relations between Egypt and Israel continued to evolve, however, and in 1982, full diplomatic relations were established between the two nations. Egypt was the only nation to recognize Israel until 1994, when Jordan signed a peace treaty with Israel.

—*Bethany Groff Dorau, MA*

Bibliography and Additional Reading

Lesch, David W. *1979: The Year That Shaped the Modern Middle East.* Boulder: Westview, 2001. Print.

Meital, Yoram. *Peace in Tatters: Israel, Palestine, and the Middle East.* Boulder: Rienner, 2006. Print.

Wright, Lawrence. *Thirteen Days in September: Carter, Begin, and Sadat at Camp David.* New York: Knopf, 2014. Print.

■ Documents Relating to the Soviet Invasion of Afghanistan

Date(s): September 23, 1980; November 5, 1982; March 21, 1986
Authors: Central Intelligence Agency (CIA), Defense Intelligence Agency (DIA), President Ronald Reagan
Geographic region: Afghanistan
Genre: Report

Summary Overview

During the Cold War, two sizeable military conflicts each directly involved one of the two superpowers: Vietnam (the United States) and Afghanistan (the Soviet Union). Earlier in the 1970s, communism had expanded in Vietnam after the United States decided to withdraw its forces. In Afghanistan in the late 1970s, the government was transformed from a non-aligned one into a Communist-headed one, even while much of the rest of the country stood at odds with that result. Factional fighting and political assassinations ensued, and in December 1979 Soviet troops entered Afghanistan to install a Soviet-backed regime and extend its authority to the rest of the nation. Many Americans, both inside and outside the government, advocated not only a forceful diplomatic response but also military assistance to the Afghani *mujahedeen* fighters resisting the Soviet occupation. The CIA and Defense Intelligence Agency (DIA) sought to learn more about what was happening, and which Afghan groups' interests might align with those of the United States. Thus did the CIA/DIA produce reports such as the ones reprinted here, while also arranging the shipment of military supplies to anti-Soviet groups in Afghanistan. Meanwhile, President Reagan made public statements intended to keep pressure on the Soviets to withdraw their troops. If the Soviets prevailed, it was thought, it could give them a significant victory in the ongoing Cold War.

Defining Moment

Throughout the Cold War, both the United States and the Soviet Union tried to expand their spheres of influence and block each other's geopolitical maneuvers. Entering the 1970s, Afghanistan had been a non-aligned country and was relatively inactive on the international stage. This changed in 1973, however, when a coup overthrew the Afghan monarchy. King Mohammad Zahir Shah had recently appointed a prime minister who was anti-Communist and who advocated instituting some liberal Western ideas. Mohammad Daoud Khan, a former prime minister, led the 1973 coup and was more open to communist ideas. Strongly supported by the Soviet Union, Daoud Khan tried to balance Soviet interests against American desires. In 1978, the Soviets seemed to tire of dealing with him, resulting in a Communist takeover under Nur Mohammad Taraki. Taraki signed a treaty with the Soviet Union, which the Soviets used as justification for their invasion in December 1979. However, in September 1979, Taraki was overthrown and killed by Hafizullah Amin. On December 27th, Amin himself was overthrown by Soviet-backed forces and replaced by a strong friend of the Soviet Union, Babrak Karmal. The Afghan Communist Party now firmly controlled the government, and during the last week of 1979 about 40,000 Soviet troops entered Afghanistan to insure that Karmal stayed in power and carried out policies in line with Soviet desires.

Prior to 1978, the central government in Afghanistan had allowed tribal and regional leaders a substantial amount of freedom in the handling of local affairs. Karmal and his Soviet allies, on the other hand, wanted total control of the nation. Although not everyone in every region opposed that idea, there was widespread opposition to the attempt to radically strengthen the central government. The effort to enforce the central government's policy of total control placed a heavy burden on Soviet troops charged with enforcing the policy. In addition, Moscow's policy virtually insured that the United States would provide supplies and assistance to those opposing the Communists. The CIA coordinated most of the American assistance going to the anti-Soviet leaders. After Reagan was elected president, he supported many anti-Communist efforts, through both covert and overt means.

Author Biographies

The Central Intelligence Agency, a civilian agency, was created in 1948 to gather information on foreign governments and foreign operatives both openly and covertly. It grew out of the Office of Strategic Services, a World War II agency. The Directorate of Analysis was established in 1952 and reorganized in 1981, with several sub-offices including Political Analysis.

The Defense Intelligence Agency was established in the early 1961. It is a joint operation of all branches of the military. Its mission is to provide needed information for the Department of Defense and the armed forces, not the government as a whole.

Ronald Wilson Reagan (1911-2004) was born in Illinois, although most of his adult life was spent in California, where he served as governor (1966-73). He was president of the United States from 1981 to 1989, being noted for his political vision and conservative views.

HISTORICAL DOCUMENT

[Central Intelligence Agency, Directorate of Intelligence, Office of Political Analysis]

23 September 1980
MEMORANDUM
SUBJECT: The Soviets and the Tribes of Southwest Asia

SUMMARY

The Tribes

There are hundreds of tribes belonging to more than a dozen ethnic groups in Afghanistan and neighboring areas of Iran and Pakistan. Most are loosely organized with little or no central authority, but in some the power of the tribal chief is nearly absolute. Some have only a few thousand members; others, several hundred thousand. Some tribesmen are nomadic, most are settled farmers, and a few have abandoned the tribal way of life almost entirely.

These variations occur even with tribes. Pushtun [or Pashtun] Mohmands (living on both sides of the Pakistan-Afghan border near the Khyber Pass) include both nomads and farmer, and some members of the tribe have broken with traditional ways altogether to become urban laborers or even physicians or lawyers.

Tribes in Afghanistan

Tribal loyalties have more importance among the Pushtun of eastern and southern Afghanistan than among most of the other ethnic groups. Among the Uzbeks of northern Afghanistan, for example, tribal ties are weak, and they probably are not much stronger for many of the Turkmen of northwest Afghanistan. Even for the Pushtuns, tribal membership usually means little more than a feeling of identity with others in the tribe. Organized action by an entire tribe is rare. An attack on one part of a tribe may bring some response from other tribesmen not directly affected, but each extended family or village usually determines its own course without reference to the rest of the tribe or to the ostensible tribal leaders.

Those who cling most closely to the tradition tribal ways are the least likely to be influenced by Communism. To the extent that the tribesmen have an ideology it is a belief that a combination of Islam and even older tribal traditions is the proper guide for action. Among most tribes, the traditional views include such things as the obligation to seek revenge, masculine superiority, an emphasis on personal bravery and honor, and suspicion of outsiders. Tradition also tends to sanctify everything from rules governing property ownership to ways of treating illness. Any change in the traditional way of life is considered wrong, and modern ideas–whether Communist or Western–are seen as a threat.

The Afghan insurgency has been strongest among the most traditionally minded such as the Pushtuns of Paktia Province and the Nuristanis and Tajiks farther north along the Pakistani border. They resist the Afghan Marxists and the Soviets more to preserve their old ways than to fight Communism. Some of the reforms that have incensed the tribes–education of women, for example–are neither Communist nor anti-Islamic, but they conflict with the tribesman's perceptions of what is right. . . .

In the tribal villages, it is in the interests of the most influential men—local landowners, religious leaders, or both—to reject reforms, especially Communist ones, that threaten both their property and their political power. Nevertheless, Communist programs might have some appeal to the settled tribes. . . .

A major problem for the Soviets is to convince the tribes that it is to their advantage to support the government. The Soviets can bolster their arguments with offers of weapons and money. They can also threaten retaliation against tribesmen who will not cooperate, or threaten to support their traditional enemies. . . .

Even were the tribesmen motivated by more than an opportunity to steal, they would probably regard any arrangement with the Soviets as a temporary expedient and would turn against them as soon as it seemed advantageous to do so. . . In the past, tribesmen fighting for outsiders have changed alliance in response to offers of better pay, or even when they decided their pay [was] inadequate. A recent book review published in Tashkent made much of Britain's problems in the 19th century in trying to keep Afghan tribes loyal.

* * *

[Defense Intelligence Agency, Directorate for Research, 5 November 1982]

Assessment of Insurgent Equipment
All six major resistance groups appear to have adequate supplies of modern assault weapons and ammunition but still lack the heavier weaponry needed to turn the military situation in their favor. Smaller groups in isolated provinces, however, are still affected by shortages of small arms and ammunition.

While Soviets can and do temporarily disrupt the two-way flow of men and supplies through the major mountain passes, we do not believe the Soviets can permanently seal off Afghanistan from the rest of the world. The rugged terrain, limited manpower thus far available to Soviet/Afghan commanders, hostility of the local populace and the resourcefulness of the resistance argue against a successful effort to permanently close the passes.

Insurgent Equipment Deficiencies
Major military equipment deficiencies among resistance forces include more and better surface-to-air missiles and anti-aircraft guns, heavy machine guns, antitank missiles, antitank mines, man-pack mortars and tactical radio equipment. . . .

Resolve of the Resistance Forces
The resistance forces could continue the insurgency for the foreseeable future at its present level against current Soviet forces. We believe the Soviets would have to double their strength to break the current stalemate . . .

* * *

Proclamation 5450—Afghanistan Day, 1986
March 21, 1986
By the President of the United States of America

A Proclamation
The people of Afghanistan celebrate March 21 as the beginning of their new year. In ordinary times, it is an occasion of joy, renewal, and hope for a better future. March 21, 1986, however, does not mark the passage of an ordinary year, nor does it bring cause to celebrate. For the heroic Afghan people it marks the beginning of yet another year in their struggle for national liberation against the ruthless Soviet military force that seeks to conquer them.

Over six years ago, on December 27, 1979, the Soviet army invaded Afghanistan, a small, friendly, nonaligned, and deeply religious neighbor. For six long years, the Soviets have sought to obliterate Afghan culture and remold that ancient nation into a replica of their own system, causing millions of Afghan refugees to flee the country. To achieve their goals, the Soviets installed the quisling regime of Babrak Karmal, in which Soviet advisors now man the key positions. They have transported thousands of young Afghans to the Soviet Union for reeducation in summer camps, universities, and specialized institutions, and they have set up a secret police apparatus matched in brutality only by their own KGB.

These tactics hardly begin to describe the continuing horror of the Soviet attempt to subjugate Afghanistan, a violation of international law repeatedly condemned by the United Nations. Despite calculated destruction of crops, irrigation systems, and livestock, indiscriminate air and artillery bombardments of civilian areas, brutal reprisals against noncombatants, and other unspeakable atrocities, the Afghan people remain determined to defend their liberty. The resistance has in fact become more effective than ever.

The Soviet failure to quell the Afghan people is not surprising. The Afghans have a long history of resisting invasion and of defending their homes, their faith, and their culture. Since December 1979, resistance fighters have acquitted themselves well in many engagements against larger and better armed Soviet forces. The Afghan freedom fighters have shown they can render all of their country unsafe for the invader. After six years of hard, bloody fighting, the Soviets are far from achieving their military goals.

Recently the Afghan resistance has taken major steps toward achieving unity and making its presence felt on the international scene, strengthening its ability to publicize the Afghan cause. We welcome these developments. With the support of the community of civilized nations, the Afghan resistance has also increased its efforts to aid civilians remaining inside Afghanistan. This will improve the Afghan people's ability to carry on the fight and counter the deliberate Soviet attempt to drive the civilian population away from resistance-controlled areas.

Throughout the period of their brutal occupation, the Soviets have tried—but failed—to divide the international supporters of the cause of Afghan freedom. They cannot be divided. The overwhelming votes in the United Nations General Assembly, year after year, are but one expression of the ongoing commitment of the world community to this cause. For our part we reaffirm our commitment to support this just struggle until the Soviets withdraw; until the people of Afghanistan regain their liberties, their independence, and the right to self-determination; and until the refugees can return in safety to their native land. Only such a settlement can command the support of the Afghan people; a settlement that does not command their support will not end this war.

Today, we pay tribute to the brave men, women, and children of Afghanistan and remind them that their sacrifice is not and will not be forgotten.

The Congress, by Senate Joint Resolution 272, has authorized and requested the President to issue a proclamation designating March 21, 1986, as "Afghanistan Day."

Now, Therefore, I, Ronald Reagan, President of the United States of America, do hereby proclaim March 21, 1986, as Afghanistan Day.

In Witness Whereof, I have hereunto set my hand this twenty-first day of March, in the year of our Lord nineteen hundred and eighty-six, and of the Independence of the United States of America the two hundred and tenth.

Ronald Reagan

Document Analysis

Although the United States was officially an outside observer, these documents demonstrate that the Americans were involved in the Afghan wars of the 1980s. The first two documents were for internal use by government agencies, while the proclamation by Reagan was for the general public. American intelligence agencies sought out weaknesses in the Soviet position and ways to help the resistance. The American president conducted a public relations campaign that likewise helped the resistance. Although few Americans paid much attention to Afghanistan prior to the Soviet invasion in 1979, throughout the 1980s events in and related to Afghanistan moved to the forefront of public awareness.

The CIA analysis of the socio-political situation in Afghanistan was necessary because, previously, the United States had had only moderate involvement with the country. Although formal diplomatic relations had been established in 1921, there was little interaction prior to the onset of the Cold War, and even then it was limited to a few economic projects. While some were intended to strengthen the central government, as can be seen from the CIA analysis, this had not happened in this case. Tribal loyalties took precedence over national ones, although even tribes were "loosely organized." The CIA accurately understood this to be a positive factor in resisting the Communist incursion, as most local tribal and religious leaders were ready to help the highest bidder, provided it did not interfere in local affairs. In 1980, then, this fit American needs perfectly.

The DIA report represents the more controversial aspect of American involvement in Afghanistan: providing weapons to the resistance. The DIA's analysis of what weapons and weapon systems were available to the tribes fighting the Soviets, was at the heart of this matter. The 1982 list of resistance groups' "deficiencies" in military equipment was basically a requisition by the DIA for the weapons listed. The DIA accurately understood that local forces resisting the non-native troops could sustain a conflict at a much lower cost than could those from the outside. Thus, it was left to the Soviets as to how much of their resources they were willing to expend to obtain a military victory.

President Reagan campaigned on a strong anti-Communist platform. In Afghanistan, this included covert operations supporting the resistance. In addition, he also harshly criticized Communism in public forums. Thus the proclamation of Afghanistan Day in 1986 was not a simple statement applauding Afghan society. What he issued was a short history of the Soviet incursion into that country and the resulting war—at that time more than six years old. Reagan closed with the dramatic statement of tribute, "to the brave men, women, and children of Afghanistan and remind them that their sacrifice is not and will not be forgotten." The Afghan sacrifice as opposed to the brutality of the Soviets was the president's constant message. This message was designed to strengthen support for the Afghan resistance both within the United States and internationally. In the end, the Soviet Union did not want to increase its effort to the level reflected in the DIA report, and, facing strong international opposition, the Soviets withdrew from Afghanistan in 1989.

Essential Themes

Examining the three documents, in the Historical Document section, it can be seen that each one has a central theme. The CIA report's theme is the tribal nature of the country, and the advantages that that gives to those resisting the central government. For the DIA, it is the types of heavy weapons needed to augment those already available in the nation (mostly side arms). Finally, for Reagan, it is the dichotomy between the heroic Afghan people and the invading forces of the Soviet Union, which three years earlier he had called the "Evil Empire." In spite of the fact that each document differs in its specifics, the group is united in so far as seeking ways to support the anti-Communist movement.

The fact that Afghanistan has never been a strongly unified nation is seen in these documents as key to being able to develop anti-Soviet forces. Tradition normally triumphs over change in Afghanistan, and the implication in the CIA document is that the U.S. could assist this through giving the right type of support. The slightly later DIA document focuses on military items that might be supplied to the tribal divisions for them to prevail in the conflict. Sticking to military matters, the DIA's analysis projected a positive outcome for the resistance, unless the Soviets decide to greatly increase their support of the Afghan government.

President Reagan, in his proclamation, very definitely interprets the situation from an American, anti-Communist, point of view. (As is often the case, one person's "freedom fighter" is another person's "terrorist.") Ultimately, the hopeful optimism of the DIA report and Reagan's observations proved correct. The Soviets could not bear up under the long-term strain of a foreign war. However, when the United States became involved in Afghanistan as a result of the September 11 al-Qaida attacks on American targets, things in Afghanistan were both the same and yet different. One can recognize in the 1980 CIA analysis a picture of tribal and regional differences that still held true in 2001 (and after), the main difference being the growth of the Taliban and al-Qaida.

—*Donald A. Watt, PhD*

Bibliography and Additional Reading

Braithwaite, Rodric. *Afgantsy: The Russians in Afghanistan 1979-89*. Oxford: Oxford UP, 2011. Print.

Feifer, Gregory. *The Great Gamble: The Soviet War in Afghanistan*. New York: HarperCollins, 2009. Print.

Office of the Historian. "The Soviet Invasion of Afghanistan and the U.S. Response, 1978-1980." *U.S. Department of State: Bureau of Public Affairs*. Washington: U.S. Department of State, 2016. Web.

Savranskaya, Svetlana. "The Soviet Experience in Afghanistan: Russian Documents and Memoirs." *The September 11th Sourcebooks: Volume II: Afghanistan: Lessons from the Last War*. Washington: The National Security Archive, 2016. Web.

Wilson Center. "Soviet Invasion of Afghanistan." *Wilson Center Digital Archive: International History Declassified*. Washington, D.C.: Woodrow Wilson International Center for Scholars, 2016. Web.

■ Oslo Accords (Oslo I and Oslo II)

Date: September 13, 1993 (Oslo I); September 24, 1995 (Oslo II)
Authors: Various; Yasser Arafat (signatory); Yitzhak Rabin (signatory)
Geographic region: Palestine; Israel
Genre: Treaty

Summary Overview

The Oslo Accords represent an important pair of documents in that for the first time the Palestinian Authority and Israel recognized one another's right to exist. In many ways, this was the land-for-peace deal that had been suggested many times over the years but rejected by one side or the other. The process of developing the document (which can be thought of as a single treaty) seemed to prove what had been known for years: that progress was better reached in secret, outside of the limelight of external scrutiny. The authors here show how much had changed in the process, as Yitzhak Rabin and Yasser Arafat had been enemies for years—both personally and as representatives of their people or nations. Rabin, for instance, had ordered a brutal repression of the First Intifada (uprising) in the late 1980s, and Arafat had launched attacks on Israel from Lebanon. Both, however, ultimately switched tactics and went from war to negotiation to acceptance of the other's claim. Such acceptance is shown here in the two accords and in an exchange of letters that occurred right before the first accord (Oslo I). Arafat sent a letter to Rabin that recognized Israel and promised no more violence, and Rabin sent one in return that recognized the Palestine Liberation Organization (PLO). Observers had for years assumed that neither would ever happen. The Oslo Accords, then, were in some way the high-water mark for the Palestinian-Israeli peace process, for it has since become bogged down, and Rabin was assassinated shortly after Oslo II by an Israeli opposed to the peace process.

Defining Moment

The Oslo Accords signified the first time that the PLO and Israel had mutually signed a peace treaty. There had been treaties before between Israel and Egypt (notably, 1979), and one was made between Israel and Jordan (1994) in the period between Oslo I and Oslo II, but this—Oslo I, specifically—was the first treaty between the PLO and Israel, which heretofore had largely sought to destroy one another. (Israel had suc-

ceeded in forcing the PLO out of the country but not in eliminating it). The agreement is also significant in that it shows the acceptance by both parties of a two-state (or two-entity) solution. Israel had for a time wanted to wipe out the PLO and toyed with the idea of sticking with a single-state solution, while the PLO had called for the eradication of Israel and the return of all lands to Palestinian control.

Thus, while Oslo may have been the high-water mark, its success did not last long. The peace process began to stall soon afterward, Rabin being killed in 1995 and Arafat dying in 2004—after being detained by the Israelis for much of his last two years. Israeli opinion of the peace process did not improve in the interim. The Palestinians, too, started to favor the more radical Hamas organization/party over the Palestinian Authority (existing government), which in turn caused increased repression from the Israelis. In many ways, this trend came to a head in 2006, when violence erupted in the Hamas-controlled Gaza Strip area on both sides, and, in the West Bank region, the Fatah government, which had succeeded Arafat's authority, continued pursuing its own course somewhat.

Since 2006, the West Bank has continued to operate under Fatah leadership and has continued to deal with Israel and the issue of Israeli settlements there. The Gaza Strip, on the other hand, has become more of an occupied state with a closed border and Israel controlling the sea and airspace around it as well.

Author Biographies

Yasser Arafat was born in Egypt in 1929 and was educated as a civil engineer. After World War II, he joined the fight against Israel, siding with the Muslim Brotherhood faction. He was one of the founders of Fatah, which aimed to attack Israel. In the late 1960s, Arafat joined the Palestinian Liberation Organization (PLO) and moved up in its ranks to become leader. After being in Jordan for a time, he relocated to Lebanon and from there attacked Israel. Being driven to Tunisia by 1983, he then aimed to negotiate a solution and eventually become involved in the Oslo peace talks. In the early 2000s, the Israeli army confined him to his house in Ramallah and it was there that he died in 2004.

Yitzhak Rabin was born in Jerusalem in 1922 and grew up there. In 1941 he joined the Haganah (the Jewish paramilitary) and trained secretly while the British still controlled Palestine. Following World War II, he opposed Britain's continued occupation and, in 1948, fought against Egypt in the war following Israel's cre-

ation. He remained in the Israeli Defense Force until 1967 and became chief of staff. He was prime minister from 1974 to 1977 and then served as minister of defense in the 1980s. In 1993, he became prime minister again and negotiated a peace treaty with Jordan in addition to the two Oslo accords. He, along with Arafat and Shimon Peres (another Israeli leader) were jointly awarded the Nobel Peace Prize in 1994. In 1995, Rabin was assassinated by a right-wing Israeli opposed to the Oslo Accords.

HISTORICAL DOCUMENT

Declaration of Principles on Interim Self-Government Arrangements (Oslo I)
September 13, 1993

The Government of the State of Israel and the P.L.O. team (in the Jordanian-Palestinian delegation to the Middle East Peace Conference) (the "Palestinian Delegation"), representing the Palestinian people, agree that it is time to put an end to decades of confrontation and conflict, recognize their mutual legitimate and political rights, and strive to live in peaceful coexistence and mutual dignity and security and achieve a just, lasting and comprehensive peace settlement and historic reconciliation through the agreed political process. Accordingly, the two sides agree to the following principles:

Article I: Aim of the Negotiations

The aim of the Israeli-Palestinian negotiations within the current Middle East peace process is, among other things, to establish a Palestinian Interim Self-Government Authority, the elected Council (the "Council"), for the Palestinian people in the West Bank and the Gaza Strip, for a transitional period not exceeding five years, leading to a permanent settlement based on Security Council Resolutions 242 and 338.

It is understood that the interim arrangements are an integral part of the whole peace process and that the negotiations on the permanent status will lead to the implementation of Security Council Resolutions 242 and 338.

Article II: Framework for the Interim Period

The agreed framework for the interim period is set forth in this Declaration of Principles.

Article III: Elections

In order that the Palestinian people in the West Bank and Gaza Strip may govern themselves according to democratic principles, direct, free and general political elections will be held for the Council under agreed supervision and international observation, while the Palestinian police will ensure public order.

An agreement will be concluded on the exact mode and conditions of the elections in accordance with the protocol attached as Annex I, with the goal of holding the elections not later than nine months after the entry into force of this Declaration of Principles.

These elections will constitute a significant interim preparatory step toward the realization of the legitimate rights of the Palestinian people and their just requirements.

Article IV: Jurisdiction

Jurisdiction of the Council will cover West Bank and Gaza Strip territory, except for issues that will be negotiated in the permanent status negotiations. The two sides view the West Bank and the Gaza Strip as a single territorial unit, whose integrity will be preserved during the interim period.

Article V: Transitional Period and Permanent Status Negotiations

The five-year transitional period will begin upon the withdrawal from the Gaza Strip and Jericho area.

Permanent status negotiations will commence as soon as possible, but not later than the beginning of the third year of the interim period, between the Government of Israel and the Palestinian people representatives.

It is understood that these negotiations shall cover remaining issues, including: Jerusalem, refugees, settlements, security arrangements, borders, relations and cooperation with other neighbors, and other issues of common interest.

The two parties agree that the outcome of the permanent status negotiations should not be prejudiced or preempted by agreements reached for the interim period.

Article VI: Preparatory Transfer of Powers and Responsibilities

Upon the entry into force of this Declaration of Principles and the withdrawal from the Gaza Strip and the Jericho area, a transfer of authority from the Israeli military government and its Civil Administration to the authorised Palestinians for this task, as detailed herein, will commence. This transfer of authority will be of a preparatory nature until the inauguration of the Council.

Immediately after the entry into force of this Declaration of Principles and the withdrawal from the Gaza Strip and Jericho area, with the view to promoting economic development in the West Bank and Gaza Strip, authority will be transferred to the Palestinians on the following spheres: education and culture, health, social welfare, direct taxation, and tourism. The Palestinian side will commence in building the Palestinian police force, as agreed upon. Pending the inauguration of the Council, the two parties may negotiate the transfer of additional powers and responsibilities, as agreed upon.

Article VII: Interim Agreement

The Israeli and Palestinian delegations will negotiate an agreement on the interim period (the "Interim Agreement")

The Interim Agreement shall specify, among other things, the structure of the Council, the number of its members, and the transfer of powers and responsibilities from the Israeli military government and its Civil Administration to the Council. The Interim Agreement shall also specify the Council's executive authority, legislative authority in accordance with Article IX below, and the independent Palestinian judicial organs.

The Interim Agreement shall include arrangements, to be implemented upon the inauguration of the Council, for the assumption by the Council of all of the powers and responsibilities transferred previously in accordance with Article VI above.

In order to enable the Council to promote economic growth, upon its inauguration, the Council will establish, among other things, a Palestinian Electricity Authority, a Gaza Sea Port Authority, a Palestinian Development Bank, a Palestinian Export Promotion Board, a Palestinian Environmental Authority, a Palestinian Land Authority and a Palestinian Water Administration Authority, and any other Authorities agreed upon, in accordance with the Interim Agreement that will specify their powers and responsibilities.

After the inauguration of the Council, the Civil Administration will be dissolved, and the Israeli military government will be withdrawn.

Article VIII: Public Order and Security

In order to guarantee public order and internal security for the Palestinians of the West Bank and the Gaza Strip, the Council will establish a strong police force, while Israel will continue to carry the responsibility for defending against external threats, as well as the responsibility for overall security of Israelis for the purpose of safeguarding their internal security and public order.

Article IX: Laws and Military Orders

The Council will be empowered to legislate, in accordance with the Interim Agreement, within all authorities transferred to it.

Both parties will review jointly laws and military orders presently in force in remaining spheres.

Article X: Joint Israeli-Palestinian Liaison Committee

In order to provide for a smooth implementation of this Declaration of Principles and any subsequent agreements pertaining to the interim period, upon the entry into force of this Declaration of Principles, a Joint Israeli-Palestinian Liaison Committee will be established in order to deal with issues requiring coordination, other issues of common interest, and disputes.

Article XI: Israeli-Palestinian Cooperation in Economic Fields

Recognizing the mutual benefit of cooperation in promoting the development of the West Bank, the Gaza Strip and Israel, upon the entry into force of this Declaration of Principles, an Israeli-Palestinian Economic Cooperation Committee will be established in order to develop and implement in a cooperative manner the programs identified in the protocols attached as Annex III and Annex IV.

Article XII: Liaison and Cooperation with Jordan and Egypt

The two parties will invite the Governments of Jordan and Egypt to participate in establishing further liaison and cooperation arrangements between the Government of Israel and the Palestinian representatives, on the one hand, and the Governments of Jordan and Egypt, on the other hand, to promote cooperation between them. These arrangements will include the constitution of a Continuing Committee that will decide by agreement on the modalities of admission of persons displaced from the West Bank and Gaza Strip in 1967, together with necessary measures to prevent disruption and disorder. Other matters of common concern will be dealt with by this Committee.

Article XIII: Redeployment of Israeli Forces

After the entry into force of this Declaration of Principles, and not later than the eve of elections for the Council, a redeployment of Israeli military forces in the West Bank and the Gaza Strip will take place, in addition to withdrawal of Israeli forces carried out in accordance with Article XIV.

In redeploying its military forces, Israel will be guided by the principle that its military forces should be redeployed outside populated areas.

Further redeployments to specified locations will be gradually implemented commensurate with the assumption of responsibility for public order and internal security by the Palestinian police force pursuant to Article VIII above.

Article XIV: Israeli Withdrawal from the Gaza Strip and Jericho Area

Israel will withdraw from the Gaza Strip and Jericho area, as detailed in the protocol attached as Annex II.

Article XV: Resolution of Disputes

Disputes arising out of the application or interpretation of this Declaration of Principles, or any subsequent agreements pertaining to the interim period, shall be resolved by negotiations through the Joint Liaison Committee to be established pursuant to Article X above.

Disputes which cannot be settled by negotiations may be resolved by a mechanism of conciliation to be agreed upon by the parties.

The parties may agree to submit to arbitration disputes relating to the interim period, which cannot be settled through conciliation. To this end, upon the agreement of both parties, the parties will establish an Arbitration Committee.

Article XVI: Israeli-Palestinian Cooperation Concerning Regional Programs

Both parties view the multilateral working groups as an appropriate instrument for promoting a "Marshall Plan", the regional programs and other programs, including special programs for the West Bank and Gaza Strip, as indicated in the protocol attached as Annex IV.

Article XVII: Miscellaneous Provisions

This Declaration of Principles will enter into force one month after its signing.

All protocols annexed to this Declaration of Principles and Agreed Minutes pertaining thereto shall be regarded as an integral part hereof.

Done at Washington, D.C., this thirteenth day of September, 1993.

Annexes

Annex I: Protocol on the Mode and Conditions of Elections

Palestinians of Jerusalem who live there will have the right to participate in the election process, according to an agreement between the two sides.

In addition, the election agreement should cover, among other things, the following issues:

the system of elections;

the mode of the agreed supervision and international observation and their personal composition; and

rules and regulations regarding election campaign, including agreed arrangements for the organizing of mass media, and the possibility of licensing a broadcasting and TV station.

The future status of displaced Palestinians who were registered on 4th June 1967 will not be prejudiced because they are unable to participate in the election process due to practical reasons.

Annex II: Protocol on Withdrawal of Israeli Forces from the Gaza Strip and Jericho Area

The two sides will conclude and sign within two months from the date of entry into force of this Declaration of Principles, an agreement on the withdrawal of Israeli military forces from the Gaza Strip and Jericho area. This agreement will include comprehensive arrangements to apply in the Gaza Strip and the Jericho area subsequent to the Israeli withdrawal.

Israel will implement an accelerated and scheduled withdrawal of Israeli military forces from the Gaza Strip and Jericho area, beginning immediately with the signing of the agreement on the Gaza Strip and Jericho area and to be completed within a period not exceeding four months after the signing of this agreement.

The above agreement will include, among other things:

Arrangements for a smooth and peaceful transfer of authority from the Israeli military government and its Civil Administration to the Palestinian representatives.

Structure, powers and responsibilities of the Palestinian authority in these areas, except: external security, settlements, Israelis, foreign relations, and other mutually agreed matters.

Arrangements for the assumption of internal security and public order by the Palestinian police force consisting of police officers recruited locally and from abroad holding Jordanian passports and Palestinian documents issued by Egypt). Those who will participate in the Palestinian police force coming from abroad should be trained as police and police officers.

A temporary international or foreign presence, as agreed upon.

Establishment of a joint Palestinian-Israeli Coordination and Cooperation Committee for mutual security purposes.

An economic development and stabilization program, including the establishment of an

Emergency Fund, to encourage foreign investment, and financial and economic support. Both sides will coordinate and cooperate jointly and unilaterally with regional and international parties to support these aims.

Arrangements for a safe passage for persons and transportation between the Gaza Strip and Jericho area.

The above agreement will include arrangements for coordination between both parties regarding passages:

    Gaza—Egypt; and

    Jericho—Jordan.

The offices responsible for carrying out the powers and responsibilities of the Palestinian authority under this Annex II and Article VI of the Declaration of Principles will be located in the Gaza Strip and in the Jericho area pending the inauguration of the Council.

Other than these agreed arrangements, the status of the Gaza Strip and Jericho area will continue to be an integral part of the West Bank and Gaza Strip, and will not be changed in the interim period.

Annex III: Protocol on Israeli-Palestinian Cooperation in Economic and Development Programs

The two sides agree to establish an Israeli-Palestinian continuing Committee for Economic Cooperation, focusing, among other things, on the following:

Cooperation in the field of water, including a Water Development Program prepared by experts from both sides, which will also specify the mode of cooperation in the management of water resources in the West Bank and Gaza Strip, and will include proposals for studies and plans on water rights of each party, as well as on the equitable utilization of joint water resources for implementation in and beyond the interim period.

Cooperation in the field of electricity, including an Electricity Development Program, which will also specify the mode of cooperation for the production, maintenance, purchase and sale of electricity resources.

Cooperation in the field of energy, including an Energy Development Program, which will provide for the exploitation of oil and gas for industrial purposes, particularly in the Gaza Strip and in the Negev, and will encourage further joint exploitation of other energy resources. This Program may also provide for the construction of a Petrochemical industrial complex in the Gaza Strip and the construction of oil and gas pipelines.

Cooperation in the field of finance, including a Financial Development and Action Program for the encouragement of international investment in the West Bank and the Gaza Strip, and in Israel, as well as the establishment of a Palestinian Development Bank.

Cooperation in the field of transport and communications, including a Program, which will define guidelines for the establishment of a Gaza Sea Port Area, and will provide for the establishing of transport and communications lines to and from the West Bank and the Gaza Strip to Israel and to other countries. In addition, this Program will provide for carrying out the necessary construction of roads, railways, communications lines, etc.

Cooperation in the field of trade, including studies, and Trade Promotion Programs, which will encourage local, regional and inter-regional trade, as well as a feasibility study of creating free trade zones in the Gaza Strip and in Israel, mutual access to these zones, and cooperation in other areas related to trade and commerce.

Cooperation in the field of industry, including Industrial Development Programs, which will provide for the establishment of joint Israeli-Palestinian Industrial Research and Development Centers, will promote Palestinian-Israeli joint ventures, and provide guidelines for cooperation in the textile, food, pharmaceutical, electronics, diamonds, computer and science-based industries.

A program for cooperation in, and regulation of, labor relations and cooperation in social welfare issues.

A Human Resources Development and Cooperation Plan, providing for joint Israeli-Palestinian workshops and seminars, and for the establishment of joint vocational training centers, research institutes and data banks.

An Environmental Protection Plan, providing for joint and/or coordinated measures in this sphere.

A program for developing coordination and cooperation in the field of communication and media.

Any other programs of mutual interest.

Annex IV: Protocol on Israeli-Palestinian Cooperation Concerning Regional Development Programs

The two sides will cooperate in the context of the multilateral peace efforts in promoting a Development Program for the region, including the West Bank and the Gaza Strip, to be initiated by the G-7. The parties will request the G-7 to seek the participation in this program of other interested states, such as members of the Organisation for Economic Cooperation and Development, regional Arab states and institutions, as well as members of the private sector.

The Development Program will consist of two elements:

An Economic Development Program for the 'West Bank and the Gaza Strip.

A Regional Economic Development Program:

The Economic Development Program for the West Bank and the Gaza strip will consist of the following elements:

A Social Rehabilitation Program, including a Housing and Construction Program.

A Small and Medium Business Development Plan.

An Infrastructure Development Program (water, electricity, transportation and communications, etc.)

A Human Resources Plan.

Other programs.

The Regional Economic Development Program may consist of the following elements:

The establishment of a Middle East Development Fund, as a first step, and a Middle East Development Bank, as a second step.

The development of a joint Israeli-Palestinian-Jordanian Plan for coordinated exploitation of the Dead Sea area.

The Mediterranean Sea (Gaza)—Dead Sea Canal.

Regional Desalinization and other water development projects.

A regional plan for agricultural development, including a coordinated regional effort for the prevention of desertification.

Interconnection of electricity grids.

Regional cooperation for the transfer, distribution and industrial exploitation of gas, oil and other energy resources.

A Regional Tourism, Transportation and Telecommunications Development Plan.

Regional cooperation in other spheres.

The two sides will encourage the multilateral working groups, and will coordinate towards their success. The two parties will encourage intersessional activities, as well as pre-feasibility and feasibility studies, within the various multilateral working groups.

Agreed Minutes to the Declaration of Principles on Interim Self-Government Arrangements

A. General Understandings and Agreements

Any powers and responsibilities transferred to the Palestinians pursuant to the Declaration of Principles prior to the inauguration of the Council will be subject to the same principles pertaining to Article IV, as set out in these Agreed Minutes below.

B. Specific Understandings and Agreements

Article IV

It is understood that:

Jurisdiction of the Council will cover West Bank and Gaza Strip territory, except for issues that will be negotiated in the permanent status negotiations: Jerusalem, settlements, military locations, and Israelis.

The Council's jurisdiction will apply with regard to the agreed powers, responsibilities, spheres and authorities transferred to it.

Article VI (2)

It is agreed that the transfer of authority will be as follows:

The Palestinian side will inform the Israeli side of the names of the authorised Palestinians who will assume the powers, authorities and responsibilities that will be transferred to the Palestinians according to the Declaration of Principles in the following fields: education and culture, health, social welfare, direct taxation, tourism, and any other authorities agreed upon.

It is understood that the rights and obligations of these offices will not be affected.

Each of the spheres described above will continue to enjoy existing budgetary allocations in accordance with arrangements to be mutually agreed upon. These arrangements also will provide for the necessary adjustments required in order to take into account the taxes collected by the direct taxation office.

Upon the execution of the Declaration of Principles, the Israeli and Palestinian delegations will immediately commence negotiations on a detailed plan for the transfer of authority on the above offices in accordance with the above understandings.

Article VII (2)

The Interim Agreement will also include arrangements for coordination and cooperation.

Article VII (5)

The withdrawal of the military government will not prevent Israel from exercising the powers and responsibilities not transferred to the Council.

Article VIII

It is understood that the Interim Agreement will include arrangements for cooperation and coordination between the two parties in this regard. It is also agreed that the transfer of powers and responsibilities to the Palestinian police will be accomplished in a phased manner, as agreed in the Interim Agreement.

Article X

It is agreed that, upon the entry into force of the Declaration of Principles, the Israeli and Palestinian delegations will exchange the names of the individuals designated by them as members of the Joint Israeli-Palestinian Liaison Committee.

It is further agreed that each side will have an equal number of members in the Joint Committee. The Joint Committee will reach decisions by agreement. The Joint Committee may add other technicians and experts, as necessary. The Joint Committee will decide on the frequency and place or places of its meetings.

Annex II

It is understood that, subsequent to the Israeli withdrawal, Israel will continue to be responsible for external security, and for internal security and public order of settlements and Israelis. Israeli military forces and civilians may continue to use roads freely within the Gaza Strip and the Jericho area.

Israeli-Palestinian Interim Agreement on the West Bank and the Gaza Strip

Washington, D.C., September 28, 1995

Preamble

The Government of the State of Israel and the Palestine Liberation Organization (hereinafter "the PLO"), the representative of the Palestinian people;

Within the framework of the Middle East peace process initiated at Madrid in October 1991;

REAFFIRMING their determination to put an end to decades of confrontation and to live in peaceful coexistence, mutual dignity and security, while recognizing their mutual legitimate and political rights;

REAFFIRMING their desire to achieve a just, lasting and comprehensive peace settlement and historic reconciliation through the agreed political process;

RECOGNIZING that the peace process and the new era that it has created, as well as the new relationship established between the two Parties as described above, are irreversible, and the determination of the two Parties to maintain, sustain and continue the peace process;

RECOGNIZING that the aim of the Israeli-Palestinian negotiations within the current Middle East peace process is, among other things, to establish a Palestinian Interim Self-Government Authority, i.e. the elected Council (hereinafter "the Council" or "the Palestinian Council"), and the elected Ra'ees of the Executive Authority, for the Palestinian people in the West Bank and the Gaza Strip, for a transitional period not exceeding five years from the date of signing the Agreement on the Gaza Strip and the Jericho Area (hereinafter "the Gaza-Jericho Agreement") on May 4, 1994, leading to a permanent settlement based on Security Council Resolutions 242 and 338;

REAFFIRMING their understanding that the interim self-government arrangements contained in this Agreement are an integral part of the whole peace process, that the negotiations on the permanent status, that will start as soon as possible but not later than May 4, 1996, will lead to the implementation of Security Council Resolutions 242 and 338, and that the Interim Agreement shall settle all the issues of the interim period and that no such issues will be deferred to the agenda of the permanent status negotiations;

REAFFIRMING their adherence to the mutual recognition and commitments expressed in the letters dated September 9, 1993, signed by and exchanged between the Prime Minister of Israel and the Chairman of the PLO;

DESIROUS of putting into effect the Declaration of Principles on Interim Self-Government Arrangements signed at Washington, D.C. on September 13, 1993, and the Agreed Min-

utes thereto (hereinafter "the DOP") and in particular Article III and Annex I concerning the holding of direct, free and general political elections for the Council and the Ra'ees of the Executive Authority in order that the Palestinian people in the West Bank, Jerusalem and the Gaza Strip may democratically elect accountable representatives;

RECOGNIZING that these elections will constitute a significant interim preparatory step toward the realization of the legitimate rights of the Palestinian people and their just requirements and will provide a democratic basis for the establishment of Palestinian institutions;

REAFFIRMING their mutual commitment to act, in accordance with this Agreement, immediately, efficiently and effectively against acts or threats of terrorism, violence or incitement, whether committed by Palestinians or Israelis;

FOLLOWING the Gaza-Jericho Agreement; the Agreement on Preparatory Transfer of Powers and Responsibilities signed at Erez on August 29, 1994 (hereinafter "the Preparatory Transfer Agreement"); and the Protocol on Further Transfer of Powers and Responsibilities signed at Cairo on August 27, 1995 (hereinafter "the Further Transfer Protocol"); which three agreements will be superseded by this Agreement;

Hereby agree as follows:

Chapter I—The Council

Article I: Transfer of Authority

1. Israel shall transfer powers and responsibilities as specified in this Agreement from the Israeli military government and its Civil Administration to the Council in accordance with this Agreement. Israel shall continue to exercise powers and responsibilities not so transferred.

2. Pending the inauguration of the Council, the powers and responsibilities transferred to the Council shall be exercised by the Palestinian Authority established in accordance with the Gaza-Jericho Agree-

ment, which shall also have all the rights, liabilities and obligations to be assumed by the Council in this regard. Accordingly, the term "Council" throughout this Agreement shall, pending the inauguration of the Council, be construed as meaning the Palestinian Authority.

3. The transfer of powers and responsibilities to the police force established by the Palestinian Council in accordance with Article XIV below (hereinafter "the Palestinian Police") shall be accomplished in a phased manner, as detailed in this Agreement and in the Protocol concerning Redeployment and Security Arrangements attached as Annex I to this Agreement (hereinafter "Annex I").

4. As regards the transfer and assumption of authority in civil spheres, powers and responsibilities shall be transferred and assumed as set out in the Protocol Concerning Civil Affairs attached as Annex III to this Agreement (hereinafter "Annex III").

5. After the inauguration of the Council, the Civil Administration in the West Bank will be dissolved, and the Israeli military government shall be withdrawn. The withdrawal of the military government shall not prevent it from exercising the powers and responsibilities not transferred to the Council.

6. A Joint Civil Affairs Coordination and Cooperation Committee (hereinafter "the CAC"), Joint Regional Civil Affairs Subcommittees, one for the Gaza Strip and the other for the West Bank, and District Civil Liaison Offices in the West Bank shall be established in order to provide for coordination and cooperation in civil affairs between the Council and Israel, as detailed in Annex III.

7. The offices of the Council, and the offices of its Ra'ees and its Executive Authority and other committees, shall be located in areas under Palestinian territorial jurisdiction in the West Bank and the Gaza Strip.

Article II: Elections

1. In order that the Palestinian people of the West Bank and the Gaza Strip may govern themselves according to democratic principles, direct, free and general political elections will be held for the Council and the Ra'ees of the Executive Authority of the Council in accordance with the provisions set out in the Protocol concerning Elections attached as Annex II to this Agreement (hereinafter "Annex II").

2. These elections will constitute a significant interim preparatory step towards the realization of the legitimate rights of the Palestinian people and their just requirements and will provide a democratic basis for the establishment of Palestinian institutions.

3. Palestinians of Jerusalem who live there may participate in the election process in accordance with the provisions contained in this Article and in Article VI of Annex II (Election Arrangements concerning Jerusalem).

4. The elections shall be called by the Chairman of the Palestinian Authority immediately following the signing of this Agreement to take place at the earliest practicable date following the redeployment of Israeli forces in accordance with Annex I, and consistent with the requirements of the election timetable as provided in Annex II, the Election Law and the Election Regulations, as defined in Article I of Annex II.

Article III: Structure of the Palestinian Council

1. The Palestinian Council and the Ra'ees of the Executive Authority of the Council constitute the Palestinian Interim Self-Government Authority, which will be elected by the Palestinian people of the West Bank, Jerusalem and the Gaza Strip for the transitional period agreed in Article I of the DOP.

2. The Council shall possess both legislative power and executive power, in accordance with Articles VII and IX of the DOP. The Council shall carry out and be responsible

for all the legislative and executive powers and responsibilities transferred to it under this Agreement. The exercise of legislative powers shall be in accordance with Article XVIII of this Agreement (Legislative Powers of the Council).

3. The Council and the Ra'ees of the Executive Authority of the Council shall be directly and simultaneously elected by the Palestinian people of the West Bank, Jerusalem and the Gaza Strip, in accordance with the provisions of this Agreement and the Election Law and Regulations, which shall not be contrary to the provisions of this Agreement.

4. The Council and the Ra'ees of the Executive Authority of the Council shall be elected for a transitional period not exceeding five years from the signing of the Gaza-Jericho Agreement on May 4,.   1994.

5. Immediately upon its inauguration, the Council will elect from among its members a Speaker. The Speaker will preside over the meetings of the Council, administer the Council and its committees, decide on the agenda of each meeting, and lay before the Council proposals for voting and declare their results.

6. The jurisdiction of the Council shall be as determined in Article XVII of this Agreement (Jurisdiction).

7. The organization, structure and functioning of the Council shall be in accordance with this Agreement and the Basic Law for the Palestinian Interim Self-government Authority, which Law shall be adopted by the Council. The Basic Law and any regulations made under it shall not be contrary to the provisions of this Agreement.

8. The Council shall be responsible under its executive powers for the offices, services and departments transferred to it and may establish, within its jurisdiction, ministries and subordinate bodies, as necessary for the fulfillment of its responsibilities.

9. The Speaker will present for the Council's approval proposed internal procedures that will regulate, among other things, the decision-making processes of the Council.

Article IV: Size of the Council

The Palestinian Council shall be composed of 82 representatives and the Ra'ees of the Executive Authority, who will be directly and simultaneously elected by the Palestinian people of the West Bank, Jerusalem and the Gaza Strip.

Article V: The Executive Authority of the Council

1. The Council will have a committee that will exercise the executive authority of the Council, formed in accordance with paragraph 4 below (hereinafter "the Executive Authority").

2. The Executive Authority shall be bestowed with the executive authority of the Council and will exercise it on behalf of the Council. It shall determine its own internal procedures and decision making processes.

3. The Council will publish the names of the members of the Executive Authority immediately upon their initial appointment and subsequent to any changes.

4. a. The Ra'ees of the Executive Authority shall be an ex officio member of the Executive Authority.

   b. All of the other members of the Executive Authority, except as provided in subparagraph c. below, shall be members of the Council, chosen and proposed to the Council by the Ra'ees of the Executive Authority and approved by the Council.

   c. The Ra'ees of the Executive Authority shall have the right to appoint some persons, in number not exceeding twenty percent of the total membership of the Executive Authority, who are not members of the Council, to exercise executive authority and participate in government tasks. Such appointed members may not vote in meetings of the Council.

d. Non-elected members of the Executive Authority must have a valid address in an area under the jurisdiction of the Council.

Article VI: Other Committees of the Council

1. The Council may form small committees to simplify the proceedings of the Council and to assist in controlling the activity of its Executive Authority.
2. Each committee shall establish its own decision-making processes within the general framework of the organization and structure of the Council.

Article VII: Open Government

1. All meetings of the Council and of its committees, other than the Executive Authority, shall be open to the public, except upon a resolution of the Council or the relevant committee on the grounds of security, or commercial or personal confidentiality.
2. Participation in the deliberations of the Council, its committees and the Executive Authority shall be limited to their respective members only. Experts may be invited to such meetings to address specific issues on an ad hoc basis.

Article VIII: Judicial Review

Any person or organization affected by any act or decision of the Ra'ees of the Executive Authority of the Council or of any member of the Executive Authority, who believes that such act or decision exceeds the authority of the Ra'ees or of such member, or is otherwise incorrect in law or procedure, may apply to the relevant Palestinian Court of Justice for a review of such activity or decision.

Article IX: Powers and Responsibilities of the Council

1. Subject to the provisions of this Agreement, the Council will, within its jurisdiction, have legislative powers as set out in Article XVIII of this Agreement, as well as executive powers.

2. The executive power of the Palestinian Council shall extend to all matters within its jurisdiction under this Agreement or any future agreement that may be reached between the two Parties during the interim period. It shall include the power to formulate and conduct Palestinian policies and to supervise their implementation, to issue any rule or regulation under powers given in approved legislation and administrative decisions necessary for the realization of Palestinian self-government, the power to employ staff, sue and be sued and conclude contracts, and the power to keep and administer registers and records of the population, and issue certificates, licenses and documents.

3. The Palestinian Council's executive decisions and acts shall be consistent with the provisions of this Agreement.

4. The Palestinian Council may adopt all necessary measures in order to enforce the law and any of its decisions, and bring proceedings before the Palestinian courts and tribunals.

5. a. In accordance with the DOP, the Council will not have powers and responsibilities in the sphere of foreign relations, which sphere includes the establishment abroad of embassies, consulates or other types of foreign missions and posts or permitting their establishment in the West Bank or the Gaza Strip, the appointment of or admission of diplomatic and consular staff, and the exercise of diplomatic functions.

   b. Notwithstanding the provisions of this paragraph, the PLO may conduct negotiations and sign agreements with states or international organizations for the benefit of the Council in the following cases only:

   (1) economic agreements, as specifically provided in Annex V of this Agreement:

(2) agreements with donor countries for the purpose of implementing arrangements for the provision of assistance to the Council,

(3) agreements for the purpose of implementing the regional development plans detailed in Annex IV of the DOP or in agreements entered into in the framework of the multilateral negotiations, and

(4) cultural, scientific and educational agreements. Dealings between the Council and representatives of foreign states and international organizations, as well as the establishment in the West Bank and the Gaza Strip of representative offices other than those described in subparagraph 5.a above, for the purpose of implementing the agreements referred to in subparagraph 5.b above, shall not be considered foreign relations.

6. Subject to the provisions of this Agreement, the Council shall, within its jurisdiction, have an independent judicial system composed of independent Palestinian courts and tribunals.

Chapter 2—Redeployment and Security Arrangements

Article X: Redeployment of Israeli Military Forces

1. The first phase of the Israeli military forces redeployment will cover populated areas in the West Bank—cities, towns, villages, refugee camps and hamlets—as set out in Annex I, and will be completed prior to the eve of the Palestinian elections, i.e., 22 days before the day of the elections.

2. Further redeployments of Israeli military forces to specified military locations will commence after the inauguration of the Council and will be gradually implemented commensurate with the assumption of responsibility for public order and

internal security by the Palestinian Police, to be completed within 18 months from the date of the inauguration of the Council as detailed in Articles XI (Land) and XIII (Security), below and in Annex I.

3. The Palestinian Police shall be deployed and shall assume responsibility for public order and internal security for Palestinians in a phased manner in accordance with XIII (Security) below and Annex I.

4. Israel shall continue to carry the responsibility for external security, as well as the responsibility for overall security of Israelis for the purpose of safeguarding their internal security and public order.

5. For the purpose of this Agreement, "Israeli military forces" includes Israel Police and other Israeli security forces.

Article XI: Land

1. The two sides view the West Bank and the Gaza Strip as a single territorial unit, the integrity and status of which will be preserved during the interim period.

2. The two sides agree that West Bank and Gaza Strip territory, except for issues that will be negotiated in the permanent status negotiations, will come under the jurisdiction of the Palestinian Council in a phased manner, to be completed within 18 months from the date of the inauguration of the Council, as specified below:

a. Land in populated areas (Areas A and B), including government and Al Waqf land, will come under the jurisdiction of the Council during the first phase of redeployment.

b. All civil powers and responsibilities, including planning and zoning, in Areas A and B, set out in Annex III, will be transferred to and assumed by the Council during the first phase of redeployment.

c. In Area C, during the first phase of redeployment Israel will transfer to the

Council civil powers and responsibilities not relating to territory, as set out in Annex III.

d. The further redeployments of Israeli military forces to specified military locations will be gradually implemented in accordance with the DOP in three phases, each to take place after an interval of six months, after the inauguration of the Council, to be completed within 18 months from the date of the inauguration of the Council.

e. During the further redeployment phases to be completed within 18 months from the date of the inauguration of the Council, powers and responsibilities relating to territory will be transferred gradually to Palestinian jurisdiction that will cover West Bank and Gaza Strip territory, except for the issues that will be negotiated in the permanent status negotiations.

f. The specified military locations referred to in Article X, paragraph 2 above will be determined in the further redeployment phases, within the specified timeframe ending not later than 18 months from the date of the inauguration of the Council, and will be negotiated in the permanent status negotiations.

3. For the purpose of this Agreement and until the completion of the first phase of the further redeployments:

a. "Area A" means the populated areas delineated by a red line and shaded in brown on attached map No. 1;

b. "Area B" means the populated areas delineated by a red line and shaded in yellow on attached map No. 1, and the built-up area of the hamlets listed in Appendix 6 to Annex I, and

c. "Area C" means areas of the West Bank outside Areas A and B, which, except for the issues that will be negotiated in the permanent status negotiations,

will be gradually transferred to Palestinian jurisdiction in accordance with this Agreement.

Article XII: Arrangements for Security and Public Order

1. In order to guarantee public order and internal security for the Palestinians of the West Bank and the Gaza Strip, the Council shall establish a strong police force as set out in Article XIV below. Israel shall continue to carry the responsibility for defense against external threats, including the responsibility for protecting the Egyptian and Jordanian borders, and for defense against external threats from the sea and from the air, as well as the responsibility for overall security of Israelis and Settlements, for the purpose of safeguarding their internal security and public order, and will have all the powers to take the steps necessary to meet this responsibility.

2. Agreed security arrangements and coordination mechanisms are specified in Annex I.

3. A Joint Coordination and Cooperation Committee for Mutual Security Purposes (hereinafter "the JSC"), as well as Joint Regional Security Committees (hereinafter "RSCs") and Joint District Coordination Offices (hereinafter "DCOs"), are hereby established as provided for in Annex I.

4. The security arrangements provided for in this Agreement and in Annex I may be reviewed at the request of either Party and may be amended by mutual agreement of the Parties. Specific review arrangements are included in Annex I.

5. For the purpose of this Agreement, "the Settlements" means, in the West Bank the settlements in Area C; and in the Gaza Strip—the Gush Katif and Erez settlement areas, as well as the other settlements in the Gaza Strip, as shown on attached map No. 2.

Article XIII: Security

1. The Council will, upon completion of the redeployment of Israeli military forces in each district, as set out in Appendix 1 to Annex I, assume the powers and responsibilities for internal security and public order in Area A in that district.

2. a. There will be a complete redeployment of Israeli military forces from Area B. Israel will transfer to the Council and the Council will assume responsibility for public order for Palestinians. Israel shall have the overriding responsibility for security for the purpose of protecting Israelis and confronting the threat of terrorism.

   b. In Area B the Palestinian Police shall assume the responsibility for public order for Palestinians and shall be deployed in order to accommodate the Palestinian needs and requirements in the following manner:

      (1) The Palestinian Police shall establish 25 police stations and posts in towns, villages, and other places listed in Appendix 2 to Annex I and as delineated on map No. 3. The West Bank RSC may agree on the establishment of additional police stations and posts, if required.

      (2) The Palestinian Police shall be responsible for handling public order incidents in which only Palestinians are involved.

      (3) The Palestinian Police shall operate freely in populated places where police stations and posts are located, as set out in paragraph b (1) above.

      (4) While the movement of uniformed Palestinian policemen in Area B outside places where there is a Palestinian police station or post will be carried out after coordination and confirmation through the relevant DCO, three months after the completion of redeployment from Area B, the DCOs may decide that movement of Palestinian policemen from the police stations in Area B to Palestinian towns and villages in Area B on roads that are used only by Palestinian traffic will take place after notifying the DCO.

      (5) The coordination of such planned movement prior to confirmation through the relevant DCO shall include a scheduled plan, including the number of policemen, as well as the type and number of weapons and vehicles intended to take part. It shall also include details of arrangements for ensuring continued coordination through appropriate communication links, the exact schedule of movement to the area of the planned operation, including the destination and routes thereto, its proposed duration and the schedule for returning to the police station or post.

      The Israeli side of the DCO will provide the Palestinian side with its response, following a request for movement of policemen in accordance with this paragraph, in normal or routine cases within one day and in emergency cases no later than 2 hours.

      (6) The Palestinian Police and the Israeli military forces will conduct joint security activities on the main roads as set out in Annex I.

      (7) The Palestinian Police will notify the West Bank RSC of the names of the policemen, number plates of police vehicles and serial numbers of weapons, with respect to each police station and post in Area B.

(8) Further redeployments from Area C and transfer of internal security responsibility to the Palestinian Police in Areas B and C will be carried out in three phases, each to take place after an interval of six months, to be completed 18 months after the inauguration of the Council, except for the issues of permanent status negotiations and of Israel's overall responsibility for Israelis and borders.

(9) The procedures detailed in this paragraph will be reviewed within six months of the completion of the first phase of redeployment.

Article XIV: The Palestinian Police

1. The Council shall establish a strong police force. The duties, functions, structure, deployment and composition of the Palestinian Police, together with provisions regarding its equipment and operation, as well as rules of conduct, are set out in Annex I.

2. The Palestinian police force established under the Gaza-Jericho Agreement will be fully integrated into the Palestinian Police and will be subject to the provisions of this Agreement.

3. Except for the Palestinian Police and the Israeli military forces, no other armed forces shall be established or operate in the West Bank and the Gaza Strip.

4. Except for the arms, ammunition and equipment of the Palestinian Police described in Annex I, and those of the Israeli military forces, no organization, group or individual in the West Bank and the Gaza Strip shall manufacture, sell, acquire, possess, import or otherwise introduce into the West Bank or the Gaza Strip any firearms, ammunition, weapons, explosives, gunpowder or any related equipment, unless otherwise provided for in Annex I.

Article XV: Prevention of Hostile Acts

1. Both sides shall take all measures necessary in order to prevent acts of terrorism, crime and hostilities directed against each other, against individuals falling under the other's authority and against their property and shall take legal measures against offenders.

2. Specific provisions for the implementation of this Article are set out in Annex I.

Article XVI: Confidence Building Measures

With a view to fostering a positive and supportive public atmosphere to accompany the implementation of this Agreement, to establish a solid basis of mutual trust and good faith, and in order to facilitate the anticipated cooperation and new relations between the two peoples, both Parties agree to carry out confidence building measures as detailed herewith:

1. Israel will release or turn over to the Palestinian side, Palestinian detainees and prisoners, residents of the West Bank and the Gaza Strip. The first stage of release of these prisoners and detainees will take place on the signing of this Agreement and the second stage will take place prior to the date of the elections. There will be a third stage of release of detainees and prisoners. Detainees and prisoners will be released from among categories detailed in Annex VII (Release of Palestinian Prisoners and Detainees). Those released will be free to return to their homes in the West Bank and the Gaza Strip.

2. Palestinians who have maintained contact with the Israeli authorities will not be subjected to acts of harassment, violence, retribution or prosecution. Appropriate ongoing measures will be taken, in coordination with Israel, in order to ensure their protection.

3. Palestinians from abroad whose entry into the West Bank and the Gaza Strip is approved pursuant to this Agreement, and to whom the provisions of this Article are applicable, will not be prosecuted for offenses committed prior to September 13, 1993.

Chapter 3—Legal Affairs

Article XVII: Jurisdiction

1. In accordance with the DOP, the jurisdiction of the Council will cover West Bank and Gaza Strip territory as a single territorial unit, except for:
   a. issues that will be negotiated in the permanent status negotiations: Jerusalem, settlements, specified military locations, Palestinian refugees, borders, foreign relations and Israelis; and
   b. powers and responsibilities not transferred to the Council.

2. Accordingly, the authority of the Council encompasses all matters that fall within its territorial, functional and personal jurisdiction, as follows:
   a. The territorial jurisdiction of the Council shall encompass Gaza Strip territory, except for the Settlements and the Military Installation Area shown on map No. 2, and West Bank territory, except for Area C which, except for the issues that will be negotiated in the permanent status negotiations, will be gradually transferred to Palestinian jurisdiction in three phases, each to take place after an interval of six months, to be completed 18 months after the inauguration of the Council. At this time, the jurisdiction of the Council will cover West Bank and Gaza Strip territory, except for the issues that will be negotiated in the permanent status negotiations.
      Territorial jurisdiction includes land, subsoil and territorial waters, in accordance with the provisions of this Agreement.
   b. The functional jurisdiction of the Council extends to all powers and responsibilities transferred to the Council, as specified in this Agreement or in any future agreements that may be reached between the Parties during the interim period.

   c. The territorial and functional jurisdiction of the Council will apply to all persons, except for Israelis, unless otherwise provided in this Agreement.
   d. Notwithstanding subparagraph a. above, the Council shall have functional jurisdiction in Area C, as detailed in Article IV of Annex III.

3. The Council has, within its authority, legislative, executive and judicial powers and responsibilities, as provided for in this Agreement.

4. a. Israel, through its military government, has the authority over areas that are not under the territorial jurisdiction of the Council, powers and responsibilities not transferred to the Council and Israelis.
   b. To this end, the Israeli military government shall retain the necessary legislative, judicial and executive powers and responsibilities, in accordance with international law. This provision shall not derogate from Israel's applicable legislation over Israelis in personam.

5. The exercise of authority with regard to the electromagnetic sphere and air space shall be in accordance with the provisions of this Agreement.

6. Without derogating from the provisions of this Article, legal arrangements detailed in the Protocol Concerning Legal Matters attached as Annex IV to this Agreement (hereinafter "Annex IV") shall be observed. Israel and the Council may negotiate further legal arrangements.

7. Israel and the Council shall cooperate on matters of legal assistance in criminal and civil matters through a legal committee (hereinafter "the Legal Committee"), hereby established.

8. The Council's jurisdiction will extend gradually to cover West Bank and Gaza Strip territory, except for the issues to be negotiated in the permanent status negotiations,

through a series of redeployments of the Israeli military forces. The first phase of the redeployment of Israeli military forces will cover populated areas in the West Bank—cities, towns, refugee camps and hamlets, as set out in Annex I—and will be completed prior to the eve of the Palestinian elections, i.e. 22 days before the day of the elections. Further redeployments of Israeli military forces to specified military locations will commence immediately upon the inauguration of the Council and will be effected in three phases, each to take place after an interval of six months, to be concluded no later than eighteen months from the date of the inauguration of the Council.

Article XVIII: Legislative Powers of the Council

1. For the purposes of this Article, legislation shall mean any primary and secondary legislation, including basic laws, laws, regulations and other legislative acts.

2. The Council has the power, within its jurisdiction as defined in Article XVII of this Agreement, to adopt legislation.

3. While the primary legislative power shall lie in the hands of the Council as a whole, the Ra'ees of the Executive Authority of the Council shall have the following legislative powers

   a. the power to initiate legislation or to present proposed legislation to the Council;

   b. the power to promulgate legislation adopted by the Council; and

   c. the power to issue secondary legislation, including regulations, relating to any matters specified and within the scope laid down in any primary legislation adopted by the Council.

4. a. Legislation, including legislation which amends or abrogates existing laws or military orders, which exceeds the jurisdiction of the Council or which is otherwise inconsistent with the provisions of the DOP, this Agreement, or of any other agreement that may be reached between the two sides during the interim period, shall have no effect and shall be void ab initio.

   b. The Ra'ees of the Executive Authority of the Council shall not promulgate legislation adopted by the Council if such legislation falls under the provisions of this paragraph.

5. All legislation shall be communicated to the Israeli side of the Legal Committee.

6. Without derogating from the provisions of paragraph 4 above, the Israeli side of the Legal Committee may refer for the attention of the Committee any legislation regarding which Israel considers the provisions of paragraph 4 apply, in order to discuss issues arising from such legislation. The Legal Committee will consider the legislation referred to it at the earliest opportunity.

Article XIX: Human Rights and the Rule of Law

Israel and the Council shall exercise their powers and responsibilities pursuant to this Agreement with due regard to internationally-accepted norms and principles of human rights and the rule of law.

Article XX: Rights, Liabilities and Obligations

1. a. The transfer of powers and responsibilities from the Israeli military government and its civil administration to the Council, as detailed in Annex III, includes all related rights, liabilities and obligations arising with regard to acts or omissions which occurred prior to such transfer. Israel will cease to bear any financial responsibility regarding such acts or omissions and the Council will bear all financial responsibility for these and for its own functioning.

   b. Any financial claim made in this regard against Israel will be referred to the Council.

c. Israel shall provide the Council with the information it has regarding pending and anticipated claims brought before any court or tribunal against Israel in this regard.

d. Where legal proceedings are brought in respect of such a claim, Israel will notify the Council and enable it to participate in defending the claim and raise any arguments on its behalf.

e. In the event that an award is made against Israel by any court or tribunal in respect of such a claim, the Council shall immediately reimburse Israel the full amount of the award.

f. Without prejudice to the above, where a court or tribunal hearing such a claim finds that liability rests solely with an employee or agent who acted beyond the scope of the powers assigned to him or her, unlawfully or with willful malfeasance, the Council shall not bear financial responsibility.

2. a. Notwithstanding the provisions of paragraphs l.d through l.f above, each side may take the necessary measures, including promulgation of legislation, in order to ensure that such claims by Palestinians including pending claims in which the hearing of evidence has not yet begun, are brought only before Palestinian courts or tribunals in the West Bank and the Gaza Strip, and are not brought before or heard by Israeli courts or tribunals.

b. Where a new claim has been brought before a Palestinian court or tribunal subsequent to the dismissal of the claim pursuant to subparagraph a. above, the Council shall defend it and, in accordance with subparagraph l.a above, in the event that an award is made for the plaintiff, shall pay the amount of the award.

c. The Legal Committee shall agree on arrangements for the transfer of all materials and information needed to enable the Palestinian courts or tribunals to hear such claims as referred to in subparagraph b. above, and, when necessary, for the provision of legal assistance by Israel to the Council in defending such claims.

3. The transfer of authority in itself shall not affect rights, liabilities and obligations of any person or legal entity, in existence at the date of signing of this Agreement.

4. The Council, upon its inauguration, will assume all the rights, liabilities and obligations of the Palestinian Authority.

5. For the purpose of this Agreement, "Israelis" also includes Israeli statutory agencies and corporations registered in Israel.

Article XXI: Settlement of Differences and Disputes

Any difference relating to the application of this Agreement shall be referred to the appropriate coordination and cooperation mechanism established under this Agreement. The provisions of Article XV of the DOP shall apply to any such difference which is not settled through the appropriate coordination and cooperation mechanism, namely:

1. Disputes arising out of the application or interpretation of this Agreement or any related agreements pertaining to the interim period shall be settled through the Liaison Committee.

2. Disputes which cannot be settled by negotiations may be settled by a mechanism of conciliation to be agreed between the Parties.

3. The Parties may agree to submit to arbitration disputes relating to the interim period, which cannot be settled through conciliation. To this end, upon the agreement of both Parties, the Parties will establish an Arbitration Committee.

Chapter 4—Cooperation

Article XXII: Relations between Israel and the Council

1. Israel and the Council shall seek to foster mutual understanding and tolerance and

shall accordingly abstain from incitement, including hostile propaganda, against each other and, without derogating from the principle of freedom of expression, shall take legal measures to prevent such incitement by any organizations, groups or individuals within their jurisdiction.

2. Israel and the Council will ensure that their respective educational systems contribute to the peace between the Israeli and Palestinian peoples and to peace in the entire region, and will refrain from the introduction of any motifs that could adversely affect the process of reconciliation.

3. Without derogating from the other provisions of this Agreement, Israel and the Council shall cooperate in combating criminal activity which may affect both sides, including offenses related to trafficking in illegal drugs and psychotropic substances, smuggling, and offenses against property, including offenses related to vehicles.

Article XXIII: Cooperation with Regard to Transfer of Powers and Responsibilities

In order to ensure a smooth, peaceful and orderly transfer of powers and responsibilities, the two sides will cooperate with regard to the transfer of security powers and responsibilities in accordance with the provisions of Annex I, and the transfer of civil powers and responsibilities in accordance with the provisions of Annex III.

Article XXIV: Economic Relations

The economic relations between the two sides are set out in the Protocol on Economic Relations signed in Paris on April 29, 1994, and the Appendices thereto, and the Supplement to the Protocol on Economic Relations all attached as Annex V, and will be governed by the relevant provisions of this Agreement and its Annexes.

Article XXV: Cooperation Programs

1. The Parties agree to establish a mechanism to develop programs of cooperation between them. Details of such cooperation are set out in Annex VI.

2. A Standing Cooperation Committee to deal with issues arising in the context of this cooperation is hereby established as provided for in Annex VI.

Article XXVI: The Joint Israeli-Palestinian Liaison Committee

1. The Liaison Committee established pursuant to Article X of the DOP shall ensure the smooth implementation of this Agreement. It shall deal with issues requiring coordination, other issues of common interest and disputes.

2. The Liaison Committee shall be composed of an equal number of members from each Party. It may add other technicians and experts as necessary.

3. The Liaison Committee shall adopt its rules of procedures, including the frequency and place or places of its meetings.

4. The Liaison Committee shall reach its decisions by agreement.

5. The Liaison Committee shall establish a subcommittee that will monitor and steer the implementation of this Agreement (hereinafter "the Monitoring and Steering Committee"). It will function as follows:

   a. The Monitoring and Steering Committee will, on an ongoing basis, monitor the implementation of this Agreement, with a view to enhancing the cooperation and fostering the peaceful relations between the two sides.

   b. The Monitoring and Steering Committee will steer the activities of the various joint committees established in this Agreement (the JSC, the CAC, the Legal Committee, the Joint Economic Committee and the Standing Cooperation Committee) concerning the ongoing implementation of the Agreement, and will report to the Liaison Committee.

c. The Monitoring and Steering Committee will be composed of the heads of the various committees mentioned above.

d. The two heads of the Monitoring and Steering Committee will establish its rules of procedures, including the frequency and places of its meetings.

Article XXVII: Liaison and Cooperation with Jordan and Egypt

1. Pursuant to Article XII of the DOP, the two Parties have invited the Governments of Jordan and Egypt to participate in establishing further liaison and cooperation arrangements between the Government of Israel and the Palestinian representatives on the one hand, and the Governments of Jordan and Egypt on the other hand, to promote cooperation between them. As part of these arrangements a Continuing Committee has been constituted and has commenced its deliberations.

2. The Continuing Committee shall decide by agreement on the modalities of admission of persons displaced from the West Bank and the Gaza Strip in 1967, together with necessary measures to prevent disruption and disorder.

3. The Continuing Committee shall also deal with other matters of common concern.

Article XXVIII: Missing Persons

1. Israel and the Council shall cooperate by providing each other with all necessary assistance in the conduct of searches for missing persons and bodies of persons which have not been recovered, as well as by providing information about missing persons.

2. The PLO undertakes to cooperate with Israel and to assist it in its efforts to locate and to return to Israel Israeli soldiers who are missing in action and the bodies of soldiers which have not been recovered.

Chapter 5—Miscellaneous Provisions

Article XXIX: Safe Passage between the West Bank and the Gaza Strip

Arrangements for safe passage of persons and transportation between the West Bank and the Gaza Strip are set out in Annex I.

Article XXX: Passages

Arrangements for coordination between Israel and the Council regarding passage to and from Egypt and Jordan, as well as any other agreed international crossings, are set out in Annex I.

Article XXXI: Final Clauses

1. This Agreement shall enter into force on the date of its signing.

2. The Gaza-Jericho Agreement, except for Article XX (Confidence-Building Measures), the Preparatory Transfer Agreement and the Further Transfer Protocol will be superseded by this Agreement.

3. The Council, upon its inauguration, shall replace the Palestinian Authority and shall assume all the undertakings and obligations of the Palestinian Authority under the Gaza-Jericho Agreement, the Preparatory Transfer Agreement, and the Further Transfer Protocol.

4. The two sides shall pass all necessary legislation to implement this Agreement.

5. Permanent status negotiations will commence as soon as possible, but not later than May 4, 1996, between the Parties. It is understood that these negotiations shall cover remaining issues, including: Jerusalem, refugees, settlements, security arrangements, borders, relations and cooperation with other neighbors, and other issues of common interest.

6. Nothing in this Agreement shall prejudice or preempt the outcome of the negotiations on the permanent status to be conducted pursuant to the DOP. Neither Party shall be deemed, by virtue of having entered

into this Agreement, to have renounced or waived any of its existing rights, claims or positions.

7. Neither side shall initiate or take any step that will change the status of the West Bank and the Gaza Strip pending the outcome of the permanent status negotiations.

8. The two Parties view the West Bank and the Gaza Strip as a single territorial unit, the integrity and status of which will be preserved during the interim period.

9. The PLO undertakes that, within two months of the date of the inauguration of the Council, the Palestinian National Council will convene and formally approve the necessary changes in regard to the Palestinian Covenant, as undertaken in the letters signed by the Chairman of the PLO and addressed to the Prime Minister of Israel, dated September 9, 1993 and May 4, 1994.

10. Pursuant to Annex I, Article IX of this Agreement, Israel confirms that the permanent checkpoints on the roads leading to and from the Jericho Area (except those related to the access road leading from Mousa Alami to the Allenby Bridge) will be removed upon the completion of the first phase of redeployment.

11. Prisoners who, pursuant to the Gaza-Jericho Agreement, were turned over to the Palestinian Authority on the condition that they remain in the Jericho Area for the remainder of their sentence, will be free to return to their homes in the West Bank and the Gaza Strip upon the completion of the first phase of redeployment.

12. As regards relations between Israel and the PLO, and without derogating from the commitments contained in the letters signed by and exchanged between the Prime Minister of Israel and the Chairman of the PLO, dated September 9, 1993 and May 4, 1994, the two sides will apply between them the provisions contained in Article XXII, paragraph 1, with the necessary changes.

13. a. The Preamble to this Agreement, and all Annexes, Appendices and maps attached hereto, shall constitute an integral part hereof.

   b. The Parties agree that the maps attached to the Gaza-Jericho Agreement as:

      a. map No. 1 (The Gaza Strip), an exact copy of which is attached to this Agreement as map No. (in this Agreement "map No. 2");

      b. map No. 4 (Deployment of Palestinian Police in the Gaza Strip), an exact copy of which is attached to this Agreement as map No. 5 (in this Agreement "map No. 5"); and

      c. map No. 6 (Maritime Activity Zones), an exact copy of which is attached to this Agreement as map No. 8 (in this Agreement "map No. 8"; are an integral part hereof and will remain in effect for the duration of this Agreement.

14. While the Jeftlik area will come under the functional and personal jurisdiction of the Council in the first phase of redeployment, the area's transfer to the territorial jurisdiction of the Council will be considered by the Israeli side in the first phase of the further redeployment phases.

Done at Washington D.C., this 28th day of September, 1995

GLOSSARY

Al Waqf land: land that belonged to the religious foundations

Basic Law: a code of law that was supposed to be created by the governing authority to replace the Israeli law

Marshall Plan: the U.S. effort after World War II to rebuild Europe

permanent status: the achievement of independent statehood

Ra'ees: a chief or leader, used to signify those who lead the Executive Authority

Document Analysis

Oslo I, in 1993, started the process toward creation of an independent Palestinian state (or was supposed to have). This is essentially what was hailed as the Oslo Accords, with less attention being paid to the second installment of agreements two years later. The first part of the first agreement notes that both parties wish to work toward peace and the implementation of U.N. Resolutions 242 and 338 (both of which sought a withdrawal of Israeli forces from territories occupied in 1967). The second part of Oslo I notes that there is supposed to be a five-year interim period during which both parties work toward implementation of the Oslo accords and iron out other details. The agreement also held that the Gaza Strip and West Bank, which are not physically connected, were to be one state for Palestinians. It goes on to identify the areas of government that would immediately be transferred, such as education, and those that would await transfer, such as a police force, even as the Palestinians begin preparing for such transfers (as by training a police force). The next part notes how the interim agreement is to start at once and how the Palestinians are expected to maintain a strong police force in order to establish order. The agreement then looks at liaisons that are planned to take place. Withdrawal of forces and resolutions of disputes complete the agreement. There is also, however, a six-page annex that notes a number of points concerning cooperation.

The second agreement starts out with a preamble and thus is a bit more formal than the first. It notes that powers are to be transferred first to the Palestinian Authority and then to an elected council, and that only the powers specified are to be so transferred. After the council is established, the Israelis will be expected to withdraw. The second part of the second agreement deals with elections and notes that the people in Jerusalem are to be allowed to vote. It should be noted that the agreement treats Jerusalem as a separate area distinct from the West Bank, which partly surrounds it.

The agreement then notes that the council will be both legislative and executive in nature, thus resembling a parliamentary system in which the winning candidate picks members of the executive. The council would serve five years. Once an executive is picked, that executive could name up to sixteen people to serve on the council. The council would have open meetings, generally, would allow judicial review of its decisions, and could have committees. The council is given no power in the area of foreign relations other than in cultural affairs. The council is specifically banned from having embassies or making agreements with foreign powers—those things were left for future negotiations. The agreement specifies that Israeli military forces would be redeployed outside the areas covered by the agreement, and notes that such redeployment is to be accomplished within 18 months. The issue of land is noted, with the land being divided up into three parts—"A" "B" and "C"—with power in areas A and B being given first to the Palestinians along with limited power over area C. In the areas of police and security, the Israelis are supposed to be given power outside of the West Bank and Gaza Strip, with the Palestinian police being given power inside. The agreement describes the Palestinian police force that needs to be created as a "strong" one. One difference between areas A and B is that, in area A, police forces are to be allowed early on while in area B it would be delayed somewhat. The agreement also notes that confidence-building measures should be undertaken to ensure success. It describes how the council is to be given general powers over the area, except in the area C parts, which would be transferred generally. The agreement includes a set of articles noting how the Israelis and Palestinians are to work together to handle disagreements. It closes with a series of notes, including one about permanent status negotiation to begin in early 1996.

Essential Themes

The main theme here is that of peace and compromise after a period of extended conflict. The Oslo Accords essentially sought to exchange land (occupied by Israel) for peace. They gave the Palestinians some level of control over their land, particularly the Gaza Strip and parts of the West Bank, and expected the Palestinians to cease hostilities against Israel. However, over time, the people of both sides seem largely to have moved away from the agreements. Israel has dragged its feet on implementing the Oslo Accords, while the Palestinian Authority has been slow to oppose terrorism. More fatal to the agreement has been the rising power of Hamas among the Palestinians; for Hamas never agreed to the accords in the place. In 2006 Hamas gained power in the Gaza Strip, leading to retaliation and hostilities on both sides. For their part, voters in Israel have been unwilling to push the peace process forward, leading to administrations that are unwilling to expend effort in that direction and more inclined, in fact, to follow a hard line.

In Gaza, for example, a buffer zone has been imposed by Israel, which takes up much of Gaza's land (Gaza is only 141 square miles, about 25 miles long and 6 miles wide). Israel's main concern here is stopping attacks from the region. Its main concern regarding the West Bank, in contrast, is land, where it has allowed Jewish settlers to take up residence. A sizable portion of what is now the West Bank has either already been taken up by Jewish settlements or eyed for future Jewish settlements. The question persists as to what is to be done regarding those areas. Some have suggested swapping land in the West Bank currently set up as Jewish settlements with land in Israel, but the details of that arrangement remain hazy and no concrete action has been taken. As for the Gaza Strip, the problem for Israel is how to force Hamas, which controls the area, to cease attacks. Israel continues to retaliate against such attacks, but that has not proved effective in any lasting way so far. Most recently, the U.S. president, Donald Trump, has stated that the American Embassy is to be moved to West Jerusalem, a move that bolsters the hardliners inside Israel. Some observers have remarked that, as a result, the two-state solution is more threatened than it ever has been.

—*Scott A. Merriman, PhD*

Bibliography and Additional Reading

Brown, Nathan J. *Palestinian Politics after the Oslo Accords: Resuming Arab Palestine.* Berkeley: University of California Press, 2003.

Rosler, Nimrod. "Leadership and Peacemaking: Yitzhak Rabin and the Oslo Accords." *International Journal of Intercultural Relations*, vol. 54, 01 Sept. 2016, pp. 55-67.

Somdeep Sen, author. ""It's Nakba, Not a Party": Re-Stating the (Continued) Legacy of the Oslo Accords." *Arab Studies Quarterly*, no. 2, 2015, p. 161.

Watson, Geoffrey R. *The Oslo Accords: International Law and the Israeli-Palestinian Peace Agreements.* New York: Oxford University Press, 2000.

Yitzhak Rabin Speaks at Signing of the Oslo Accords (1993) Ca. 1993. [Place of publication not identified]: *WPA Film Library*, [1993], 2008. EBSCOhost

RECENT REALITIES

Unfortunately, a great deal of violence marks the history of the Middle East in the twenty-first century. Much of that violence was sparked, initially at least, by massive U.S. military interventions in response to the 9/11 attacks of 2001. Shortly after those attacks, the United States initiated a campaign in Afghanistan that lasted over a decade (indeed, U.S. military involvement continues there today). In 2003, without U.N. approval, it invaded Iraq and removed Saddam Hussein. That part of the Iraq War (Operation Iraqi Freedom) proved relatively easy, albeit devastating for the inhabitants. The country, however, soon descended into chaos, and U.S. occupation forces (the Coalition Provisional Authority) had neither plans nor the means to deal with the situation. After eight years of occupation, the United States finally withdrew from Iraq at the end of 2011, leaving a country ruined by war and paralyzed by political crisis. From out of the ashes, moreover, arose an even greater regional threat: the so-called Islamic State (ISIL or ISIS), an ultra-extremist jihadist organization seeking to establish a new Middle Eastern (or world) caliphate. After yet another few years of war and devastation, extending from Syria to Kurdish northern Iraq, ISIL was broken up, in the main, in late 2017. (Pockets of both it and allied groups still exist.)

In Afghanistan, meanwhile, the longest-ever war fought by the United States produced little in the way of tangible, enduring change. Osama bin Laden, the chief instigator of 9/11, remained at large until 2011, when he was killed by U.S. forces—in Pakistan. The most that can be said beyond that is that Afghanistan remains Afghanistan, a hard-knock nation that has, more than once, survived attempts by great foreign powers to subdue it. In this case, however, U.S. efforts have been directed not against the Afghan government but against extremist-jihadist elements inside the country.

Popular uprisings that came to be known as the Arab Spring erupted in Tunisia in late 2010 and soon spread to other areas in the region. Long-standing, autocratic rulers fell in Egypt, Libya, Tunisia, and Yemen. Libya and Syria, however, erupted in civil war. The Syrian civil war in particular has proved troublesome, generating great numbers of refugees and resulting in something of a proxy war between Russia (which backs the Syrian regime) and the United States (which opposes it). Elsewhere, such as in the Gulf States and Iran, popular uprisings were contained or quelled. In Egypt, in a backlash, a military regime has taken hold. In Turkey, a coup was attempted in 2016 but put down by the regime of Recep Tayyip Erdoğan. In Saudi Arabia, a "reverse coup," or purge, took place in 2017: prominent princes, government ministers, and business people were arrested by Saudi authorities and forced to turn over much of their wealth as part of an anti-corruption effort.

And then there is the Palestine-Israel conflict. This conflict involves not only Israel and the Israeli-occupied territories of the West Bank and Gaza Strip, as well as Jerusalem, but also Lebanon, Syria, and Jordan. In 2005 Israel decided to end 38 years of occupation in Gaza, leaving it largely to Palestinian control but under Israeli surveillance. Two years later, in response to an internal dispute between the two major Palestinian political parties, Hamas and Fatah, Israel and Egypt began a blockade of Gaza to prevent the importation of a range of materials that Israel claimed could be used to support attacks against its territory. Then, in winter 2008–2009, 2012, and again in 2014 Israel launched offensives against Gaza that killed thousands of people, mainly civilians. Since then, violence has become the norm for Palestinians in Gaza—particularly after the demise of the Oslo peace process (started in 1994). Today, the Israel-Palestine conflict revolves around the same issues it always has: the occupied territories, the status of Jerusalem, the final borders, and the return of Palestinians from camps in Syria, Jordan, and Lebanon.

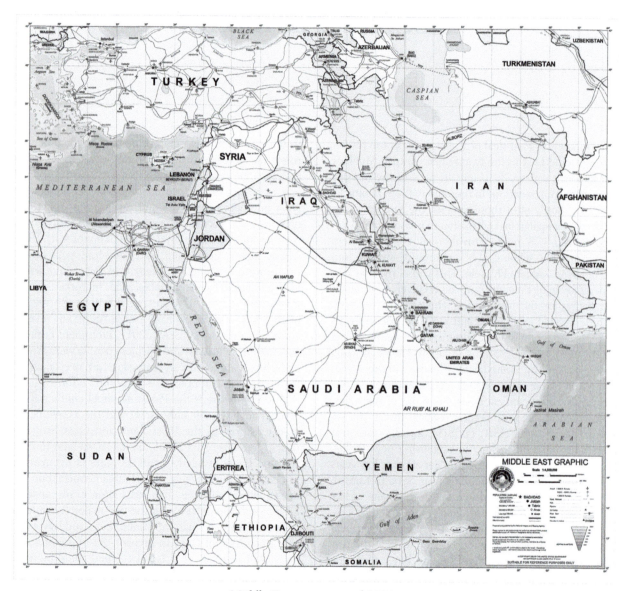

Middle East map, around 2006.

■ George W. Bush's Address to the Nation on Military Operations in Iraq

Date: March 19, 2003
Author: George W. Bush
Geographic region: Iraq
Genre: Address; speech

Summary Overview

This document examined here is historically significant because it announced the United States' pending invasion of Iraq (it took place the following day) and signaled a major broadening of the so-called war on terror. Before this point, U.S. forces had invaded Afghanistan, which had harbored al-Qaida and its leader Osama Bin Laden, who was behind the 9/11 attacks against Washington. The Afghanistan invasion was widely viewed in the United States and worldwide as necessary and justified. On the other hand, the Iraq invasion was different. The United States had become an ally with Iraq in the 1980s, when Iraq opposed Iran in the Iran-Iraq war. Allies became enemies in 1990, however, when Iraq took over Kuwait. The United States then forced Iraq out of Kuwait but did not remove Iraq's leader, Saddam Hussein, from power. After the U.S. invasion of Iraq, Saddam was removed from power; he was captured in late 2003 and, after questioning, was turned over to the Iraqi government that the U.S. had helped come to power. In 2006 he was found guilty of a long list of charges, and in December 2006 he was executed. After the U.S. invasion, the provisional Iraqi government did not gain full control of the country and chaos erupted. This chaos, in turn, eventually allowed such rogue, ultra-militant groups as the Islamic State (ISIS) to emerge, creating havoc in the region and destabilizing Syria. Thus, the invasion announced here ultimately led to long period of instability and destruction in the Middle East.

Defining Moment

The United States, along with Britain, played a key role in shaping the modern Middle East. Following World War I, Britain took control of southern parts of the (including most of Iraq) and ruled it under a mandate from the League of Nations. The Iraqi government, however, moved away from the monarchy imposed on it in the 1950s and became an ally of the Soviet Union. Britain continued to control the Iraqi oil industry—until the Iraqi government nationalized it in the 1970s. Both of these moves by Iraq caused Britain and the United States to step back from it. Yet the Americans favored Iraq in the 1980s during its war with Iran. With nothing to show from that war, however, Iraq invaded Kuwait in 1990, and the United States led a coalition organized to expel it from that small country. Nevertheless, Saddam Hussein remained in power. With the 9/11 attacks against the United States by al-Qaida in 2001, the United States immediately moved into Afghanistan. On comparatively scanty evidence that Iraq was also a threat, it nevertheless chose to do the same there in 2003.

President George W. Bush's speech, delivered on television the day before the Iraq invasion, attempted to justify the action and the widening of the war. Questions existed at the time (and since) as to what extent, if any, Iraq was connected to 9/11. The judgment of history is that the Bush administration pushed for war despite ongoing efforts to prevent it (such as a U.N. weapons inspection team operating in the country) and little clear necessity for it. In fact, the Iraq War turned out to be a debacle. After initial hostilities ended, U.S. military and diplomatic teams undertook a major nation-building effort there that only seemed to make matters worse. The speech reprinted here in many ways represents a tipping point in U.S. policy in that the United States had not been directly attacked by Iraq but felt it incumbent on itself—or at least in the eyes of the Bush administration it did—to launch a "pre-emptive" war.

Author Biography

George W. Bush was the 43rd president of the United States, serving from 2001 to 2009.

Bush is the son of the 41st president, George H.W. Bush. George W. was educated at Yale University. His first foray into politics was assisting his father with his presidential election campaigns. He won election as governor of Texas in 1995 and served as governor there from 1995 to 2000. He defeated Al Gore for the presidency in 2000, after a highly disputed tally of the ballots in Florida. Nationwide, he had lost the popular vote but won in the electoral college. Soon after becoming president, the attack on the World Trade Center and the Pentagon (also known as 9/11) occurred. Bush rallied U.S. and world opinion against Islamic extremism/ terrorism, launching what he called a war on terror. Besides invading Afghanistan and Iraq, Bush, somewhat controversially, detained terrorist suspects at Guanta-namo Bay Naval Base and pushed for passage of the USA PATRIOT Act, which gave the government broad surveillance powers. In domestic policy, Bush passed tax cuts and the No Child Left Behind Act (in education). Since leaving the presidency, Bush has kept a relatively low profile, although he did speak out against the candidacy of Donald J. Trump in order to promote the candidacy of his brother, Jeb Bush in 2016.

HISTORICAL DOCUMENT

My fellow citizens, at this hour, American and coalition forces are in the early stages of military operations to disarm Iraq, to free its people, and to defend the world from grave danger.

On my orders, coalition forces have begun striking selected targets of military importance to undermine Saddam Hussein's ability to wage war. These are opening stages of what will be a broad and concerted campaign. More than 35 countries are giving crucial support, from the use of naval and air bases, to help with intelligence and logistics, to the deployment of combat units. Every nation in this coalition has chosen to bear the duty and share the honor of serving in our common defense.

To all the men and women of the United States Armed Forces now in the Middle East, the peace of a troubled world and the hopes of an oppressed people now depend on you. That trust is well-placed. The enemies you confront will come to know your skill and bravery. The people you liberate will witness the honorable and decent spirit of the American military.

In this conflict, America faces an enemy who has no regard for conventions of war or rules of morality. Saddam Hussein has placed Iraqi troops and equipment in civilian areas, attempting to use innocent men, women, and children as shields for his own military, a final atrocity against his people. I want Americans and all the world to know that coalition forces will make every effort to spare innocent civilians from harm.

A campaign on the harsh terrain of a nation as large as California could be longer and more difficult than some predict. And helping Iraqis achieve a united, stable, and free country will require our sustained commitment. We come to Iraq with respect for its citizens, for their great civilization, and for the religious faiths they practice. We have no ambition in Iraq except to remove a threat and restore control of that country to its own people.

I know that the families of our military are praying that all those who serve will return safely and soon. Millions of Americans are praying with you for the safety of your loved ones and for the protection of the innocent. For your sacrifice, you have the gratitude and respect of the American people. And you can know that our forces will be coming home as soon as their work is done.

Our Nation enters this conflict reluctantly. Yet our purpose is sure. The people of the United States and our friends and allies will not live at the mercy of an outlaw regime that threatens the peace with weapons of mass murder. We will meet that threat now with our Army, Air Force, Navy, Coast Guard, and Marines, so that we do not have to meet it later with armies of firefighters and police and doctors on the streets of our cities.

Now that conflict has come, the only way to limit its duration is to apply decisive force. And I assure you, this will not be a campaign of half measures, and we will accept no outcome but victory.

My fellow citizens, the dangers to our country and the world will be overcome. We will pass through this time of peril and carry on the work of peace. We will defend our freedom. We will bring freedom to others, and we will prevail.

May God bless our country and all who defend her.

Document Analysis

The major claims here fall into four related areas. First, Bush argues that the U.S. invasion is justified. Second, he posits that the United States is not alone, but one partner in a coalition. Third, he thanks the American troops (and families) and tells them that their work is justified. Fourth, he argues that the U.S. invasion is aimed to remove a dictator and prevent future harm, particularly to the United States.

There are several different audience groups here, and some are addressed throughout the speech while others are focus on only briefly. The first audience, and one that is addressed throughout, is the American people. They are also the ones formally the focus of the speech. Bush is trying to convince them both that the invasion is necessary and that a quagmire will not be created. The second are the nations who are helping the Americans. While most of the coalition partners aided the U.S. effort for political or diplomatic reasons, they naturally expect to be commended for their contribution.

The third audience group is the U.S. military and those closely affiliated with it. While Bush points out that "I know that the families of our military are praying that all those who serve will return safely and soon. Millions of Americans are praying with you for the safety of your loved ones and for the protection of the innocent," his point is something more. He argues that the invasion is justified as a protective (or preventive) measure. He maintains that if Saddam is not removed, he will be responsible for more terror similar to 9/11—even though 9/11 is not explicitly named; it is implied. He states that Saddam's overthrow will take some effort, but he pledges that enough force will be applied to avoid a quagmire. (Subsequently, the attack was said to have been designed specifically to "shock and awe" the Iraqi regime and its supporters.)

The fourth audience is the Iraqi people. Bush tells them that he respects their faith(s) and only wants to give them the power to rule themselves. In the event, there turned out to be numerous civilian casualties—"collateral damage" was the term later used. The implication is that "regime change," as the need to remove Saddam was called, was more important to the Americans than limiting the use of U.S. weapons to safeguard civilians.

Essential Themes

The speech lays out the belief that the actions the United States was taking were justified and lays out those justifications. Iraq, according to the administration, possessed nuclear, biological, and chemical weapons. The fact that a U.N. weapons inspection team was nearing the end of its survey in Iraq, under strict protocols that applied to Saddam and his regime, is not mentioned by Bush in his speech. (Bush consistently downplayed the effectiveness of the U.N. effort and highlighted instead some questionable findings by U.S. intelligence agencies.) Another thing that he does not say, because he cannot, is that the United Nations, as a body, had authorized the invasion. As a matter of fact, the Bush administration did not press for a U.N. vote on the matter because it knew that France, and probably other nations, would veto the move.

One claim that Bush does make is that Iraq was linked to terrorism. The claim is not made directly, yet terrorist groups are mentioned as wanting to keep Saddam in power. No particular group is named. The vagueness of the claim tends to highlight how speculative the connection between Iraq and terrorist groups was at the time—something that was proved to be patently false later on.

It is notable, too, that nearly a hundred years after the end of World War I, western powers—here, the United States—are claiming the right to shape the destiny of Iraq. While the words may be different, the ideas embedded in the speech are not terribly different from those of the earlier era. The point is clear that, given the right rationale, the Great Powers are free to do as they see fit on the world stage.

—*Scott A. Merriman, PhD*

Bibliography and Additional Reading

Coe, Kevin. "George W. Bush, Television News, and Rationales for the Iraq War." *Journal of Broadcasting & Electronic Media*, vol. 55, no. 3, July 2011, pp. 307-324.

Grossman, Michael Orlov, and Ronald Eric Matthews Jr. *Perspectives on the Legacy of George W. Bush.* London: Cambridge Scholars Publishing, 2009.

Kinzer, Stephen. *Overthrow: America's Century of Regime Change from Hawaii to Iraq.* New York: Times Books/Henry Holt, 2007

Melanson, Richard A. *American Foreign Policy since the Vietnam War: The Search for Consensus from Richard Nixon to George W. Bush.* Armonk, NY: M.E. Sharpe, 2005.

Moens, Alexander. *The Foreign Policy of George W. Bush: Values, Strategy and Loyalty.* Burlington, VT: Ashgate Pub., 2004.

■ Declaration of Abu Musab al-Zarqawi at the Execution of Nicholas Berg

Date: 2004
Author: Abu Musab al-Zarqawi
Geographic region: Middle East
Genre: Speech

Summary Overview

In 2004, the world was introduced to the Islamic State of Iraq and Syria (ISIS) in horrific fashion. The group's de facto leader, going by the alias Abu Musab al-Zarqawi, took a hapless American contractor as a hostage, the electrician Nicholas Berg, and executed him on video by cutting his head off with a knife. The shock of Berg's execution, the brutality of the executioner and his demented speech distorting the history and language of Islam marked a turning point in the U.S. war in Iraq then taking place. From being a war involving the world's major political and military force trying to remake a much-divided Arab state along ethnic or economic lines, the Iraq War became a religious conflict, between Muslim Sunnis and Shiites on the one hand, and between Muslims and a predominantly Christian state and its occupying army on the other.

Al-Zarqawi's goal with ISIS was to re-establish a Muslim caliphate—the successor regime to Muhammad's leadership—and to reunite Muslims in the twenty-first century. Nearly all Muslims despised ISIS and its methods, but there was some sympathy for the project: an organization that united Muslims as a people across borders and boundaries in the face of the modern decadence represented by the west and its influence in world culture. As a result, despite the hatred ISIS inspired, it survived, and after al-Zarqawi's death, briefly thrived as an alternative state in the Muslim Arab Middle East.

Defining Moment

Like all religions, Islam's focus is on peace and concern for one's fellow man. In the Judeo-Christian tradition from which it derives, Islam is a religion whose message is centered around social justice, sharing one's bounty, values and gifts with the people around them: a fitting message from a religion developed in Arabia, a peninsula populated by nomadic tribes that needed to share everything in order to survive.

After Muhammad's death in 632, his closest followers struggled to keep the Muslim community in Arabia together. They chose amongst themselves a successor—caliph, in Arabic—who would continue to spread the recitations (Qur'an) Muhammad received from Allah and keep Muslims united in faith. One way all Arab nomads found unity was in battle; raiding other tribes in a desert wasteland like Arabia was a means of getting the resources necessary to stay alive. So the second caliph, Umar, began to send Muslim armies to raid communities outside Arabia, not to spread the faith but to give his people a focus; the expansion of the Muslim caliphate as an empire was not a Muslim act but a nomadic one. Yet it immediately created problems for the religion, because the caliph was now not just a religious figure—he was an emperor, and rich as well. How could he distribute the bounty, values, and gifts of his wealth and maintain the principles of social justice across such a huge geographic expanse in the seventh century? Over more than a millennium, the caliphate became more and more corrupted by wealth and power until the last man to claim the caliphate—the Ottoman sultan—was deposed by the president of Turkey, Mustafa Kemal Ataturk, after the collapse of the Ottoman Empire in 1924. With that, a quarter of a billion people lost their spiritual center.

Nothing could replace the caliphate as a central focus of proper worship in Sunni Islam—it would be of similar devastation as if the Catholic Church were to lose the papacy at its center, or if Buddhists lost the Dalai Lama and Panchen Lama as leaders. The closest replacement, if one could call it that, was the modern family of monarchs managing the holy cities in Arabia, the Sauds. Saudi Arabia was home to a puritanical version of Sunni Islam called Wahhabism, a sect developed in opposition to the degenerate Ottomans. Disgusted by materialism and idolatry, Wahhabis wanted to live in the manner of the prophet Muhammad himself as he lived in Medina in the seventh century, to avoid modernity as a corrupting influence. In 1926, King Abdul Aziz Saud founded Saudi Arabia as a Wahhabi kingdom with the intention of remaking Arabia in the image of the seventh century, to expose Muslims making the *hajj* to Mecca to the piety of a religious life unspoiled by the modern world. But in 1937, oil was discovered in Arabia, and the Saudi kingdom accepted the wealth oil provided them—and, like the Ottoman sultans, became immediately reviled by pious Muslims for their hypocrisy.

One of these pious Muslims was born in 1957, the seventeenth child of a billionaire Arab construction magnate, Osama bin Laden. Despite his family's close relationship with the Sauds, Osama bin Laden was disgusted with the Saudi royal family's accommodations with Israel and the United States and its inability to take care of poor Muslims in the Arab world. Bin Laden became famous in the Muslim world for supplying and organizing the jihad declared against the Soviet Union's invasion of Afghanistan in the 1980s; he became even more infamous around the world for plotting the destruction of the World Trade Center buildings in New York City on September 11, 2001. Bin Laden's stated long-term goal was to re-establish the caliphate, to wake up Muslims to the real threats to their religion—globalism and world trade—and reunite the Muslim community around a pious religious center.

Bin Laden's jihadist terrorist organization, al-Qaeda, was considered heroic to a tiny disaffected minority in the Sunni Muslim world. Al-Qaeda appeared to be the only group taking the fight to the west, in pursuit of Muslim unity across national borders that divided the world's Muslim population. One such troubled person was Abu Musab al-Zarqawi, a Jordanian terrorist who joined al-Qaeda. In 2003 al-Zarqawi was tracked by the CIA when he moved to Iraq just before the U.S. invasion; his presence there was used falsely as evidence of al-Qaeda's connection with the government of Saddam Hussein. The move to Iraq brought the Bush Administration in the U.S. into the war it wanted with Saddam, and brought al-Zarqawi a notoriety he had so far not earned.

The U.S.-led invasion of Iraq began in March 2003, and the invaders easily destroyed the Iraqi army and toppled Saddam's regime. In assembling a new provisional government, one of the orders issued by the Bush administration's envoy in Iraq, L Paul Bremer, was to dismantle the Iraqi army and government and rid them of all members of Saddam Hussein's political party, the

Ba'ath Party, This threw thousands of innocent people out of work, and made a small percentage of them angry enough to be recruited by al-Zarqawi for his own version of jihad. After launching terrorist attacks on the United Nations headquarters in Baghdad, western embassies and Shiite shrines, al-Zarqawi's forces captured a hostage, Nicholas Berg, and decided to declare their goals on video at Berg's execution.

Author Biography

Abu Musab al-Zarqawi has long been identified by U.S. military intelligence as the hooded figure standing in the middle of the group of jihadists in the video, who read off his speech and then cut off Nicholas Berg's head. Several more videos followed, all attributed to al-Zarqawi and his terrorist group, al-Tawhid wal-Jihad, or Monotheism and Jihad. It is distinctly possible that the identification of the speechmaker is wrong; al-Zarqawi was a short man while the knife-wielder seemed to be of average height, and while the knife is held in the figure's right hand, some people who knew al-Zarqawi claimed he was left-handed. Nevertheless, by all accounts, the sentiment expressed in the speech is purely attributable to al-Zarqawi and his beliefs.

Abu Musab al-Zarqawi was born in 1966 as Ahmad Fadhil Nazal al-Khalayleh, in the Jordanian border town of Zarqa; his alias means "of Zarqa." Zarqa was well-known in Jordan as the home of many fundamentalist Muslim radicals. Al-Khalayleh, on the other hand, was by all accounts a thug, barely literate, a member of street gangs and in trouble often for dealing drugs, bootlegging, and pimping women. In 1989, with a criminal rap sheet that was thirty-seven violations long, al-Khalayleh left Zarqa, likely on the run from the law, to go fight as a jihadist in Afghanistan. There, he took on his alias al-Zarqawi. He proved to be an adept soldier, not talented as a commander but courageous and tough.

Al-Zarqawi also turned his life over to Islam while he was fighting in Afghanistan, to purge himself of the sins his crimes represented. In the process, he became a loose member of Osama bin Laden's jihadist group, al-Qaeda. He made contacts with thousands of warriors from all over the Muslim world in Afghanistan, contacts he would later use to set up his own terrorist organization. The most important of these was Sheikh Abu Muhammad al-Maqdisi, a fundamentalist Muslim cleric from Jordan. Al-Maqdisi taught al-Zarqawi a severe, puritanical form of Sunni Islam similar to Wahhabism, where even Shiite Muslims—a minority who separated from the Muslim community in the 650s over the succession to the caliphate—were considered demonic heretics that needed stamping out. The only countries where Shiite Muslims are in the majority of the population are Iran and Iraq.

Al-Zarqawi and al-Maqdisi returned to Jordan in 1993 and tried to apply al-Qaeda's principles to the establishment of a revolutionary Muslim organization dedicated to jihad in Jordan. They were instead arrested and thrown in prison in 1994 for trying to overthrow the Jordanian monarchy. In prison, al-Zarqawi became a celebrity of sorts, meeting other jihadists sympathetic to Wahhabism; his street-tough lifestyle made him their leader, and he spent five years studying the *Qur'an* and recruiting future soldiers for his terrorist group.

In 1999, al-Zarqawi got out of prison and promptly returned to Afghanistan, where bin Laden's al-Qaeda organization prepared for future attacks on the world in opposition to Muslim unity. Al-Zarqawi shared this goal, with two major differences, which he revealed to bin Laden when the two finally met in 1999. First, al-Zarqawi wanted to carry the fight to Shiite Muslims; bin Laden, whose mother was a Shiite, believed all Muslims should be a part of the unification effort. Second, bin Laden saw the goal of al-Qaeda as preparing the stage for the return of the caliphate, uniting Muslims against the decadence that divided them and then using the resulting consensus to establish a caliphate—a goal he did not expect to see in his lifetime. Al-Zarqawi had no such patience: he wanted to re-establish a caliphate first, and now, and demand that Muslims abandon national differences to submit to its authority. Not surprisingly, the unaccomplished and atavistic al-Zarqawi and the learned and refined bin Laden came away from the meeting despising each other. Nevertheless, al-Zarqawi needed al-Qaeda's money and blessing, and remained a member of the organization all the way until his notoriety was finally established with the execution of Nicholas Berg in 2004.

Bin Laden was disgusted with the Nicholas Berg video; there seemed no theological purpose to such a gruesome execution. In contrast, Al-Zarqawi defined his purpose for the execution in his speech, and the purpose for making such a graphic murder so public was not just theological but strategic. He wanted to attract recruits to join him in a sectarian war with the vast Shiite population in Iraq. By executing an American and continuing attacks on Shiite sites, al-Zarqawi believed the Shiites would turn to the U.S. military occupation for protection and launch their own attacks on Sunni Muslim Iraqis. The attacks would drive Sunnis to turn to al-Qaeda for protection, and al-Qaeda could then take this population as a part of an "Islamic State" beneath an appointed caliph and spread its authority throughout the Muslim world.

Instead of approving of these methods, bin Laden and al-Qaeda demanded that al-Zarqawi stop using the al-Qaeda brand; al-Zarqawi needed to publicize himself and his ideas on his own. His messages in videos electrified a small fundamentalist section of the Muslim world: al-Zarqawi did what Bin Laden merely promised to accomplish in the future. But by exposing his face to cameras and allowing his location to be seen on the internet, al-Zarqawi could be tracked by the CIA. In 2006, an American air strike was called in on al-Zarqawi's hideout, and he was finally killed.

HISTORICAL DOCUMENT

Praise to Allah who honored Islam with His support, humiliated the infidels with His power, controlled everything with His Command, and tricked the infidels. Prayers and peace be upon the one that raised the banner of Islam with his sword.

Nation of Islam, great news! The signs of dawn have begun and the winds of victory are blowing. Allah has granted us a great victory, in one of his battles in Fallujah. Thanks to Allah alone.

Nation of Islam, is there any excuse left to sit idly by? How can a free Muslim sleep soundly while Islam is being slaughtered, its honor bleeding and the images of shame in the news of the satanic abuse of the Muslim men and women in the prison of Abu-Ghraib? Where is your zeal and where is the anger for the religion of Allah? And where is the jealousy over the honor of the Muslims and where is the revenge for the honor of the

Muslim men and women in the prisons of the Crusaders?

As for you, scholars of Islam, it is to Allah that we complain about you. Don't you see that Allah has established the evidence against you by the youth of Islam, who have humiliated the greatest power in history and broken its nose and destroyed its arrogance?

Hasn't the time come for you to learn from them the meaning of reliance on God and to learn from their actions the lessons of sacrifice and forbearance? How long will you remain like the women, knowing no better than to wail, scream and cry?

One scholar appeals to the free people of this world, another begs Kofi Annan, a third seeks help from 'Amr Musa and a fourth calls for peaceful demonstrations, as if they did not hear the words of Allah: "O Messenger, rally the believers to fight!"

Aren't you fed up with the jihad of conferences and the battles of sermons? Has the time not come for you to lift the sword, which the master of the Messengers was sent with?

And we hope that you will not intervene as usual by denouncing what we do to please the Americans. The Prophet, the master of the merciful has ordered to cut off the heads of some of the prisoners of Badr in patience. He is our example and a good role model.

As for you, Bush dog of the Christians, we promise you things that will displease you. With Allah's assistance, hard days are coming to you. You and your soldiers are going to regret the day that you stepped foot in Iraq and dared to violate the Muslims.

Another message for the collaborator and traitor Pervez Musharraf; we say to you, we cannot wait to welcome your soldiers. By Allah, we will target them before the Americans and will avenge the blood of our brothers in Wana and others.

As for you, mothers and wives of the American soldiers, we say to you that we offered the American Administration the chance to exchange this prisoner for some of the prisoners in Abu-Ghraib, but they refused. We say to you, the dignity of the Muslim men and women in the prison of Abu Ghraib and others will be redeemed by blood and souls. You will see nothing from us except corpse after corpse and casket after casket of those slaughtered in this fashion.

"So kill the infidels wherever you see them, take them, sanction them, and await them in every place."

GLOSSARY

jihad: literally, "struggle" in Arabic; the term usually applied to violence conducted in the name of Islam, though it is really meant to apply to the struggle to maintain the faith in all its forms, and defense of the religion should be only a small part of that struggle

infidels: unbelievers

the Crusaders; a pejorative term used by fundamentalist Muslims to talk about western Christians, who tried to retake Jerusalem from the caliphate in the medieval wars known as the Crusades

Document Analysis

Al-Zarqawi, or the hooded figure purported to be al-Zarqawi, opens with the standard praise for Allah, with one difference: he depicts Allah as a military commander, "rais[ing] the banner of Islam with his sword." Such a depiction would immediately signal to his intended audience—disaffected Muslims—that al-Zarqawi intended to carry the same fight to the "infidels" in Iraq. He celebrates the recent uprising in the city of Fallu-

jah against the American occupation, a brutal citywide battle that would not be completely finished for more than a year to follow, and would cost many American soldiers their lives.

Then al-Zarqawi demands that Muslims around the world rise in anger to oppose the Americans, due to the abuses they perpetuated on Iraqi prisoners housed in a military prison in Abu Ghraib, a district in western Baghdad. A month earlier, in April 2004, the world was shocked when pictures of torture and humiliation practiced by American military police on Iraqi prisoners housed in Abu Ghraib came to light.

Al-Zarqawi roars his anger at Muslim clerics who did not join in the war against the United States, claiming that young Muslims had taken up the defense of Islam, and that their actions "have humiliated the greatest power in history and broken its nose and destroyed its arrogance". He asserts that verbal complaints are not enough, and his rhetoric implies that the only appropriate response to Abu Ghraib and the U.S. presence in Iraq is violence and war. He mocks the clerics' efforts as "the jihad of conferences and the battles of sermons": meeting with the United Nations Secretary General Kofi Annan or the president of the Arab League, 'Amr Musa to hope for sanctions against the U.S., which al-Zarqawi implies will never happen. Instead, al-Zarqawi says that Allah would have exhorted Muslims to "rally the believers to fight!" In an ominous display of the distortion of his knowledge, he references the story of the fate of the prisoners taken by Muhammad in the Battle of Badr in 624—the two enemies who led their peoples and armies in opposition to Islam were ordered beheaded by Muhammad, by direction from Allah. Al-Zarqawi has no use for the rest of the story or the relevant passages in the *Qur'an,* which exhort Muslims to treat their captives better than they treat themselves in a show of Muslim generosity.

Al-Zarqawi then makes threats against President Bush and the U.S. forces in Iraq, promising that "you and your soldiers are going to regret the day that you stepped foot in Iraq and dared to violate the Muslims." He also references the Muslim president or Pakistan, Pervez Musharraf, who at that time was launching military attacks on the Pakistani city of Wana, near the Afghan border, because it was allegedly where bin Laden and his al-Qaeda operatives were hiding out from the U.S. invasion of Afghanistan. Al-Zarqawi promises to take vengeance on Pakistani troops before even American troops.

Finally, al-Zarqawi offers an excuse to the mothers and wives of the soldiers he intends to kill, claiming he had asked for a prisoner exchange with "the American Administration"; no one in Baghdad or Washington confirmed any such contact at the time. Then he repeats his intention to avenge the humiliation of Muslims at Abu-Ghraib, and ends with a paraphrased quote from the Qur'an: "So kill the infidels wherever you see them, take them, sanction them, and await them in every place." He does not finish the appropriate passage with the sentence that follows: "But, in case they repent, and keep up the prayer . . . then let them go their way; surely Allah is Ever-Forgiving, Ever-Merciful."

Essential Themes

With Zarqawi dead at last in 2006, the caliphate project appeared to be dead too. In the next year, the Bush administration authorized a U.S. army "surge," flooding Iraq with troops to establish some level of control and peace. The newly elected Iraqi government began to unite Iraqis across ethnic or religious lines—everyone was tired of war. By 2009, al-Zarqawi's branch of al-Qaeda in Iraq, the so-called Islamic State, had only 37 members left alive.

In 2009, however, the Obama administration took office in the United States, with the declared intent of removing American troops from its long-lasting wars in Iraq and Afghanistan. A withdrawal date was set for the beginning of 2012—and no one accounted for those final thirty-seven terrorists in Iraq. One of them was a PhD student in Islamic theology who went by the alias Abu Bakr al-Baghdadi. In 2003, he had been wrongly imprisoned (though not at Abu Ghraib) by American forces because he was assumed to be a terrorist. His time in prison radicalized al-Baghdadi just as it did al-Zarqawi, and when he got out, he joined al-Zarqawi's team. Like al-Zarqawi, al-Baghdadi wanted to reestablish the caliphate, now as opposed to later; unlike Zarqawi, his studies meant that he could use language and traditions that would attract more average Muslims to the cause.

Between 2009 and 2011, Iraq remained quiet, but without interference or attention, al-Baghdadi recruited disaffected Sunni and Iraqi soldiers who were out of work to join the Islamic State that he now led. These recruits were not untrained future suicide bombers—they were soldiers who knew how to occupy and hold territory, and they had American weapons they had attained from the U.S. forces over the previous decade. They would prove to be a much more flexible and powerful group than al-Zarqawi's terrorists, now awaiting their moment to assert themselves.

The moment arrived with the so-called Arab Spring of 2011-2012. Next door in Syria, protestors rose against the most brutal dictator left in the region after Saddam, Bashar al-Assad. Al-Assad had no compunction about putting down his own people in revolt: he simply bombed them, starting in the city of Homs on the Mediterranean coast, thus triggering a civil war. Al-Assad was also a member of a minority Muslim sect, the Alawites, who were associated with the Shiites—which provided al-Baghdadi with the excuse he was looking for to use his forces and invade Syria to protect a frightened and persecuted Sunni majority. In 2014, the Shiite government of Nouri al-Maliki in Iraq launched a crackdown on its dissident Sunni population, thus providing al-Baghdadi's army with another excuse to fight in Iraq. By 2014, the famous black flag of the Islamic State flew over a third of Syria and a third of Iraq, and the army had recruited 3500 Saudis, 5000 French, German and British Muslims, 6000 Tunisians, and 5000 from the republics of the former USSR. While these were formidable numbers for a small army, they amounted to a mere .005% of all Muslims on earth; 60 times as many Americans—0.3%—identified themselves as witches, druids or pagans at the same time, so ISIS' popularity should not be exaggerated. Nevertheless, on July 4, 2014, Abu Bakr al-Baghdadi entered Mosul's grand mosque and announced his claim to the Muslim caliphate. While ISIS has not succeeded in establishing itself as a state, it has certainly attracted more than enough attention to its cause to worry secularists and nationalists around the world.

—*David Simonelli*

Bibliography and Additional Reading

Books

Armstrong, Karen. *Islam: A Short History.* London: Phoenix Press, 2001.

Cockburn, Patrick. *The Age of Jihad: Islamic State and the Great War for the Middle East.* London: Verso 2016.

Filiu, Jean-Pierre. *From Deep State to Islamic State: The Arab Counter-Revolution and Its Jihadi Legacy.* New York: Oxford University Press, 2015.

Juergensmeyer, Mark. *Terror in the Mind of God: The Global Rise of Religious Violence.* Berkeley, CA: University of California Press, 2000.

Lynch, Marc. *The New Arab Wars: Uprisings and Anarchy in the Middle East.* New York: PublicAffairs, 2016.

McCants, William. *The ISIS Apocalypse: The History, Strategy, and Doomsday Vision of the Islamic State.* New York: Picador, 2015.

Moubayed, Sami M. *Under the Black Flag: At the Frontier of the New Jihad.* New York: I.B. Tauris, 2015.

Zepp, Ira G. *A Muslim Primer: Beginner's Guide to Islam.* Westminster, MD: Wakefield Editions, 1992.

Web Sites

"ISIS Fast Facts". *CNN.com* (November 1, 2016) http://www.cnn.com/2014/08/08/world/isis-fast-facts/ [accessed March 14, 2017].

"The Rise of Isis". *Frontline*, October 28, 2014. *PBS.org* http://www.pbs.org/wgbh/frontline/film/rise-of-isis/ [accessed March 14, 2017].

The Noble *Qur'an*. https://quran.com/ [accessed March 14, 2017].

Muir, Jim. "Islamic State Group: The Full Story". *BBC News* (June 20, 2016) http://www.bbc.com/news/ world-middle-east-35695648 [accessed March 14, 2017].

■ U.N. Security Council Resolution 1973 on Libya

Date: March 17, 2011
Author: United Nations Security Council
Geographic region: Middle East, Libya
Genre: Diplomatic resolution

Summary Overview

United Nations (U.N.) Security Council Resolution 1973 was a measure adopted in March of 2011 by the Security Council as a response to the Libyan civil war and the threat to Libya's civilian population. The resolution was proposed by France, Lebanon, and the United Kingdom.

Resolution 1973 formed the basis for military intervention by the Security Council in the Libyan civil war. In early 2011 a wave of popular protest via peaceful demonstrations against entrenched regimes in countries throughout the Middle East and Northern Africa, including Egypt and Tunisia, culminated in transfers of power. However, in Libya an uprising against the four-decade rule of Muammar al-Qaddafi led to a violent civil war. Anti-government rallies were held in Benghazi by protesters angered at the arrest of human rights lawyer, Fethi Tarbel. The protesters demanded Qaddafi step down and for the release of political prisoners. Libyan security forces used water cannons and rubber bullets, resulting in many injuries. The protests intensified and the protesters took control of Benghazi and moved into Tripoli. The Libyan government began using lethal force against the protesters. Security forces and hired mercenaries began firing live ammunition into crowds of protesters. Protesters were also attacked with tanks as well as from the air with warplanes and helicopter gunships. Communication restrictions were put in place including the blocking of the internet and telephone service.

The Libyan government's sudden escalation of violence against the protesters drew international condemnation from foreign governments and international human rights organizations. Some top Libyan officials resigned in protest, including the Libyan ambassador to the United Nations. On February 22, 2011 Qaddafi delivered an angry, inflammatory speech on Libyan state television, refusing to step down and vowing to continue to use violence to remain in power. Attacks against the protesters continued, including the attack of unarmed protesters as they emerged from mosques after Friday prayers. International efforts to intervene were complicated by the number of foreign nationals that remained in Libya. The violence continued to escalate and foreign nationals were evacuated.

The United Nations unanimously approved a measure that included implementing sanctions against the Qaddafi regime, imposing a travel ban and arms embargo, and freezing the Qaddafi family's assets. By February 28, 2011 the United States announced that it had frozen approximately $30 billion in Libyan assets.

Qaddafi invited Western journalists to Tripoli in an attempt to demonstrate that the capitol was under control and that the protests were conducted by a small number of anti-government rebel groups. He asserted that the Western governments were calling for him to step down in order to colonize Libya. However, the condition in Libya worsened and thousands of migrant workers mostly from Egypt and Tunisia began fleeing for the borders. The Libyan government continued its attacks on the rebel forces and was able to maintain control of Tripoli. The forces loyal to Qaddafi began to gain momentum and at an emergency summit on March 11, 2011, the European Union unanimously called for Qaddafi to step down. The international community was divided about using military intervention in Libya. France and the United Kingdom signaled support for intervention while Germany and the United States remained concerned about the long-term consequences of intervention.

On March 15, 2011, pro-Qaddafi Libyan forces launched a heavy attack on the eastern city of Ajdabiya, the last rebel-held city on the way to Benghazi. On March 17, 2011, the U.N. Security Council voted 10-0 with abstentions from Russia, China, Germany, India, and Brazil, to authorize military action, including the imposition of a no-fly zone to protect Libyan civilians. Although all member states were in agreement that the situation in Libya had deteriorated, Germany was concerned that there would be large-scale loss of life and that the Resolution would result in a prolonged military conflict. Brazil felt that a humanitarian intervention in Libya would exacerbate the situation and ultimately cause more harm to the civilians. Russia warned against unpredictable consequences and concern about who would enforce the measures and how enforcement would take place. India was also concerned about implementation and any unintended consequences. China simply disagreed with the resolution and felt that all peaceful means had not been exhausted. Ultimately, the concerns of the five abstaining member states proved largely unfounded were far fewer civilians dying through the implementation than were projected if the U.N. had done nothing. And although not as brief as originally anticipated, the military campaign wound down in just over six months. Moreover, in the end the Libyan people were no longer under the rule of a brutal dictator.

Defining Moment

Resolution 1973 presented a clear instance where the Security Council created a blueprint that authorized all measures necessary to protect Libyan civilians, and an international coalition swiftly and aggressively implemented the mandate created by the Resolution.

Although certain member states expressed hesitation at utilizing force as an intervention during a humanitarian crisis, the member states and later NATO, following the careful language of the Resolution, combined forces to protect Libyan civilians. The additional sanctions including the no-fly zone, freezing of assets and the provision of a panel for oversight of the measures, demonstrated that a Resolution by the U.N. Security Council could effectively and swift address a humanitarian crisis within the permissible bounds of the U.N. Charter.

Author Biography

The U.N. Security Council is comprised of five permanent nation states (China; France; Russia; United Kingdom and the United States) as well as ten nonpermanent members that are elected on a regional basis and serve two-year terms. The Security Council is responsible for maintaining peace and security, accepting new members into the United Nations as well as setting up peacekeeping operations; implementing international sanctions and authorizing military action by issuing resolutions.

HISTORICAL DOCUMENT

The Security Council,

RECALLING its resolution 1970 (2011) of 26 February 2011,

DEPLORING the failure of the Libyan authorities to comply with resolution 1970 (2011),

EXPRESSING grave concern at the deteriorating situation, the escalation of violence, and the heavy civilian casualties,

REITERATING the responsibility of the Libyan authorities to protect the Libyan population and reaffirming that parties to armed conflicts bear the primary responsibility to take all feasible steps to ensure the protection of civilians,

CONDEMNING the gross and systematic violation of human rights, including arbitrary detentions, enforced disappearances, torture and summary executions,

FURTHER CONDEMNING acts of violence and intimidation committed by the Libyan authorities against journalists, media professionals and associated personnel and urging these authorities to comply with their obligations under international humanitarian law as outlined in resolution 1738 (2006),

CONSIDERING that the widespread and systematic attacks currently taking place in the Libyan Arab Jamahiriya against the civilian population may amount to crimes against humanity,

RECALLING paragraph 26 of resolution 1970 (2011) in which the Council expressed its readiness to consider taking additional appropriate measures, as necessary, to facilitate and support the return of humanitarian agencies and make available humanitarian and related assistance in the Libyan Arab Jamahiriya,

EXPRESSING its determination to ensure the protection of civilians and civilian populated areas and the rapid and unimpeded passage of humanitarian assistance and the safety of humanitarian personnel,

RECALLING the condemnation by the League of Arab States, the African Union, and the Secretary General of the Organization of the Islamic Conference of the serious violations of human rights and international humanitarian law that have been and are being committed in the Libyan Arab Jamahiriya,

TAKING NOTE of the final communiqué of the Organisation of the Islamic Conference of 8 March 2011, and the communiqué of the Peace and Security Council of the African Union of 10 March 2011 which established an ad hoc High Level Committee on Libya,

TAKING NOTE ALSO of the decision of the Council of the League of Arab States of 12 March 2011 to call for the imposition of a no-fly zone on Libyan military aviation, and to establish safe areas in places exposed to shelling as a precautionary measure that allows the protection of the Libyan people and foreign nationals residing in the Libyan Arab Jamahiriya,

TAKING NOTE FURTHER of the Secretary-General's call on 16 March 2011 for an immediate cease-fire,

RECALLING its decision to refer the situation in the Libyan Arab Jamahiriya since 15 February 2011 to the Prosecutor of the International Criminal Court, and stressing that those responsible for or complicit in attacks targeting the civilian population, including aerial and naval attacks, must be held to account,

REITERATING its concern at the plight of refugees and foreign workers forced to flee the violence in the Libyan Arab Jamahiriya, welcoming the response of neighbouring States, in particular Tunisia and Egypt, to address the needs of those refugees and foreign workers, and calling on the international community to support those efforts,

DEPLORING the continuing use of mercenaries by the Libyan authorities,

CONSIDERING that the establishment of a ban on all flights in the airspace of the Libyan Arab Jamahiriya constitutes an important element for the protection of civilians as well as the safety of the delivery of humanitarian assistance and a decisive step for the cessation of hostilities in Libya,

EXPRESSING CONCERN also for the safety of foreign nationals and their rights in the Libyan Arab Jamahiriya,

WELCOMING THE APPOINTMENT by the Secretary General of his Special Envoy to Libya, Mr Abdel-Elah Mohamed Al-Khatib and supporting his efforts to find a sustainable and peaceful solution to the crisis in the Libyan Arab Jamahiriya,

REAFFIRMING its strong commitment to the sovereignty, independence, territorial integrity and national unity of the Libyan Arab Jamahiriya,

DETERMINING that the situation in the Libyan Arab Jamahiriya continues to constitute a threat to international peace and security,

ACTING UNDER CHAPTER VII OF THE CHARTER OF THE UNITED NATIONS,

1. Demands the immediate establishment of a cease-fire and a complete end to violence and all attacks against, and abuses of, civilians;

2. Stresses the need to intensify efforts to find a solution to the crisis which responds to the legitimate demands of the Libyan people and notes the decisions of the Secretary-General to send his Special Envoy to Libya and of the Peace and Security Council of the African Union to send its ad hoc High Level Committee to Libya with the aim of facilitating dialogue to lead to the political reforms necessary to find a peaceful and sustainable solution;

3. Demands that the Libyan authorities comply with their obligations under international law, including international humanitarian law, human rights and refugee law and take all measures to protect civilians

and meet their basic needs, and to ensure the rapid and unimpeded passage of humanitarian assistance;

[Protection of civilians]

4. Authorizes Member States that have notified the Secretary-General, acting nationally or through regional organizations or arrangements, and acting in cooperation with the Secretary-General, to take all necessary measures, notwithstanding paragraph 9 of resolution 1970 (2011), to protect civilians and civilian populated areas under threat of attack in the Libyan Arab Jamahiriya, including Benghazi, while excluding a foreign occupation force of any form on any part of Libyan territory, and requests the Member States concerned to inform the Secretary-General immediately of the measures they take pursuant to the authorization conferred by this paragraph which shall be immediately reported to the Security Council;

5. Recognizes the important role of the League of Arab States in matters relating to the maintenance of international peace and security in the region, and bearing in mind Chapter VIII of the Charter of the United Nations, requests the Member States of the League of Arab States to co-operate with other Member States in the implementation of paragraph 4;

[No fly zone]

6. Decides to establish a ban on all flights in the airspace of the Libyan Arab Jamahiriya in order to help protect civilians;

7. Decides further that the ban imposed by paragraph 6 shall not apply to flights whose sole purpose is humanitarian, such as delivering or facilitating the delivery of assistance, including medical supplies, food, humanitarian workers and related assis-

tance, or evacuating foreign nationals from the Libyan Arab Jamahiriya, nor shall it apply to flights authorised by paragraphs 4 or 8, nor other flights which are deemed necessary by States acting under the authorisation conferred in paragraph 8 to be for the benefit of the Libyan people, and that these flights shall be coordinated with any mechanism established under paragraph 8;

8. Authorizes Member States that have notified the Secretary-General and the Secretary-General of the League of Arab States, acting nationally or through regional organizations or arrangements, to take all necessary measures to enforce compliance with the ban on flights imposed by paragraph 6 above, as necessary, and requests the States concerned in cooperation with the League of Arab States to coordinate closely with the Secretary General on the measures they are taking to implement this ban, including by establishing an appropriate mechanism for implementing the provisions of paragraphs 6 and 7 above,

9. Calls upon all Member States, acting nationally or through regional organizations or arrangements, to provide assistance, including any necessary over-flight approvals, for the purposes of implementing paragraphs 4, 6, 7 and 8 above;

10. Requests the Member States concerned to coordinate closely with each other and the Secretary-General on the measures they are taking to implement paragraphs 4, 6, 7 and 8 above, including practical measures for the monitoring and approval of authorised humanitarian or evacuation flights;

11. Decides that the Member States concerned shall inform the Secretary-General and the Secretary-General of the League of Arab States immediately of measures taken in exercise of the authority conferred by paragraph 8 above, including to supply a concept of operations;

12. Requests the Secretary-General to inform the Council immediately of any actions taken by the Member States concerned in exercise of the authority conferred by paragraph 8 above and to report to the Council within 7 days and every month thereafter on the implementation of this resolution, including information on any violations of the flight ban imposed by paragraph 6 above;

Enforcement of the arms embargo

13. Decides that paragraph 11 of resolution 1970 (2011) shall be replaced by the following paragraph : "Calls upon all Member States, in particular States of the region, acting nationally or through regional organisations or arrangements, in order to ensure strict implementation of the arms embargo established by paragraphs 9 and 10 of resolution 1970 (2011), to inspect in their territory, including seaports and airports, and on the high seas, vessels and aircraft bound to or from the Libyan Arab Jamahiriya, if the State concerned has information that provides reasonable grounds to believe that the cargo contains items the supply, sale, transfer or export of which is prohibited by paragraphs 9 or 10 of resolution 1970 (2011) as modified by this resolution, including the provision of armed mercenary personnel, calls upon all flag States of such vessels and aircraft to cooperate with such inspections and authorises Member States to use all measures commensurate to the specific circumstances to carry out such inspections";

14. Requests Member States which are taking action under paragraph 13 above on the high seas to coordinate closely with each other and the Secretary General and further requests the States concerned to inform the Secretary-General and the Committee established pursuant to paragraph 24 of resolution 1970 (2011) ("the Committee") immediately of measures taken in the exercise of the authority conferred by paragraph 13 above;

15. Requires any Member State whether acting nationally or through regional organisations or arrangements, when it undertakes an inspection pursuant to paragraph 13 above, to submit promptly an initial written report to the Committee containing, in particular, explanation of the grounds for the inspection, the results of such inspection, and whether or not cooperation was provided, and, if prohibited items for transfer are found, further requires such Member States to submit to the Committee, at a later stage, a subsequent written report containing relevant details on the inspection, seizure, and disposal, and relevant details of the transfer, including a description of the items, their origin and intended destination, if this information is not in the initial report;

16. Deplores the continuing flows of mercenaries into the Libyan Arab Jamahiriya and calls upon all Member States to comply strictly with their obligations under paragraph 9 of resolution 1970 (2011) to prevent the provision of armed mercenary personnel to the Libyan Arab Jamahiriya;

[Ban on flights]

17. Decides that all States shall deny permission to any aircraft registered in the Libyan Arab Jamahiriya or owned or operated by Libyan nationals or companies to take off from, land in or overfly their territory unless the particular flight has been approved in advance by the Committee, or in the case of an emergency landing;

18. Decides that all States shall deny permission to any aircraft to take off from, land in or overfly their territory, if they have information that provides reasonable grounds to

believe that the aircraft contains items the supply, sale, transfer, or export of which is prohibited by paragraphs 9 and 10 of resolution 1970 (2011) as modified by this resolution, including the provision of armed mercenary personnel, except in the case of an emergency landing;

[Asset freeze]

19. Decides that the asset freeze imposed by paragraph 17, 19, 20 and 21 of resolution 1970 (2011) shall apply to all funds, other financial assets and economic resources which are on their territories, which are owned or controlled, directly or indirectly, by the Libyan authorities, as designated by the Committee, or by individuals or entities acting on their behalf or at their direction, or by entities owned or controlled by them, as designated by the Committee, and decides further that all States shall ensure that any funds, financial assets or economic resources are prevented from being made available by their nationals or by any individuals or entities within their territories, to or for the benefit of the Libyan authorities, as designated by the Committee, or individuals or entities acting on their behalf or at their direction, or entities owned or controlled by them, as designated by the Committee, and directs the Committee to designate such Libyan authorities, individuals or entities within 30 days of the date of the adoption of this resolution and as appropriate thereafter;

20. Affirms its determination to ensure that assets frozen pursuant to paragraph 17 of resolution 1970 (2011) shall, at a later stage, as soon as possible be made available to and for the benefit of the people of the Libyan Arab Jamahiriya;

21. Decides that all States shall require their nationals, persons subject to their jurisdiction and firms incorporated in their territory or subject to their jurisdiction to exercise vigilance when doing business with entities incorporated in the Libyan Arab Jamahiriya or subject to its jurisdiction, and any individuals or entities acting on their behalf or at their direction, and entities owned or controlled by them, if the States have information that provides reasonable grounds to believe that such business could contribute to violence and use of force against civilians;

[Designations]

22. Decides that the individuals listed in Annex I shall be subject to the travel restrictions imposed in paragraphs 15 and 16 of resolution 1970 (2011), and decides further that the individuals and entities listed in Annex II shall be subject to the asset freeze imposed in paragraphs 17, 19, 20 and 21 of resolution 1970 (2011);

23. Decides that the measures specified in paragraphs 15, 16, 17, 19, 20 and 21 of resolution 1970 (2011) shall apply also to individuals and entities determined by the Council or the Committee to have violated the provisions of resolution 1970 (2011), particularly paragraphs 9 and 10 thereof, or to have assisted others in doing so;

Panel of experts

24. Requests the Secretary-General to create for an initial period of one year, in consultation with the Committee, a group of up to eight experts ("Panel of Experts"), under the direction of the Committee to carry out the following tasks:

(a) Assist the Committee in carrying out its mandate as specified in paragraph 24 of resolution 1970 (2011) and this resolution;

(b) Gather, examine and analyse information from States, relevant United Nations bodies, regional organisations and other interested parties regarding the implementation of the measures decided in resolution 1970 (2011) and this resolution, in particular incidents of non-compliance;

(c) Make recommendations on actions the Council, or the Committee or State, may consider to improve implementation of the relevant measures;

(d) Provide to the Council an interim report on its work no later than 90 days after the Panel's appointment, and a final report to the Council no later than 30 days prior to the termination of its mandate with its findings and recommendations;

25. Urges all States, relevant United Nations bodies and other interested parties, to co-operate fully with the Committee and the Panel of Experts, in particular by supplying any information at their disposal on the implementation of the measures decided in resolution 1970 (2011) and this resolution, in particular incidents of non-compliance;

26. Decides that the mandate of the Committee as set out in paragraph 24 of resolution 1970 (2011) shall also apply to the measures decided in this resolution;

27. Decides that all States, including the Libyan Arab Jamahiriya, shall take the necessary measures to ensure that no claim shall lie at the instance of the Libyan authorities, or of any person or body in the Libyan Arab Jamahiriya, or of any person claiming through or for the benefit of any such person or body, in connection with any contract or other transaction where its performance was affected by reason of the measures taken by the Security Council in resolution 1970 (2011), this resolution and related resolutions;

28. Reaffirms its intention to keep the actions of the Libyan authorities under continuous review and underlines its readiness to review at any time the measures imposed by this resolution and resolution 1970 (2011), including by strengthening, suspending or lifting those measures, as appropriate, based on compliance by the Libyan authorities with this resolution and resolution 1970 (2011).

29. Decides to remain actively seized of the matter.

GLOSSARY

United Nations: An international organization formed in 1945 for the purpose of increasing political and economic cooperation among its member countries.

U.N. Security Council: A division of the United Nations comprised of five permanent members (United States, Britain, China, France, and Russia) and ten other rotating members who serves to address issues regarding the maintenance of international peace and security.

U.N. sanctions: After adopting a resolution, the United Nations may implement sanctions, such as arms embargoes, asset freezes or travel bans against a particular country for political reasons and in response to the target country's improper conduct.

U.N. no-fly zone: An area designated by the U.N. over which no aircraft from that country can fly in order to protect civilians or U.N. personnel on the ground.

Document Analysis

Resolution 1973 is written in somewhat broad terms to provide for a wide range of actions, including strikes on air-defense systems and missile attacks from ships with the purpose of averting a bloody rout of rebels by forces which were loyal to Qaddafi. The U.N. emphasized that it was not seeking to divide or dismember Libya but, rather, that the situation in Libya presented "a threat to international peace and security."

Resolution 1973 has several key points. First, it demanded an immediate ceasefire and a complete end to violence and all attacks against Libyan civilians. The overall stated purpose of this provision of the Resolution was to halt the fighting and to achieve a ceasefire. It did not explicitly call for the removal of Qaddafi although there was strong sentiment that Qaddafi should not remain in power and several representatives from member states expressly stated such at the time of the Resolution.

Second, the Resolution also imposed an immediate no-fly zone over Libya to protect Libyan civilians against attacks from pro-Qaddafi forces. The no-fly ban was most discussed before the passage of the Resolution. Military experts that Qaddafi's ground forces were more powerful than his air force. However, it was agreed that a no-fly zone would definitively constrain and most likely halt the use of Qaddafi's air forces. The "ban on all flights" all includes helicopters which are seen as more difficult to control. Thus, the Resolution created a ban on all Libyan designated flights.

Paragraph 4 of Resolution also authorized the taking of "all necessary measures" to protect civilians as well as civilian-populated areas with the exception of a "foreign occupation force." The utilization of the phrase "all necessary measures" indicated the ability to use force to implement the no-fly zone. "All necessary measures" is the language employed by the Security Council to authorize the use of force under Chapter VII, Article 42 of the U.N. Charter. The Resolution authorized states to arm and train the Libyan rebel forces so long as necessary for the protection of the civilian population. It did so by creating an exception to paragraph 9 of Resolution 1970 which required states "to prevent the . . . supply, sale or transfer to the Libyan Arab Jamahiriya . . . of arms and related material of all types . . . and technical assistance, training, financial or other assistance, related to military activities . . ." Thus, in paragraph 4 of the Resolution, the Security Council authorized states to take all necessary measures to protect civilians "notwithstanding paragraph 9 of resolution 1970 (2011)." Thus, it created an exception to the paragraph 9

arms embargo for measures that were necessary to protect civilians, including arming and training civilians to protect themselves. The U.S. was concerned that this created a blanket exception to the arms embargo. France was the first and only NATO leader to confirm that it actually provided weapons to the Libyan opposition.

The Resolution also allowed states flexibility of putting limited foreign intelligence and military personnel on the ground in Libya so long as they did not constitute a "foreign occupation force of any form on any part of Libyan territory." Thus, it did not prevent any "boots on the ground" but, rather, any "occupying force" which, under the Hague Convention IV, a territory is considered to be occupied when it is placed under the actual authority of the foreign, hostile army.

It strengthened the already existing arms embargo with particular enforcement against mercenaries by allowing for forcible inspections of all ships and planes entering and leaving Libya. The Resolution also imposed a freeze on all assets owned by Libyan authorities and reaffirmed that those assets should be used to benefit the Libyan civilian population. Finally, the Resolution also established a panel of experts who would be charged with monitoring and promoting the implementation of sanctions.

Essential Impact

Proponents of the Resolution have argued that it provided an effective blueprint for effective humanitarian intervention. The Resolution was characterized by swift action by the Security Council to authorize military intervention when diplomacy appeared to be futile and was drafted utilizing language that provided the mandate necessary for an immediate implementation by an international coalition. Others have argued that although Resolution 1973 was a seminal act in its time, other countries have engaged in equally offensive conduct with the Security Council being slow to act.

However, it took less than a month for the Security Council to authorize the use of force to protect the civilians in Libya. Less than one month after Qaddafi first ordered helicopters and snipers to kill protesters, the Security Council authorized the use of force to protect those civilians. Just two days after the Resolution was adopted, French planes attacked Qaddafi's forces advancing on Benghazi and the U.S. and U.K. launched over 110 cruise missiles into Libya. In less than two weeks after the Resolution, NATO assumed full responsibility for the mission in Libya and conducted over 9,000 strike sorties in six months.

Before that time, the Security Council had rarely responded so quickly in an attempt to stop a humanitarian crisis. In Bosnia, over a year had passed from the time forces fired on peaceful civilian demonstrators in Sarajevo until the Security Council authorized the use of force to deter attacks.

The immediate and aggressive implementation of "all necessary measures" was a dramatic shift from the slow moving response to attacks on civilians in other instances. Unlike in other conflicts where use of military force was authorized by rarely used, Resolution 1973 was swiftly put into action to protect Libyan civilians on the ground.

—*Michelle McBride Simonelli, JD*

Bibliography

Bellamy, AJ "Libya and the Responsibility to Protect: The Exception and the Norm" *Ethics and International Affairs,* 25(3) (2011): 263-269.

Gifkins, J. "R2P in the U.N. Security Council: Darfur, Libya and Beyond," *Cooperation and Conflict,* 51(2) (2016): 157-158.

S.C. Res. 1970, ¶¶ 1-23, U.N. Doc. S/RES/1970 (Feb. 26, 2011).

Thakur, R. "R2P after Libya and Syria: Engaging Emerging Powers," *The Washington Quarterly,* 36:2 (2013): 61-76.

Wheeler, NJ. *Saving Strangers: Humanitarian Intervention in International Society.* Oxford: Oxford University Press, 2000.

■ U.N. Report on the Alleged Use of Chemical Weapons in the Ghouta Area of Damascus on 21 August 2013

Date: September 13, 2013
Author: United Nations Mission to Investigate Alleged Uses of Chemical Weapons in the Syrian Arab Republic (Dr. Ake Sellstrom, Head of Mission)
Geographic region: Damascus
Genre: International government report

Summary Overview

On the morning of August 21, 2013, a series of rockets was fired into the neighborhoods of Eastern and Western Ghouta, a pair of towns outside Damascus in Syria. The towns were considered strongholds of rebel groups looking to oust Syrian president Bashar al-Assad, whose dictatorship was a continuation of his father's rule since 1971 and had been deemed as comparatively brutal as that of Saddam Hussein, his one-time next-door neighbor in Iraq. Like Saddam, Assad had long been thought to maintain chemical weapons in his military arsenal, and the attacks on Ghouta were believed to confirm it. Hundreds of people were killed, combatants and non-combatants, men, women and especially children.

The United Nations' Secretary-General, Ban Ki-moon, had already assigned a team of experts representing the World Health Organization (WHO) and the Organization for the Prohibition of Chemical Weapons (OPCW) to go to Damascus and investigate claims that the Syrian government had launched chemical weapons earlier at another site. He reassigned the team to look into the atrocities at Ghouta, and the team assembled a report, the U.N. Report on the Alleged Use of Chemical Weapons in the Ghouta Area of Damascus on 21 August 2013, delivered three weeks later and released to the public on September 16, 2018. The team concluded that Assad's forces had fired the nerve gas sarin into Ghouta, regardless of Assad's denials of responsibility. The report focused international attention on the Syrian conflict, which would become, along with the rise of the Islamic State, a major focus of international rivalries and tensions in the next five years.

Defining Moment

Syria's borders were drawn as a French mandate newly independent of the Ottoman Empire after 1919. Its people were largely impoverished and conflicted by ethnicity and religion, a hodgepodge of Arab-speaking Assyrians, Kurds and Armenians, religiously split between Sunni and Shia Muslims, Christians and some smaller religious sects combining the beliefs of several religions, even including the polytheistic beliefs of the original Assyrian Empire that had once dominated the region. Its people united only in their hatred of French rule—once the colonial period ended for good after the Second World War, Syrians set upon each other, holding coups d'état and counter-coups regularly until 1970, when Syria's Minister of Defense, Hafez al-Assad, took control permanently.

Assad was an Alawi Shia Muslim, a religious sect that combined Shia Islam with the Christian Holy Trinity. More important than its theology was the fact that Alawis, representing about a tenth of the Syrian population, were generally poor and were perceived in Syria as deserving of little respect. Upon assuming his dictatorship, Assad allowed Sunnis in Syria to achieve high political position in the government, but Alawis retained the highest positions in the military, the police, and the intelligence community in Syria. Assad cultivated a cult of personality and destroyed his opposition; when a militant sect of the Muslim Brotherhood challenged his rule with guerrilla attacks and an assassination attempt, he besieged their home city of Hama and massacred thousands of its citizens, regardless of their support for the Muslim Brotherhood or not. By the time he died in 2000, Hafez al-Assad had solidified his total control over Syria and its many ethnic and religious divisions. His son Bashar al-Assad succeeded him, and though he did not have to assert his power over the Syrian people as his father had, there was little question that the Assad family and their Alawi brethren were the dominant power in Syria for the next decade.

Then came the Arab Spring. Like several other Arab nations, Syrians in the southern city of Deraa launched a peaceful series of street demonstrations against Bashar al-Assad in 2011, in defiance of the Assad regime's corruption, a poor economy, and a lack of political freedom. Unlike in other Arab states, Assad had no problem calling on his army to brutally crush the demonstrators—the perception of his supporters was that if Alawis did not maintain power in Syria, they would be reduced in power to the extent that they might be slaughtered themselves. The demonstrations spread from Deraa to other cities, while Assad claimed it to be an incidence of "foreign-backed terrorism" and demanded even more reprisals. Instead of overthrowing their government as in Egypt or Tunisia, Syrians found their state collapsing into civil war—a civil war that in some respects had been brewing between the country's disparate peoples since its foundation.

The Syrian army concentrated its attacks on Sunni strongholds of rebellion around Syria, which were mostly near major cities. One such area was Khan al-Assal outside the northwestern city of Aleppo. In March 2013, rockets containing sarin gas, a nerve agent, landed in the city, killing and injuring about a hundred soldiers and civilians in a government-held sector of Khan al-Assal. No one seemed certain who had launched the attack, but there was already much evidence that another four sarin gas attacks had occurred already in the civil war.

Outside Assad's capital of Damascus, the suburbs of Eastern and Western Ghouta were full of Sunni rebels and sat around major roadways connecting Damascus with the rest of Syria. The civil war was therefore most intense around the Ghouta area, and in early August 2013, Assad's forces launched an offensive to drive the rebel opposition out of the area. On August 21, 2013, at 2:30 in the morning, somewhere between eight and twelve rockets fell in Eastern Ghouta within a 500-meter radius of each other. Another seven rockets were launched into Western Ghouta at 5:00 am. According to eyewitnesses and survivors, the rockets emitted a poisonous gas that had people writhing in pain—their eyes tearing, mouths and noses frothing—before thousands collapsed and hundreds died.

Just two days earlier, United Nations agents from the World Health Organization (WHO) and the Organization for the Prohibition of Chemical Weapons (OPCW) had arrived in Damascus, expecting to travel to Aleppo to investigate the alleged chemical weapons attack at Khan al-Assal from back in March. Immediately, the United Nations Secretary-General,

Ban Ki-moon, called for a ceasefire in the war and ordered the investigators to stay in Damascus to look into the attacks at Ghouta. Even then, the U.N. team was fired on by snipers and experienced mortar attacks as they tried to assess what had happened at Ghouta. Nevertheless, since the delivery system was the same as at Khan al-Assal and there was little doubt from anyone surrounding the area that Assad's army had launched the attack, the investigation went quickly. In a matter of five and a half total hours, the team inspected the area, interviewed survivors, and took samples to determine if sarin gas had indeed been used as a weapon in Ghouta. Three weeks later, their report was issued, detailing the worst atrocity of the Syrian Civil War and prompting shock in the international community.

Author Biography

The U.N. Mission's report was a collaboration between scientists and investigators for the U.N., the Organization for the Prohibition of Chemical Weapons and the World Health Organization. Though the precise author of the report is difficult to assess, the writer was certainly transcribing the collective thoughts and findings of the three leaders of the Mission—Dr. Ake Sellstrom, the head of the Mission; Scott Cairns, the head of the OPCW component; and Dr. Maurizio Barbeschi, the head of the WHO component. Sellstrom was a renowned Swedish expert on chemical warfare; Cairns was a chemist and munitions expert from the University of Manitoba; and Barbeschi was a chemist serving with WHO's World Health Emergencies Program.

Assad's regime had requested the initial U.N. investigation into the Khan al-Assal attack, blaming it on rebel forces in the area. Sellstrom's group was sent to investigate, without having a mandate to determine who the perpetrators of the attack were supposed to be, but they were also supposed to investigate other allegations of the use of chemical weapons in Syria as well. This apparently annoyed Assad, since a whole series of complications arose before the U.N. Mission was cleared for entry into Syria, five months after the attack on Khan al-Assal. Two days after their arrival, on August 21, 2013, the U.N. team watched from the balcony of their hotel in Damascus as rockets rained down on the suburb of Ghouta to their north—it is likely that they actually watched the chemical weapons attack occur in real time. Secretary-General Ban reached the team right away and ordered them to move their investigation to Ghouta. Assad's government again tried to delay the investigation and was admonished by the U.N. to adhere to a ceasefire so the Mission could begin its work.

While the Mission took evidence, its investigators noticed people sneaking around the neighborhoods, apparently carrying munitions similar to those of the rockets dropped on Ghouta. Eventually, the U.N. investigators had to be protected by a rebel commander so as not to be shot at and to protect witnesses during their investigations.

HISTORICAL DOCUMENT

I. Terms of Reference

1. The Secretary-General decided to establish the U.N. Mission to Investigate Allegations of the Use of Chemical Weapons in the Syrian Arab Republic based on his authority under General Assembly resolution 42/37C and Security Council 620 (1988). The purpose of this Mission is to ascertain the facts related to the allegations of use of chemical weapons and to gather relevant data and undertake the necessary analyses for this purpose and to deliver a report to the Secretary-General.

2. For the purpose of ascertaining the facts related to the allegations of use of chemical weapons, gathering relevant data and undertaking the necessary analyses, the Secretary-General has requested the Organisation for the Prohibition of Chemical Weapons ("OPCW") to put its resources at his disposal, including providing a team of experts to conduct fact-finding activities. The Secretary-General has also requested the World Health Organization ("WHO") to provide technical support in assessing the public health, clinical and event-specific health aspects of the allegations that have been brought to his attention.

3. The U.N. Mission has conducted its investigation and all related activities in accordance with the terms of reference issued by the Secretary-General to the U.N. Mission including the above provisions as well as others on cooperation, methods of work and scope and reporting. As such, the terms of reference applied in respect of its investigation of the Ghouta allegations on which this report is submitted without prejudice to the continuing investigation of, and final report on, all allegations involving the use of chemical weapons in the Syrian Arab Republic.

4. In discharging its mandate, the Mission was guided by the United Nations Guidelines and Procedures for the timely and efficient investigation of reports of the possible use of chemical and bacteriological (biological) or toxin weapons (A/44/561) and, as appropriate and to the extent applicable, the OPCW provisions as identified in Article I(5)(a) of the Supplementary Arrangement to the Agreement concerning the Relationship between the United Nations and the Organization for the Prohibition of Chemical Weapons. . . .

II. Methodological Considerations

6. In its investigation of the alleged use of chemical weapons in the Ghouta area of Damascus on 21 August 2013, the Mission visited Moadamiyah on 26 August 2013 and Ein Tarma and Zamalka on 28-29 August. During its on-site visits, the U.N. Mission carried out the following activities:

- Interviews with survivors and other witnesses;
- Documentation of munitions and their sub-components;
- Collection of environmental samples for subsequent analysis;

- Assessment of symptoms of survivors;
- Collection of hair, urine and blood samples for subsequent analysis;

7. Doing so, the Mission adhered to the most stringent protocols available for such an investigation. Key to investigation methods of alleged use of chemical weapons are concepts like traceability, documentation, use of standardized and recognized procedures as well as relevant and up-to-date training of inspectors.

8. Traceability means that all processes and procedures are recorded and continuity is maintained for transparency and to withstand future scrutiny.

9. For example, the chain of custody procedures for sampling involved the following: The retrieval of samples is recorded and witnessed, samples are sealed, detailed documentation is prepared, transported to the preparatory laboratory under supervision of the members of the Mission, seals are confirmed and then broken, and the samples are representatively subdivided. The re-sealed samples are then distributed to the OPCW-designated laboratories with guidance documents, again, under the same supervision. The laboratories conduct their activities using standardized procedures (including quality assurance/quality control checks) for receiving, storing, and analyzing samples. The results are then returned under supervision to the investigation Mission for review. Each transfer of material is accompanied by handover receipts.

10. All information received, be it witness statements, pictures, videos, audios or patient records and other documentation, is recorded and registered for filing and archiving with the United Nations.

11. Methods for interviews, sampling, and documentation follow well established standard operating procedures (SOPs), developed and enforced by the OPCW and the WHO and in accordance with the Guidelines.

12. Mission members are regularly trained and periodically updated on aspects of their respective specializations, including risk assessments, epidemiology, sampling, scene assessment, acquisition and processing of bio-medical samples, the performance of interviews, munition designs, unexploded ordnances, epidemiology as well as safety and security.

13. The selection process used was designed to primarily identify survivors who had severe clinical presentations, since these were also expected to have had significant exposure to the chemical agent. The ability to provide a sound history of the event and identify the alleged impact sites was also considered in selecting survivors.

14. The selection process was guided by a standardized checklist that aimed to identify individuals who either demonstrated moderate to severe symptoms and signs or were able to provide a clear and detailed history of the event. These survivors were requested to present to the local hospital on the day of the field visit to meet with the investigation Mission. Physicians at Zamalka were also asked to provide a purposive sample of eight medical records of patients with significant symptoms and signs.

III. Narrative and Results of the Mission

15. Having arrived in the Syrian Arab Republic on 18 August 2013, we were in Damascus on the 21 August preparing to conduct on-site inspections in connection with our investigation into the allegations concerning the use of chemical weapons in Khan al-Assal and in Sheik Maqsood and Saraqueb. Based on several reports of allegations on the use of chemical weapons in the Ghouta area of Damascus on 21 August 2013, you instructed us to focus our investigation efforts on the Ghouta allegations. We, therefore, proceeded to conduct on-site inspections in Moadamiyah in

West Ghouta and Ein Tarma and Zamalka in East Ghouta.

16. Pursuant to the joint understanding reached with the Syrian Government and separate arrangements agreed on an ad-hoc basis with the other parties to the conflict, a temporary ceasefire was effectively in place for five hours daily between 26-29 August.

17. The planning of this Mission was therefore complex and highly delicate. The time window for operations was determined by actual hours of access. The route of entry into the areas remained uncertain until the final moments. Finally, the understanding of what the Mission could be expected to find once in opposition-controlled area was also uncertain. Crucial elements for the planning, such as the number of patients affected or the surface area covered by the attacks remained undefined until the actual arrival of the Mission on the affected sites. . . .

18. On 26 August, the Mission visited Moadamiyah of West Ghouta for two hours. On 28-29 August the Mission visited Zamalka and Ein Tarma of East Ghouta for a total time of five and a half hours. In spite of the imposed time constraints, and repeated threats of harm, including an actual attack on the convoy by an unidentified sniper on 26 August, the Mission was nonetheless able to gather a considerable amount of information and to collect the necessary amount of samples.

19. The Mission was also able to collect primary statements from more than fifty exposed survivors including patients, health workers and first-responders. Based on these statements and the information gathered from various reports, the surface-to-surface rockets impacted in the early morning hours of 21 August.

20. Survivors reported an attack with shelling, followed by the onset of a common range of symptoms, including shortness of breath, disorientation, rhinorrhea (runny nose), eye irritation, blurred vision, nausea, vomiting, general weakness, and eventual loss of consciousness. Those who went to assist other community members described seeing a large number of individuals lying on the ground, many of whom were deceased or unconscious. These individuals reported observing labored breathing and excessive salivation among a large proportion of the survivors. Several of these "first responders" also became ill, with one describing the onset of blurred vision, generalized weakness, shaking, a sensation of impending doom, followed by fainting.

21. Nine nurses and seven treating physicians were interviewed by the Mission. Most were at their respective homes at the time of incident, with several responding immediately to assist exposed individuals at the site of the incident. Those clinicians who responded in the field described seeing a large number of ill or deceased persons lying in the streets without external signs of injury. Most survivors were described as being unconscious, with many demonstrating laboured breathing. The responders attempted to assist the survivors through the provision of first aid, decontamination with water where possible, and transfer to the nearest hospital by whatever means possible—usually by private car.

Weather conditions in Damascus on 21 August:

22. Weather information from Damascus on the morning of 21 August shows a falling temperature between 0200h and 0500h in the morning (Worldweatheronline.com). This means that the air is not moving from the ground upwards, but rather the opposite. Chemical weapons use in such meteorological conditions maximizes their potential impact as the heavy gas can stay close to the ground and penetrate into lower levels of buildings and constructions where many people were seeking shelter.

Information about munitions:

23. Information gathered about the delivery systems used was essential for the investigation. Indeed, several surface to surface rockets capable of delivering significant chemical payloads were identified and recorded at the investigated sites. These were carefully measured, photographed and sampled. Samples later confirmed to contain Sarin were recovered from a majority of the rockets or rocket fragments. . . .

Information concerning environmental samples:

24. In total, 30 environmental samples were recovered during the investigation. The samples were taken from impact sites and surrounding areas   . . . . Samples were subsequently processed and sent for analysis. According to the reports received from the OPCW-designated laboratories, the presence of Sarin, its degradation and/ or production by-products were observed in a majority of the samples. . . .

Information concerning symptoms:

25. The Mission requested to see 80 survivors who met the criteria established by the Mission. Of the 80 presented the Mission selected 36 who were diagnosed by the medical experts of the Mission. Patients clearly showed symptoms, such as: loss of consciousness (78%), shortness of breath (61%), blurred vision (42%), eye irritation/ inflammation (22%), excessive salivation (22%), vomiting (22%), and convulsions/ seizures (19%). These symptoms are consistent with an organophosphate intoxication. . . .

Information concerning bio-medical samples:

26. Blood, urine and hair samples were withdrawn from 34 of the 36 patients selected by the Mission who had signs of intoxication. The positive blood and urine specimens provide definitive evidence of exposure to Sarin by almost all of the survivors assessed by the Mission. These results are corroborated by the clinical assessments, which documented symptoms and signs that are consistent with nerve agent exposure, including shortness of breath, eye irritation, excessive salivation, convulsions, confusion/disorientation, and miosis. The findings of the clinical assessments were consistent with information derived from both the interviews with clinicians and the review of medical records, which each reported symptoms and signs consistent with nerve agent exposure. . . .

Conclusions

27. On the basis of the evidence obtained during our investigation of the Ghouta incident, the conclusion is that, on 21 August 2013, chemical weapons have been used in the ongoing conflict between the parties in the Syrian Arab Republic, also against civilians, including children, on a relatively large scale.

28. In particular, the environmental, chemical and medical samples we have collected provide clear and convincing evidence that surface-to-surface rockets containing the nerve agent Sarin were used in Ein Tarma, Moadamiyah and Zamalka in the Ghouta area of Damascus.

29. The facts supporting this conclusion are:

- Impacted and exploded surface-to-surface rockets, capable to carry a chemical payload, were found to contain Sarin.
- Close to the rocket impact sites, in the area where patients were affected, the environment was found to be contaminated by Sarin.

- Over fifty interviews given by survivors and health care workers provided ample corroboration of the medical and scientific results.
- A number of patients/survivors were clearly diagnosed as intoxicated by an organophosphorous compound.

- Blood and urine samples from the same patients were found positive for Sarin and Sarin signatures.

30. This result leaves us with the deepest concern.

GLOSSARY

organophosphates: chemical compounds found in insecticides and herbicides, toxic to humans in that they induce attacks on the nervous system

miosis: excessive constriction of the pupil of the eye, the opposite of dilation

Document Analysis

In analyzing the U.N. Mission's report on the use of chemical weapons in Syria, it is important to note that the Mission was not expected to determine, and did not undertake to determine, who was the perpetrator that launched rockets containing sarin gas at Ghouta. To do so might have brought violence down on the Mission itself, and it would have made it extremely unlikely that future missions would be allowed into Syria to keep tabs on the conduct of the war. Even in later interviews, the three leaders of the Mission did not speculate on who launched the rockets, though interviewers prompted them numerous times to do so. Nevertheless, as the interviewers noted, there were traces of other gases and compounds derived from the rockets that the Mission found chemically attached to evidence of the presence of sarin gas that pointed the finger at the Syrian government's likelihood as the perpetrator, and Sellstrom, Cairns and Barbeschi each acknowledged the existence of that evidence in the interviews. The report itself, however, does nothing whatsoever to acknowledge a perpetrator, only the existence of evidence that sarin gas had been used as a weapon at Ghouta.

The Mission opens its report with its terms of reference. Back in 1988, Saddam Hussein of Iraq had dropped chemical weapons bombs on the Iraqi Kurdish town of Halabja, simply as a test of their effectiveness; he had earlier used them liberally against Iranian troops during the Iran-Iraq War. Therefore, the U.N. Security Council passed a resolution, number 620, that encour-

aged the U.N. Secretary-General to investigate allegations concerning the possible use of chemical weapons and to take appropriate actions if positive evidence of such use was identified. The attack on Eastern Ghouta was considered the worst chemical weapons attack since the time of Halabja and the passage of the resolution, so this sort of Mission had been established specifically on the resolution's terms. The U.N. requested the help of the OPCW and WHO, who were to investigate the evidence at Ghouta and move on to other reports at other locations without prejudice.

Next, the Mission detailed its methods for obtaining the evidence. It conducted interviews; documented evidence of weapons used in the area; collected environmental samples; assessed the symptoms of survivors of the attacks; and took samples of hair, urine, and blood from survivors as further potential evidence. They detailed the means of obtaining samples and the procedures to make sure they remained uncontaminated before they were processed and assessed in laboratories, and recorded the evidence through "witness statements, pictures, videos, audios or patient records and other documentation." The Mission described their own expertise and the standard operating procedures under which they were expected to operate and noted the definition of a "survivor" as someone "who either demonstrated moderate to severe symptoms and signs or were able to provide a clear and detailed history of the event. These survivors were requested to present to the local hospital on the day of the field visit to meet with the investigation Mission", at Zamalka, a town near Ghouta where the U.N. Mission set up its investigation headquarters.

There follows a narrative of the history of the Mission and its investigation. Upon arriving in Syria on August 18, 2013, they were to investigate chemical attacks at Khan al-Assal, Sheik Maqsood and Saraqueb, but the investigation changed focus to Ghouta just three days later. A temporary ceasefire went into effect for five hours a day for three days between the twenty-sixth and twenty-ninth of August, giving the Mission very little time to determine logistics such as how it would enter the area, who controlled the area surrounding Ghouta, where they could find survivors and the surface area in which the attack had taken place. Yet "[i]n spite of the imposed time constraints, and repeated threats of harm, including an actual attack on the convoy by an unidentified sniper on 26 August, the Mission was nonetheless able to gather a considerable amount of information and to collect the necessary amount of samples" and fifty survivor statements.

The Mission's report of the attack itself is harrowing. Rockets had landed early in the morning of August 21; people on the scene found themselves experiencing "shortness of breath, disorientation, rhinorrhea (runny nose), eye irritation, blurred vision, nausea, vomiting, general weakness, and eventual loss of consciousness ... [as well as] labored breathing and excessive salivation." Thousands lost consciousness, and many of those people died as well. First responders, nurses and doctors also reported experiencing the symptoms themselves, while their patients often should no externals signs of being hurt by the rockets—bruises, lacerated skin and bleeding, shrapnel or other foreign objects in their skin, etc. There were so many victims that private cars had to be commandeered by ambulances to get them to hospitals.

Conditions were ripe for a chemical weapons attack, according to the information the Mission found in the area. Weather reports saw a temperature drop between 2:00 and 5:00 am, thus allowing poisonous gases to travel close to the ground before dissipating. Rocket shell fragments were confirmed to contain sarin, and environmental samples produced the same evidence. The symptoms of survivors were consistent with what was known of "an organophosphate intoxication," a toxic nerve attack. Blood, urine, and hair samples identified the nerve agent present as sarin gas. Therefore, "[o]n

the basis of the evidence obtained during our investigation of the Ghouta incident, the conclusion is that, on 21 August 2013, chemical weapons [were] used in the ongoing conflict between the parties in the Syrian Arab Republic, also against civilians, including children, on a relatively large scale. . . . This result leaves us with the deepest concern."

Essential Themes

The report came out three days after being accepted at the U.N.; Ban Ki-Moon said its findings presented "overwhelming and indisputable evidence that a majority of the rockets or rocket fragments recovered were found to be carrying sarin." The international community was mostly horrified. The Ghouta attack was the first (and unfortunately, not the last) incident that exposed the horrific nature of the Syrian civil war, and tacitly, the depravity of the Assad regime. The OPCW would win the Nobel Peace Prize for its work at Ghouta.

Crucially, however, not every power denounced Bashar al-Assad. The Russian government dismissed the Mission report, saying that they believed that the opposition forces had launched the sarin gas attack because the serial numbers on the rockets were from old weapons produced in the Soviet Union in the 1960s and abandoned by the Syrian government. Though most members of the United Nations dismissed such objections, the idea that the Russians supported Assad's regime seemed to give pause to the international community in crafting a response to the attacks. The Obama administration in the U.S. had hinted at military retaliation if Assad was found likely to have used chemical weapons on his own people, but instead, the U.S. negotiated through the Russians to have Assad surrender his chemical weapons arsenal to the U.N.'s inspectors.

Since 2013, the Syrian Civil War has only gotten more complicated. The chaos in Syria briefly allowed the Islamic State to flourish, distracting American and European attentions from the war itself. The Kurdish peoples in northeastern Syria attracted international attention to their cause by warring with ISIS using American weapons, but also destabilized the borders between Syria, Turkey, Iraq, and Iran as they sought autonomy from those states. The Russians and Iranians continued to support Assad, Russia through air strikes on rebel strongholds, Iran with troops. The rebels received sympathy—but not soldiers—from the American, Turkish and Saudi Arabian governments, but each of these allies seemed more concerned to prevent the spread of ISIS than to stop the civil war. Worse, by 2018, the Turks concentrated mostly on crushing Kurdish support for autonomy within Turkish borders, as opposed to stopping the Assad regime from killing its own people.

Between them all, the U.N. was able to document approximately 400,000 people dead or missing in the conflict, with another 100,000 impossible to document—meaning that 3% of the Syrian population had died in the war, let alone been injured or had their lives ruined. At least six million more fled the country as refugees, some to die trying to escape their homeland under dangerous circumstances. Another six million were rendered homeless.

—*Michelle McBride Simonelli, JD*

Bibliography and Additional Reading

Books

Harris, William. *Quicksilver War: Syria, Iraq and the Spiral of Conflict*. London: Hurst & Company, 2018.

Van Dam, Nikolaos. *Destroying a Nation: The Civil War in Syria*. London: I.B. Tauris, 2017.

Saleh, Yassin al-Haj. *The Impossible Revolution: Making Sense of the Syrian Tragedy*. London: Hurst & Co., 2017.

Di Giovanni, Janine. The Morning They Came for Us: Dispatches from Syria. New York: Liveright Publishing Corporation, 2017.

Websites

Beauchamp, Zack, editor. "The Syria War: A History". *Vox* (September 21, 2015) https://www.vox.com/cards/syrian-refugees-war-assad/syria-chemical-weapons

Rodgers, Lucy, David Gritten, James Offer, and Patrick Asare. "Syria: The Story of the Conflict". *BBC News* (March 11, 2016) http://www.bbc.com/news/world-middle-east-26116868 [accessed March 18, 2018].

"Syria's Civil War Explained from the Beginning." *Al Jazeera* (March 3, 2018) https://www.aljazeera.com/news/2016/05/syria-civil-war-explained-160505084119966.html [accessed March 18, 2018].

"Attacks on Ghouta: Analysis of Alleged Use of Chemical Weapons in Syria". *Human Rights Watch* (September 10, 2013) https://www.hrw.org/report/2013/09/10/attacks-ghouta/analysis-alleged-use-chemical-weapons-syria [accessed March 18, 2018].

■ Hassan Rouhani's Address Before the U.N. General Assembly

Date: September 25, 2014
Author: President Hassan Rouhani
Geographic region: Islamic Republic of Iran
Genre: Speech

Summary Overview

In 2014, Iran was engaged in negotiations with the world's major powers to settle issues surrounding Iran's ongoing nuclear-development program, a program that Iranians across the political spectrum supported but outside powers viewed as a threat. Iran was also engaged in supporting Shiites (Shias) in conflicts in several countries across the Middle East. Again, Iranians viewed this as a largely defensive or protective action, but outsiders saw it as aggressive.

Defining Moment

Following heightened tensions between Iran and the West under President Mahmoud Ahmadinejad, who had close ties to the Islamic Revolutionary Guard Corps, the election in 2013 of Hassan Rouhani, a moderate cleric with a Western education, created an opportunity for improved relations between the Islamic Republic and the outside world. In his 2014 address to the General Assembly of the United Nations, outlining his hopes for the future, Rouhani hinted at his strategy for Iranian foreign policy and alluded to the contradictions that he would have to overcome.

Author Biography

Hassan Rouhani (born Hassan Fereydoun, 1948) was elected president of the Islamic Republic of Iran in 2013 and was reelected in 2017. Earlier, he had studied at Qom Seminary, University of Tehran (B.A., 1972), and Scotland's Glasgow Caledonian University (PhD, 1999), specializing in religious law. He served as secretary (1989–2005) of Iran's Supreme National Security Council and as national security adviser to the president (1989–97, 2000–05) under presidents Akbar Hashemi Rafsanjani and Mohammad Khatami.

HISTORICAL DOCUMENT

In the name of God, the Compassionate, the Merciful.
Praise be to God, the Lord of the worlds. Blessing and Peace be upon our Prophet Mohammad and his kin and companions.

Mr. President, Mr. Secretary-General, Excellencies, Ladies and Gentlemen,

At the outset, I would like to offer my most sincere felicitations on your deserved election to the presidency of the General Assembly and seize the moment to express appreciation for the valuable efforts of our distinguished Secretary-General.

Our world today is replete with fear and hope; fear of war and hostile regional and global relations; fear of deadly confrontation of religious, ethnic and national identities; fear of institutionalization of violence and extremism; fear of poverty and destructive discrimination; fear of decay and destruction of life-sustaining resources; fear of disregard for human dignity and rights; and fear of neglect of morality. Alongside these fears, however, there are new hopes; the hope of universal acceptance by the people and the elite all across the globe of "yes to peace and no to war"; and the hope of preference of dialogue over conflict, and moderation over extremism.

The recent elections in Iran represent a clear, living example of the wise choice of hope, rationality and moderation by the great people of Iran. The realization of democracy consistent with religion and the peaceful transfer of executive power manifested that Iran is the anchor of stability in an otherwise ocean of regional instabilities. The firm belief of our people and government in enduring peace, stability, tranquility, peaceful resolution of disputes and reliance on the ballot box as the basis of power, public acceptance and legitimacy, has indeed played a key role in creating such a safe environment.

Mr. President, Ladies and Gentlemen,

The current critical period of transition in international relations is replete with dangers, albeit with unique opportunities. Any miscalculation of one's position, and of course, of others, will bear historic damages; a mistake by one actor will have negative impact on all others.

Vulnerability is now a global and indivisible phenomenon.

At this sensitive juncture in the history global relations, the age of zero-sum games is over, even though a few actors still tend to rely on archaic and deeply ineffective ways and means to preserve their old superiority and domination. Militarism and the recourse to violent and military means to subjugate others are failed examples of the perpetuation of old ways in new circumstances.

Coercive economic and military policies and practices geared to the maintenance and preservation of old superiorities and dominations have been pursued in a conceptual mindset that negates peace, security, human dignity, and exalted human ideals. Ignoring differences between societies and globalizing Western values as universal ones represent another manifestation of this conceptual mindset. Yet another reflection of the same cognitive model is the persistence of Cold War mentality and bi-polar division of the world into "superior us" and "inferior others."

Fanning fear and phobia around the emergence of new actors on the world scene is another. In such an environment, governmental and non-governmental, religious, ethnic, and even racial violence has increased, and there is no guarantee that the era of quiet among big powers will remain immune from such violent discourses, practices and actions. The catastrophic impact of violent and extremist narratives should not—in fact, must not—be underestimated.

In this context, the strategic violence, which is manifested in the efforts to deprive regional players from their natural domain of action, containment policies, regime change from outside, and the efforts towards redrawing of political borders and frontiers, is extremely dangerous and provocative.

The prevalent international political discourse depicts a civilized center surrounded by un-civilized peripheries. In this picture, the relation between the center of world power and the peripheries is hegemonic. The discourse assigning the North the center stage and relegating the South to the periphery has led to the establishment of a monologue at the level of international relations. The creation of illusory identity distinctions and the current prevalent violent forms of xenophobia are the inevitable outcome of such a discourse. Propagandistic and unfounded faithphobic, Islamophobic, Shia-phobic, and Iran-phobic discourses do indeed represent serious threats against world peace and human security.

This propagandistic discourse has assumed dangerous proportions through portrayal and inculcation of presumed imaginary threats. One such imaginary threat is the so-called "Iranian threat" -which has been employed as an excuse to justify a long catalogue of crimes and catastrophic practices over the past three decades. The arming of the Saddam Hussein regime with chemical weapons and supporting the Taliban and A1-Qaida are just two examples of such catastrophes. Let me say this in all sincerity before this august world assembly, that based on irrefutable evidence, those who harp on the so-called threat of Iran are either a threat against international peace and security themselves or promote such a threat. Iran poses absolutely no threat to the world or the region. In Fact, in ideals as well as in actual practice, my country has been a harbinger of just peace and comprehensive security.

President, Ladies and Gentlemen,

Nowhere in the world has violence been so deadly and destructive as in North Africa and West Asia. Military intervention in Afghanistan, Saddam Hussein's imposed war against Iran, occupation of Kuwait, military interventions against Iraq, brutal repression of the Palestinian people, assassination of common people and political figures in Iran, and terrorist bombings in countries such as Iraq, Afghanistan and Lebanon are examples of violence in this region in the last three decades.

What has been—and continues to be—practiced against the innocent people of Palestine is nothing less than structural violence. Palestine is under occupation; the basic rights of the Palestinians are tragically violated, and they are deprived of the right of return and access to their homes, birthplace and homeland. Apartheid as a concept can hardly describe the crimes and the institutionalized aggression against the innocent Palestinian people.

The human tragedy in Syria represents a painful example of catastrophic spread of violence and extremism in our region. From the very outset of the crisis and when some regional and international actors helped to militarize the situation through infusion of arms and intelligence into the country and active support of extremist groups, we emphasized that there was no military solution to the Syrian crisis. Pursuit of expansionist strategies and objectives and attempts to change the regional balance through proxies cannot be camouflaged behind humanitarian rhetoric. The common objective of the international community should be a quick end to the killing of the innocent. While condemning any use of chemical weapons, we welcome Syria's acceptance of the Chemical Weapons Convention, and believe that the access by extremist terrorist groups to such weapons is the greatest danger to the region that must be considered in any disarmament plan. Simultaneously, I should underline that illegitimate and ineffective threat to use or the actual use of force will only lead to further exacerbation of violence and crisis in the region.

Terrorism and the killing of innocent people represent the ultimate inhumanity of extremism and violence. Terrorism is a violent scourge and knows no country or national borders. But, the violence and extreme actions such as the use of drones against innocent people in the name of combating terrorism should also be condemned. Here, I should also say a word about the criminal assassination of Iranian nuclear scientists. For what crimes have they been assassinated? The United Nations and the Security Council should answer the question: have the perpetrators been condemned?

Unjust sanctions, as manifestation of structural violence, are intrinsically inhumane and against peace. And contrary to the claims of those who pursue and impose them, it is not the states and the political elite that are targeted, but rather, it is the common people who are victimized by these sanctions. Let us not forget millions of Iraqis who, as a result of sanctions covered in international legal jargon, suffered and lost their lives, and many more who continue to suffer all through their lives. These sanctions are violent, pure and simple; whether called smart or otherwise, unilateral or multilateral. These sanctions violate inalienable human rights, inter alia, the right to peace, fight to development, right to access to health and education, and above all, the right to life. Sanctions, beyond any and all rhetoric, cause belligerence, war-mongering and human suffering. It should be borne in mind, however, that the negative impact is not merely limited to the intended victims of sanctions; it also affects the economy and livelihood of other countries and societies, including the countries imposing sanctions.

Mr. President, Excellencies,

Violence and extremism nowadays have gone beyond the physical realm and have unfortunately afflicted and tarnished the mental and spiritual dimensions of life in human societies. Violence and extremism leave no space for understanding and moderation as the necessary foundations of collective life of human beings and the modern society. Intolerance is the predicament of our time. We need to promote and reinforce tolerance in light of the religious teachings and appropriate cultural and political approaches. The human society should be elevated from a state of mere tolerance to that of collective collaboration. We should not just tolerate others. We should rise above mere tolerance and dare to work together.

People all over the world are tired of war, violence and extremism. They hope for a change in the status quo. And this is a unique opportunity—for us all. The Islamic Republic of Iran believes that all challenges can be managed—successfully—through a smart, judicious blend of hope and moderation. Warmongers are bent on extinguishing all hope. But hope for change for the better is an innate, religious, widespread, and universal concept.

Hope is founded on the belief in the universal will of the people across the globe to combat violence and extremism, to cherish change, to oppose imposed structures, to value choice, and to act in accordance with human responsibility. Hope is no doubt one of the greatest gifts bestowed upon human beings by their All-Loving Creator. And moderation is to think and move in a wise, judicious manner, conscious of the time and the space, and to align exalted ideals with choice of effective strategies and policies, while cognizant of objective realities.

The Iranian people, in a judiciously sober choice in the recent elections, voted for the discourse of hope, foresight and prudent moderation—both at home and abroad. In foreign policy, the combination of these elements means that the Islamic Republic of Iran, as a regional power, will act responsibly with regard to regional and international security, and is willing and prepared to cooperate in these fields, bilaterally as well as multilaterally, with other responsible actors. We defend peace based on democracy and the ballot box everywhere, including in Syria, Bahrain, and other countries in the region, and believe that there are no violent solutions to world crises. The bitter and ugly realities of the human society can only be overcome through recourse to and reliance on human wisdom, interaction and moderation. Securing peace and democracy and ensuring the legitimate rights of all countries in the world, including in the Middle East, cannot—and will not—be realized through militarism.

Iran seeks to resolve problems, not to create them. There is no issue or dossier that cannot be resolved through reliance on hope and prudent moderation, mutual respect, and rejection of violence and extremism. Iran's nuclear dossier is a case in point. As clearly stated by the Leader of the Islamic Revolution, acceptance of the inalienable right of Iran constitutes the best and the easiest way of resolving this issue. This is not political rhetoric. Rather, it is based on a profound recognition of the state of technology in Iran, global political environment, the end of the era of zero-sum games, and the imperative of seeking common objectives and interests towards reaching common understanding and shared security. Put otherwise, Iran and other actors should pursue two common objectives as two mutually inseparable parts of a political solution for the nuclear dossier of Iran.

Iran's nuclear program—and for that matter, that of all other countries—must pursue exclusively peaceful purposes. I declare here, openly and unambiguously, that, notwithstanding the positions of others, this has been, and will always be, the objective of the Islamic Republic of Iran. Nuclear weapon and other weapons of mass destruction have no place in Iran's security and defense doctrine, and contradict our fundamental religious and ethical convictions. Our national interests make it imperative that we remove any and all reasonable concerns about Iran's peaceful nuclear program.

The second objective, that is, acceptance of and respect for the implementation of the right to enrichment inside Iran and enjoyment of other related nuclear rights, provides the only path towards achieving the first objective. Nuclear knowledge in Iran has been domesticated now and the nuclear technology, inclusive of enrichment, has already reached industrial scale. It is, therefore, an illusion, and extremely unrealistic, to presume that the peaceful nature of the nuclear program of Iran could be ensured through impeding the program via illegitimate pressures.

In this context, the Islamic Republic of Iran, insisting on the implementation of its rights and the imperative of international respect and cooperation in this exercise, is prepared to engage immediately in time-bound and result-oriented talks to build mutual confidence and removal of mutual uncertainties with full transparency.

Iran seeks constructive engagement with other countries based on mutual respect and common interest, and within the same framework does not seek to increase tensions with the United States. I listened carefully to the statement made by President Obama today at the General Assembly. Commensurate with the political will of the leadership in the United States and hoping that they will refrain from following the short-sighted interest of warmongering pressure groups, we can arrive at a framework to manage our differences. To this end, equality, mutual respect, and the recognized principles of international law should govern the interactions. Of course, we expect to hear a consistent voice from Washington.

Mr. President, Ladies and Gentlemen,

In recent years, a dominant voice has been repeatedly heard: "The military option is on the table." Against the backdrop of this illegal and ineffective contention, let me say loud and clear that "peace is within reach." So, in the name of the Islamic Republic of Iran I propose, as a starting step, the consideration by the United Nations of the project: "the World Against Violence and Extremism." (WAVE) Let us all join this "WAVE." I invite all states, international organizations and civil institutions to undertake a new effort to guide the world in this direction.

We should start thinking about "Coalition for Enduring Peace" all across the globe instead of the ineffective "Coalitions for War" in various parts of the world.

Today, the Islamic Republic of Iran invites you and the entire world community to take a step forward; an invitation to join the WAVE: World Against Violence and Extremism. We should accept and be able to open a new horizon in which peace will prevail over war, tolerance over violence, progress over bloodletting, justice over discrimination, prosperity over poverty, and freedom over despotism. As beautifully said by Ferdowsi, the renowned Iranian epic poet:

"Be relentless in striving for the cause of Good
Bring the spring, you must, Banish the winter, you should."

Notwithstanding all difficulties and challenges, I am deeply optimistic about the future. I have no doubt that the future will be bright with the entire world solidly rejecting violence and extremism. Prudent moderation will ensure a bright future for the world. My hope, aside from personal and national experience, emanates from the belief shared by all divine religions that a good and bright future awaits the world. As stated in the Holy Qur'an:

"And We proclaimed in the Psalms, after We had proclaimed in the Torah, that My virtuous servants will inherit the earth." (21:105)

GLOSSARY

hegemonic: having a predominant, controlling influence or authority over others

Islamic Revolutionary Guard Corps: an Iranian military organization, separate from the army, founded after the Iranian Revolution of 1979 to assure the integrity of the Islamic Republic; it is noted for its hardline political stances and active involvement in the economy

Shiites: (also, Shias): with Sunnis, one of the two principal divisions of Islam, dating from a split in the seventh century; most Muslims are Sunnis, but Shiites make up the majority population in Iran, Iraq, Bahrain, and Azerbaijan and also are a plurality in Lebanon; minority Shiite populations exist, as well, in other Middle Eastern countries

Document Analysis

Rouhani's speech, repeating many themes from his U.N. address of the previous years, spoke against violence and extremism and for tolerance and understanding. Written from an Iranian perspective, it will strike many American audiences as strange, even backward. He posits Iran and similar countries as the victims of international violence. He sees the United States and former colonial powers as trying to dominate them and tell them what to believe and how to live, and he decries the "structural violence" perpetrated against the Palestinians. He does not promise to abandon Iranian policies to which the West objects, but he presents them as nonthreatening and subject to solution if underlying issues can be resolved.

He blames the violence in Syria, where Iran supports the existing government at its invitation, on outsiders who have armed and encouraged extremists. He condemns extremist terrorism and the use of chemical weapons but also the U.S. use of drones, which he says kill innocents. Rouhani notes that no one seems to care when Iranian scientists are assassinated (acts generally believed to have been carried out by Israeli agents). He also condemns the use of economic sanctions, which he argues harm innocent people and undermine the economies of the countries that impose them as well as those of the targeted countries. Those who call Iran a threat, in his view, are the actual threats to peace.

Rouhani goes on to offer a more positive counternarrative. Members of human society should not just tolerate each other but actively work together. In this way the Middle East's conflicts can be overcome. He presents the controversy over Iran's nuclear program as an issue that can be dealt with cooperatively if others would only recognize Iran's right to develop nuclear power. Iran has no need of nuclear weapons and is willing to address other countries' concerns. At the same time he continues to assert that Iran has the right to process uranium for peaceful purposes and that the program had already advanced too far to be stopped. Negotiations on the nuclear program—which were ongoing at the time of his speech, having already missed one deadline in July 2014 and been extended—should aim to build mutual confidence and remove uncertainties. This, in his view, was opposed only by "the shortsighted interest of warmongering pressure groups" in the United States.

Rouhani also spoke in favor of the creation of an antiwar coalition, the World Against Violence and Extremism (WAVE), a slogan he had already used on various occasions, and averred that "Prudent moderation will ensure a bright future for the world." In a tacit appeal to unity, he finished with an optimistic Koranic quote that in turn cited the Psalms and the Torah.

Essential Themes

It is important to note that Iran has a hybrid political system. The supreme religious leader—first, Ayatollah Ruhollah Khomeini (1979–89), then, Ayatollah Ali Khamenei (1989–)—is the ultimate authority and determines the limits of policy but rarely interferes in day-to-day decisions. The parliament and president are elected by the people, but the Guardian Council, an appointed body consisting of experts in religious law, may disqualify any candidate it sees as unfit, and it regularly disqualifies liberals and reformists. Nevertheless, despite the relatively narrow range of choice, electoral outcomes have consequences.

After the hardline conservative presidency of Mahmoud Ahmadinejad (2005–13), Rouhani, a moderate, saw a need for change in both politics and the stagnant economy, Realizing that it was pointless to ally himself with reformers, who would be eliminated by the Guardian Council, he formed a coalition of moderates and those conservatives who were willing to see Iran opened to the outside world in order to spur economic growth through trade. On the other side were conservatives who opposed any opening to foreign influences of any kind. With its ties to conservatives, the strategy would not bring immediate systemic change, but if successful, the opening might lay the groundwork for the future evolution of the social and political system. This is why the hardline conservatives opposed it.

The key to Rouhani's plan was an agreement with the United States and other powers in which Iran would give up any claim to nuclear weapons but maintain a nuclear-processing industry for peaceful purposes in return for the lifting of economic sanctions. That agreement was reached with representatives of the United States, China, France, Germany, Russia, the United Kingdom, and the European Union in April 2015. Under the agreement, the first multinational arms-control accord to restrict the capabilities of only one participant, Iran foreswore nuclear weapons in perpetuity and agreed, also in perpetuity, to one of the world's most extensive verification regimes (run by the International Atomic Energy Agency) to assure that it did not divert nuclear material from its permitted processing program to any other facility. In addition, as a confidence-building measure, Iran agreed to extraordinary restrictions that would expire in 10, 15, or 25 years, depending on the restriction. In return, the United States released Iranian funds that it had frozen at the time of the Iranian Revolution of 1979 (with interest), and the United States, the United Nations, and others agreed to lift economic sanctions that had been imposed in order to compel Iran to negotiate on its nuclear program. Opponents to the agreement, who did not believe that it went far enough, were prominent only in the United States. They focused attention on the temporary provisions, sometimes depicting the accord as allowing Iran to have nuclear weapons in ten years.

Rouhani's strategy fell short in two respects. First, the agreement did not boost the Iranian economy as much as he had hoped. While some of the economy's problems resulted from international sanctions, others were indigenous to Iran and not aided by the agreement. In addition, the United States retained sanctions that had not been tied to negotiations on the nuclear program. Moreover, U.S. banks and many corporations were reluctant to involve themselves in any Iranian deal for fear of a policy reversal in the future, given the continuing political opposition to the agreement.

Second, in an apparent desire to "balance" Rouhani's deal with the Americans and other outsiders, Ayatollah Khamenei permitted Iran's hard-liners to pursue an aggressive policy in support of Shiite and related populations in Iraq, Syria, and Yemen, at the invitation of the government in the case of Iraq and Syria. (This should not be viewed as a policy driven purely by religion. Theologically, the "Fiver" Shiites of Yemen are quite distinct from the "Twelver" Shiites of Iran, Iraq, and Lebanon, and the Alawites of Syria are treated as Shiites primarily for geopolitical purposes.) While Rouhani may well share the hard-liners' view that these groups are oppressed and under threat, as his speech implies, this policy has foreclosed any hope he might have had of building on the nuclear agreement to improve relations with the United States, at the very least in the near term.

—*Scott C. Monje, PhD*

Bibliography and Additional Reading

Akbarzadeh, Shahram, and Dara Conduit, eds. *Iran in the World: President Rouhani's Foreign Policy.* New York: Palgrave Macmillan, 2016.

Nasr, Vali. "Iran among the Ruins." *Foreign Affairs* 97:2 (March/April 2018): 108–18.

Parsi, Trita. *Losing an Enemy: Obama, Iran, and the Triumph of Diplomacy.* New Haven, CT: Yale University Press, 2017.

■ Remarks by Abdullah II of Jordan Before the U.N. General Assembly

Date: September 24, 2014
Author: Abdullah II bin Al-Hussein
Geographic region: Jordan
Genre: Address, speech

Summary Overview

In the nineteenth century the territory of present day Jordan was part of the Ottoman Empire. In 1916 the Great Arab Revolt against Ottoman rule started under the leadership of Hussein bin Ali (Sharif Hussein) and his sons: Feisal and Abdullah. They had significant help and advice from a British major, T.E. Lawrence (who was popularized in the 1962 movie *Lawrence of Arabia*). The revolt succeeded in capturing some Turkish strongholds (Aqaba) and securing British help. Till the end of the war Hussein bin Ali's Bedouin tribal forces fought a guerrilla war against the Turks from their headquarters in Petra.

Following the war, and ignoring Hussein's aspirations, the Arab territories were divided between France (Syria, Lebanon) and Great Britain (Palestine and Transjordan).

In 1925 Abdullah became the first Emir of Jordan, thus initiating the present ruling family. He successfully steered Jordan thorough the 1920s, a second Arab Revolt in the 1930s, and World War II, after which Jordan gained independence from Britain. Abdullah became the first king of the Hashemite Kingdom of Jordan as Abdullah I.

In 1948, during the Arab-Israeli War, Jordan annexed part of Palestine—specifically, the so-called West Bank, which attracted a large number of migrants and Palestinian refugees.

King Abdulla I was assassinated in 1951 and his grandson Hussein bin Talal acceded to the throne as King Hussein—a monarch who was very popular in the West and in other Arab countries as well as among the Jordanian population. In 1952 the country received a new constitution and formed a bicameral parliament. Throughout the 1950s Jordan was considered the most liberal and free of all the Middle Eastern countries.

The Arab-Israeli wars of 1967 and 1973 resulted in a worsening of the situation, the imposition of martial law, the loss of control of the West Bank, and a large inflow of Palestinian refugees. In 1970 a clash between the monarchy and extremist Palestinian groups led to the forming of the Black September Organization and the expulsion of the most radical Palestinian fighters. Because of events of the 1960s and 1970s, over one third of Jordan's population consists of descendants of Palestinian refugees.

Eventually, King Hussein decided to follow a policy independent of Soviet advice, recognize the Palestinian Liberation Organization as the representative of Arabs in the West Bank, and enter into a peaceful dialogue with Israel, signing a formal treaty in 1994. In domestic policy he worked toward establishing a stable democracy in Jordan, pursuing economic development, and opening up Jordan to free international trade. In 1999 Hussein was succeeded by his son Abdullah II, who has continued his father's policies and is the person delivering this address before the United Nations General Assembly.

Defining Moment

Upon ascending to the throne, Abdullah II continued to pursue his father's reforms. Economic liberalization, foreign investments, and free trade resulted in technological progress and substantial economic growth until the 2008 global recession. Attempts to liberalize political life met with opposition. On one hand, some groups found them not fast and democratic enough; on the other hand, they were considered to progressive by conservative Muslim organizations.

In 2005 al-Qaeda launched several terrorist attacks in Jordan, killing about 60 people and injuring over 100. These attacks caused anger in the country and were seen as an attempt to sabotage the nation's peaceful relations with Israel.

Six years later massive demonstrations shook the Arab world from North Africa and elsewhere in the Middle

East. The Arab Spring, as such calls for democratization were called, did not spare Jordan—although their consequences there were not as severe for the ruling family as in other countries. In response to domestic protests, Abdullah changed the government, introduced constitutional reforms, and guaranteed elections and new public freedoms. Thus, Jordan managed to avoid the fate of a number of other Arab countries, where civil wars broke out, governments were overthrown, domestic chaos reigned, and opportunities arose for extremist Islamist groups.

North of Jordan, on the border of Syria and Iraq, for example, the Islamic State of Iraq and the Levant (ISIL; also known as the Islamic State of Iraq and al-Sham, or ISIS) emerged. The new "state," claiming to be an Islamic caliphate, started to conduct extremely brutal and aggressive activities in Iraq, in Kurdish areas, and in Syria, leading to hundreds of thousands of civilians fleeing the region. Simultaneously, a civil war in Syria, which started in when opposition tried to remove the president, Bashar al-Assad, broke out in 2011 with many outside forces (the United States, Russia, Turkey, and Iran) involved in the conflict. Again, there was widespread destruction of the country and the creation of additional hundreds of thousands of civilian refugees.

Additionally, in the summer of 2014 conflict between Israel and Hamas (a fundamentalist political-military organization representing the Palestinians and working against Israel) intensified, leading to a full-scale Gaza War. That conflict proved to be far more devastating and deadlier than one occurring five years earlier.

Trying to secure and manage fragile peace and stability, the kingdom of Jordan with a population reaching 10 million, accepted approximately 3 million refugees from Syria in the years 2011-14. In October 2014, the United Nations registered 619,000 refugees in Jordan. At the time of Abdullah's speech before the General Assembly, the registered refugees constituted only about 20 percent of the total. These people require food, health care, education, and work.

Thus, at the moment of King Abdullah II's speech at the U.N. session, Jordan was trying to cope with supplying humanitarian aid to several million refugees on its soil, and to limit the activity and influence of extremist Islamic groups, particular those connected with ISIL/ISIS.

Author Biography

Abdullah II bin Al-Hussein (1962-) has, since 1999, been the king of Jordan. He inherited the throne after the death of his father, King Hussein. Abdullah II was Hussein's first son, born in the capital city of Amman. After attending school in Jordan, he studied abroad, including at the Royal Military Academy Sandhurst (1980), Pembroke College in Oxford (1982), Edmund A. Walsh School of Foreign Service at Georgetown University (1987), and the British Staff College in Camberley, U.K. (1990). Simultaneously he pursued a military career in the Jordanian armed forces, serving also in the British army. In 1994 he assumed command of Jordan's special forces and other elite units. He became a brigadier general and, in 1996, a major general. In 1998 he commanded elite special forces.

In 1999, after his father's death, he was crowned king of Jordan. Although Jordan is a constitutional monarchy, the king has significant prerogatives. In the first years of his rule Abdullah decided to liberalize the economy and, with foreign help, managed to overcome an economic crisis (the legacy of the 1990 Gulf War) and set the country's economy on a path of growth for a decade. Abdullah also took decisive action against Hamas, forcing them to take their operations outside the country. In the year 2000 his family was an al-Qaeda terrorist target. After the World Trade Center attack of 9/11, Abdullah provided assistance to United States and its allies in their fight against al-Qaeda.

In 2004 Abdullah introduced the term "Shia Crescent," warning about the growing importance of the Shia Muslim separatists in the region between Damascus and Iran. During the 2010 Arab Spring, Abdullah managed to overcome opposition and a growing crisis, offering political concessions. In 2012, in an attempt to calm unrest and protests, Abdullah introduced significant reforms, amended the constitution, organized a constitutional court, and an independent electoral commission. He also initiated a large-scale information campaign regarding planned reforms and his vision for the country. Abdullah is popular both domestically and internationally. He is praised for his input concerning the Arab-Israeli conflict and also for his contributions to the ongoing dialogue between Islam, Christianity, and Judaism.

HISTORICAL DOCUMENT

The United Nations, New York
September 24, 2014

Bismillah ar-Rahman ar-Rahim

Mr. President, Mr. Secretary General, thank you; Distinguished Heads of Delegations, Members of the General Assembly:

What and where is global power? I say global power is here, and it is ours. If our countries work as one.

This is the great promise of the General Assembly. The times demand we exercise that power, now, and to the full.

In my region, the challenges have grown significantly since I spoke here last. Those who say, 'This is not our business,' are wrong. The security of every nation will be shaped by the fate of the Middle East. Together, we can and must undertake urgent humanitarian and security measures, create durable solutions for today's crises and provide new opportunities for dialogue, reconciliation, prosperity and peace.

My friends,

The terrorists and criminals targeting Syria, Iraq, and other countries today are extreme reflections of a global threat. Our international community needs a collective strategy to contain and defeat these groups.

My country is at the forefront of this effort. We are leading a number of initiatives to counter extremism. As representative of the Asia-Pacific bloc on the U.N. Security Council, we look for a strong outcome of the Council's Summit on Threats to International Peace and Security caused by Terrorist Acts, chaired by President Obama.

Another critical global focus must be a decisive affirmation of mutual respect, within and among religions and peoples.

The teachings of true Islam are clear: sectarian conflict and strife are utterly condemned. Islam prohibits violence against Christians and other communities that make up each country. Let me say once again: Arab Christians are an integral part of my region's past, present, and future.

I call on Muslim and other leaders to work together against falsehoods and divisive actions. Jordan is honoured to have spearheaded global interfaith and intra-religious initiatives. Building on this, Jordan will introduce a draft resolution covering the general proposition that a new international offence, falling under the crimes of Genocide and Crimes Against Humanity, be considered, on the basis of the aberrant new crimes against religious communities seen recently in Syria and Iraq.

Together, let us also address the conditions that extremists exploit. Radicalisation thrives on injustice, insecurity and marginalisation. This Assembly's "Transformative Development Agenda" can give the world's people a better way forward, through concrete programs and investments that will change lives.

My friends,

We must also work actively for consensus-driven political solutions to regional crises. The security situation in Syria, Iraq and Lebanon must be addressed comprehensively. Jordan supports a united and stable Iraq, with an inclusive, national political process. In Syria, there must be a political solution based on reforms that give all communities a role in rebuilding their country. International influence is vital, to get the moderate opposition and the regime back to the negotiating table immediately.

The heavy flow of Syrian refugees continues. My country is sheltering nearly 1.4 million Syrians. We are now the world's third largest host of refugees. This is placing an overwhelming burden on Jordan's people, infrastructure and already limited resources.

The refugee crisis is a recognised global responsibility, and demands a global solution. To date, the response has not kept pace with the real needs. There must be a concerted effort to get humanitarian assistance flowing inside Syria, and to support host countries and communities, including Jordan.

My friends,

We cannot address the future of my region without addressing its central conflict: the denial of Palestinian rights and statehood.

This year, yet again, we have seen a dangerous halt in the progress towards peace and a Palestinian state. Instead, in Gaza, we have seen another violent detour into conflict. How shall we heal the families who have lost so much? How shall we offer hope to young people whose futures are at risk?

A first, imperative step is to mobilise international efforts to rebuild Gaza. As we do so, we must also marshal the united, global response needed to achieve a once-and-for-all, lasting settlement. Such action can create the environment necessary to re-launch final-status negotiations on the basis of the Arab Peace Initiative.

This approach offers a clear path, the only path, to a comprehensive settlement—based on the two-state solution and international legitimacy and terms of reference. For Israel, security and normal diplomatic and economic relations with Arab and Muslim states. For Palestinians, a viable, independent, sovereign state, along the 1967 lines, with East Jerusalem as its capital.

Unilateral actions that seek to pre-empt negotiations must end. Jordan strongly opposes threats to Jerusalem's Arab Muslim and Christian identity. As Hashemite custodian of Jerusalem's Muslim and Christian Holy Sites, I will continue to oppose any violation of Al Aqsa Mosque's sanctity.

My friends,

The people of Palestine seek what all humanity seeks. It is the common cause of this General Assembly: justice, dignity, opportunity, and hope.

This is our global responsibility, it is in our global power, and we must make it our global reality. Jordan stands ready to do its part.

Thank you.

GLOSSARY

Al Aqsa Mosque: a holy mosque located on the Temple Mount (holy site for Judaism, Christianity, and Islam) in the Old City of Jerusalem; it is considered to be the third holiest site of Islam

Arab Peace Initiative: an initiative proposed in 2002 to end the Arab-Israeli conflict in the Middle East; the initiative is a short, ten-sentence proposal presented by Saudi Arabia at the Beirut Summit of the Arab League

Bismillah ar-Rahman ar-Rahim: "In the name of God, the Most Gracious, the Most Merciful"—a phrase recited before each *sura* (chapter) of the holy book of the Koran

Gaza: the Gaza Strip, a small section of land on the eastern coast of the Mediterranean Sea between Israel and Egypt (the Sinai); it is a self-governed Palestinian territory

Document Analysis

This speech was delivered at the United Nations headquarters in New York City, at a plenary session or general assembly involving all members. It is a speech addressing the situation or crisis then experienced by the people of the Middle East, in particular the people of Jordan as represented by their monarch.

Abdullah starts with a statement that the unrest and war in the Middle East should not be seen as a local conflict but must be understood as a conflict that touches all peoples, nations, and governments of the world. Although he does not state it explicitly, Abdullah suggests that peace is important in the region because the Middle East is the biggest oil producing area in the world. Disruption of oil production and transport will clearly have a global impact.

In this context he calls for general solidarity and a common front to stand against the violence and threats that are wracking the region. In particular, he refers to the struggle against terrorism, which, although most immediately affecting Syria, Iraq, and Kurdistan, north of the Jordanian border, is a global threat that must be dealt with. "My country is at the forefront of this effort," he states, referring to the need to undertake peace initiatives through different organizations with diverse stakeholders.

Many of the current problems in the Middle East are ignited by Islamic extremist groups engaging in terrorism, claiming their fight to be a religious war. Abdullah sees Islam, instead, as a force for peace: "The teachings of true Islam are clear: sectarian conflict and strife are utterly condemned. Islam prohibits violence against Christians and other communities that make up each country," he says. He calls on all Arab countries to work together towards reaching a peaceful solution to the crisis. To that end, the countries in the region should act together to address ongoing problems and dangers. Abdullah names Syria, Iraq, and Lebanon as three nations badly in need of peace, stability, and humanitarian assistance.

The result of war and terror is thousands of homeless refugees fleeing from their home countries. Jordan, says Abdullah, has provided shelter to over 1.4 million Syrian refugees, yet is not able to cope with such a large inflow of migrants on its own.

In the final part of his speech Abdullah addresses the then latest military conflict, the escalation into a full-scale war of the conflict between Palestinians of the Gaza Strip and the state of Israel. The best solution, continues Abdullah, to this long-lasting conflict would be to create two independent states: Israel and a new, fully independent Palestinian state with East Jerusalem as its capital. This was, until very recently, one of the most prominent prospective solutions to the Israeli-Palestinian conflict, and Abdullah is endorsing it here. He suggests, as have others before him, using the 1967 demarcation line as the likely border between the two nations—which actually consists of the *pre*–Six Day War borders existing between 1948 and 1967. To bolster his case, he recalls that it is his role as the Hashemite custodian of Jerusalem's Muslim and Christian Holy Sites to undertake all action to secure peace on the Temple Mount, which is a holy site for Jews, Christians, and Muslims alike.

The speech is presented in a calm tone, yet it stresses the difficult situation in which Abdullah's country finds itself. Jordan has long been affected by conflicts around it (and, to a lesser extent, from within), but, Abdullah implies, the situation is clearly getting worse, and it stands to envelope or draw in other nations, including his own.

Essential Themes

The speech by King Abdullah II at the United Nations was given in a time of severe crisis in the Middle East, which had very strong impact on the kingdom of Jordan. Many years of Jordan's efforts to modernize itself, to stabilize its economy, and guarantee its security, were being jeopardized by hostilities unfolding in neighboring states and territories, especially in Syria, Iraq, and the Gaza region.

King Abdullah II, who has tried to maintain a relatively neutral stance with respect to the recent war in Iraq and the more general war against terrorism, speaks out for the first time here, with full conviction and commitment, against the self-proclaimed caliphate of the Islamic State (ISIL). He labels their actions as terrorist ones contrary to Islamic religion. He stresses the guiding principles of Islam, a religion of peace that does not sanction religious wars between factions within Islam nor such untoward aggression against Christianity. He emphasizes the attempts that were undertaken by his family and his country to solve peacefully differences between religions, stressing that, in the end, "Jordan strongly opposes threats to Jerusalem's Arab Muslim and Christian identity. As Hashemite custodian of Jerusalem's Muslim and Christian Holy Sites, I will continue to oppose any violation of Al Aqsa Mosque's sanctity."

Referring to the Israeli-Palestinian conflict, which produced another war at about the time of his speech, he points to the need to mobilize the international community to solve the problem of bringing peace and stability to Gaza. His suggestion is to "achieve a once-and-for-all lasting settlement" between the Palestinians of Gaza and the state of Israel. He further states that such a solution should be based on respect for both sides and should incorporate elements that can be accepted internationally. The Arab Peace Initiative of 2002, he notes, would be a good place to start and might lead to the forming of an independent and sovereign Palestinian state with East Jerusalem as its capital.

—*Jakub Basista, PhD, DLitt*

Bibliography and Additional Reading

Abdullah II, King of Jordan, *Our Last Best Chance: The Pursuit of Peace in a Time of Peril*. London: Penguin Books Ltd. 2012.

Fishman, Ben, *Jordan: Caught in the Middle Again*. [in:] "Survival", vol. 56 no. 6, December 2014–January 2015, pp. 39–48.

George, Alan, *Jordan: Living in the Crossfire*. London and New York: Zed Books 2005.

Salibi, Kamal S., *The Modern History of Jordan*. London: I.B.Tauris 2006

Benjamin Netanyahu: Speech Before the U.N. General Assembly

Date: September 29, 2014
Author: Benjamin Netanyahu
Geographic region: Gaza Strip
Genre: Speech

Summary Overview

From July-August 2014, hostilities broke out between Israel and Hamas again in the Gaza Strip; this conflict resulted in the deaths of over 2,000 Palestinians, 66 Israeli soldiers, and 5 Israeli civilians. International reaction was divided in the aftermath: a number of human rights organizations condemned both Hamas and Israel for violations of international humanitarian law. On July 23, 2014, while missiles were still falling, the United Nations Human Rights Council determined that there should be an investigation on human rights violations on both sides. Consequently, Prime Minister Benjamin Netanyahu condemned the decision of the Human Rights Council in a speech before the United Nations General Assembly on September 29, 2014; he even accused the organization of supporting terrorism by condemning Israel. The Israeli Prime Minister's speech had a larger focus, however: he asserted that his nation's military was on the front lines of an ideological fight against militant Islamists, and blamed Iran as a primary instigator of bloody conflict in the Middle East.

Defining Moment

Hamas, a Sunni Islamic fundamentalist organization, has existed since 1987, and has the stated goals of liberating Palestine from Israeli occupation and establishing an Islamic state. Since its founding, Hamas has waged a war against Israel through suicide bombings and rocket attacks, as well as frequently disrupted the abilities of Fatah, the more secular and nationalist Palestinian party, to negotiate for a two-state solution to the Israeli-Palestinian conflict. When Hamas won a majority of seats in the 2006 legislative election for the Palestinian Authority, the governing body of the West Bank and Gaza Strip, Hamas' refusal to recognize previous agreements with Israel ignited an internecine conflict amongst Palestinians. The factional fighting resulted in the de facto governance of Gaza by Hamas and the West Bank by the PA Next, Israel waged war against Hamas-led Gaza in two campaigns (2008-9,

or Operation Cast Lead, and 2012, or Operation Pillar of Defense). Since the conclusion of open warfare between Hamas and Fatah, President Abbas, leader of the Palestinian Authority, has been under considerable pressure both to reject Hamas as well as to unify the Palestinian government. Prime Minister Benjamin Netanyahu, with support from the United States, has repeatedly asserted that Israel could never cooperate with an organization that has aimed at Israel's destruction.

On June 12, 2014, three Israeli teenagers were abducted at a hitchhiking stop in the West Bank. Prime Minister Netanyahu claimed it was the work of Hamas, and blamed President Abbas, who had recently created a unity government with Hamas. However, at the time neither Netanyahu nor the IDF offered immediate evidence that proved Hamas was behind the abduction. The Palestinian Authority blamed the Qawasmeh tribe, a group that frequently undermined Hamas' attempts at ceasefires with Israel. Meanwhile, the IDF swept across the West Bank, where they conducted raids and searches and arrested hundreds of Palestinians during the ensuing week in Operation Brother's Keeper. The IDF did not announce that they suspected that the teenagers had already been killed.

On June 30, 2014, the bodies of the abducted teenagers were found, which sparked anti-Arab rioting after their burial the next day. Then, a group of Israelis extremists killed a Palestinian teenager in revenge, which sparked Arab rioting. At the same time, the IDF carried out air strikes on Hamas targets in the Gaza Strip, and retaliatory rocket attacks from the Gaza Strip bombarded southern Israel ensued. On July 8 Israel began an official military campaign against Gaza, named Operation Protective Edge, and hostilities would continue for the next fifty days. The relationship between the Palestinian Authority and Hamas, as well as Israel's refusal to meet Hamas' terms, complicated repeated attempts to institute ceasefires throughout July by Egypt, the United States, and the United Nations. Finally, Israeli operations appeared to be winding down on

August 3 when the IDF began withdrawing its ground troops and destroyed a number of tunnels to facilitate militant troops. Although ceasefires continued to be implemented and broken, the height of the conflict had passed. On August 20, Saleh al-Arouri, a Hamas leader in exile in Turkey, claimed responsibility for the kidnapping of the three Israeli teenagers and admitted to hoping to ignite widespread violent conflict again. A final and more lasting truce only came on August 26, but sporadic violence would continue into the fall of 2014.

Estimates of the conflict's cost total the deaths at over 2,100 Palestinians, of whom 1,462 were civilians, and 72 Israelis, of whom 66 were military personnel. The 2014 conflict also displaced thousands of Palestinians by wrecking massive portions of Gaza's housing; the cost of rebuilding housing and repairing damaged industry sites also significantly impaired Gaza's already weakened economy and infrastructure. Agencies like Amnesty International and Human Rights Council alleged violations of international humanitarian laws on both sides of the conflict. The IDF responded to these claims that they were not targeting civilians, they provided warnings before any attack, and Hamas both manipulated the optics of the casualties and militants used civilians for cover. On September 26, 2014, President Abbas delivered a speech to the U.N. General Assembly, in which he accused Israeli of perpetuating a "new war of genocide" against the Palestinian people. In return, Netanyahu delivered his own speech defending Israel's tactics and ideology three days later.

Author Biography

Benjamin "Bibi" Netanyahu is a former commando and long-term Israeli politician; his policies have mostly supported hardline attitudes towards terrorism and an increase in Israeli settlements; economically, he has supported privatization and considers himself an "advocate of the free market." He was born in 1949 in Tel Aviv, which would later make him the first prime minister to have been born in Israel after the formation of the modern state. After attending secondary school in the United States, Netanyahu returned to Israel to enlist in the Israel Defense Force in 1967. Netanyahu alternated between completing his higher education back in the United States and serving in the IDF for the next few years. After serving in the Yom Kippur War in 1973, he completed his bachelor's degree in architecture at MIT in 1975 as well as a master's in management from MIT in 1976. However, in the same year the death

of his older brother Yonatan Netanyahu in Operation Entebbe became a watershed moment for the younger Netanyahu. He left his work at the lucrative Boston Consulting Group, where he met future U.S. presidential candidate Mitt Romney, and returned to Israel. In 1978 he formed the Jonathan Netanyahu Anti-Terror Institute; he also began making the connections that would enable his political rise during this time.

Netanyahu spent the greater part of the 1980s in the United States on behalf of the Israeli government. From 1982-4, Netanyahu was the Deputy Chief of Missions at the Israeli embassy in Washington, D.C.; then, from 1984-1988 he served as Israel's permanent representative to the United Nations in New York. Once again he returned to Israel in 1988 and joined the center-right Likud party; he won a seat in the Knesset, Israel's parliament, and was elevated to deputy foreign minister. After Likud was defeated in the 1992 general election, Netanyahu became the leader of the party. This position put him in the right place to catapult to victory after elections were called in the wake of Prime Minister Yitzhak Rabin's assassination in 1996; his hard-right positions on national security helped him succeed in the midst of a wave of suicide bombings in Israel shortly before the elections. Netanyahu's victory in 1996 made him the youngest person elected to be prime minister in Israel and the first prime minister elected directly by the general Israeli public.

Charges of corruption, waning support from the right because of his concessions to the Palestinians, and strong opposition from members of the left marked his first tenure as prime minister. Ehud Barak, his former commander, defeated him in the 1999 general elections. Netanyahu served first as foreign minister, then as finance minister for the next few years until he resigned in protest over Israeli withdrawal from the Gaza Strip in 2005. Prime Minister Ariel Sharon's withdrawal from Likud, and his incapacitation by a stroke in 2006, opened a path for Netanyahu to begin his political rise anew. Netanyahu's second premiership began in 2009. He won another term in 2013 and in 2015, which made him the only Israeli prime minister to be elected three times in a row and also has nearly tied him with David Ben Gurion for longest time in the position. Netanyahu frequently chafed with Obama administration, which attempted to facilitate peace talks between the Israelis and the Palestinians. The culmination of the antagonism between the two administrations would show in 2016, after the United States abstained from a U.N.

resolution condemning Israeli settlements in Palestinian territory. John Kerry, the U.S. Secretary of State at the time, delivered a blistering speech condemning Israeli settlement policies; in return, Netanyahu delivered his own strong response and Israel withdrew its dues from the U.N..

Netanyahu has been more supportive of the Trump administration's policies toward the Middle East. He has been a vocal supporter of President Trump's proposal of moving the United States embassy to Jerusalem and his hardline attitude toward Iran. However, criminal charges may once again destabilize Netanyahu's premiership: in February 2018, the Israeli police announced that sufficient evidence existed to charge him with bribery, fraud, and breach of trust.

HISTORICAL DOCUMENT

Thank you, Mr. President. Distinguished delegates, I come here from Jerusalem to speak on behalf of my people, the people of Israel. I've come here to speak about the dangers we face and about the opportunities we seek. I've come here to expose the brazen lies spoken from this very podium against my country and against the brave soldiers who defend it.

Ladies and gentlemen, the people of Israel pray for peace, but our hopes and the world's hopes for peace are in danger because everywhere we look militant Islam is on the march. It's not militants. It's not Islam. It's militant Islam. And typically its first victims are other Muslims, but it spares no one: Christians, Jews, Yazidis, Kurds. No creed, no faith, no ethnic group is beyond its sights. And it's rapidly spreading in every part of the world.

You know the famous American saying, all politics is local? For the militant Islamists, all politics is global, because their ultimate goal is to dominate the world. Now, that threat might seem exaggerated to some since it starts out small, like a cancer that attacks a particular part of the body. But left unchecked, the cancer grows, metastasizing over wider and wider areas. To protect the peace and security of the world, we must remove this cancer before it's too late.

Last week, many of the countries represented here rightly applauded President Obama for leading the effort to confront ISIS, and yet weeks before, some of these same countries, the same countries that now support confronting ISIS, opposed Israel for confronting Hamas. They evidently don't understand that ISIS and Hamas are branches of the same poisonous tree.

ISIS and Hamas share a fanatical creed, which they both seek to impose well beyond the territory under their control. Listen to ISIS's self-declared caliph, Abu Bakr al-Baghdadi. This is what he said two months ago: "A day will soon come when the Muslim will walk everywhere as a master. The Muslims will cause the world to hear and understand the meaning of terrorism and destroy the idol of democracy." Now listen to Khaled Mashal, the leader of Hamas. He proclaims a similar vision of the future: "We say this to the West—by Allah you will be defeated. Tomorrow our nation will sit on the throne of the world."

As Hamas charter makes clear, Hamas' immediate goal is to destroy Israel, but Hamas has a broader objective. They also want a caliphate. Hamas shares the global ambitions of its fellow militant Islamists, and that's why its supporters wildly cheered in the streets of Gaza as thousands of Americans were murdered in 9/11, and that's why its leaders condemn the United States for killing Osama bin Laden whom they praised as a holy warrior.

So when it comes to their ultimate goals, Hamas is ISIS and ISIS is Hamas. And what they share in common all militant Islamists share in common. Boko Haram in Nigeria, Al-Shabab in Somalia, Hezbollah in Lebanon, Al-Nusra in Syria, the Mahdi army in Iraq, and the Al-Qaida branches in Yemen, Libya, the Philippines, India and elsewhere.

Some are radical Sunnis, some are radical Shiites, some want to restore a pre-medieval caliphate from the seventh century, others want to trigger the apocalyptic return of an imam from the ninth century. They operate in different lands, they target different victims and they even kill each other in their battle for supremacy. But they all share a fanatic ideology. They all seek to create ever-expanding enclaves of militant Islam where there is no freedom and no tolerance, where women are treated as chattel, Christians are decimated and minorities are subjugated, sometimes given the stark choice, convert or die. For them, anyone can be considered an infidel, including fellow Muslims.

Ladies and gentlemen, militant Islam's ambition to dominate the world seems mad, but so too did the global ambitions of another fanatic ideology that swept into power eight decades ago. The Nazis believed in a master race. The militant Islamists believe in a master faith. They just disagree who among them will be the master of the master faith. That's what they truly disagree about. And therefore, the question before us is whether militant Islam will have the power to realize its unbridled ambitions.

There is one place where that could soon happen—the Islamic State of Iran. For 35 years, Iran has relentlessly pursued the global mission which was set forth by its founding ruler, Ayatollah Khomeini, in these words: "We will export our revolution to the entire world until the cry 'there is no god but Allah' will echo throughout the world over." And ever since, the regimes brutal enforcers, Iran's revolutionary guards, have done exactly that.

Listen to its current commander, General Mohammad Ali Jafari. And he clearly stated his goal. He said: "Our imam did not limit the Islamic revolution to this country; our duty is to prepare the way for an Islamic world government."

Iran's President Rouhani stood here last week and shed crocodile tears over what he called the globalization of terrorism. Maybe he should spare us those phony tears and have a word instead with the commanders of Iran's revolutionary guards. He could ask them to call off Iran's global terror campaign, which has included attacks in two dozen countries on five continents since 2011 alone.

You know, to say that Iran doesn't practice terrorism is like saying Derek Jeter never played shortstop for the New York Yankees. This is—this bemoaning by the Iranian president of the spread of terrorism has got to be one of history's greatest displays of doubletalk.

Now, some argue that Iran's global terror campaign, its subversion of countries throughout the Middle East and well beyond the Middle East, some

argue that this is the work of the extremists. They say things are changing. They point to last year's election in Iran. They claim that Iran's smooth-talking president and foreign minister, they've changed not only the tone of Iran's foreign policy but also its substance. They believe that Rouhani and Zarif generally want to reconcile with the West, that they've abandoned the global mission of the Islamic Revolution. Really?

So lets look at what Foreign Minister Zarif wrote in his book just a few years ago:

"We have a fundamental problem with the West, and especially with America. This is because we are heirs to a global mission which is tied to our raison d'être, a global mission which is tied to our very reason for being."

And then Zarif asks a question—I think an interesting one. He says: "How come Malaysia"—he's referring to an overwhelmingly Muslim country—"how come Malaysia doesn't have similar problems?" And he answers: "Because Malaysia is not trying to change the international order."

That's your moderate. So don't be fooled by Iran's manipulative charm offensive. It's designed for one purpose and for one purpose only: to lift the sanctions and remove the obstacles to Iran's path to the bomb. The Islamic Republic is now trying to bamboozle its way to an agreement that will remove the sanctions it still faces and leave it with a capacity of thousands of refugees—of centrifuges, rather—to enrich uranium. This would effectively cement Iran's place as a threshold military nuclear power. And in the future, at the time of its choosing, Iran, the world's most dangerous regime, in the world's most dangerous region, would obtain the world's most dangerous weapons. Allowing that to happen would pose the gravest threat to us all. It's one thing to confront militant Islamists on pickup trucks armed with Kalashnikov rifles. It's another thing to confront militant Islamists armed with weapons of mass destruction.

I remember that last year, everyone here was rightly concerned about the chemical weapons in Syria, including the possibility that they would fall into the hands of terrorists. Well, that didn't happen, and President Obama deserves great credit for leading the diplomatic effort to dismantle virtually all of Syria's chemical weapons capability. Imagine how much more dangerous the Islamic State, ISIS, would be if it possessed chemical weapons. Now imagine how much more dangerous the Islamic State of Iran would be if it possessed nuclear weapons.

Ladies and gentlemen, would you let ISIS enrich uranium? Would you let ISIS build a heavy water reactor? Would you let ISIS develop intercontinental ballistic missiles? Of course you wouldn't. Then you mustn't let the Islamic state of Iran do those things either, because here's what will happen. Once Iran produces atomic bombs, all the charms and all the smiles will suddenly disappear. They'll just vanish. And it's then that the ayatollahs will show their true face and unleash their aggressive fanaticism on the entire world.

There's only one responsible course of action to address this threat. Iran's nuclear military capabilities must be fully dismantled. Make no mistake: ISIS must be defeated. But to defeat ISIS and leave Iran as a threshold nuclear power is to win the battle and lose the war. To defeat ISIS and leave Iran as a threshold nuclear power is to win the battle and lose the war.

Ladies and gentlemen, the fight against militant Islam is indivisible. When militant Islam succeeds anywhere, it's emboldened everywhere. When it suffers a blow in one place, it's set back in every place. That's why Israel's fight against Hamas is not just our fight; it's your fight. Israel is fighting a fanaticism today that your countries may be forced to fight tomorrow. For 50 days this past summer Hamas fired thousands of rockets at Israel, many of them supplied by Iran. I want you to think about what your countries would do if thousands of rockets were fired at your cities. Imagine millions of your citizens having seconds at most to scramble to bomb shelters day after day. You wouldn't let terrorists fire rockets at your cities with impunity, nor would you let terrorists dig dozens of terror tunnels under your borders to infiltrate your towns in order to murder and kidnap your citizens. Israel justly defended itself against both rocket attacks and terror tunnels.

Yet Israel faced another challenge. We faced a propaganda war because in an attempt to win the world sympathy, Hamas cynically used Palestinian civilians as human shields. It used schools—not just schools, U.N. schools—private homes, mosques, even hospitals to store and fire rockets at Israel. As Israel surgically struck at the rocket launchers and at the tunnels, Palestinian civilians were tragically but unintentionally killed. There are heartrending images that resulted, and these fueled libelous charges that Israel was deliberately targeting civilians. We were not. We deeply regret every single civilian casualty.

And the truth is this. Israel was doing everything to minimize Palestinian civilian casualties. Hamas was doing everything to maximize Israeli civilian casualties and Palestinian civilian casualties. Israel dropped flyers, made phone calls, sent text messages, broadcast warnings in Arabic on Palestinian television, all this to enable Palestinian civilians to evacuate targeted areas. No other country and no other army in history have gone to greater lengths to avoid casualties among the civilian population of their enemies.

Now this, this concern for Palestinian life was all the more remarkable given that Israel civilians were being bombarded by rockets day after day, night after night. And as their families were being rocketed by Hamas, Israel's citizen army, the brave soldiers of the IDF, our young boys and girls, they upheld the highest moral values of any army in the world. Israel's soldiers deserve not condemnation, but admiration, admiration from decent people everywhere.

Now, here is what Hamas did. Here is what Hamas did. Hamas embedded its missile batteries in residential areas and told Palestinians to ignore Israel's warnings to leave. And just in case people didn't get the message, they executed Palestinian civilians in Gaza who dared to protest. And no less reprehensible, Hamas deliberately placed its rockets where Palestinian children live and play. Let me show you a photograph. It was taken by a France24 crew during the recent conflict. It shows two Hamas rocket launchers, which were used to attack us. You see three children playing next to them. Hamas deliberately put its rockets in hundreds of residential areas like this—hundreds of them.

Ladies and gentlemen, this is a war crime. And I say to President Abbas, these are the crimes, the war crimes, committed by your Hamas partners in the national unity government which you head and you are responsible for. And these are the real war crimes you should have investigated or spoken out against from this podium last week.

Ladies and gentlemen, as Israel's children huddle in bomb shelters and Israel's Iron Dome missile defense knocked Hamas rockets out of the sky, the profound moral difference between Israel and Hamas couldn't have been clearer. Israel was using its missiles to protect its children. Hamas was using its children to protect its missiles.

By investigating Israel rather than Hamas for war crimes, the U.N. Human Rights Council has betrayed its noble mission to protect the innocent. In fact, what it's doing is to turn the laws of war upside down. Israel, which took unprecedented steps to minimize civilian casualties—Israel is condemned. Hamas, which both targeted and hid behind civilians—that's a double war crime—Hamas is given a pass.

The Human Rights Council is thus sending a clear message to terrorists everywhere: Use civilians as a human shield. Use them again and again and again. And you know why? Because, sadly, it works. By granting international legitimacy to the use of human shields, the U.N. Human Rights Council has thus become a terrorist rights council, and it will have repercussions—it probably already has—about the use of civilians as human shields. It's not just our interests. It's not just our values that are under attack. It's your interests and your values.

Ladies and gentlemen, we live in a world steeped in tyranny and terror, where gays are hanged from cranes in Tehran, political prisoners are executed in Gaza, young girls are abducted en masse in Nigeria, and hundreds of thousands are butchered in Syria, Libya and Iraq, yet nearly half—nearly half of the U.N. Human Rights Councils resolutions focusing on a single country have been directed against Israel, the one true democracy in the Middle East,

Israel, where issues are openly debated in a boisterous parliament, where human rights are protected by the—by independent courts, and where women, gays and minorities live in a genuinely free society.

The human rights—that's an oxymoron, the human—U.N. Human Rights Council, but I'll use it just the same. The council's biased treatment of Israel is only one manifestation of the return of one of the world's largest prejudices. We hear mobs today in Europe call for the gassing of Jews. We hear some national leaders compare Israel to the Nazis. This is not a function of Israel's policies. It's a function of diseased minds. And that disease has a name. It's called anti-Semitism. It is now spreading in polite society where it masquerades as legitimate criticism of Israel.

Ladies and gentlemen, despite the enormous challenges facing Israel, I believe we have a historic opportunity. After decades of seeing Israel as their enemy, leading states in the Arab world increasingly recognize that together, we and they face many of the same dangers, and principally, this means a nuclear-armed Iran and militant Islamist movements gaining ground in the Sunni world. Our challenge is to transform these common interests to create a productive partnership, one that would build a more secure, peaceful and prosperous Middle East. Together, we can strengthen regional security, we can advance projects in water and agricultural, in transportation and health and energy in so many fields.

I believe the partnership between us can also help facilitate peace between Israel and the Palestinians. Now, many have long assumed that an Israeli-Palestinian peace can help facilitate a broader rapprochement between Israel and the Arab world. But these days, I think it may work the other way around, namely that a broader rapprochement between Israel and the Arab world may help facilitate an Israeli-Palestinian peace. And therefore, to achieve that peace, we must look not only to Jerusalem and Ramallah but also to Cairo, to Amman, Abu Dhabi, Riyadh and elsewhere.

I believe peace can be realized with the active involvement of Arab countries—those that are willing to provide political, material and other indispensable support. I'm ready to make a historic compromise, not because Israel occupies a foreign land. The people of Israel are not occupiers in the land of Israel. History, archaeology and common sense all make clear that we have had a singular attachment to this land for over 3,000 years.

I want peace because I want to create a better future for my people, but it must be a genuine peace—one that is anchored in mutual recognition and enduring security arrangements—rock solid security arrangements on the ground, because you see, Israeli withdrawals from Lebanon and Gaza created two militant Islamic enclaves on our borders for which tens of thousands of rockets have been fired at Israel, and these sobering experiences heightens Israel's security concerns (regarding ?) potential territorial concessions in the future.

Now, those security concerns are even greater today. Just look around you. The Middle East is in chaos, states are disintegrating, and militant Islamists are filling the void. Israel cannot have territories from which it withdraws taken over by Islamic militants yet again, as happened in Gaza and Lebanon. That would place the likes of ISIS within mortar range, a few miles, of 80 percent of our population.

Now think about that. The distance between the 1967 lines and the suburbs of Tel Aviv is like the distance between the U.N. building here and Times Square. Israel is a tiny country. That's why in any peace agreement, which will obviously necessitate a territorial compromise, I will always insist that Israel be able to defend itself by itself against any threat.

And yet despite everything that has happened, some still don't take Israel's security concerns seriously. But I do and I always will—(applause)—because as prime minister of Israel, I'm entrusted with the awesome responsibility of ensuring the future of the Jewish people and the future of the Jewish state. And no matter what pressure is brought to bear, I will never waiver in fulfilling that responsibility.

Now, those security concerns are even greater today. Just look around you. The Middle East is in chaos, states are disintegrating, and militant Islamists are filling the void. Israel cannot have territories from which it withdraws taken over by Islamic militants yet again, as happened in Gaza and Lebanon. That would place the likes of ISIS within mortar range, a few miles, of 80 percent of our population.

Now think about that. The distance between the 1967 lines and the suburbs of Tel Aviv is like the distance between the U.N. building here and Times Square. Israel is a tiny country. That's why in any peace agreement, which will obviously necessitate a territorial compromise, I will always insist that Israel be able to defend itself by itself against any threat.

And yet despite everything that has happened, some still don't take Israel's security concerns seriously. But I do and I always will—(applause)—because as prime minister of Israel, I'm entrusted with the awesome responsibility of ensuring the future of the Jewish people and the future of the Jewish state. And no matter what pressure is brought to bear, I will never waiver in fulfilling that responsibility.

Isaiah, our great prophet of peace, taught us nearly 3,000 years ago in Jerusalem to speak truth to power. (Speaks in Hebrew.) For the sake of Zion, I will not be silent, for the sake of Jerusalem, I will not be still until her justice shines bright and her salvation glows like a flaming torch.

Ladies and gentlemen, let us light a torch of truth and justice to safeguard our common future. Thank you.

Document Analysis

Prime Minister Netanyahu's speech is ostensibly a defense of his country's actions, but it also functions as a persuasive strategy to redefine the nature of the 2014 Gaza conflict. Instead of a small and local struggle between Palestinians and Israelis, Netanyahu reframes the conflict as part of a larger global battle between good and evil. He accomplishes this in two ways: by encouraging his audience to identify with Israel, and by conflating Hamas with larger and greater security threats to world order so that the Palestinian conflict appears less like a territorial dispute gone awry and more like a war with clear moral sides.

To start, Netanyahu uses his familiarity with American culture to encourage his Western audience to sympathize with his message, and thus with Israel. He twists "the famous American saying, all politics is local" in a colloquial beginning to emphasize that Israel's struggle is really a struggle for the whole world's safety. If his global audience at the U.N. cares about their own safety, they ought to care about Israel's safety. As Netanyahu describes the recent conflict in Gaza, he asks his audience to consider the Israeli conflict personally: "Imagine millions of your citizens having seconds at most to scramble to bomb shelters day after day." Rather than asking his audience to imagine their citizens waging a righteous war, the prime minister seeks a sympathetic connection between his country and his listeners. He is even more blatant later on in the speech when he says: "That's why Israel's fight against Hamas is not just our fight; it's your fight." Once his audience identifies emotionally with Israel, Netanyahu then hopes to prove how unfairly the Human Rights Council has treated Israel's actions.

On the other hand, Netanyahu conflates Hamas' goals with a host of other Islamic organizations across the world in order to encourage his audience to oppose the Palestinians. He connects Hamas to the deaths of Americans during the 9/11 tragedy and Osama bin Laden, a Saudi national who primarily targeted American interests; Netanyahu also says "Hamas is ISIS and ISIS is Hamas" as far as their interests are concerned, although this is a reductive assessment of the goals of each group. The prime minister has also made a slight change in referring to the official title of Iran: he calls it "the Islamic State of Iran," instead of its official name, the "Islamic Republic of Iran;" this subtle change allows him to conflate the country with the terrorist organization ISIS (Islamic state of Iraq and Syria), and further encourages his audience to consider all Islamic organizations as essentially the same. Finally, Netanyahu's comparison between these groups and Nazis, combined with long passages about atrocities committed by Hamas, Iran, and ISIS, supplement this rhetorical tactic to make the struggle with Gaza appear like a contest with clear moral divisions.

Netanyahu wants the choice to be clear for his audience: do they support Israel, a tolerant democracy unfairly besieged, or Hamas, a terrorist group with fanatic aspirations for global domination? As the leader of Israel with hawkish policies, Netanyahu's rhetorical tactics are transparent. However, this speech eclipses the fact that the Israeli-Palestinian conflict is a complicated issue with years of abuses on both sides; Netanyahu also minimizes the fact that very often politics is local: the grand narrative he attempts to impose on the nature of Middle East history is a mirage, and that many smaller and interconnected histories, such as Fatah's conflict with Hamas, and Iran's conflict with Iraq, have contributed to the Gordian knot of finding peaceful solutions to regional stability.

Essential Themes

The end of the 2014 war brought neither side any closer to a peaceful solution to the decades-long conflict. Israeli settlements in land claimed by the Palestinian Authority continued; people and goods have been restricted from entering or leaving the Gaza Strip; and infrastructure remains weak. Despite and in response to this pressure, Palestinian armed groups have continued to launch rocket attacks into Israel, although these rockets have caused relatively few casualties; periodic violent attacks by isolated groups have also continued, such as the deaths of four people at a Jewish synagogue on November 18, 2014. Animosity between the Palestinian Authority and Hamas has continued as well: Abbas' political party, Fatah, immediately blamed the attempted assassination of Abbas' prime minister, Rami Hamdallah, while he visited Gaza on March 13, 2018, on Hamas.

One place where the conflict between Israel and Palestine has changed has been the diplomatic position of the United States in attempting to resolve this crisis. The Obama administration pointedly abstained on December 23, 2016 from a U.N. resolution condemning Israeli settlements which have antagonized peace negotiations: this abstention, instead of an outright veto, expressed for the first time that the United States disapproved of the actions of Netanyahu's government. However, the ensuing Trump administration's policies promised in turn to be much more pro-Netanyahu. President Trump's decision in December 2017 to move the U.S. embassy to Jerusalem enraged Palestinians, since the move effectively recognizes the disputed land of Jerusalem as Israel's capital and thus questions the diplomatic capabilities of the United States to facilitate a two-state solution.

It could be argued, however, that progress was made regarding another topic of Netanyahu's speech: Iran. Netanyahu in this speech anticipates that if Iran were to acquire the means to produce nuclear weapons, the Iranians would use this military advantage to threaten the existence of a Jewish state in the Middle East. In

2015, the United States and Iran, along with China, France, Russia, the United Kingdom, and Germany, signed an agreement to relax nuclear-related sanctions against Iran; in return, Iran would limit its uranium enrichment and permit international observers to inspect nuclear facilities and ensure that they were only being used for peaceful reasons. Many countries lauded the Joint Comprehensive Plan of Action, also known as the Iran deal, as a promising move toward Middle East stability. On the other hand, Netanyahu saw the Iran deal as a sly move that would allow Iran to continue working toward Israel's destruction; President Trump has called the Iran deal the "worst deal ever," and mulled withdrawing from the agreement because of the ways the agreement does not go far enough in curtailing Iran's troubling behavior, such as providing support to terrorist organizations and conducting missile tests. These tumultuous changes prove that the only consistency in Middle East politics has been how much effort it takes to maintain peaceful negotiations and how little it takes to undo years of diplomatic work.

—*Ashleigh Fata, MA*

Bibliography and Additional Reading

Brenner, Björn. *Gaza under Hamas: From Islamic Democracy to Islamist Governance*. New York: I.B. Tauris, 2017.

Caspitt, Ben. *The Netanyahu Years*. Translated by Ora Cummings, New York: Thomas Dunne, 2017.

Finkelstein, Norman. *Gaza: An Inquest into Its Martyrdom*. Oakland: University of California Press, 2018.

Jeffries, Jennifer. *Hamas: Terrorism, Governance, and Its Future in Middle East Politics*. Santa Barbara, CA: ABC-CLIO, 2016.

Gaza—Ten Years Later

Date: July 2017
Author: United Nations Country Team
Geographic region: Occupied Palestinian Territory
Genre: Report

Summary Overview

The document examined here is the official report of the United Nations Country Team as it worked to coordinate efforts to improve the conditions in the Gaza Strip, home to about two million Palestinians. Gaza is a small piece of land just under 141 square miles in size and surrounded by Israel, Egypt, and the Mediterranean Sea. For comparison, it is half the size of New York City, or a little larger than the small island nation of Malta. This piece of land is home to some of the most important sites for the Jewish, Christian, and Islamic faiths and its ownership is hotly contested, although it is currently under the control of Hamas, a Palestinian political organization and government services agency with a history of militant opposition to Israel. The United Nations team has for the past several years sought to organize international bodies to help improve living conditions in Gaza, which have become increasingly squalid and unsustainable, with serious shortages of water and medical aid. The inhabitants of the region, moreover, are constantly under pressure from their own governing authority (Hamas) and from Israeli surveillance and retaliations.

Defining Moment

Gaza has been a place of turmoil and instability for over 60 years. Modern Palestine, home to a substantial Arab population, was a British-administered territory, or "mandate," carved out from the collapsing Ottoman Empire at the end of World War I. At the time, a plan was already in place to establish the area as a homeland for repatriated European Jews involved in the Zionist movement. Thus, in 1948, the modern state of Israel was created and the British mandate ended. Immediately, however, war broke out between Israel and its Arab neighbor states. The conflict was compounded by the large number of Palestinians who had been displaced under the political and territory changes taking place from 1946-48. Under Egyptian control until 1967, Gaza became a place often disrupted by conflicts between Israel and Egypt, Jordan, and Syria.

After the 1967 Six-Day War, Israel occupied the territory and took over control from the Egyptians. Integrating it into their own territory, to a degree, the Israelis located military units there and allowed Israeli settlers to move in. Controversy remains as to whether the Israelis had intended to remove the Palestinian refugees from Gaza as part of their own state-building efforts. In any case, the Israeli government, in 2005, instead removed Jewish settlers from Gaza in connection with renewed tensions with the Palestinian Authority, a governing body for the Palestinians.

In 1994, the Israeli government and the Palestinians came to an agreement that shifted control of areas (those not deemed military targets) from Israel to an independent Palestinian parliamentary government. A year later, Palestinian authority was also extended to many West Bank areas (a contested area outside of Jerusalem), although tensions between Gaza and Israel remained high. These issues came to a head in 2006 when Hamas won in elections and refused to acknowledge existing treaties and decisions regarding the status of other nations, particularly that of Israel. This led to a distinct breakdown of the tentative peace in the region and to massive in-fighting between Hamas and the other Palestinian political party, Fatah. Hamas won a violent conflict in 2007 and remains in power.

The United Nations (U.N.) has been involved in Gaza since its creation in 1947, beginning with a resolution to find a way for Palestinian refugees to return to their homes. Over time, however, the U.N. has played different roles in the region, such as attempting to broker peace, settling political crises, and, as highlighted in the document reproduced here, organizing international aid for the people of Gaza. With varied success, the U.N. has tried to alleviate some of the tensions in the region; however, they have often been hindered by their own requirements, by previous resolutions concerning the situation, and by the interventions of other nations working unilaterally, such as the United States and Russia.

Author Biography

The United Nations' involvement in the Middle East is geared toward finding peace for the region. The Office of the United Nations Special Coordinator for the Middle East Peace Process was created in 1999 out of the earlier office of the United Nations Special Coordinator. These offices were created after the signing of the Oslo Accords (part of a peace process) in 1993 and 1995. The Oslo Accords authorized the creation of the Palestinian Authority, a limited government for the West Bank and Gaza, but they did not create an independent Palestinian state. When Hamas won the Palestinian Authority election in 2006 (and assured its control through military force), the U.N. used the opportunity to evaluate the state of Gaza and assess the negative consequences of continued Israeli external control over the area. *Gaza—Ten Years Later* is follow-up report to that earlier examination. One of the continuing goals of the U.N.'s Country Team is to find ways to aid the displaced persons of the region, including the Palestinian refugees. To do this, it tries to bring together Israeli, Hamas, and other governmental leaders to alleviate the humanitarian crisis facing the residents of the region.

HISTORICAL DOCUMENT

United Nations Country Team in the occupied Palestinian Territory, July 2017

SUMMARY: GAZA'S DE-DEVELOPMENT TRAJECTORY AND PROJECTIONS FOR THE FUTURE

Since the publication in 2012 of the UNCT's report on "Gaza 2020," Gaza's population has increased by 400,000, reaching 2 million people by the end of 2016. Gaza's population is projected to further increase to 2.2 million by 2020 and to 3.1 million by 2030—just 12 years away.

Reviewing the indicators which in 2012 led the U.N. to question whether Gaza would become 'unlivable' by 2020, it is clear that very little progress has been made to change the basic trajectory identified in 2012. The population has actually grown slightly faster than projected and neither the economy nor basic infrastructure and services have been able—even remotely—to keep pace. The findings of this report indicate that most of the projections for 2020 have in fact deteriorated even further and faster than anticipated.

In 2012, the U.N. projected an annual growth rate of real GDP per capita in Gaza of 0.6-1.5%, or even as high as 5.7-6.6% if a significant easing of trade and other restrictions were to take place. Since then, real GDP per capita in Gaza has instead decreased. Provision of basic services, including health and education, has continued to decline, as the needs for additional health clinics and classrooms and doctors, nurses and teachers, outlined in the 2020 report, have not been met. Instead, the number of doctors, nurses and hospital beds, relative to the population, declined by 15, 12 and 5 percentage points respectively between 2010 and 2017; and the teacher/student ratio declined by more than five percentage points over the past five years. It should be noted that these reductions do not apply to services provided by UNRWA, where the teacher-student ratio has improved in recent years.

The only indicator which has not deteriorated as quickly as was projected in 2012 relates to the water aquifer. The projection in 2012 that the aquifer would become unusable by 2016 has now been shifted to the end of 2017, thanks mainly to a doubling of water supplied by the Israeli water company and paid for by the Palestinian Authority (PA). But there is little to celebrate as by the end of this year, Gaza's only water source will be depleted, and irreversibly so by 2020, unless immediate remedial action is taken.

In addition to the impact of the violent Hamas takeover and ensuing Israeli measures imposed in 2007, three rounds of armed hostilities between Israel and Hamas—with the most devastating round in 2014—have dealt repeated blows to the Gazan economy and damaged essential infrastructure. As a result, the past three years have been focused mainly on the reconstruction of conflict-damages, drawing attention away from the desperate needs that Gaza faced even before the conflict in 2014. Huge reconstruction needs triggered an easing in imports of construction material to Gaza, particularly through the temporary Gaza Reconstruction Mechanism (GRM), but access to material necessary to allow the Gazan economy to recover and expand remains highly restricted.

Despite the warnings issued by the U.N. in 2012, Gaza has continued on its trajectory of de-development, in many cases even faster than the U.N. had originally projected. Ongoing humanitarian assistance and international service delivery, especially through UNRWA's services, are helping slow this descent, but the downward direction remains clear.

Key Indicators

Indicator	2011/12	2016/17	2020 (est.)
Population	1.6 million	2 million	2.2 million
Density	4,383/sq km	5,479 sq km	6,197 sq km
GDP per cap.	$1,165	$1,038	$1,058
Unemployment	29%	42%	44.4%
Energy—% demand met	60%	26-46%	25-71%
Water—% safe	10%	3.8%	0%
Yr. aquifer unusable	~2016	~2017	Irreversibly damaged
Hospital beds per 1,000 people	1.8	1.58	Over 1,000 new beds needed
Doctors per 1,000 people	1.68	1.42	Over 1,000 new doctors needed

GLOSSARY

aquifer: an underground layer of water-bearing permeable rock, rock fractures, or unconsolidated materials (gravel, sand, or silt) from which groundwater can be extracted using a water well

conflict-damages: damages done to property and/or person in the carrying out of violent attacks, i.e. bombings, etc.

de-development: the degradation or falling off of development; often used to describe underdeveloped nations

GDP: gross domestic product, a measure of economic growth

Hamas: a Palestinian Sunni-Islamic fundamentalist organization founded in 1987; currently, the elected leaders of Gaza

Palestinian Authority: the limited government of Gaza and the West Bank; its current controlling political party is Hamas

UNCT: United Nations Country Team

UNRWA: United Nations Relief and Works Agency for Palestine Refugees in the Near East

Document Analysis

This document provides a brief analysis of a few main points concerning the health and well-being of the inhabitants of the Gaza region, following up on similar earlier reports. It is intended for an audience that is already invested in the affairs of the region and, as such, often references events or systems that are indicative of deeper problems for Gaza without stating the specifics. By understanding the history behind these references, the meaning of the document becomes clearer. In its essence, this is a report on the sad state of Gaza and its continued decline.

In the second paragraph, the report makes reference to "basic infrastructure and services." Infrastructure can include power plants, electrical connection, water utilities, and so on, as well as significant structures such as bridges and roads. Basic services include access to doctors, medicine, and school teachers, just to name a few. The reference to infrastructure is further illuminated by the table at the end of the document. As can be seen, the energy demands of Gaza are met only between 26-49 percent of the time. Perhaps worse, there is only one doctor for about every 500 residents, despite the presence of international aid organizations such as Doctors Without Borders and the World Health Organization.

Gaza is further restricted in its access to resources and external interaction owing to the "trade and other restrictions" that were put in place by Israel after Hamas' takeover of Gaza. Trade restrictions drastically limit Gaza's ability to provide anything of value to outside markets. Without trade, modern economies cannot survive. Although the report states that Israel has eased some of those restrictions, the economy, clearly, continues to decline. Unfortunately for Gaza, with so many overlapping areas of decline, economic growth becomes an impossibility. Basic needs, such as clean water and access to medical care, must be met before addressing matters of economic growth. According to this report, Gaza is on the brink of systemic failure, or total breakdown.

As the U.N. warned in 2012, Gaza was edging toward precipitous decline then. In 2014, moreover, any potential upturn in the economy and living conditions was dampened by hostilities erupting between Hamas and Israel. That conflict is known as the Gaza War or (on the Israeli side) Operation Protective Edge. For seven weeks bombs and rockets exploded in both Gaza and Israel, resulting in many deaths on both sides. Hundreds of thousands of civilians were injured or displaced during the conflict (hence the term "conflict-damages" in the report). With a mixed international response, a tentative peace returned; but the damage to Gaza's infrastructure and civilian population was extensive.

Essential Themes

One fact that this report brings to light is the poor state of the Gazan aquifer. Identified as the only thing not in the negative column in this report, the aquifer has yet to completely cease to function. Yet it functions at only 3.8 percent of optimal, even as it outlives its projected end date. The Gaza region is expected to be out of clean water by 2020, and the governing body there has neither the infrastructure nor the economic resources to address the problem.

Gaza has not been an independent region for over 50 years, and has changed hands fairly frequently for an inhabited area. This complex situation, with its instability, discourages positive growth and development. States or territories not possessing stability are unable to attract investments or other potential growth opportunities, such as trade relationships, grants for development, or even the personnel resources needed to build and staff schools for the children. In this way, conflict creates a self-perpetuating cycle of "de-development," as the document notes, even as the region remains under scrutiny by the rest of the world. In addition, the huge number of displaced persons in Gaza (and the surrounding areas) adds to the sense of impermanence and instability. People who have been forced out of their homes, for any reason, are not easily resettled, especially in such a small area as Gaza. Moreover, situations like this create feelings of hopelessness that make growth and development all the more difficult.

In some ways, the decline of Gaza (and the very existence of the situation) can be seen as a consequence of modern state creation. When Israel was formed in 1948, it was a victory for many people but also destabilized an area that already had a history of conflict and tension. The ensuing decades of conflict between Israel and the surrounding nations attest to this. Regardless of one's political views concerning Israel and/or Palestine, when Israel was created not enough attention was paid to the displaced populations or to finding ways to mediate long-standing cultural, ethnic, political, and religious differences. The lasting effects of those decisions and actions (or lack thereof) are what we find in Gaza today. The most important thing for the writers of this report is that this problem is an ongoing one with serious ramifications and no end in sight.

—Anna Accettola, MA
—Michael Shally-Jensen, PhD

Bibliography and Additional Reading

Butt, Gerald. *Life at the Crossroads: A History of Gaza.* Rimal Publications, 2009.

Tessler, Mark A. *A History of the Israeli-Palestinian Conflict.* 2nd ed., Indiana University Press, 2009.

"United Nations Country Team in Palestine." *United Nations Country Team in Palestine*, UNSCO, unsco. unmissions.org/un-country-team-0.

"Who We Are." *United Nation Relief and Works Agency for Palestine Refugees in the Near East*, www.unrwa. org/who-we-are.

■ Statement by President Donald Trump on Jerusalem

Date: December 6, 2017
Author: Donald J. Trump
Geographic region: Israel
Genre: Speech

Summary Overview

In December 2017, U.S. President Donald J. Trump announced that the United States would be moving its embassy in Israel from the city of Tel Aviv to the contested capital city of Jerusalem, spurring both domestic and international controversy. The city of Jerusalem, a locus of controversy and a holy spot for a number of different religions and peoples for millennia, had always been the spiritual center of the modern nation of Israel. Even before the modern nation of Israel was founded in May 1948, Jerusalem stood as a controversial point when the United Nations debated how to divide the peoples, lands, and holy sites that were within what since 1917 had been the British Mandate of Palestine (a state administered under League of Nations auspices).

At the end of the 1948 Arab-Israeli War, the city of Jerusalem was divided into West Jerusalem, governed by Israel, and the "Old City" of East Jerusalem, governed by Jordan. Though the Knesset (Israeli legislature) had resolved that Jerusalem was to be Israel's capital in 1950, the city remained split until East Jerusalem was taken by Israel during the Six Day War in 1967. Although Israel guarantees access to the holy sites to Muslims, Christians, and Jews, most nations did not and still do not recognize Israel's authority over East Jerusalem and the vast majority of foreign embassies have remained in Tel Aviv.

Most analysts, with the notable exception of conservative American and Israeli commentators, viewed Trump's announcement as an unnecessary provocation of the tense situation both between Palestinians and Jews in Israel, as well as in the Middle East as a whole. Whereas the United States had long worked for a "two-state" solution to the endless conflict between Palestinians and Jews, Trump's announcement signaled a shift in U.S. foreign policy in the region—away from the traditional two-state approach and toward recognizing Israel's national rights as paramount.

Defining Moment

Jerusalem has been both holy ground and a contested place almost since its founding. As one of the holiest sites for three major world religions—Judaism, Islam, and Christianity—it has been occupied, besieged, conquered, and divided numerous times throughout its history. It has also served as the political capital of the region under numerous Arab, European, and Jewish regimes and governments. At the beginning of the twentieth century, the city was under the control of the Muslim Ottoman Empire, based in Turkey. With the defeat of the Ottoman Empire, which had allied itself with Germany during World War I, control of the region passed to the British, who under the League of Nations were mandated to govern the area until the peoples living there were capable of self-government. Though the British worked to remain neutral amid renewed rivalries between Palestinian and Jewish populations of the region, the Balfour Declaration of 1917—written by British Foreign Secretary Arthur Balfour—demonstrated an affinity that many in the Western nations felt for the Jewish people, many of whom were involved in Zionist efforts to repopulate the area as a Jewish homeland.

When the British Mandate came to an end in 1948, the (new) United Nations envisioned the creation of both Palestinian and Jewish states, with neither side controlling a neutral Jerusalem. However, Zionists were positioned to make their vision of a single Jewish nation—which included Jerusalem—a reality, and the modern State of Israel was founded on May 14, 1948. Almost immediately, warfare broke out that resulted in the Israelis seizing the western half of the city, while Jordan took the so-called Old City, which contained the vast majority of the sacred sites. In 1950 Israel declared Jerusalem—the entire city—to be its capital, and in the Six Day War of 1967, Israel was able to consolidate its control over both halves, which it has controlled ever since. The United Nations and most of its members have never recognized Israeli control over East Jerusalem,

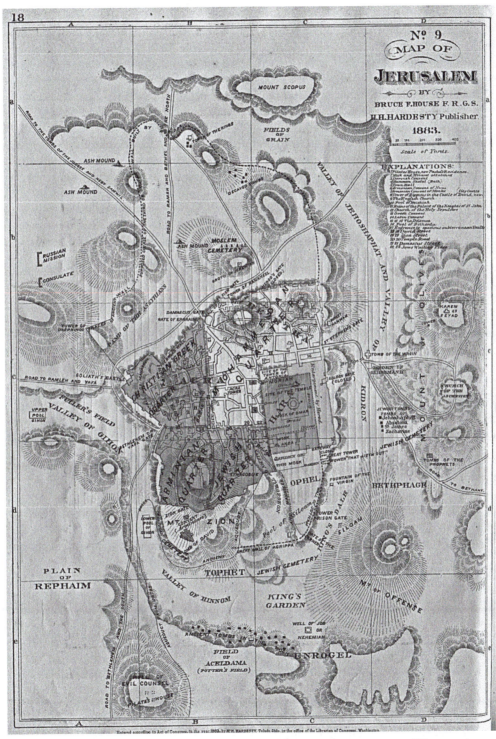

Map of Jerusalem 1883. Courtesy of The General Libraries, The University of Texas at Austin.

despite a 1980 act by the Knesset declaring an "undivided" Jerusalem to be the nation's capital.

As Israel's staunchest ally, the United States has long supported Israeli sovereignty. However, while seeking peace through initiatives such as Jimmy Carter's 1978 Camp David Accords between Israel and Egypt, and Bill Clinton's 2000 Camp David Summit between the leaders of Israel and the Palestinian Authority, American presidents have long positioned themselves as neutral on the question of Jerusalem. When Donald Trump was elected president in 2016, however, his position on Israel and Jerusalem was clear. Though prior U.S. Presidents such as Bill Clinton and George W. Bush had talked favorably about moving the U.S. embassy from Tel Aviv to Jerusalem, none of them had the political will to follow through, knowing that controversy would ensue. Trump vowed—much to the delight of conservative Israeli, American Jewish, and Evangelical Christian audiences—to fulfill his pro-Israel, anti-Muslim campaign rhetoric with action.

Author Biography

Most of the American presidents since the 1970s have hinged their hopes on peace in the Middle East on brokering a long-term solution to the centuries-long conflict between the Jewish and Palestinian populations of the modern State of Israel. However, even before the 2016 presidential election, Donald Trump had publicly committed himself to pursuing a foreign policy that would be much more favorable to the government of Israel than to the Palestinian populations. Though much of his campaign rhetoric was isolationist in nature, Evangelical Christians and American conservative Jewish leaders had his ear, leading him to espouse positions that opposed the "two-state solution" favored by prior administrations. His daughter, Ivanka—who converted to Judaism in 2006, after marrying Jared Kushner—declared on the campaign trail that her father would, indeed, move the American embassy to Jerusalem. Combined with his anti-Muslim rhetoric and his cordial relations and policy affinities with Prime Minister Benjamin Netanyahu of Israel's conservative Likud Party, it was clear to most that Trump's presidency would be characterized by actions that were quite different from prior presidents' efforts to be perceived as both a "friend of Israel" and, at the same time, neutral in its conflict with its Palestinian people.

HISTORICAL DOCUMENT

Thank you. When I came into office, I promised to look at the world's challenges with open eyes and very fresh thinking. We cannot solve our problems by making the same failed assumptions and repeating the same failed strategies of the past. Old challenges demand new approaches.

My announcement today marks the beginning of a new approach to conflict between Israel and the Palestinians.

In 1995, Congress adopted the Jerusalem Embassy Act, urging the federal government to relocate the American embassy to Jerusalem and to recognize that that city — and so importantly — is Israel's capital. This act passed Congress by an overwhelming bipartisan majority and was reaffirmed by a unanimous vote of the Senate only six months ago.

Yet, for over 20 years, every previous American president has exercised the law's waiver, refusing to move the U.S. embassy to Jerusalem or to recognize Jerusalem as Israel's capital city.

Presidents issued these waivers under the belief that delaying the recognition of Jerusalem would advance the cause of peace. Some say they lacked courage, but they made their best judgments based on facts as they understood them at the time. Nevertheless, the record is in. After more than two decades of waivers, we are no closer to a lasting peace agreement between Israel and the Palestinians. It would be folly to assume that repeating the exact same formula would now produce a different or better result.

Therefore, I have determined that it is time to officially recognize Jerusalem as the capital of Israel.

While previous presidents have made this a major campaign promise, they failed to deliver. Today, I am delivering.

I've judged this course of action to be in the best interests of the United States of America and the pursuit of peace between Israel and the Palestinians. This is a long-overdue step to advance the peace process and to work towards a lasting agreement.

Israel is a sovereign nation with the right like every other sovereign nation to determine its own capital. Acknowledging this as a fact is a necessary condition for achieving peace.

It was 70 years ago that the United States, under President Truman, recognized the State of Israel. Ever since then, Israel has made its capital in the city of Jerusalem — the capital the Jewish people established in ancient times. Today, Jerusalem is the seat of the modern Israeli government. It is the home of the Israeli parliament, the Knesset, as well as the Israeli Supreme Court. It is the location of the official residence of the Prime Minister and the President. It is the headquarters of many government ministries.

For decades, visiting American presidents, secretaries of state, and military leaders have met their Israeli counterparts in Jerusalem, as I did on my trip to Israel earlier this year.

Jerusalem is not just the heart of three great religions, but it is now also the heart of one of the most successful democracies in the world. Over the past seven decades, the Israeli people have built a country where Jews, Muslims, and Christians, and people of all faiths are free to live and worship according to their conscience and according to their beliefs.

Jerusalem is today, and must remain, a place where Jews pray at the Western Wall, where Christians walk the Stations of the Cross, and where Muslims worship at Al-Aqsa Mosque.

However, through all of these years, presidents representing the United States have declined to officially recognize Jerusalem as Israel's capital. In fact, we have declined to acknowledge any Israeli capital at all.

But today, we finally acknowledge the obvious: that Jerusalem is Israel's capital. This is nothing more, or less, than a recognition of reality. It is also the right thing to do. It's something that has to be done.

That is why, consistent with the Jerusalem Embassy Act, I am also directing the State Department to begin preparation to move the American embassy from Tel Aviv to Jerusalem. This will immediately begin the process of hiring architects, engineers, and planners, so that a new embassy, when completed, will be a magnificent tribute to peace.

In making these announcements, I also want to make one point very clear: This decision is not intended, in any way, to reflect a departure from our strong commitment to facilitate a lasting peace agreement. We want an agreement that is a great deal for the Israelis and a great deal for the Palestinians. We are not taking a position of any final status issues, including the specific boundaries of the Israeli sovereignty in Jerusalem, or the resolution of contested borders. Those questions are up to the parties involved.

The United States remains deeply committed to helping facilitate a peace agreement that is acceptable to both sides. I intend to do everything in my power to help forge such an agreement. Without question, Jerusalem is one of the most sensitive issues in those talks. The United States would support a two-state solution if agreed to by both sides.

In the meantime, I call on all parties to maintain the status quo at Jerusalem's holy sites, including the Temple Mount, also known as Haram al-Sharif.

Above all, our greatest hope is for peace, the universal yearning in every human soul. With today's action, I reaffirm my administration's longstanding commitment to a future of peace and security for the region.

There will, of course, be disagreement and dissent regarding this announcement. But we are confident that ultimately, as we work through these disagreements, we will arrive at a peace and a place far greater in understanding and cooperation.

This sacred city should call forth the best in humanity, lifting our sights to what it is possible; not pulling us back and down to the old fights that have become so totally predictable. Peace is never beyond the grasp of those willing to reach.

So today, we call for calm, for moderation, and for the voices of tolerance to prevail over the purveyors of hate. Our children should inherit our love, not our conflicts.

I repeat the message I delivered at the historic and extraordinary summit in Saudi Arabia earlier this year: The Middle East is a region rich with culture, spirit, and history. Its people are brilliant, proud, and diverse, vibrant and strong. But the incredible future awaiting this region is held at bay by bloodshed, ignorance, and terror.

Vice President Pence will travel to the region in the coming days to reaffirm our commitment to work with partners throughout the Middle East to defeat radicalism that threatens the hopes and dreams of future generations.

It is time for the many who desire peace to expel the extremists from their midst. It is time for all civilized nations, and people, to respond to disagreement with reasoned debate — not violence.

And it is time for young and moderate voices all across the Middle East to claim for themselves a bright and beautiful future.

So today, let us rededicate ourselves to a path of mutual understanding and respect. Let us rethink old assumptions and open our hearts and minds to possible and possibilities. And finally, I ask the leaders of the region — political and religious; Israeli and Palestinian; Jewish and Christian and Muslim — to join us in the noble quest for lasting peace.

Thank you. God bless you. God bless Israel. God bless the Palestinians. And God bless the United States. Thank you very much. Thank you.

(The proclamation is signed.)

GLOSSARY

British Mandate of Palestine: the League of Nations–established temporary government of what would become Israel, from 1918 until 1948

Jerusalem Embassy Act: a 1995 act by the U.S. Congress, signed by President Bill Clinton, committing the United States to moving its embassy in Israel from Tel Aviv to Jerusalem, but allowing presidents to delay its implementation as necessary to maintain peace in the Middle East

Knesset: the popularly-elected legislative body of the nation of Israel

Temple Mount: the East Jerusalem site of the Jewish temple built by King Solomon, which includes both a Jewish holy site, the Western Wall, and a Muslim holy site, the Al-Aqsa Mosque

Document Analysis

On December 6, 2017, U.S. President Donald J. Trump announced to the world that he would move the United States Embassy in Israel from Tel Aviv—where the vast majority of foreign embassies are—to Jerusalem, which Israel had claimed as its capital city since 1950. Though this announcement was met with dismay by many Democrats, some Republicans, and many other governments around the world, it was not an action without precedent and support in the United States—something that Trump went to great lengths to reinforce in his speech.

Almost immediately, Trump refers to the 1995 Jerusalem Embassy Act, passed by Congress and signed by President Bill Clinton, which committed the United States to recognizing Jerusalem as the capital of Israel, and eventually moving its embassy there. While noting the act, Trump accuses his predecessors of not living up to the terms of the law, by invoking its waiver, which allowed them to delay its implementation in the name of promoting peace in the region. Trump, however, assesses that regardless of the nobility of the motive, the delays had failed, noting that "[a]fter more than two decades of waivers, we are no closer to a lasting peace agreement between Israel and the Palestinians."

Trump refers to the campaign promise that both he and numerous prior presidents had made to move the embassy, noting that where they "failed to deliver . . . I am delivering." He couches his decision in the terms of promoting peace in the Middle East, though he does not state exactly how that is to take place or what it might look like, other than to restate his belief—and the long-held U.S. position—supporting the continued sovereignty of Israel. Trump couches his statements about sovereignty in historical terms, noting that it was President Harry S Truman who first recognized the State of Israel, and that American government officials had usually met with Israeli government officials in Jerusalem when visiting Israel.

Jerusalem contains some of the holiest sites of three world religions—Judaism, Islam, and Christianity—and Trump reinforces the view that the city and those sites will continue to be open to people of all religions and backgrounds. Trump explicitly states that the decision is not to represent a departure from prior policy seeking an equitable peace for both Israelis and Palestinians, and that the decision does not mean that the United States is "taking a position of any final status issues, including the specific boundaries of the Israeli sovereignty in Jerusalem, or the resolution of contested borders." However, while realizing that many Palestinians would react negatively, Trump calls "for calm, for moderation, and for the voices of tolerance to prevail over the purveyors of hate."

Though speaking of his desire for peace and what he terms a "great deal" for both the Israelis and the Palestinians, Trump speaks at the same time of moving the American embassy to Jerusalem. Though he states that this move is being made in an effort to achieve peace, Trump provides no arguments as to how moving the embassy might lead to peace, but rather, he recognizes that many may react negatively to his decision. Regardless, based upon his administration's pro-Israel foreign policy, Trump proceeded with the decision that the three presidents before him all considered to be detrimental to peace between the Israelis and Palestinians, moving the embassy and recognizing the entire city of Jerusalem as the capital of the State of Israel.

Essential Themes

By announcing his intention to follow through with the directives of the 1995 Jerusalem Embassy Act, Trump tacitly endorsed Israel's view that its conquest of East Jerusalem in the 1967 Six Day War gave it a legitimate claim to governing all of Jerusalem, and utilizing it as its capital city. What he did not recognize in his speech or in any of his other foreign policy statements related to Israel is that the Palestinians also may view Jerusalem as their capital city. This represented a significant departure from prior U.S. foreign policy regarding Israel, in which the United States sought to remain neutral on questions about how the final peace would look. This was done both to retain American credibility as negotiators in the region, and to keep both Israelis and Palestinians at the bargaining table. With the United States apparently taking Israel's side on the question of Jerusalem, that neutrality is diminished.

Many commentators have seen Trump's positions on Israel and Jerusalem as being aimed at shoring up his support among American Evangelical Christians. Many Evangelicals favor a strongly pro-Israel policy, on the basis of a shared Judeo-Christian tradition. Combined with the support of some conservative American Jews, Trump's shift away from prior policy restraints is understandable. Add to that the fact that at the time of his speech the peace process between the Israelis and Palestinians was largely stagnant, and it is understandable that Trump saw little downside to announcing a decision that would appease many of his supporters.

At the time of the announcement, some commentators speculated that the decision was a reward for Israel's cooperation with many of the Arab Gulf states, arrayed against Iran, which Trump and his advisors have seen as the primary threat in the region. Others saw it as in line with prior administrations' efforts to appear pro-Israel in order to make Israeli leaders secure enough to pursue peace. Trump was silent on both of these possible motives. But in the short term, the decision has only resulted in increased unrest and protest in the region. Palestinians, already dubious of American motives in its policies regarding their struggle with the Israelis, have seen this as a continuation and escalation of America's pro-Israel policies. Protests against Israel and the American decision erupted almost immediately after Trump's announcement. Many other Arab nations have viewed American Israeli policy in much the same way.

Making American support of Israel more explicit may make it even more difficult to convince Arab nations and the Palestinians that they are willing to work in good faith for a solution that benefits both the Israelis and the Palestinians. Israel, knowing that Trump just made a major diplomatic concession for nothing, could emerge even more unmotivated to make concessions of their own. Additionally, Trump runs the risk of alienating the more moderate Palestinian factions that the United States supports, making them more likely to align with the more militant groups such as Hamas. Though the years following the decision will demonstrate the long-term effects of moving the U.S. embassy to Jerusalem, it is clear that most governments and politicians both in the Middle East and around the world are doubtful that it will enhance the chances for peace in the region.

—*Steven L. Danver, PhD*

Bibliography and Additional Reading

Cohen, Hillel. *The Rise and Fall of Arab Jerusalem: Palestinian Politics and the City since 1967.* New York: Routledge, 2011. Print.

Cortellessa, Eric. What a Trump Presidency Would Mean for Israel. *The Times of Israel*, November 6, 2016. Online. https://www.timesofisrael.com/what-a-donald-trump-presidency-would-mean-for-israel/

Landler, Mark. Trump Recognizes Jerusalem as Israel's Capital and Orders U.S. Embassy to Move. *The New York Times*, December 6, 2017. Online. https://www.nytimes.com/2017/12/06/world/middleeast/trump-jerusalem-israel-capital.html

Shlay, Anne B. and Gillad Rosen. *Jerusalem: The Spatial Politics of a Divided Metropolis.* Malden, MA: Polity Press, 2015. Print

Shragai, Nadav. *Demography, Geopolitics, and the Future of Israel's Capital: Jerusalem's Proposed Master Plan.* Jerusalem: Jerusalem Center for Public Affairs, 2010. Print.

U.S. Congress, Jerusalem Embassy Act of 1995, Pub.L. 104–45, November 8, 1995, 109 Stat. 398.

APPENDIXES

Chronological List

Web Resources

https://www.al-islam.org/

Al-Islam is a large collection of online resources on every aspect of Islam.

http://library.columbia.edu/locations/global/mideast.html

Middle East & Islamic Studies, a collection of websites and other useful tools and information, from Columbia University Libraries.

http://www.merip.org/

The Middle East Research & Information Project provides an informative website on Middle East politics, culture, and society.

http://teachmideast.org/background-context/history/

TeachMideast, an educational initiative of the Middle East Policy Council, offers a range of resources for teaching and learning about the Middle East.

https://sourcebooks.fordham.edu/halsall/islam/islamsbook.asp

The Internet Islamic History Sourcebook, from Fordham University, provides a wide selection of texts and images concerning Islamic history.

https://sourcebooks.fordham.edu/halsall/jewish/jewishsbook.as

The Internet Jewish History Sourcebook, from Fordham University, provides a wide selection of texts and images concerning Jewish history.

https://sourcebooks.fordham.edu/Halsall/mod/modsbook54.asp

The Middle East Since 1944, from Fordham University, provides a wide selection of texts and images concerning modern Middle Eastern history.

https://ottomanhistorians.uchicago.edu/

Historians of the Ottoman Empire, from the University of Chicago, is an expanding project that serves as a reference work and an archive of primary sources concerning the Ottoman Empire.

http://mesana.org/

The Middle East Studies Association is a learned society that fosters the study of the Middle East, including Iran, Turkey, Afghanistan, Israel, Pakistan, and the countries of the Arab World from the seventh century to modern times.

http://www.mei.edu/

The Middle East Institute works to provide non-partisan, expert information and analysis on the Middle East.

http://aimsnorthafrica.org/

The American Institute for Maghrib Studies is an educational organization specializing in topics related to North Africa.

Bibliography

Abdullah II, King of Jordan, *Our Last Best Chance: The Pursuit of Peace in a Time of Peril*. London: Penguin Books Ltd. 2012.

Abrahamian, Ervand. *The Coup: 1953, the CIA, and the Roots of Modern US-Iranian Relations*. New York: New, 2013. Print.

Aburish, Said K. *Nasser: The Last Arab*. New York: Thomas Dunne Books, 2004. Print.

Addi, Lahouari. *Radical Arab Nationalism and Political Islam*. Translated by Anthony Roberts, Washington, D.C.: Georgetown University Press, 2017.

Adel, Ezzat. "The Day Nasser Nationalised the Canal." *BBC News*. London: The British Broadcasting Corporation, 2006. Web. 2 March 2018.

Aharoni, Reuven. *The Pasha's Bedouin: Tribes and State in the Egypt of Mehemet Ali, 1805–1848*. Routledge, 2010.

Akbarzadeh, Shahram, and Dara Conduit, eds. *Iran in the World: President Rouhani's Foreign Policy*. New York: Palgrave Macmillan, 2016.

Akcam, Tanar. 2013. *The Young Turks' Crime against Humanity: The Armenian Genocide and Ethnic Cleansing in the Ottoman Empire*. Princeton University Press.

Alkhateeb, Firas. "Granada – The Last Muslim Kingdom of Spain." *Lost Islamic History*. Chicago: Lost Islamic History, 2013. Web. 17 January 2017.

al-Mawardi, Muhammed. *The Ordinances of Government*. Reading, UK: Garnet Publishing, 2000. Print.

Ambrose, Stephen E. *Eisenhower, Vol. II: The President*. New York: Simon, 1984. Print.

Ansary, Tamim. *Destiny Disrupted: A History of the World through Islamic Eyes*. Washington, DC: PublicAffairs, 2010.

Antonius, George. *The Arab Awakening: The Story of the Arab National Movement*. Philadelphia: J.B. Lippincott Company, 1939. Online - Toronto: McGill University Rare Books, 2018. Web. 4 March 2018.

Armstrong, Karen. *Islam: A Short History*. London: Phoenix Press, 2001.

Ashton, Nigel John. "The Hijacking of a Pact: The Formation of the Baghdad Pact and Anglo-American Tensions in the Middle East, 1955–1958." *Review of International Studies* 19.2 (1993): 123–37. Print.

"Attacks on Ghouta: Analysis of Alleged Use of Chemical Weapons in Syria". *Human Rights Watch* (September 10, 2013) https://www.hrw.org/report/2013/09/10/attacks-ghouta/analysis-alleged-use-chemical-weapons-syria [accessed March 18, 2018].

Atiya, Aziz. 1991. "Sawirus Ibn Al-Muqaffa." In *The Coptic Encyclopedia* (volume 4). Claremont Graduate University.

Avineri, Shlomo. *Herzl's Vision: Theodor Herzl and the Foundation of the Jewish State*. BlueBridge, 2014.

Axworthy, Michael. *Revolutionary Iran: A History of the Islamic Republic*. New York: Oxford UP, 2016. Print.

Baracskay, Daniel. *The Palestine Liberation Organization: Terrorism and Prospects for Peace in the Holy Land*. (Praeger Security International) Santa Barbara CA: Praeger, 2011. Print.

Barr, James. *A Line in the Sand: The Anglo-French Struggle for the Middle East, 1914–1948*. New York: W.W. Norton & Co, 2012. Print.

Barry, Quintin. *War in the East: A Military History of the Russo-Turkish War of 1877–78*. Solihull, UK: Helion & Co., 2012.

Barton, Simon. *A History of Spain*. 2nd ed. (Palgrave Essential Histories series) New York: Palgrave Macmillan, 2009. Print.

Beaten, Roderick and David Ricks, eds. *The Making of Modern Greece: Nationalism, Romanticism, and the Uses of the Past (1797–1896)*. New York: Routledge, 2016.

_____. *Byron's War: Romantic Rebellion, Greek Revolution*. New York: Cambridge UP, 2013.

Beauchamp, Zack, editor. "The Syria War: A History". *Vox*(September 21, 2015) https://www.vox.com/cards/syrian-refugees-war-assad/syria-chemical-weapons

Bellamy, AJ "Libya and the Responsibility to Protect: The Exception and the Norm" *Ethics and International Affairs*, 25(3) (2011): 263-269.

Ben-Arieh, Alex. "Independence Day 1948" *Historama*. Tel Aviv: Historama, 2018. Web. 27 February 2018.

Bennison, Amira K. *The Great Caliphs: The Golden Age of the 'Abbasid Empire*. New Haven, CT: Yale University Press, 2010. Print.

Bennoune, Mahfoud. *The Making of Contemporary Algeria, 1830–1987: Colonial Upheavals and Post-Independence Development*. Cambridge University Press, 2002.

Benson, Michael T. *Harry S. Truman and the Founding of Israel*. Westport: Greenwood, 1997. Print.

Berkowitz, Michael. *Zionist Culture and West European Jewry before the First World War*. Cambridge University Press, 1993.

Beshara, Adel (ed.). *The Origins of Syrian Nationhood: Histories, Pioneers, and Identity*. Routledge Studies in Middle Eastern History. Abingdon UK: Routledge, 2014. Print.

Black, Eric. "Resolution 242 and the Aftermath of 1967." *Frontline*. Boston: WGBH Educational Foundation, 1995. Web. 6 March 2018.

Boahen, A. Adu *African Perspective on Colonialism*. Johns Hopkins, 1987.

_____. *Africa under Colonial Domination, 1880–1935*. New Africa Education, 2003.

Boghoziyan, Albert. "One for Us, Six for Britons!: William Knox D'Arcy in History of Iran". *Iran Review* (May 25, 2016) http://www.iranreview.org/content/Documents/One-for-Us-Six-for-Britons-.htm [accessed March 17, 2018].

Bostdorff, Denise M. *Proclaiming the Truman Doctrine: The Cold War Call to Arms*. College Station: Texas A&M UP, 2008. Print.

Bowie, Robert R. & Richard H. Immerman. *Waging Peace: How Eisenhower Shaped an Enduring Cold War Strategy*. New York: Oxford UP, 1998. Print.

Braithwaite, Rodric. *Afgantsy: The Russians in Afghanistan 1979-89*. Oxford: Oxford UP, 2011. Print.

Bredero, Adriaan. *Christendom and Christianity in the Middle Ages*. Grand Rapids: Eerdmans, 1987. Print.

Brenner, Björn. *Gaza under Hamas: From Islamic Democracy to Islamist Governance*. New York: I.B. Tauris, 2017.

Brewer, David. *Greece, the Hidden Centuries: Turkish Rule from the Fall of Constantinople to Greek Independence*. New York: I.B. Tauris, 2010.

Brown, Nathan J. *Palestinian Politics after the Oslo Accords: Resuming Arab Palestine*. Berkeley: University of California Press, 2003.

Burke, Edmund. *The Ethnographic State: France and the Invention of Moroccan Islam*. Univ. of Calif. Press, 2014.

Butt, Gerald. *Life at the Crossroads: A History of Gaza*. Rimal Publications, 2009.

Calder, Norman, Jawid Mojaddedi, & Andrew Rippin, ed. *Classical Islam: A Sourcebook of Religious Literature*. 2nd ed. New York: Routledge. 2012. Print.

Caspitt, Ben. *The Netanyahu Years*. Translated by Ora Cummings, New York: Thomas Dunne, 2017.

Churchill, Winston. *My Early Life: 1874–1904*. New York: Scribner, 1996. Print.

_____. *The River War: An Account of the Reconquest of the Sudan*. New York: Skyhorse Publishing, 2013. Print.

Clarke, Nicola. *The Muslim Conquest of Iberia: Medieval Arabic Narratives*. London: Routledge, 2013. Print.

Claster, Jill N. *Sacred Violence: The European Crusades to the Middle East, 1095–1396*. Toronto: U of Toronto P, 2009. Digital file.

Cockburn, Patrick. *The Age of Jihad: Islamic State and the Great War for the Middle East*. London: Verso 2016.

Coe, Kevin. "George W. Bush, Television News, and Rationales for the Iraq War." *Journal of Broadcasting & Electronic Media*, vol. 55, no. 3, July 2011, pp. 307-324.

Cohen, Hillel. *The Rise and Fall of Arab Jerusalem: Palestinian Politics and the City since 1967*. New York: Routledge, 2011. Print.

Cohen, Mark. "What Was the Pact of 'Umar? A Literary- Historical Study." *Jerusalem Studies in Arabic and Islam* 23 (1999): 100–157. Print.

Cohen, Michael Joseph. *Britain's Moment in Palestine: Retrospect and Perspectives, 1917-48*. London: Routledge/Taylor & Francis Group, 2014.

Cohn, Henry J. "Theodor Herzl's Conversion to Zionism." *Jewish Social Studies* (1970): 101–110.

Collelo, Thomas (ed.) "Syria: World War I." *Syria: A Country Study*. Washington: General Printing Office/ Library of Congress, 1987. Web. 4 March 2018.

Cortellessa, Eric. What a Trump Presidency Would Mean for Israel. *The Times of Israel*, November 6, 2016. Online. https://www.timesofisrael.com/what-a-donald-trump-presidency-would-mean-for-israel/

Cotton, Henry. *The Five Books of Maccabees in English: With Notes and Illustrations*. London: Forgotten Books, 2017. Print.

Danilevskii, Nikolai Iakovlevich. *Woe to the Victors: The Russo-Turkish War, the Congress of Berlin, and the Future of Slavdom*, tr. by Stephen M. Woodburn. Bloomington, IN: Slavica Publishers, 2015. [A collection of articles first published in the 1870s.]

Davies, Brian L. *The Russo-Turkish War, 1768–1774: Catherine II and the Ottoman Empire.* New York: Bloomsbury Academic, 2016.

Davison, Roderic H. "'Russian Skill and Turkish Imbecility': The Treaty of Kuchuk Kainardji Reconsidered." *Slavic Review* 35:3 (September 1976): 463–83; reprinted in Roderic H. Davison, *Essays in Ottoman and Turkish History, 1774–1923: The Impact of the West.* Austin: University of Texas Press, 1990; 29–50.

De Heijer, Johannes. 1991. "History of the Patriarchs of Alexandria." In *The Coptic Encyclopedia* (volume 4). Claremont Graduate University.

Derfler, Steven L. *Hasmonean Revolt: Rebellion or Revolution.* Lewiston, NY: Edwin Mellen Press, 1990. Print.

Di Giovanni, Janine. The Morning They Came for Us: Dispatches from Syria. New York: Liveright Publishing Corporation, 2017.

Doran, Michael. *Ike's Gamble: American's Rise to Dominance in the Middle East.* New York: Free Press, 2016. Print.

Doran, Michael. *Pan-Arabism Before Nasser: Egyptian Power Politics and the Palestinian Question.* New York: Oxford University Press, 1999.

Dunn, Ross E. *The Adventures of Ibn Battuta, a Muslim Traveler of the Fourteenth Century.* Berkeley: U of California P, 1986. Print.

Duri, Abd al-Aziz. *Early Islamic Institutions: Administration and Taxation from the Caliphate to the Umayyads and Abbasids.* London: I.B.Tauris, 2011. Print.

Elleman, Bruce A., et al. *Piracy and Maritime Crime: Historical and Modern Case Studies.* CreateSpace, 2014.

Emon, Anver M. *Religious Pluralism and Islamic Law: Dhimmīs and Others in the Empire of Law.* Oxford: Oxford UP, 2012. Print.

Ezzati, A. *The Spread of Islam: The Contributing Factors.* London: Saqi, 2002. Print.

Fahmy, Khaled. *All the Pasha's Men: Mehmed Ali, His Army and the Making of Modern Egypt.* Cambridge Univ. Press, 2009.

Farsoun, Samih K, and Naseer H. Aruri. *Palestine and the Palestinians: A Social and Political History.* Boulder, CO: Westview Press, 2006. Print.

Feifer, Gregory. *The Great Gamble: The Soviet War in Afghanistan.* New York: HarperCollins, 2009. Print.

Feron, James. "Menachem Begin, Guerilla Leader Who Became Peacemaker." *New York Times.* New York Times, 10 Mar. 1992. Web. 30 Mar. 2016.

Filiu, Jean-Pierre. *From Deep State to Islamic State: The Arab Counter-Revolution and Its Jihadi Legacy.* New York: Oxford University Press, 2015.

Fine, Steven, ed. *Sacred Realm: The Emergence of the Synagogue in the Ancient World.* New York: Oxford UP, 1996. Print.

Finkelstein, Norman. *Gaza: An Inquest into Its Martyrdom.* Oakland: University of California Press, 2018.

Fishman, Ben, *Jordan: Caught in the Middle Again.* [in:] "Survival", vol. 56 no. 6, December 2014–January 2015, pp. 39–48.

Florinksy, Michael T. *Russia: A History and an Interpretation,* v. 2. New York: Macmillan, 1953.

Friedman, Uri. "The 'Peace Process': A Short History." *Foreign Policy.* Foreign Policy, 27 Feb. 2012. Web. 30 Mar. 2016.

Fromkin, David. *A Peace to End All Peace: The Fall of the Ottoman Empire and the Creation of the Modern Middle East.* New York: Holt, 2001. Print.

Gasiorowski, Mark J. *Mohammad Mosaddeq and the 1953 Coup in Iran.* Syracuse, NY: Syracuse UP, 2004. Print.

Gelvin, James L. *The Modern Middle East: A History,* 4th ed. New York: Oxford University Press, 2015.

George, Alan, *Jordan: Living in the Crossfire.* London and New York: Zed Books 2005.

Gibson, Roy K. & Ruth Morello. *Reading the Letters of Pliny the Younger: An Introduction.* New York: Cambridge UP, 2012. Print.

Gifkins, J. "R2P in the U.N. Security Council: Darfur, Libya and Beyond," *Cooperation and Conflict,* 51(2) (2016): 157-158.

Gilbert, Martin. *Israel: A History.* New York: Harper Perennial, 1998 and 2008. Print.

Glenny, Misha. *The Balkans: Nationalism, War, and the Great Powers, 1804–2011.* New York: Penguin Books, 2012.

Goodman, Martin, ed. *Jews in a Graeco-Roman World.* New York: Oxford UP, 1998. Print.

Grabar, Andre. *The Golden Age of Justinian: From the Death of Theodosius to the Rise of Islam.* New York: Odyssey, 1967. Print.

Grossman, Michael Orlov, and Ronald Eric Matthews Jr. *Perspectives on the Legacy of George W. Bush.* London: Cambridge Scholars Publishing, 2009.

Hadas-Lebel, Mireille. *Flavius Josephus: Eyewitness to Rome's First-Century Conquest of Judea.* Trans. Richard Miller. London: Macmillan, 1993. Print.

Hanioglu, M. Sükrü. *A Brief History of the Late Ottoman Empire.* Princeton University Press. 2010. Print

Harris, William. *Quicksilver War: Syria, Iraq and the Spiral of Conflict.* London: Hurst & Company, 2018.

Hayes, John H. & Sara R. Mandell. *The Jewish People in Classical Antiquity: From Alexander to Bar Kochba.* Louisville, KY: Westminster, 1998. Print.

"Herzl Law." *World Zionist Organization.* knesset.gov.il/vip/herzl/eng/Herz_Law_eng.html.

Howard, Douglas A. *A History of the Ottoman Empire.* New York: Cambridge University Press, 2017.

Husain, Shahnaz. *The Muslim Conquest of Spain and the Legacy of Al-Andalus.* London: Ta-Ha Publishers, 2010. Print.

"ISIS Fast Facts". *CNN.com* (November 1, 2016) http://www.cnn.com/2014/08/08/world/isis-fast-facts/ [accessed March 14, 2017].

Jamal, Amal. *The Palestinian National Movement.* Bloomington IN: Indiana University Press, 2005. Print.

James, Lawrence. *Churchill and Empire: A Portrait of an Imperialist.* New York: Pegasus Books, 2014. Print.

Jeffries, Jennifer. *Hamas: Terrorism, Governance, and Its Future in Middle East Politics.* Santa Barbara, CA: ABC-CLIO, 2016.

"Jewish Population of Europe in 1945." *Holocaust Encyclopedia.* United States Holocaust Memorial Museum, 20 Jun. 2014. Web. 2 Jan. 2015.

Jewish Virtual Library. "U.N. Security Council: The Meaning of Resolution 242." *Jewish Virtual Library.* Chevy Chase MD: American-Israeli Cooperative Enterprise, 2018. Web. 7 March 2018.

Jones, Howard. "A New Kind of War": *America's Global Strategy and the Truman Doctrine in Greece.* New York: Oxford UP, 1989. Print.

Judis, John B. "Seeds of Doubt: Harry Truman's Concerns about Israel and Palestine Were Prescient—and Forgotten." *New Republic.* The New Republic, 15 Jan. 2014. Web. 2 Jan. 2015.

Juergensmeyer, Mark. *Terror in the Mind of God: The Global Rise of Religious Violence.* Berkeley, CA: University of California Press, 2000.

Kattan, Victor. *From Coexistence to Conquest: International Law and the Origins of the Arab-Israeli Conflict, 1891–1949.* London: Pluto Press, 2009. Internet resource.

King, Henry Churchill and Charles R. Crane. "The King-Crane Commission Report, August 28, 1919." *WWI Document Archive.* Provo UT: Brigham Young University Library, 2008. Web. 4 March 2018.

Kinzer, Stephen. *All the Shah's Men: An American Coup and the Roots of Middle East Terror.* Hoboken: Wiley, 2003. Print.

_____. *Overthrow: America's Century of Regime Change from Hawaii to Iraq.* New York: Times Books/Henry Holt, 2007

Kyle, Keith. *Suez.* New York: St. Martin's Press, 1991. Print.

Landler, Mark. Trump Recognizes Jerusalem as Israel's Capital and Orders U.S. Embassy to Move. *The New York Times,* December 6, 2017. Online. https://www.nytimes.com/2017/12/06/world/middleeast/trump-jerusalem-israel-capital.html

Lansford, Tom. *The Lords of Foggy Bottom: American Secretaries of State and the World They Shaped.* Baldwin Place: Encyclopedia Soc., 2001. Print.

Law, Timothy Michael, and Alison Salvesen, eds. *Greek Scripture and the Rabbis.* Leuven: Peeters, 2012. Print.

Le Strange, G. *Baghdad During the Abbasid Caliphate.* Whitefish, MT: Kessinger Publishing, 2010. Print.

Lesch, David W. *1979: The Year That Shaped the Modern Middle East.* Boulder: Westview, 2001. Print.

"London Conference on Palestine Suddenly Adjourns until after U.N. General Assembly." *JTA.* Jewish Telegraphic Agency, 2015. Web. 2 Jan. 2015.

Lowney, Chris. *A Vanished World: Muslims, Christians, and Jews in Medieval Spain.* Oxford: Oxford University Press, 2006. Print.

Lust, Ellen, ed. *The Middle East,* 14th ed. Thousand Oaks, CA: CQ Press/SAGE Publications, 2016.

Lustick, Ian. *Arab-Israeli Relations: Historical Background and Origins of the Conflict.* New York: Garland, 1994. Print.

Lynch, Marc. *The New Arab Wars: Uprisings and Anarchy in the Middle East.* New York: PublicAffairs, 2016.

MacDonald, Robert W. *The League of Arab States: A Study in Dynamics of Regional Organization.* Princeton: Princeton University Press, 1965.

Mastny, Vojtech. *The Cold War and Soviet Insecurity: The Stalin Years.* New York: Oxford UP, 1996. Print.

Matthews, Weldon C. *Confronting an Empire, Constructing a Nation: Arab Nationalists and Popular Politics in Mandate Palestine.* London: I.B. Tauris, 2006.

McCants, William. *The ISIS Apocalypse: The History, Strategy, and Doomsday Vision of the Islamic State.* New York: Picador, 2015.

McCullough, David. *Truman.* New York: Simon, 2003. Print.

McDougall, James. 2017. *A History of Algeria*. Cambridge University Press.

McMeekin, Sean. *The Ottoman Endgame: War, Revolution, and the Making of the Modern Middle East, 1908–1923*. New York: Penguin, 2015. Print.

Medlicott, W. N. *The Congress of Berlin and After: A Diplomatic History of the Near Eastern Settlement, 1878–1880*, 2ᵈ ed. Hamden, CT: Archon Books, 1963.

Meinardus, Otto. 2016. *Two Thousand Years of Coptic Christianity*. American University in Cairo.

Meital, Yoram. *Peace in Tatters: Israel, Palestine, and the Middle East*. Boulder: Rienner, 2006. Print.

Melanson, Richard A. *American Foreign Policy since the Vietnam War: The Search for Consensus from Richard Nixon to George W. Bush*. Armonk, NY: M.E. Sharpe, 2005.

Milner, Laurie. "History: The Suez Crisis." *BBC*. London: The British Broadcasting Corporation, 2014. Web. 28 February 2018.

Mina, Parviz. "Oil Agreements in Iran". *Encyclopaedia Iranica* (July 20, 2004) [accessed March 17, 2018].

Moens, Alexander. *The Foreign Policy of George W. Bush: Values, Strategy and Loyalty*. Burlington, VT: Ashgate Pub., 2004.

Morris, Benny. *1948: A History of the First Arab-Israeli War*. New Haven: Yale University Press, 2008. Print.

Moubayed, Sami M. *Under the Black Flag: At the Frontier of the New Jihad*. New York: I.B. Tauris, 2015.

Muir, Jim. "Islamic State Group: The Full Story". *BBC News* (June 20, 2016) http://www.bbc.com/news/world-middle-east-35695648 [accessed March 14, 2017].

Nasr, Vali. "Iran among the Ruins." *Foreign Affairs* 97:2 (March/April 2018): 108–18.

Neiberg, Michael S. *The World War I Reader: [primary and Secondary Sources]*. New York: New York University Press, 2007. Print.

Neill, Lochery. "Review Article: Lion in the Sand: British Policy in the Middle East, 1945–67." *Middle Eastern Studies*, no. 5, 2008, p. 807.

Nicoll, Fergus. *The Mahdi of Sudan and the Death of General Gordon*. Stroud, UK: Sutton Publishing, 2004. Print.

O'Callaghan, Joseph F. *The Last Crusade in the West: Castile and the Conquest of Granada*. (The Middle Ages Series) Philadelphia: University of Pennsylvania Press, 2014. Print.

Odeh, Adnan Abu (ed.) *U.N. Security Council Resolution 242: The Building Block of Peacemaking: A Washington Institute Monograph*. Washington: Washington Institute for Near East Policy. 1993. Print.

Office of the Historian. "The Arab-Israeli War of 1948" *Milestones in U.S. Foreign Relations*. Washington: Department of State, 2018. Web. 27 February 2018.

_____. "The Soviet Invasion of Afghanistan and the U.S. Response, 1978-1980." *U.S. Department of State: Bureau of Public Affairs*. Washington: U.S. Department of State, 2016. Web.

Offner, Arnold A. *Another Such Victory: President Truman and the Cold War, 1945–1953*. Stanford: Stanford UP, 2002. Print.

Ogot, Bethwell A. *Africa from the Sixteenth to the Eighteenth Century*. East African Educational Publishers Ltd., 2014.

Pace, Eric. "Anwar el-Sadat, the Daring Arab Pioneer of Peace with Israel." *New York Times*. New York Times, 7 Oct. 1981. Web. 30 Mar. 2016.

Palestine Ministry of Information. "The Palestinian Charter." *Palestine Affairs Council*. Houston: Palestine American Council, 2018. Web. 7 March 2018.

Pappé, Ilan. *A History of Modern Palestine: One Land, Two Peoples*. New York: Cambridge UP, 2004. Print.

Parra, Francisco R. *Oil Politics: A Modern History of Petroleum*. London: I.B. Tauris, 2004.

Parsi, Trita. *Losing an Enemy: Obama, Iran, and the Triumph of Diplomacy*. New Haven, CT: Yale University Press, 2017.

"Peace Talks at Camp David, September 1978." *PBS*. WGBH, n.d. Web. 30 Mar. 2016.

Pechatnov, Vladimir O. "The Soviet Union and the World, 1944–1953." *The Cambridge History of the Cold War: Origins*. Vol. 1. Ed. Melvyn P. Leffler and Odd Arne Westad. New York: Cambridge UP, 2010. 90–111. Print.

Pennell, C. R. *Morocco since 1830: A History*. New York Univ. Press, 2000.

Peters, Edward. *The First Crusade: "The Chronicle of Fulcher of Chartres" and Other Source Materials*. 2ⁿᵈ ed. Philadelphia: U of Pennsylvania P, 1998. The Middle Ages Ser. Print.

Phillips, William D. Jr., and Carla Rahn Phillips. *A Concise History of Spain*. 2ⁿᵈ ed. (Cambridge Concise Histories) Cambridge: Cambridge University Press, 2016. Print.

Pressman, Jeremy. "Explaining the Carter Administration's Israeli-Palestinian Solution." *Diplomatic History* 37.5 (2013): 1117–47. Print.

"The Recognition of the State of Israel." *Harry S. Truman Library and Museum*. Harry S. Truman Library and Museum, 2014. Web. 2 Jan. 2015.

"The Rise of Isis". *Frontline*, October 28, 2014. *PBS. org* http://www.pbs.org/wgbh/frontline/film/rise-of-isis/ [accessed March 14, 2017].

Robenne, Meir. "Understanding U.N. Security Council Resolution 242." *Jerusalem Center for Public Affairs: Israeli Security, Regional Diplomacy, and International Law.* Jerusalem: Jerusalem Center for Public Affairs, 2018. Web. 7 March 2018.

Robins, Philip. *A History of Jordan.* Cambridge: Cambridge University Press, 2004. Print.

Rodgers, Lucy, David Gritten, James Offer, and Patrick Asare. "Syria: The Story of the Conflict". *BBC News* (March 11, 2016) http://www.bbc.com/news/world-middle-east-26116868 [accessed March 18, 2018].

Rogan, Eugene L. *The Fall of the Ottomans: the Great War in the Middle East.* New York: Basic Books, 2015. Print.

Rosler, Nimrod. "Leadership and Peacemaking: Yitzhak Rabin and the Oslo Accords." *International Journal of Intercultural Relations*, vol. 54, 01 Sept. 2016, pp. 55-67.

Rostow, Eugene V. "The Drafting of Security Council Resolution 242: The Role of Non-Regional Actors." *Yale Law School Legal Scholarship Repository: Faculty Scholarship Series.* New Haven: Yale Law School, 1993. Web. 6 March 2018.

S.C. Res. 1970, ¶¶ 1-23, U.N. Doc. S/RES/1970 (Feb. 26, 2011).

Sachar, Howard M. *A history of Israel: From the rise of Zionism to our time.* Knopf, 2013.

Saleh, Yassin al-Haj. *The Impossible Revolution: Making Sense of the Syrian Tragedy.* London: Hurst & Co., 2017.

Salibi, Kamal S., *The Modern History of Jordan.* London: I.B.Tauris 2006

Sanjian, Ara. "The Formulation of the Baghdad Pact." *Middle Eastern Studies* 33.2 (1997): 226–66. Print.

Savranskaya, Svetlana. "The Soviet Experience in Afghanistan: Russian Documents and Memoirs." *The September 11th Sourcebooks: Volume II: Afghanistan: Lessons from the Last War.* Washington: The National Security Archive, 2016. Web.

Schayegh, Cyrus and Andrew Arsan (eds.). *The Routledge Handbook of the Middle East Mandates.* Routledge History Handbooks. London: Routledge, 2015. Print.

SchlichimMetrowest. "Declaration of Independence of the State of Israel (English subtitles)" *YouTube.* San Bruno CA: YouTube, 2010. Web. 27 February 2018.

Schneer, Jonathan. *The Balfour Declaration: The Origins of the Arab-Israeli Conflict.* New York: Random House, 2010. Print.

Scott, H. M. *The Emergence of the Eastern Powers, 1756–1775.* New York: Cambridge University Press, 2001.

Segev, Tom. *One Palestine, Complete: Jews and Arabs under the Mandate.* New York: Metropolitan Books, 2000.

Sessions, Jennifer E. *By Sword and Plow: France and the Conquest of Algeria.* Cornell University Press, 2014.

Shapira, Anita. (Anthony Berris, trans.) *Ben-Gurion: Father of Modern Israel.* (Jewish Lives) New Haven: Yale University Press, 2014. Print.

Sharkey, Heather J. *Living with Colonialism: Nationalism and Culture in the Anglo-Egyptian Sudan.* University of California Press, 2003.

Sharkey, Heather J. *Living with Colonialism: Nationalism and Culture in the Anglo-Egyptian Sudan.* Berkeley, CA: University of California Press, 2003. Print.

Shepard, Todd. 2008. *The Invention of Decolonization: The Algerian War and the Remaking of France.* Cornell University Press.

Shinder, Colin. *A History of Modern Israel.* 2nd ed. Cambridge: Cambridge University Press, 2013. Print.

Shlay, Anne B. and Gillad Rosen. *Jerusalem: The Spatial Politics of a Divided Metropolis.* Malden, MA: Polity Press, 2015. Print

Shragai, Nadav. *Demography, Geopolitics, and the Future of Israel's Capital: Jerusalem's Proposed Master Plan.* Jerusalem: Jerusalem Center for Public Affairs, 2010. Print.

Shukeiry, Ahmed. "Palestine Liberation Organization: The Original Palestine National Charter (1964)." Jewish Virtual Library. Washington: American-Israeli Cooperative Enterprise, 2018. Web. 7 March 2018.

Simon, Reeva S, and Eleanor H. Tejirian. *The Creation of Iraq, 1914–1921.* New York: Columbia University Press, 2004. Internet resource.

Slany, William Z. "Foreign Relations of the United States, 1955-1957, Suez Crisis, July 26-December 31, 1956, Volume XVI." *Office of the Historian: Department of State.* Washington: United States Department of State, 2018. Web. 2 March 2018.

Sluglett, Peter, and M. Hakan Yavuz, eds. *War and Diplomacy: The Russo-Turkish War of 1877–1878 and the Treaty of Berlin.* Salt Lake City: University of Utah Press, 2011.

Smith, Robert R., Hassaan S. Vahidy and Fereidun Fesharaki. "OPEC's Evolving Role: D'Arcy Concession Centennial and OPEC Today - An Historical Perspective". *Oil & Gas Journal* (July 9, 2001) [accessed March 17, 2018].

Somdeep Sen, author. ""It's Nakba, Not a Party": Re-Stating the (Continued) Legacy of the Oslo Accords." *Arab Studies Quarterly*, no. 2, 2015, p. 161.

Stone, Martin. 1997. *The Agony of Algeria*. Columbia University Press.

Stora, Benjamin, et al. *Algeria 1830–2000: A Short History*. Cornell University Press, 2004.

Streane, A.W. *The Age of the Maccabees*. Charleston, SC: BiblioLife, 2009. Print.

"Syria's Civil War Explained from the Beginning." *Al Jazeera* (March 3, 2018) https://www.aljazeera.com/ news/2016/05/syria-civil-war-explained-160505084119966.html [accessed March 18, 2018].

Taha, Abdulwahid Dhanun. *The Muslim Conquest and Settlement of North Africa and Spain*. London: Routledge, 2017. Print.

Tappan, Eva March, ed. *The World's Story: A History of the World in Story, Song and Art*, Vol. III. Boston: Houghton Mifflin company, 1914. Print.

Tessler, Mark A. *A History of the Israeli-Palestinian Conflict*. 2nd ed., Indiana University Press, 2009.

Thakur, R. "R2P after Libya and Syria: Engaging Emerging Powers," *The Washington Quarterly*, 36:2 (2013): 61-76.

Thomas, Evans. *Ike's Bluff: President Eisenhower's Secret Battle to Save the World*. New York: Little, Brown, 2012. Print.

Tyerman, Christopher. *God's War: A New History of the Crusades*. Cambridge: Belknap P of Harvard UP, 2006. Print.

"United Nations Country Team in Palestine." *United Nations Country Team in Palestine*, UNSCO, unsco. unmissions.org/un-country-team-0.

U.S. Congress, Jerusalem Embassy Act of 1995, Pub.L. 104–45, November 8, 1995, 109 Stat. 398.

UCC Palestine Solidarity Campaign. "Ahmad Shukairi." *Palestine: Information with Provenance (PIWP database)*. Cork IE: UCC Palestine Solidarity Campaign, 2018. Web. 7 March 2018.

Ufford, Letitia Wheeler. *The Pasha: How Mehemet Ali Defied the West, 1839–1841*. McFarland, 2007.

Van Dam, Nikolaos. *Destroying a Nation: The Civil War in Syria*. London: I.B. Tauris, 2017.

Waines, David. *The Odyssey of Ibn Battuta: Uncommon Tales of a Medieval Adventurer*. Chicago: U of Chicago P, 2010. Print.

Walker, Martin. *The Cold War: A History*. New York: Holt, 1993. Print.

Watkinson, Charles. "The Battle of Navarino." *Sandy Pylos: An Archaeological History from Nestor to Navarino*, edited by Jack Davis, University of Texas Press, 267–71.

Watson, Geoffrey R. *The Oslo Accords: International Law and the Israeli-Palestinian Peace Agreements*. New York: Oxford University Press, 2000.

Watson, William E. *Tricolor and Crescent: France and the Islamic World*. Westport, Conn: Praeger, 2003. Print.

Wheeler, NJ. *Saving Strangers: Humanitarian Intervention in International Society*. Oxford: Oxford University Press, 2000.

"Who We Are." *United Nation Relief and Works Agency for Palestine Refugees in the Near East*, www.unrwa.org/who-we-are.

Wien, Peter. *Arab Nationalism: The Politics of History and Culture in the Modern Middle East*. New York: Routledge, 2017.

Wilken, Robert Louis. *The Christians as the Romans Saw Them*. 2nd ed. New Haven: Yale UP, 2003.

Wilson Center. "Soviet Invasion of Afghanistan." *Wilson Center Digital Archive: International History Declassified*. Washington, D.C.: Woodrow Wilson International Center for Scholars, 2016. Web.

Winsbury, Rex. *Pliny the Younger: A Life in Roman Letters*. London: Bloomsbury, 2014. Print.

Wistrich, Robert S. "Theodor Herzl: Zionist icon, myth-maker and social utopian." *Israel Affairs* 1.3 (1995): 1–37.

Wright, Lawrence. *Thirteen Days in September: Carter, Begin, and Sadat at Camp David*. New York: Knopf, 2014. Print.

Wyrtzen, Jonathan. *Making Morocco: Colonial Intervention and the Politics of Identity*. Cornell University Press, 2016.

Yergin, Daniel. *The Prize: The Epic Quest for Oil, Money & Power*. New York: Free Press, 1991.

Yeşilbursa, B. Kemal. *The Baghdad Pact: Anglo-American Defence Policies in the Middle East, 1950–1959*. New York: Cass, 2005. Print.

Yitzhak Rabin Speaks at Signing of the Oslo Accords (1993) Ca. 1993. [Place of publication not identified]: *WPA Film Library*, [1993], 2008. EBSCO host

Zepp, Ira G. *A Muslim Primer: Beginner's Guide to Islam.* Westminster, MD: Wakefield Editions, 1992.

Zweig, R. W. "British Policy to Palestine, May 1939 to 1943: The Fate of the White Paper." 1978. PhD Dissertation.

Index